"In this passionate and expansive book, Andrew DeCort tells the story of Christianity with neighbor love at its core. Rooted in his experiences in Ethiopia, DeCort pushes past the clichés that swirl around love. From the Hebrew Bible to Martin Luther King Jr., from the early Jesus followers to Simone Weil, DeCort's inspiring stories will motivate readers to put neighbor love into practice in their own contexts."
Vincent Lloyd, professor of theology and religious studies at Villanova University

"This book is a rich personal, historical, and theological exploration of the most important moral questions of our earthly existence—who are my neighbors, and how should I care for them?"
Eboo Patel, founder and president of Interfaith America and author of *We Need to Build: Field Notes for Diverse Democracy*

"In *Reviving the Golden Rule*, Andrew DeCort calls Christians to rediscover the ethical demands of a faith that commands us to love everyone—neighbors, strangers, and enemies—as ourselves. With urgency and clarity, he challenges us to resist the forces that divide and dehumanize and to embody the bold, boundary-breaking love of Jesus. This book is both a moral summons and a hopeful guide for anyone who longs to live out gospel implications in a fractured world."
Noah Toly, provost at Calvin University and author of *The Gardeners' Dirty Hands*

"This is one of those exceedingly rare 'big books' in Christian ethics that traces a crucial concept historically while advancing the normative discussion for today. Andrew DeCort does that with the crucial pair of othering on the problem side and neighbor love on the solution side. What makes the book even more rare is that it really marks reflection on the radical practice of neighbor love as a movement, innovated by the author in the hard crucible of Ethiopia. So impressive. I highly recommend this book."
David P. Gushee, distinguished university professor of Christian ethics at Mercer University

"Do you want to make the world a better place? Start here. *Reviving the Golden Rule* addresses the most urgent ethical question of our time and perhaps of all time—the question of how we can expand the circle of the 'us' to encompass the 'other.' Although written from an unapologetically Christian perspective, Andrew DeCort's newest book delivers a powerful humanist message that should be heard and acted upon by believers and unbelievers alike."
David Livingstone Smith, author of *On Inhumanity*

"The perfect fusion of simple and profound. Neighbor love is the lifeline for our sin-sick souls suffocating in the quicksand of fear, scarcity, and indifference. Andrew DeCort does a masterful job diagnosing the problem and the cure."
Shane Claiborne, author, activist, and cofounder of Red Letter Christians

REVIVING THE GOLDEN RULE

HOW THE ANCIENT ETHIC OF NEIGHBOR LOVE CAN HEAL THE WORLD

ANDREW DeCORT

An imprint of InterVarsity Press
Downers Grove, Illinois

InterVarsity Press
P.O. Box 1400 | Downers Grove, IL 60515-1426
ivpress.com | email@ivpress.com

©2025 by Andrew David DeCort

All rights reserved. No part of this book may be reproduced in any form without written permission from InterVarsity Press.

InterVarsity Press® is the publishing division of InterVarsity Christian Fellowship/USA®. For more information, visit intervarsity.org.

All Scripture quotations, unless otherwise indicated, are taken from The Holy Bible, New International Version®, NIV®. Copyright © 1973, 1978, 1984, 2011 by Biblica, Inc.™ Used by permission of Zondervan. All rights reserved worldwide. www.zondervan.com. The "NIV" and "New International Version" are trademarks registered in the United States Patent and Trademark Office by Biblica, Inc.™

While any stories in this book are true, some names and identifying information may have been changed to protect the privacy of individuals.

The publisher cannot verify the accuracy or functionality of website URLs used in this book beyond the date of publication.

Cover design: Faceout Studio, Tim Green
Interior design: Daniel van Loon
Images: Faceout Studio, Tim Green

ISBN 978-1-5140-1276-5 (print) | ISBN 978-1-5140-1277-2 (digital)

Printed in the United States of America ∞

Library of Congress Cataloging-in-Publication Data
A catalog record for this book is available from the Library of Congress.

32 31 30 29 28 27 26 25 | 13 12 11 10 9 8 7 6 5 4 3 2 1

For beloved Lily, Eyob, Graham, Tekalign,

Ferdosa, Fitsum, and all the others

who inspired the Neighbor-Love Movement

While ours is a nation wherein the vast majority of citizens are followers of religious faiths that proclaim the transformative power of love . . . many of us are not sure what we mean when we talk of love or how to express love. . . . Yet schools for love do not exist. . . . We must dare to acknowledge how little we know of love in both theory and practice. . . . We want to live in a culture where love can flourish. We yearn to end the lovelessness that is so pervasive in our society. . . . Only love can heal the wounds of the past.

BELL HOOKS, *ALL ABOUT LOVE*

The revolution which was begun two thousand years ago by a disreputable Hebrew criminal may now have to be begun again by people equally disreputable and equally improbable.

JAMES BALDWIN, *COLLECTED ESSAYS*

["Love your neighbor as yourself"] is not merely a helpful suggestion, it is the fundamental law of human existence.

THOMAS MERTON, *NO MAN IS AN ISLAND*

All, everyone, everything, belongs. None is an outsider, all are insiders, all belong.

DESMOND TUTU, *NO FUTURE WITHOUT FORGIVENESS*

CONTENTS

	Gratitude	*xi*
1	**Neighbor Love**	
	The Crisis of Othering and the Hope of Humanity	*1*
2	**The Origins of Neighbor Love**	
	The Hebrew Bible	*29*
3	**The Universalization of Neighbor Love and the Abolition of Othering**	
	Jesus of Nazareth	*59*
4	**The Improbable Revolution of Neighbor Love**	
	The New Testament	*94*
5	**The Red Thread**	
	A Brief History of Jesus' Neighbor-Love Movement	*119*
6	**Twentieth-Century Exemplars of Neighbor Love**	
	Bonhoeffer, Weil, King, Romero, and Teresa	*154*
7	**Neighbor Love Now**	
	The Abolition of Othering and a New Beginning for Humanity	*193*
	An Invitation to the Neighbor-Love Movement	*223*
	Study Guide	
	Questions for Reflection and Discussion	*224*
	Recommended Readings in Neighbor Love	*231*
	Neighbor Love	
	An Extensive Bibliography for an Ancient-yet-Emerging Field of Study and Practice	*233*
	Othering	
	A Brief Bibliography	*247*

General Bibliography *249*   **General Index** *254*
Scripture Index *259*

GRATITUDE

THIS BOOK IS THE HARVEST of over two decades of labor as a scholar, practitioner, and friend. I am immensely grateful for all of my friends, teachers, and partners in this journey of discovering and living into neighbor love, which began with my beloved mother, Jane, and late father, Joe DeCort (1944–2024).

In this book, I tell some of the story of the Neighbor-Love Movement, which I cofounded in Ethiopia in 2019 with the message that the other is not our enemy; the other is our neighbor. I wish to give special thanks to my beloved wife, Lily DeCort; our dear partner, Dr. Tekalign Nega; our honorary cofounders, Eyob and Ferdosa; our brilliant designer, Fitsum Admassu; and all of the many precious others who have inspired and strengthened us. This book is dedicated to you with all of my gratitude.

Deep thanks to the board of the Institute for Faith and Flourishing, which oversees our work: James Hoey, Dr. Steve Ivester, Liz Brown Evans, Grant Henzel, and Lily DeCort. Deep thanks as well to generous friends who have seeded and sustained our work: Dan Boyce, Matthew Robinson, Dave and Kate Schmidgall, Joe DeCort, Graham Smith, Mark and Joelle Herskind, Dr. Jenna and Tyler Heath, David Ellis, Elias Schulze, Al and Kim Powers, Bob Beschel, the European Institute of Peace, and our small but mighty band of monthly partners. I also wish to thank Dr. Rich Hansen and Dr. Duane Grobman, who have been crucial guides in my vocation of neighbor love. Learn more about the Neighbor-Love Movement at www.nlmglobal.org and consider partnering in our work at www.iffglobal.org.

This book is seeing the light of day because of my dear friend Colton Bernasol, former academic associate project editor at IVP Academic. I wish to thank Colton for so generously inviting me to propose this project to IVP Academic and for his championing belief in it when I had buried it. His editorial acumen significantly improved the final book and was itself a beautiful embodiment of neighbor love. I also wish to thank Zachary Gordon, associate academic editor at IVP Academic, whose insight and encouragement significantly improved the book and saw it to the finish line. Deep thanks as well to an anonymous reviewer of my manuscript who offered many helpful suggestions, and to my young friends Mia and Caroline who accompanied me in the adventure of making final revisions. All limitations and errors remain my own.

Finally, I wish to thank all of the inspiring visionaries of neighbor love, dead and alive, explored in this book. In *All About Love: New Visions*, bell hooks observes that "only love can heal the wounds of the past" and "yet schools for love do not exist."[1] Building on these visionaries, my hope is that this book can serve as a school for love and revive what I believe is the most healing movement in human history—what I call the neighbor-love movement. I offer it to you in the spirit of James Baldwin, who called for "the revolution which was begun two thousand years ago by a disreputable Hebrew criminal" to be "begun again by people equally disreputable and equally improbable."[2] I am grateful to be among these beloved neighbors.

---

[1] bell hooks, *All About Love: New Visions* (New York: HarperCollins, 2001), xxviii.
[2] James Baldwin, "White Racism or World Community?," in *James Baldwin: Collected Essays*, ed. Toni Morrison (New York: Library of America, 1998), 750.

1

NEIGHBOR LOVE

The Crisis of Othering and the Hope of Humanity

May 1, 2010, was a day like any other in Addis Ababa, or so it seemed.

I was sitting at a roadside cafe eating lunch with dear friends. Betena was a favorite spot for Ethiopia's sizzling *tibbs* and sumptuous stews. As we chatted, the sun shined on our faces, and a refreshing breeze streamed over the mountains encircling Ethiopia's capital city. The University of Chicago had recently admitted me to its PhD program in theological ethics, and Lily and I were soon to be married. All was seemingly well.

But inside, my spirit was deeply troubled.

The previous year, I had returned to Addis Ababa to continue working as a pastor at one of the exploding Pentecostal churches in the city. This time, I was invited to serve as the personal assistant to the church's charismatic founder, an august man who was part of starting one of the fastest-growing Christian movements in the world. Later he became a personal friend to Ethiopia's Pentecostal prime minister.

But soon enough, I was forced to choose between my church community and my fiancée. Lily grew up in another church across town, and this marked her as "other" to my leaders. They warned that unless she "submitted" to them, she might infect their church with a "foreign spirit" through me and disrupt the church's "favor" with God. At the time, I expected to work with this community for the rest of my life. But after long and fruitless discussions, my mentor insisted on his ultimatum. I chose Lily, and I lost my place in the church.

This painful event heightened my attention to *othering*. By othering, I mean seeing "others" as unrelated or less than ourselves. It's a sense of separation from or even superiority to others. In Christian circles, othering can be triggered by something as simple as attending a different church, despite sharing almost identical beliefs. More often, othering revolves around perceived differences of religious conviction, ethnic identity, or political affiliation. It may sound innocuous, but it's the prerequisite for normalized injustice, mass violence, and genocide.[1] When we see others as unrelated or less than ourselves, we begin to accept treating them differently than we would want to be treated. Others can be ignored or excluded. When othering becomes severe and we see others as less than human, their grief no longer saddens us, and we may see eliminating them as an existential necessity for our survival. The basic responsibilities of ethics are suspended or inverted. In many ways, I see othering as the fundamental crisis of our humanity.[2]

Soon after being excluded from my church, I began working as the interim pastor of a much smaller community across town. To get there, I needed to commute through Mexico Square—one of the city's major hubs, with a large roundabout chaotically buzzing with blue Toyota minibuses packed with people.

Mexico Square haunted my conscience and intensified my attention to othering. From early in the morning, the roundabout was lined with suffering people begging for help. One elderly woman in particular caught my attention. Her right eye was covered with milky cataracts. Her left eye had seemingly been torn out of its socket and left to dangle. It was now cocooned in flesh on her gaunt cheekbone. She, along with many others—lepers with limbs rotting off, polio survivors with legs bowed like boomerangs, small orphaned children—would plaintively cry out for care.

---

[1] When I refer to genocide in this book, I have in mind the definition used by the United States Holocaust Memorial Museum: "Genocide is an internationally recognized crime where acts are committed with the intent to destroy, in whole or in part, a national, ethnic, racial, or religious group." See "What Is Genocide," United States Memorial Holocaust Museum, accessed January 19, 2025, www.ushmm.org/genocide-prevention/learn-about-genocide-and-other-mass-atrocities/what-is-genocide.

[2] For important studies on or adjacent to othering, see john powell and Stephen Menendian, *Belonging Without Othering: How We Save Ourselves and the World* (Stanford, CA: Stanford University Press, 2024); Isabel Wilkerson, *Caste: The Origins of Our Discontents* (New York: Random House, 2023); David Livingstone Smith, *On Inhumanity: Dehumanization and How to Resist It* (New York: Oxford University Press, 2020); Toni Morrison, *The Origin of Others* (Cambridge, MA: Harvard University Press, 2017); David Livingstone Smith, *Less Than Human: Why We Demean, Enslave, and Exterminate Others* (New York: St. Martin's, 2011); Sam Keen, *Faces of the Enemy: Reflections of the Hostile Imagination* (New York: Harper & Row, 1986).

But they were all typically ignored or, at best, tossed a few coins. The flow of bodies in Mexico Square was river-like. Shoulder to shoulder, people were there to get somewhere else. In the process, these others became little more than obstacles in our way.

Still, it always troubled me how we could rush past these suffering people as if they weren't even there, as if we didn't see them and couldn't hear their cries of distress. Each trip through Mexico Square felt like another interrogation as I grieved the loss of my church family: Was I just another othering religious leader like the ones in Jesus' parable of the good Samaritan, who didn't stop to give their time and attention to a person left for dead on the roadside? After all, I was literally on my way to church as I routinely walked past the woman with her eye torn out and the others in Mexico Square.

○ ○ ○

Back to that sunny Saturday, my friends and I were enjoying our lunch at Betena, the roadside cafe not far from Mexico Square.

A teenage boy approached our table and asked us to help him. He was skinny and wearing a filthy hoodie. But this was typical for homeless children in Addis, and he seemed healthy enough. We told him no and continued eating.

As he turned away, his hood slipped off, and I saw that he had a horrifying wound on the back of his head. This time, Mexico Square had come to me, and I was faced with a choice. Would I play the priest again and respond to this boy as yet another other—as someone unrelated or less than myself who could be ignored and excluded from the table? Or would I follow the othered Samaritan and respond to the boy as my neighbor—as someone morally related to me and equally precious as myself?

At heart, this is the meaning of *neighbor love*. Neighbor love sees and treats others as morally connected to ourselves and equally precious in value. It's a form of what john powell calls "belonging without othering."[3] This practice embodies passionate will and practical work for others' well-being. It's a way of seeing that leads to mutual flourishing rather than caste systems, status hierarchies, and power politics. Crucially, neighbor love is far more than momentary pity or random kindness. It's a chosen way of life

---

[3] See powell and Menendian, *Belonging Without Othering*.

that intentionally transgresses the boundaries of othering and actively recognizes the divine value of others, including those we have been conditioned to see as strangers or enemies. This is how Jesus describes neighbor love in his parable of the good Samaritan in Luke 10. The story itself was a daring defiance of othering, since Samaritans were seen as heretics, half-breeds, and enemies—certainly not *good*. Neighbor love is the abolition of othering, starting within ourselves and spreading between us like ripples in our world.

In that moment, I distinctly heard the voice of Jesus reverberate in my conscience. The voice told me, "If you say no to him, you've said no to me." After wrestling in my soul, I got up from the table and ran after him. It was one of many moments when I've learned the truth of Erich Fromm that love is a decision.[4]

Eyob (Amharic for "Job") was born in southern Ethiopia. As a small child, he had fallen into an open cooking fire in his parents' dwelling, and his head was badly burned. Sadly, his wound was never properly treated. Over the years, Eyob's wound worsened, and his parents removed him from school because the bleeding crater on the back of his head became so putrid. Eyob was seen as shameful to his community—as an other. As such, he was forced to hide his suffering in the shadows and didn't receive the medical care he so desperately needed.

Eventually, Eyob's suffering became so severe that his parents put him on a pickup truck and sent him to Addis. They told him to beg for help or die. And that's exactly how I met him: wandering the streets alone with an oozing head wound in excruciating pain.

When Eyob approached our table, I was wrestling with the meaning of my faith and the practice of neighbor love. Being expelled from my church and commuting through Mexico Square had acutely expanded my awareness of othering. After hearing the voice of Jesus like never before in my life, I felt responsible to take him to a local hospital and advocate for him to receive the care he urgently needed.

My friends and I fought for Eyob's life over the next several months with the help of international and local doctors. Those countless days with Eyob in the hospital were some of the most meaningful and joyful of my life. I

---

[4]Erich Fromm, *The Art of Loving* (New York: Open Road Media, 2013).

discovered that he was full of love and brilliantly gifted. Whenever we brought him food and gifts, he would immediately start sharing them with the other children beside him. Laughter filled the burn ward.

Eyob's dream was to become a pastor and professor who could teach hope and love for people in pain. This too was my dream. I learned that this "other" was anything but unrelated or less than myself. He was a precious diamond, full of complex pain and precious worth. In my countless hours with Eyob, I experienced what bell hooks observed: "I know no one who has embraced a love ethic whose life has not become joyous and more fulfilling. The widespread assumption that ethical behavior takes the fun out of life is false."[5]

Still, after several grueling surgeries, skin grafts, and months of rehab, Eyob was diagnosed with brain cancer. Despite the doctors' best efforts, his cancer could not be treated. We helped Eyob return to his family in the countryside, and he died in early 2011 at age fourteen.[6]

I will never understand why Eyob, so gentle and full of love, had to endure such horrific suffering throughout his short life. But what drills into me is that Eyob's suffering and death were preventable. Far more than cancer, othering killed Eyob. He was born into one of the most Christianized areas in his country, abounding with churches and evangelism. And yet, othered as he was, no one stopped and helped him for over a decade.

Was Eyob seen as cursed by God? Was he seen as less than human? Was he simply *not seen* as a neighbor and thus ignored as an unfortunate obstacle?

I don't have answers to these questions. But they haunt me to this day. Eyob reminds me of W. H. Auden's poem about another dying boy, in which everyone goes about their daily activities untroubled and "everything turns away quite leisurely from the disaster."[7]

I am left asking how it is possible for us—Christians, humans, whoever we may be—to "turn away quite leisurely" from the suffering of a child like Eyob. How could we leave him to die alone in the streets? Othering and its normalization in our everyday awareness and religiosity is certainly a crucial part of the answer.

---

[5]bell hooks, *All About Love: New Visions* (New York: HarperCollins, 2001), 88.
[6]See Andrew DeCort, *Bonhoeffer's New Beginning: Ethics After Devastation* (Lanham, MD: Fortress Academic, 2018), 7-8.
[7]W. H. Auden, "Musée des Beaux Arts," December 1938, www.poetryfoundation.org/poems/159364/musee-des-beaux-arts-63a1efde036cd.

○ ○ ○

In 1859, John Stuart Mill noted in *On Liberty* that our most important moral convictions easily become "dead beliefs" and fall into what he calls "the deep slumber of a decided opinion." Because we agree with them, we don't feel the need to understand or act on them. We simply check the box.[8]

Mill mentions how Christians can affirm that loving our neighbors is the revealed will of God in Holy Scripture. But rather than embracing this as "a living truth," we endorse it as a "dead dogma." Mill insists that unless our deepest convictions are "fully, frequently, and fearlessly discussed," we will affirm them as beliefs but forget what they actually mean and fail to practice them. They will become a "shell and husk . . . outside the mind, incrusting and petrifying it."[9]

Is that what happened in Eyob's Christian community? Had neighbor love become a "dead dogma" for them? Had they fallen into "the deep slumber of a decided opinion," which allowed them to remain indifferent to his suffering with "incrusted minds"? Or had the vision of neighbor love simply never taken root in their community, letting othering go unchallenged?

○ ○ ○

When I graduated from my PhD program at the University of Chicago, I had Eyob's picture over my heart under my doctoral robes. A few months later in 2016, Lily and I returned to Ethiopia, and I started working as a professor of Christian ethics with Eyob in my heart. During this time, a local organization named Hope for the Fatherless invited me to speak to their community about Jesus' vision of neighbor love.

After the session ended, Hope's director, Belay, kindly offered to drive me to my next appointment. But as we crossed Addis, we heard a child wailing on the side of the road. Belay immediately pulled his car over, got out, and went to her.[10]

---

[8] See Bob Goff, *Everybody Always: Becoming Love in a World Full of Setbacks and Difficult People* (Nashville: Nelson, 2018), 6: "I can't think of a single time [Jesus] gathered His friends around Him and said, 'Guys, I just want you to agree with Me.' He wants us to do what He said, and He said He wants us to love everybody, always."
[9] John Stuart Mill, *On Liberty* (New York: Penguin, 1974), 96-97, 101-14.
[10] I tell this story with Belay's written permission.

I was struck by the fact that this little girl was sitting directly in front of one of the largest churches in Addis Ababa. Hundreds of Christians were streaming in and out of the church. But no one stopped to help this weeping child. It seems that normalized othering had made her invisible and inaudible.

But Belay heard her voice from his car as he drove by. He pulled over and rushed to see what she needed. Belay wasn't a member of the church or its denomination. But as an orphan himself, he saw these "others" as his *neighbors*—as intimately connected to him and fully worthy of love.

When he got back to the car, Belay had the little girl with him. He said to me, "Andrew, I need to practice what you preached." He asked me to give her my seat, and he took her to the hospital. It turns out that she had an open head wound like Eyob did. Thankfully, the doctor was able to treat her wound, and a follow-up appointment was scheduled to make sure she healed properly.

This little girl's life was saved, but why? Because a complete stranger heard her cry as the cry of his neighbor. So, while hundreds of other Christians streamed in and out of church as if she didn't exist, he pulled over and helped her.

This experience shook me. If Eyob had a Belay, he would still be alive today like that little girl. Rather than a tragic memory, Eyob could be serving as a pastor and professor of hope for Ethiopia. Neighbor love would have helped him heal, and he would be helping others heal. But Eyob's Belay came too late.

This is why I've written this book: to revive the dead dogma of neighbor love and to reawaken us to the living truth that it was since the beginning—a radical vision and practice of being human for our "age of othering."[11] Like Mill urged, I aim to discuss it fully and fearlessly.

Near and far, othering is escalating and increasingly normalized in our world today. From the highest positions of power, we hear public officials mobilizing their power by describing whole groups of others as unrelated and less than ourselves, indeed, as animals who are less than human. I don't believe it is coincidental that we're also witnessing the highest number of conflict-related deaths since the 1994 Rwandan genocide. As john powell and David Menendian

---

[11]See Kim Samuel, "How to Reverse the Psychology of Othering," *Psychology Today*, May 11, 2023, www.psychologytoday.com/us/blog/the-power-of-belonging/202305/how-to-reverse-the-psychology-of-othering.

write, "the problem of the twenty-first century is the problem of 'othering.' . . . We currently inhabit a world that is nominally dictated by othering."[12]

The horrifying explosion of violence in Rwanda was made possible by labeling others as cockroaches. Othering is always the gateway to genocide. Sadly, much of the violent death in recent years has taken place in Ethiopia's ongoing civil war, which began in 2020. Ethnic, religious, and political others have been labeled as "enemies," "hyenas," "cancers," and "demons."[13] Predictably, this othering opened the door to genocidal violence and made the suffering of others "ungrievable" or even seen as an "existential necessity."[14] In the process, an estimated 1.2 million of our Ethiopian neighbors have been killed—1.5 times as many victims as the Rwandan genocide, after the world said "never again."[15]

Neighbor love was a revolutionary movement in ancient culture. As we'll see, it changed the way people saw one another across race, ethnicity, class, gender, age, physical ability, politics, and religion. It challenged societies to disestablish othering and restructure themselves around compassion, hospitality, generosity, and justice. It also redefined what it means to have an authentic relationship with the Creator of the universe—indeed, who our Creator actually is and what our Creator desires for our world. Jesus called neighbor love "the greatest commandment," the summary of God's will. He said it's the key to unlocking sacred Scripture and the heart of what it means to be truly human and live forever. Jesus promised, "Do this"—love the othered neighbor—"and you will flourish" (Lk 10:28, my translation). Two thousand years later, Jim Wallis calls neighbor love "still the most transformational social ethic the world has ever seen."[16] As bell hooks observes, "All the great movements for social justice in our society have strongly emphasized a love ethic."[17]

I believe neighbor love remains a revolutionary way of becoming human together still today. By *revolutionary*, I mean what Audre Lorde called "the

---

[12]john powell and David Menendian, *Belonging without Othering*, 3, 260.
[13]See Andrew DeCort, "Christian Nationalism Is Tearing Ethiopia Apart," *Foreign Policy*, June 17, 2022, https://foreignpolicy.com/2022/06/18/ethiopia-pentecostal-evangelical-abiy-ahmed-christian-nationalism/.
[14]See Judith Butler, *Frames of War: When Is Life Grievable?* (New York: Verso, 2009); Butler, *Precarious Life: The Powers of Mourning and Violence* (New York: Verso, 2004).
[15]See Andrew DeCort, "A Gospel of Violence," *Los Angeles Review of Books*, September 16, 2024, https://lareviewofbooks.org/article/a-gospel-of-violence/.
[16]Jim Wallis, *The (Un)Common Good: How the Gospel Brings Hope to a World Divided* (Grand Rapids, MI: Brazos, 2014), xii.
[17]hooks, *All About Love*, xix.

Neighbor Love

energy to pursue genuine change within our world, rather than merely settling for a shift of characters in the same weary drama."[18] Infinitely more than a dead dogma, neighbor love is an ancient-yet-still-emerging story that can change our lives and heal our world. When Jesus called us to love our neighbors as ourselves, he promised that doing this would transform how we see one another, how we design our societies, and how we relate to the Source and Sustainer of our universe. Neighbor love is key to overcoming our separation, healing our suffering, and energizing human flourishing with authentic faith. Its movement offers the abolition of othering and a mandate worth championing with everything we have.

And still, neighbor love has been scandalously neglected. In 1973, the Peruvian liberation theologian Gustavo Gutiérrez wrote, "A theology of the neighbor . . . has yet to be worked out."[19] Fifteen years later and with a sense of bafflement, Christian ethicist Garth Hallett noted, "Strange as this assertion may sound after nearly two millennia of Christian emphasis on agape [love], the Christian norm of neighbor-love offers relatively virgin territory for inquiry."[20] To my knowledge, this remains unchanged still today.

Like Mill's insight into neighbor love as a "dead dogma" slumbering in "incrusted minds," Ludwig Wittgenstein, a twentieth-century Austrian philosopher, helps us understand how this happened: "The aspects of things that are most important for us are hidden because of their simplicity and familiarity. . . . And this means: we fail to be struck by what, once seen, is most striking and most powerful."[21]

And so, I ask: Where did this simple and familiar yet most important and powerful vision of neighbor love emerge? How has it evolved across time, space, and human culture? And how can we practice it today as our way of life in our "age of othering"?

Most resources addressing these questions offer superficial piety or inaccessible scholarship without the pathos and urgency of the mandate that Eyob embodied outside Mexico Square. I'm not aware of another book that

---

[18] Audre Lorde, *The Master's Tools Will Never Dismantle the Master's House* (London: Penguin, 2018), 15.
[19] Gustavo Gutiérrez, *A Theology of Liberation*, trans. Caridad Inda and John Eagleson (Maryknoll, NY: Orbis Books, 1973), 203.
[20] Garth Hallett, *Christian Neighbor-Love: An Assessment of Six Rival Versions* (Washington, DC: Georgetown University Press, 1989), vii.
[21] Ludwig Wittgenstein, *Philosophical Investigations*, trans. G. E. M. Anscombe (New York: Macmillan, 1958), §129.

attempts to trace the neighbor-love movement from its ancient origins to our modern world. I offer this book in hopes that it can help revive and expand this healing movement for our time.[22]

The Question of Neighbor Love in an Age of Othering

On June 2, 1944, dissident pastor Dietrich Bonhoeffer penned a letter from his Nazi prison cell. Bonhoeffer had been jailed for his work resisting Hitler's Holocaust against the Jews, one of the most atrocious weaponizations of othering in human history. In that letter, Bonhoeffer writes, "The most important question for the future is how we are going to find a basis for living together with other people, what spiritual realities and rules we honor as the foundations for a meaningful human life."[23]

Bonhoeffer's "most important question for the future" amid Nazi genocide alerts us to the stakes of othering and neighbor love: *How are we going to find a basis for living together with other people?* How should we see others? How should we value others? How should we treat others? On this basis, how should we understand and organize our life together in our world in the face of the othering that destroys us?

Our entire lives are woven together with others from before birth until death and beyond. As Aristotle said, we are social animals. Our greatest joys and saddest sorrows, our highest hopes and worst fears, are bound together with others. From being born and named, to learning language and how to walk, to our growth and sexuality, to creating our own families and careers, to aging and being buried, our lives are unimaginable and meaningless

---

[22]Recent scholars who have done seminal work on the ethics of neighbor love include, among others, Anders Nygren, *Agape and Eros: A Study of the Christian Idea of Love* (New York: Harper & Row, 1956); Gene Outka, *Agape: An Ethical Analysis* (New Haven, CT: Yale University Press, 1972); Paul Ramsey, *Basic Christian Ethics* (Chicago: University of Chicago Press, 1977); Hallett, *Christian Neighbor-Love*; Timothy Jackson, *Love Disconsoled: Meditations on Christian Charity* (New York: Cambridge University Press, 1999); Werner Jeanrond, *A Theology of Love* (New York: T&T Clark, 2010); Timothy Jackson, *Political Agape: Christian Love and Liberal Democracy* (Grand Rapids, MI: Eerdmans, 2015); Marcus Mescher, *The Ethics of Encounter: Christian Neighbor Love as a Practice of Solidarity* (Maryknoll, NY: Orbis Books, 2020). See also Edmund Santurri, ed., *The Love Commandments: Essays in Christian Ethics and Moral Philosophy* (Eugene, OR: Wipf & Stock, 2009); Frederick Simmons and Brian Sorrels, eds., *Love and Christian Ethics: Tradition, Theory, and Society* (Washington, DC: Georgetown University Press, 2016); and Kelly James Clark, Aziz Abu Sarah, and Nancy Fuchs, *Strangers, Neighbors, Friends: Muslim-Christian-Jewish Reflections on Compassion and Peace* (Eugene, OR: Cascade Books, 2018).

[23]Dietrich Bonhoeffer, "Letter to Hans-Walter Schleicher on June 2, 1944," in *Letters and Papers from Prison*, ed. John de Gruchy, trans. Christian Gremmels et al. (Minneapolis: Fortress, 2010), 409.

without others. Our most mundane activities, such as walking down the street, shopping for groceries, and scrolling online, are surrounded by others.

Bonhoeffer's question is essential because we have a choice in how we answer it. A pack of wolves doesn't gather in the forest and discuss whether they will have mercy on neighboring lambs or devour them. They follow their instinct and hunt for prey. But human beings can stop and think. We can ask ourselves these fundamental questions: How should we see others? How should we value others? How should we treat others? How can we find a basis for living together with other people—with our neighbors near and far?

How we answer these questions determines how we spend our attention, time, energy, money, passion, and vocation. And what we do with these gifts reveals who we really are, what we truly love, and what we think the ultimate meaning of life is. Our answers to these questions become our identity and destiny.

Amid our age of othering, I agree with Bonhoeffer: how we see and relate with other people is the most important question for our present and future. Bonhoeffer's question is another way of asking that ancient question, "Who is my neighbor?"

The Ethics of Neighbor Love to Abolish Othering

At heart, the question, "Who is my neighbor?" interrogates the scope of our moral community. It asks, Who is related to us, and who is other? Who am I obligated to care for, and who can I overlook, exclude, or even attack without regret? All human beings have an inherent sense of moral right and responsibility—to tell the truth, to protect others, to share and serve. But the question is, Who counts as morally significant, and who falls off our radar?

Think of morality as a circle. Those inside the circle are people we recognize, respect, and want to see flourish, or at least to treat fairly and do justice to. Others outside the circle are those we consciously or unconsciously ignore, exclude, or attack. The question is how we draw this circle and thus who is in, who is out, and why. *Who is our neighbor?*

This question searches to the heart of Hebrew Scripture and its ethical vision for humanity. On the one hand, the Hebrew Bible or Christian Old Testament affirms that all people have been created by God, bear God's holy image, and descend as one family from shared ancestors. In this way, the

Hebrew Bible presents us with a universal moral vision in which there are no "others." This was a revolutionary breakthrough in ancient morality. Building on this vision, God's promise to Abraham was ultimately to bless "all peoples on earth" (Gen 12:3), and Moses commanded his community, "Love your neighbor as yourself" (Lev 19:18). The circle seems to surround everyone—as wide as the world.

But on the other hand, Israel was one nation among many others, surrounded by people it saw as enemies, and sometimes in danger for its survival. For Israel, *neighbor* generally meant a fellow Israelite and worshiper of Israel's God, thus potentially limiting the scope of its moral community. Israelites were called by God to be a community of love and justice for the neighbor. But Israel's qualified definition of the neighbor raises the question of just *who* counts as a neighbor.

Israel's law—the circle of its moral community—contains troubling limitations in who we're called to see as neighbors and how others should be treated in light of Israel's religious nationalism. As we wrestle with the text, we'll see that some non-Israelite neighbors could be ignored or excluded. Others could be enslaved from generation to generation. In extreme cases, whole groups of "enemies" could be hated and exterminated, including women and children.

Of course, there are places in the Old Testament that show just how groundbreaking and countercultural Israel's neighbor-love ethic truly was, especially in light of the cultures of surrounding societies. The story of Ruth and Boaz is particularly inspiring as we'll see. But Israel's ethic didn't include everyone or completely abolish othering. We'll explore this complexity in the next chapter.

But with Jesus of Nazareth, we discover a revolutionary breakthrough in culture and ethics—the radical expansion of neighbor love into a universal movement. For Jesus, the neighbor to be loved was not simply a fellow Jew or follower of Moses' law. Jesus insists the neighbor is *everyone*, including excluded outsiders and hated rivals. In fact, Jesus expands the command of neighbor love and declares for the first time in Israel's history three extraordinary words: "Love your enemies" (Mt 5:44). Indeed, in his most famous story about the meaning of neighbor love, Jesus makes his society's most hated enemy the loving neighbor who crosses every boundary of religion, ethnicity, and politics to help a suffering stranger. Jesus is provocative and profound: the one we are most tempted to other is our neighbor. A universal belonging is unlocked.

What was so revolutionary in Jesus' teaching was that he drew the moral circle of love around everyone. Now no one was left outside. Othering was abolished. For Jesus, it didn't matter whether you were a fellow citizen or foreigner, righteous or sinner, friend or enemy, man or woman, rich or poor, child or adult—all people were valued as precious neighbors. And thus all others were to be treated as *neighbors* with respect, compassion, and self-giving love.

In fact, Jesus seems to make loving our enemies a condition for enjoying an authentic relationship with God (Mt 5:45; Lk 6:35). This is the paradox of his teaching of neighbor love: we exclude ourselves from full belonging only when we exclude others from it. For Jesus, God is a neighbor lover without limits, and thus to fully participate in the life of God's family, we too must be neighbor lovers without limits. Jesus' teachings were as challenging as they were inspiring, and love for the enemy became their signature. We'll explore them in chapter three.

In the following chapters, I'll argue that the practitioners of Jesus' movement not only preserved his teaching of neighbor love; they expanded and intensified it in their world and across the earth. They hand it off to us today and invite us to continue it in the face of othering.

Having said that, I want to name immediately that Christianity does not have a monopoly on neighbor love, nor an exceptional history of practicing it. My Christian tradition has also often seen itself as separated from or superior to its neighbors. We've fallen into othering again and again. As this book's story unfolds, we'll see examples of famous Christians, such as Martin Luther, who labeled others as subhuman "enemies," which contributed to the atrocious othering of the Holocaust. Sadly, some of the gravest examples of othering in history—from America's genocidal founding and institutionalized slavery to the German Holocaust, Rwandan genocide, and Ethiopia's civil war—have been perpetrated by overwhelmingly Christian populations.[24]

This is perhaps the greatest irony of othering: it leads us to claim a superior identity to others, and yet it justifies some of the most appalling behavior imaginable. Another irony of othering is that we can reinscribe it in the very process of claiming to have overcome it, as if "we" are exceptionally

---

[24] I'm grateful to an anonymous reviewer of this book who encouraged me to underscore this important point.

moral and fundamentally different from "them." James Baldwin was right: "None of us are that different from one another, neither that much better nor that much worse."[25] In a sense, then, othering presents a third irony: recognizing it can unite us and remind us of our shared humanity. Just like no one has a monopoly on neighbor love, no one has a monopoly on othering. Neighbor love includes all of us and can be practiced by all of us. As Baldwin wrote, "Our humanity is our burden, our life; we need not battle for it; we need only to do what is infinitely more difficult—that is, to accept it."[26] Othering is our only true enemy.

I write this book as a Christian ethicist deeply inspired by the life, teaching, and practice of Jesus. The movement he started is the one I know most thoroughly, and I believe it universalized the moral circle of our humanity in extremely important, innovative ways. But I hope this book speaks to neighbors who are not Christian or are even deeply suspicious of Christianity. Most fundamentally, neighbor love is an ethic of cooperation rather than competition, of solidarity rather than supremacy. As a student of ethics, I hold deep reverence for the sacred wisdom and healing power of neighbor love in Jewish, Muslim, Buddhist, Hindu, and other religious and secular traditions. I'll return to this at the end of this book and hope to explore neighbor love in these traditions more thoroughly in the future.

For now, this mindfulness of othering's ironies takes me back to Bonhoeffer's question: "How can we find a basis for living together with other people?" Jesus and the best parts of the movement he inherited and inspired answer that neighbor love is this divine basis. It's a movement that flows from and returns to the very heart of God in our primal origins, exceeding and including all of our finite humanity. All people have been created by God. All people are loved by God. And thus all people are our neighbors, morally significant presences whom we are connected to and called to care for as equally precious to ourselves—including our enemy-neighbors, Eyobs, and the earth itself.

From this perspective, I believe that neighbor love is the most important mandate for Christian ethics and our shared moral responsibility, now and

---

[25]James Baldwin, *James Baldwin: Collected Essays*, ed. Toni Morrison (New York: Library of America, 1998), 747.
[26]Baldwin, *Collected Essays*, 18. In *The Origin of Others*, Toni Morrison identifies three motivators behind why we other people: (1) to gain power (p. 3), (2) to define our identity (pp. 5-6), and (3) to build our sense of belonging (pp. 15-16). As we'll see, neighbor love offers powerful, healing alternatives to each of othering's addictive motivators.

always. We don't live in a world of family, friends, strangers, and enemies. Every person we see and meet—young and old, rich and poor, White and Black, male and female, straight and gay, familiar and foreign, strong and weak, friend and foe, and all who don't fit into these simplistic binaries—*every* person is our neighbor. They are someone to whom we owe our moral responsibility and can share the divine gift of life. In the beginning and in the end, we don't live in a world of war torn between some *us* and an othered *them* struggling for domination. In the beginning and in the end, we live in God's one world, a universal moral community where everyone is a neighbor and no one is to be ignored, excluded, or attacked. From the start, this ethical vision calls us to open our eyes and come home to one another—in all of the beauty, complexity, and agony of being human together in our world. We are *we*.

The circle of neighbor love is as wide as the world, surrounds us all, and opens us to a universal belonging.

The Crisis of Othering in Ancient Mythology

The biblical mandate to see everybody as our neighbor was a revolutionary vision that expanded the scope of who we owe our love. But today, many of us grew up hearing "love your neighbor" as a dead doctrine with a nominal sense that a neighbor could be anyone. In our "incrusted minds," my brief summary of Jesus' vision of neighbor love, as Mill suggested, may not strike us as a revolutionary breakthrough that changed the world forever and offers us our best hope for healing our world.

But I believe that it was and is exactly that: a revolutionary moral breakthrough and a vision that can heal our world. Jesus' vision of neighbor love was a radical innovation in the ancient world and remains countercultural to this day. We can appreciate this by looking back at some of the oldest stories, philosophies, and cultural systems that have shaped our world.

In the ancient Near East's oldest and most influential storytelling about the meaning of life, we find that it was saturated with othering, and the neighbor simply didn't exist. Human imagination was dominated with hierarchy, conflict, exclusion, and violence.

For example, Enuma Elish was one of the most widespread creation stories in ancient Mesopotamia, dating back nearly five thousand years by some estimates. In it, the young god Marduk makes war on the older goddess

Tiamat. Out of his brutal act of killing her, the world is created and the moral law established. Marduk makes the earth from Tiamat's corpse and the waters from her blood. After having successfully destroyed his enemy, Marduk sets himself up as the divine king who appoints human kings to defend his religion, produce wealth through slave labor, and destroy their enemies. In fact, humans are made from another murdered god for the purpose of serving as the gods' worshipful inferiors.[27]

This mythical story imagines othering and violence as woven into the very fabric of worldly reality and human life from the beginning. Our soil, water, social order, and embodied selves are literally founded on murder—the stronger killing the weaker and setting up a system of domination over others. The moral circle is a crime scene, and only those with the power to wage violence have any place within it. The others should be conquered, enslaved, or exterminated.[28]

We find a strikingly similar culture-making story in ancient Greece with Hesiod's *Theogony*. This is a creation myth from around 700 BC that tells the prehistory of the gods and the origins of the world.[29] In *Theogony*, Father

---

[27]See Enuma Elish translated in Alexander Heidel, *The Babylonian Genesis: The Story of Creation*, 2nd ed. (Chicago: University of Chicago Press, 1963), especially 42 (the murder of Tiamat and the creation of the world) and 46-47 (the murder of Kingu and the creation of humanity).

[28]Note powell and Menendian, *Belonging Without Othering*, 280-81: "Law plays a critical role in the othering process. Ancient legal codes are replete with legal distinctions based on identity and reflect both the othering processes of the societies in which they emerge as well as contribute to ongoing othering. . . . The Code of Hammurabi [c. 1755 BC], perhaps the earliest known legal code, divides society into two genders and three classes, superiors, commoners, and slaves or servants, and ascribes different punishments depending upon the identity of a perpetrator of a crime or the victim." This is not to say that the ancient Near East did not have laws and wisdom against injustice, especially for the poor and oppressed. For example, in "The Agreement Between Ir-Addu and Niqmepa," dating to the Middle Babylonian period (1595–1155 BC), these two kings agree, "[If people of my land] enter your land to preserve themselves from starvation, you must protect them and you must feed them like (citizens of) your land" (lines 55-56). Quoted in William Hallo and K. Lawson Younger, eds., *Contexts of Scripture*, vol. 2, *Monumental Inscriptions from the Ancient World* (Leiden: Brill, 2000), 330. I'm grateful to Daniel Master for this reference. The Babylonian wisdom poem known as "The Ballad of Early Rulers" (ca. 1500–1200 BC), emphasizing the unpredictability of fate, says, "One should not speak in disrespect of others. One should not treat the weak contemptuously. The cripple may overtake the runner. The rich may beg the poor. This is the fate of the sound person. [The fates] are determined by Ea. [The lots are drawn] according to the will of the god" (lines 25-43). Quoted in Yoram Cohen, *Wisdom from the Late Bronze Age* (Atlanta: Society of Biblical Literature, 2013), 137. I'm grateful to John Walton for pointing me to this text. However, Walton wrote in an email to me on April 5, 2019, that he is aware of "no comparisons between loving others and loving self" in ancient Near Eastern literature. Othering is pervasive and dominant.

[29]See Hesiod, *Theogony, Works and Days. Testimonia* (Cambridge, MA: Harvard University Press, 2007), lines 126-206.

Heaven hates his children, and Mother Earth wants to take revenge against her violent husband, but she is afraid. So while Heaven is having sex with Earth, his son Chronos (Time) cuts his father into pieces with a machete from his mother. Time's son Zeus then becomes the supreme god who "mightily reigns and rules." The blood of Heaven falls on Earth, and thus begins the violent process of creation.[30] As the ancient Greek philosopher Heraclitus wrote, "War is the father of all and the king of all; and some he has made gods and some men, some slave and some free."[31]

Like all world-making stories, this myth had utterly profound effects on the human imagination. It inscribed othering into its hearers' most basic worldview. Where do we come from? How should we live together? What is the purpose of life? According to *Theogony*, a son murdered his father and chopped his body into pieces, and his blood is where it all begins. Violence is our father and war our king. Some are made to be free and others to be slaves, and only the strong survive this fate.

Whether we look to ancient Mesopotamia, ancient Greece, or elsewhere, again and again humanity's earliest storytelling is animated with othering and filled with violence.[32] The moral circle inscribed people in an antagonistic and often murderous relationship in which others were seen as unrelated or less than one's own community. Human life was depicted like a crime scene, surging with fear, hatred, anger, lust, conflict, and killing. And this was presented as our normal, even normative reality. There was no neighbor or moral neighborhood. There were gods and men, kings and slaves, us and them in a depressing struggle for survival. Othering is always ironic.

THE CRISIS OF OTHERING IN CLASSICAL PHILOSOPHY

We might assume that ancient mythology was primitive and barbaric—alas, terms often used to other our ancient neighbors. Perhaps classical philosophy

---

[30] *Theogony*, lines 405, 200-205.
[31] Fragment B53 in Hippolytus, *Refutation of All Heresies* 9.9.4, quoted in Bruno Snell, *Heraklit: Fragmente* (Munich: Heimeran, 1976). See also fragment 67 in Hippolytus, *Refutation of All Heresies* 9.10.8. War has been a powerful source of othering meaning-making throughout human history. See Chris Hedges, *War Is a Force That Gives Us Meaning* (New York: PublicAffairs, 2014).
[32] See Robin W. Lovin and Frank E. Reynolds, eds., *Cosmogony and Ethical Order* (Chicago: University of Chicago Press, 1985). In *Caste*, 101-2, Isabel Wilkerson analyzes India's ancient Hindu text, Manu, in which the creation process established "the Laws of all the social classes" and thus provided a primordial justification for India's caste system. In this system, even the shadow of a subordinated "untouchable" was seen as "a pollutant."

laid the foundations for an enlightened morality of human dignity, justice, and peace? But this is also myth.

Plato lived around 429–347 BC in ancient Greece. Philosopher Alfred North Whitehead famously wrote that European philosophy was simply "a series of footnotes" on Plato and his thought.[33] Plato's *Republic* is one of his most influential works—a lengthy dialogue on the nature of justice and how to create a flourishing society. His *Republic* raises many brilliant questions about the possibilities and limits of justice. It is a work foundational to political theory, aesthetics, and ethics from which we still have much to learn. But even as it critiques Greece's myths, it too explicitly inscribes othering and offers a very limited, exclusive moral circle of human responsibility.

For example, Plato believed that a just society should be hierarchically ranked into a caste system. Philosopher-kings are the golden class that rule on top, warriors are the silver class that keep order in the middle, and farmers and craftsmen are the iron and bronze who labor at the bottom.[34] Plato was, in effect, a philosopher of eugenics: he believed that only "equals" should mate and mix, and that children should be separated by caste in order to grow up untainted by others.[35] The precious rulers and warriors should never mingle with the lowly laborers beneath them.

In fact, Plato argued that the "bottom" classes shouldn't receive any education. He thought it would be a waste of the public's resources and dangerous to treat these people as if they could learn. A committee of experts should carefully observe and examine each child to determine its true "nature." (We'll often notice how othering is essentialized or justified by claiming that some have one "nature" while others have different "natures" that are, again, unrelated or less.) Once sorted, children should be assigned to their caste for the rest of their lives—with no court of appeal. In this way, Plato's republic was governed by a eugenically engineered caste system. What we call agency, opportunity, and upward mobility were dangerous and intolerable to Plato. Unsurprisingly, Plato justifies this othering order by calling it the will of "God." (We'll also need to pay attention to how "God" is often invoked as the ultimate architect and emperor of othering.[36])

---

[33] Alfred North Whitehead, *Process and Reality* (New York: Free Press, 1979), 39.
[34] Plato, *The Republic*, 2nd ed., trans. Allan Bloom (New York: Basic Books, 1991), 415a.
[35] Plato, *Republic* 459e.
[36] Wilkerson, *Caste*, 101-4, argues that claims to "divine will and the laws of nature" are the primary pillar of caste or institutionalized systems of othering.

But Plato's city was even more brutal. For example, Plato argues that the extremely sick, weak, and disabled—people like Eyob—are not worth living. The city's doctors should leave them to die or actively eliminate them. Plato writes, "And those of the worse, and any of the others born deformed, they will hide away in unspeakable and unseen places." Why? Again, Plato believes that the weak and sick waste the resources of the city and drag it down. Indeed, they risk polluting the "purity" of the golden rulers and silver warriors, so they must either be isolated or eliminated.[37] (Purity will be another powerful notion in othering's story.) Plato's policies of breeding, casting, and killing in order to protect elite purity chillingly anticipate policies used in American slavery, Nazi Germany, and other modern cases of institutionalized othering and genocide.

Finally, Plato advocates for violently xenophobic foreign policy. For example, Plato insists that Greeks and non-Greeks are completely "foreign and alien" to one another. They are, he argues, "enemies by nature, and this hatred must be called war." Thus, Plato encourages Greeks to hate "barbarians" and to burn down their houses, destroy their fields, and kill their men, women, and children. Unsurprisingly, then, Plato thinks slavery is "just," and he insists that Greeks should use foreigners only as slaves in order to "spare the Greek stock," which he sees as "entirely superior."[38] Othering is essential to Plato's philosophy.

When we examine it honestly, it's hard to see Plato's philosophy as much more civilized than ancient mythology. Plato advocates for eugenic breeding, a rigid caste system, violence against the weak and sick, and explicit othering, war, and slavery against non-Greeks. Plato's republic draws a very narrow circle indeed that excludes and kills many. In short, his republic has no neighbors—only fellow caste members, superiors and inferiors, and foreign enemies united by a sense of racial superiority willed by the gods. From this perspective, it's disturbing to think of European philosophy as "a series of footnotes" on Plato's philosophy. No wonder so much Western philosophy went on to fuel othering with its racism, colonialism, and genocide.[39]

---

[37]Plato, *Republic* 410a, 460c. Note powell and Menendian, *Belonging Without Othering*, 280-81: "One of the earliest known written legal codes, the Roman Republic's 'Twelve Tables' [c. 450 BC], required newborns with visible disabilities to be put to immediate death." In *Caste*, 115-30, Isabel Wilkerson analyzes "purity versus pollution" as a core "pillar" of caste systems.

[38]Plato, *Republic* 470c-d, 469b-c.

[39]powell and Menendian, *Belonging Without Othering*, 180-82, trace a similar pattern in the philosophy of John Locke and other Enlightenment thinkers.

Consider another classical philosopher, Aristotle, who lived around 384–322 BC. He was Plato's most famous student and the teacher of Alexander the Great. Aristotle's philosophy broke away from Plato's in important ways, but their values fundamentally overlap.

In the first part of his book on *Politics*, Aristotle famously argues that slavery is "natural" and thus *normal*. According to Aristotle, a slave is a naturally inferior, talking tool who belongs to his naturally superior, rational master as a piece of property.[40] (Notice again how nature is used as a justification for othering.) With this othering vision, Aristotle obviously didn't oppose Alexander the Great's massive campaigns to dominate and enslave others. Aristotle's argument that slavery is "natural" and right had devastating consequences in his society and throughout history.

Aristotle also dehumanizes women, children, and manual laborers. He calls women "misbegotten males"—basically men without penises who are inherently passive, weak, and less rational. About laborers, Aristotle writes that if you aren't an independently wealthy Greek man with enslaved people doing your work, you have no chance of living a truly good and worthwhile life.[41] He summarizes his position like this: "There are by nature various classes of rulers and ruled. For the free rules the slave, the male rules the female, and the man rules the child . . . for the slave doesn't have the rational part at all, and the female has it but without full authority, while the child has it but in an undeveloped form."[42]

Like Plato, then, Aristotle gives us an inherently hierarchical, othering vision of society. But unlike Plato, Aristotle's society is exclusively dominated by rich men who rule over slaves, women, and children as their masters—unprotected by law and without any say in making the law. Still like Plato, Aristotle's philosophy naturalizes inequality and has no place for liberating agency, opportunity, and upward mobility. Despite Aristotle's important differences from Plato, his moral circle is also narrow, exclusive, and oppressive.

Notice again that Aristotle's city has no neighbors. Instead, it has superiors, inferiors, and foreign enemies. Those are the basic options. Desmond

---

[40] Aristotle, *Politics*, trans. Harris Rackham, Loeb Classical Library (Cambridge, MA: Harvard University Press, 1932), 1252a30.
[41] Aristotle, *Politics* 1278a15, 1273a30.
[42] Aristotle, *Politics* 1260a, 1275a25.

Tutu, the South African archbishop who struggled against apartheid, summarizes Aristotle's position as "irrational and immoral," justifying "cruelty with impunity."[43]

Looking at these founders of Western philosophy, it's hard to argue that it was much more enlightened and civilized than ancient mythology. Instead, it presents sophisticated arguments to justify devaluing, excluding, enslaving, and slaughtering certain groups of people. Classical philosophy is especially cruel to children, women, disabled people, workers, and foreigners. Nowhere do we find a vision of God creating all people to be treated equally as neighbors who are worthy of love. Human imagination remained trapped in othering's story of hierarchy, hatred, and hegemony. The neighbor-love mandate was virtually unknown, and othering governed an exclusive (im)moral circle.

THE CRISIS OF OTHERING IN GRECO-ROMAN CULTURE

Unsurprisingly, then, Oxford historian Larry Siedentop argues that "natural inequality" was the fundamental structure of Greco-Roman culture. He writes, "At the core of ancient thinking [was] the assumption of natural inequality. Whether in the domestic sphere, in public life or when contemplating the cosmos, Greeks and Romans did not see anything like a level playing field. Rather, they instinctively saw a hierarchy or pyramid." This culture had no vision of a fully "common humanity" called to love others as neighbors. Reality was divided into a hierarchy of families, strangers, and enemies. Siedentop argues that Greco-Roman culture thus had no concept of "charity" or loving others beyond the boundaries of one's group simply for their well-being.[44]

American historian Carter Lindberg corroborates Siedentop's picture. He writes, "[The Greco-Roman] understanding of love did not envision love beyond one's own circle or status for the wellbeing of others." Lindberg quotes from Roman dramatist Plautus, who lived two hundred years before Jesus: "A man is a wolf to a man whom he does not know. . . . What is given to the poor is lost." Plautus's perspective makes toxic sense within the framework of othering: Why give to the poor if they have no value? Lindberg shows that

---

[43]Desmond Tutu, *No Future Without Forgiveness* (New York: Doubleday, 1999), 92.
[44]Larry Siedentop, *Inventing the Individual: The Origins of Western Liberalism* (London: Penguin, 2015), 51, 13, 15.

Greeks and Romans "shared a general disdain" for "women, the weak, and the marginalized."⁴⁵ Wealthy elites who gave to those "beneath" them did so to build loyalty, secure social stability for their ambitions, and immortalize their names with plaques and temples in their honor. They didn't give because they saw others as connected to themselves and equal in value.

Like Plautus, famous Roman philosopher Cicero called the poor "the scum of the city" and thought they should be washed away. Faithful to Plato and Aristotle, Cicero saw the rich and powerful as virtuous, while he viewed the poor and weak as valueless or even evil. Lindberg summarizes, "There is little evidence of pity or compassion in ancient culture. In the ancient world, one gave in order to get. . . . The reigning ideology was that the gods love the wealthy."⁴⁶

Siedentop argues that classical culture was dominated by the idea of "natural inequality." Lindberg calls classical culture "a world without love." In many ways, ancient culture reflected the basic principles that early evolutionary scientists claimed drive natural selection: kinship, competition, conquest, and killing.⁴⁷

Whether we look at ancient mythology, classical philosophy, or the popular culture that emerged with them, the moral circle was consistently drawn around "us" alone and fueled the oppression, exclusion, enslavement, and killing of "others." This wasn't by accident: the reigning imaginations and ideologies naturalized, institutionalized, and defended othering as the will of "God." In these paradigms, the world is created and organized by othering. The divine favors the domination of one group over another. And the others—women, children, workers, the sick, the weak, the poor, the foreign, the enslaved—must simply accept their lot in life or die. In this small world, Eyob doesn't deserve to live.

Surveying these traditions, at least, we find that the non-Jewish world before Jesus had no moral vision of the neighbor and certainly no universal ethic that commanded loving others as ourselves across othering's

---

⁴⁵Carter Lindberg, *Love: A Brief History Through Western Christianity* (Malden, MA: Blackwell, 2008), 36-37.
⁴⁶Lindberg, *Love*, 38, 40.
⁴⁷For seeds of opposition to violence in Greek culture, see William Klassen, *Love of Enemies: The Way to Peace* (Philadelphia: Fortress, 1984), 12-23. For a much more expansive vision of human evolution, see Robert Bellah, *Religion in Human Evolution: From the Paleolithic to the Axial Age* (Cambridge, MA: Harvard University Press, 2011).

Neighbor Love

normalized boundaries. Even the cosmopolitan Stoics who prided themselves on being "citizens of the world" defined humanity in terms of reason and judged others as less rational and thus less human—less connected and less worthy of care.[48] Again, othering is ironic: it claims superiority and reinscribes our sadness.

When we look at the evidence, Jesus' teaching of neighbor love was in fact a revolutionary breakthrough. He was challenging established religious orthodoxies and entrenched cultural systems of othering. No wonder he himself was almost immediately othered and labeled a Samaritan, friend of sinners, and demon-possessed. When we love the other, we often become the other. Jesus named the cost of this love directly in his Sermon on the Mount, the manifesto he gave at the beginning of his public movement:

> Blessed are the persecuted for the sake of justice, because theirs is the kingdom of heaven. Blessed are you when people insult you, persecute you, and falsely say all kinds of evil against you because of me. Rejoice and be happy, because great is your reward in heaven, for in the same way they persecuted the prophets who were before you.[49] (Mt 5:10-12, my translation)

For Jesus, when we exit the closed circle of othering and enter into a new path opened with compassion, peacemaking, and justice, our humanity becomes prophetic. We turn the lights on in reality and help preserve one another's humanity. We enter into a universal blessing (see Mt 5:1-16).

But Jesus was honest: the guardians of power rarely take kindly to this divergent way of becoming humanely happy and often do everything they can to crush it.

Our Crisis of Othering Today

The crisis of othering is not a thing of the past, and Jesus' vision of neighbor love remains just as prophetic today as it was in his world. Our deep habits of ignoring, excluding, and oppressing others continue to haunt us. A few examples illustrate this sobering reality and the stakes of this book in our age of othering.

---

[48]See Martha Nussbaum, *The Cosmopolitan Tradition: A Noble but Flawed Ideal* (Cambridge, MA: Harvard University Press, 2019); Kwame Anthony Appiah, *Cosmopolitanism: Ethics in a World of Strangers* (New York: Allen Lane, 2006).

[49]I interpret Jesus' Beatitudes in the context of othering in my book *Blessed Are the Others: Jesus' Way in a Violent World* (Washington, DC: BitterSweet Collective, 2024).

Philosopher Jonathan Glover estimates that war killed eighty-six million people from 1900 to 1989. On average, that means that war ended a neighbor's life almost every fifteen seconds of every minute of every hour for ninety years.[50] As I write today, the world is witnessing more conflict-related deaths than at any time since the Rwandan genocide in 1994. This catastrophic violence is often fueled by patterns of othering in which people are seen as insects, animals, aliens, or demons rather than as neighbors and fellow humans. Violence is sold as an existential necessity for our survival.[51]

Othering, then, doesn't simply kill people. It also makes our neighbors run for their lives. According to the United Nations Refugee Agency, there are over 122 million people in our world today who have been violently forced to flee from their homes. This means that we are living in perhaps the largest refugee crisis in history. Over fifteen million refugees are under the age of eighteen—enough young neighbors to fill up New York, Los Angeles, and Chicago combined. The United Nations estimates that one person is violently displaced every two seconds in the world today.[52] Of course, the reasons for our refugee crises are many: ethnic cleansing, economic disenfranchisement, neocolonialism—just to name a few. But their roots are similar: seeing others as unrelated or less than ourselves and thus justifying their suffering or remaining indifferent to it.[53]

The depredations of othering also occur at home and in intimate relationships. According to the United Nations Agency for Women, 35 percent of women experience physical or sexual violence at some point in their lives.[54]

---

[50]Jonathan Glover, *Humanity: A Moral History of the Twentieth Century*, 2nd ed. (New Haven, CT: Yale University Press, 2012), 47.

[51]See Sam Keen, *Faces of the Enemy: Reflections of the Hostile Imagination* (New York: Harper & Row, 1991); Smith, *Less Than Human*; Smith, *On Inhumanity*.

[52]Internal Displacement Monitoring Centre, "UNHCR Mid-Year Trends 2024," United Nations Refugee Agency, October 9, 2024, www.unhcr.org/en-us/figures-at-a-glance.html.

[53]See Frances D'Emilio, "Pope: Vatican Will Shelter 2 Families Fleeing War, Hunger," Associated Press, September 6, 2015, https://apnews.com/general-news-9f9a61892ab74de693b72641b42afeb1. Pope Francis is quoted as saying, "Faced with the tragedy of tens of thousands of refugees who are fleeing death by war and by hunger, and who are on a path toward a hope for life, the Gospel calls us to be neighbors to the smallest and most abandoned, to give them concrete hope."

[54]See "Facts and Figures: Ending Violence Against Women," United Nations Agency for Women, November 24, 2024, www.unwomen.org/en/what-we-do/ending-violence-against-women/facts-and-figures.

Other studies indicate that seven in ten women suffer abuse.[55] Looking back, the Nobel Prize–winning economist Amartya Sen estimated that around one hundred million women disappeared in the twentieth century due to infanticide, abduction, sex trafficking, and murder.[56] This means that as many women were lost as casualties of war in the twentieth century. We saw above how Aristotle's patriarchal philosophy degraded women into the private property of men. Explicitly or implicitly, many cultures today continue to see women as less valuable than men and thus less worthy of dignity, security, and agency. When women are othered into objects, violence is never far away. Indeed, gender-based othering is already a form of cultural violence against women that enables the epidemic of abuse, inequality, and violence to endure.[57]

Slavery is also not a thing of othering's barbaric past. Today the international slave trade is a $150 billion business and one of the fastest-growing enterprises in the world.[58] The International Labor Association estimates that there are forty million enslaved neighbors in our world. Twenty-five million suffer under forced labor; fifteen million suffer within forced marriages and sex slavery. Over seven out of ten of these forty million neighbors are girls and women; one in four are children.[59] Again, othering is the crucial precondition of people enslaving other people: if we didn't see "them" as unrelated or less than "us," we would never tolerate enslaving our neighbors or maintaining the impoverishing economic systems that depend on their "cheap" labor.

The crisis of othering also cuts deep within each one of us. When we come to see our own selves as unrelated or inferior to others, life is drained of meaning. We become isolated and lose the will to live. The World Health Organization estimates that more than seven hundred thousand people end

---

[55] See Dennis Mukwege, *The Power of Women* (New York: Flatiron Books, 2021). This book is a deeply moving account of how women are othered today and Dr. Mukwege's struggle for women's dignity in the Democratic Republic of the Congo.

[56] Amartya Sen, "More Than 100 Million Women Are Missing," *New York Times Review of Books*, December 1990.

[57] For the seminal analysis of cultural, structural, and direct violence, see Johan Galtung, "Cultural Violence," *Journal of Peace Research* 27, no. 3 (August 1990): 291-305.

[58] The International Justice Mission regularly monitors and updates the data on modern slavery. See www.ijm.org.

[59] "Global Estimates of Modern Slavery: Forced Labour and Forced Marriage," International Labor Association, 2017, www.ilo.org/wcmsp5/groups/public/@dgreports/@dcomm/documents/publication/wcms_575540.pdf.

their lives every year. Among fifteen- to twenty-nine-year-olds, suicide is the third leading cause of death.[60] Historian Yuval Harari observes that in the year after 9/11, many more people died by suicide than were killed by terrorists, soldiers, and drug dealers.[61] Contemporary culture and socioeconomic structures are mass-producing loneliness, mental illness, a sense of worthlessness, and despair. In fact, the US surgeon general declared loneliness to be a public health epidemic as deadly as smoking.[62]

Othering attacks us from without and within. At the end of this book, I'll discuss how neighbor love invites us to see not only others but also *our own selves* as beloved *neighbors*. While neighbor love challenges selfishness, it affirms self-love as vital to our flourishing. We are all neighbors, including to ourselves.

Statistics can help us see the big picture. But they can also be numbing and depersonalizing. Near and far, the consequences of seeing others as our *neighbors*—or *not*—are concrete, intimately personal, and urgent. The indifference, exclusion, and violence that othering allows cash out in the daily lives of individual people. This is why I began this book with Eyob's story and confronting my own impulse to ignore him. Even as I was grieving the acute pain of being othered by my Christian community, I initially did the same thing to him. The Persian poet Rumi insightfully observed, "Satan thought, 'I'm better than Adam,' and that *better than* is still strongly in us."[63]

A Movement That Can Heal Our World

In the face of the extreme othering that was devastating his world, Dietrich Bonhoeffer asked from his Nazi prison cell, "How are we going to find a basis for living together with other people?" His question attunes us to the stakes of neighbor love in the face of history and our tragically perennial tradition of othering—of seeing others as less than *neighbors* and thus excluding them from our moral circle of human responsibility.

---

[60]See "Suicide: Key Facts," World Health Organization, August 24, 2024, www.who.int/news-room/fact-sheets/detail/suicide.

[61]Yuval Noah Harari, *Sapiens: A Brief History of Humankind* (London: Vintage, 2011), 411.

[62]"New Surgeon General Advisory Raises Alarm About the Devastating Impact of the Epidemic of Loneliness and Isolation in the United States," US Department of Health and Human Services, May 3, 2023, www.hhs.gov/about/news/2023/05/03/new-surgeon-general-advisory-raises-alarm-about-devastating-impact-epidemic-loneliness-isolation-united-states.html.

[63]Jalal al-Din Rumi, *The Essential Rumi*, ed. Coleman Barks (San Francisco: HarperSanFrancisco, 2004), 142.

But Bonhoeffer's question also points us to the radical hope of Jesus' revolutionary movement of neighbor love: each and every person is made by God, loved by God, and thus morally connected and equally precious in value—including our "enemies." Neighbor love invites all of us into this ever-expanding moral circle that can overcome the ancient world's othering and the othering of our own today. Neighbor love was like a healing balm that worked its way through the encrusted hatred, exclusion, and oppression of human othering. It pioneered seemingly impossible pathways into a new future of shared humanity alive with dignity, compassion, justice, and hope. It remains our inestimable inheritance today.

In the eyes of neighbor love, Eyob is not simply a poor child, a suffering stranger, or even a cursed monster. Eyob is a precious neighbor whose life is worth embracing. In the ears of neighbor love, that little girl's cry outside the church is not simply a noise or annoyance. Her voice is the voice of God calling us to stop, to act, and to bring healing to our neighbor like Belay did.

How will we see others? How will we value others? How will we treat others: women, children, men, foreigners, the weak, the enslaved, enemies, ourselves—all of us others who defy any simplistic categorization? These are the questions at the heart of the human condition and this book. According to Bonhoeffer, they're the most important questions for our future.

I believe that neighbor love is the greatest treasure of Christian ethics and all of our shared moral wisdom across traditions. As we study its history, we come to see it as a global abolition movement against othering and a universal hope for all humanity. It has the power to heal our world, if only we no longer merely endorse it as a dead dogma. If we fully, frequently, and fearlessly discuss it—and then *embody* it in the *practice* of our lives—we can revive it as the living truth that it has been from the beginning.

Imagine if our eyes were healed and we no longer saw others merely as family, friends, strangers, and enemies. Imagine if our eyes could see each and every person as a precious neighbor. As C. S. Lewis argues, "There are no *ordinary* people. . . . Next to the Blessed Sacrament itself, your neighbor is the holiest object presented to your senses."[64]

What if we embraced this sacred vision of the other? What if—before we apply any label, any category, any "us" or "them" to anyone—we simply saw

---

[64]C. S. Lewis, *The Weight of Glory and Other Addresses* (Grand Rapids, MI: Eerdmans, 1965), 15.

one another as our *neighbors*? This is a universal moral vision that draws the golden circle of belonging around everyone and excludes none. In this healing movement, all reality and the universe itself become a shared moral neighborhood energized with love, justice, and flourishing for all.

This is our humanity's shared hope in our age of othering mutilated by preference, privilege, and power. I can no longer label, overlook, or attack any other because I live in the presence of my neighbor. Life becomes transfigured and astonishing: everywhere I go, I find neighbors. There are no longer any nobodies, no longer any invisible objects or valueless enemies.

This one—a neighbor.

That one—a neighbor.

Over there—a neighbor.

Behind those walls—a neighbor.

Under that bridge—a neighbor.

Buried in the ground—a neighbor.

Across that border—a neighbor.

In the past—a neighbor.

In the future—a neighbor.

In the mirror—a neighbor.

Despite my othering—a neighbor.

Mother Teresa said, "The world has never had such a need for love as it has today."[65] I share her conviction and believe that Martin Luther King Jr. was also right: "This love might well be the salvation of our civilization. . . . Love is ultimately the only answer to mankind's problems. . . . He who has love has the key that unlocks the door to the meaning of ultimate reality."[66] Neighbor love makes humanity shimmer and shine in full color like precious diamonds as if for the first time. How was it that I went through life and couldn't see the glory all around and within me? I am born again, and neighbor love sets me free.

---

[65]Mother Teresa, *Essential Writings* (Maryknoll, NY: Orbis Books, 2001), 26.

[66]Martin Luther King Jr., *A Testament of Hope: The Essential Writings and Speeches of Martin Luther King Jr.*, ed. James Washington (New York: HarperCollins, 1986), 140, 250.

2

THE ORIGINS OF NEIGHBOR LOVE

The Hebrew Bible

Stories change the world, in large part because they shape how we see ourselves and others such as Eyob. We observed their world-making power in the ancient stories of Mesopotamia, Greece, and Rome. Stories in sacred Scripture can be particularly powerful, because many of us receive them as divine revelation, as I myself do.[1] The stakes are high. These stories can enlarge our moral vision and call us into the ever-expanding circle of neighbor love. They can also reinscribe othering and justify violence. In many cases, they unfold in a liminal space between.

On October 7, 2023, the militant group Hamas launched its atrocious attack on Israel. Its fighters killed over 1,200 people and kidnapped more than 240 others, including many women and children. In reaction, Israel then launched a punishing war on Gaza and intensified its occupation of the West Bank. As I write, the Israeli military has killed more than 50,000 Palestinians, also including thousands of women and children, and displaced millions more. Its bombing has devastated over half the infrastructure of the Gaza Strip, including homes, hospitals, and schools. Gaza is now "home" to the largest per capita population of amputee children anywhere in the world.

On October 28, Prime Minister Benjamin Netanyahu invoked Hebrew Scripture to justify Israel's war. At a press conference in Tel Aviv, he told Israel, "You must remember what Amalek has done to you, says our Holy Bible. And we do remember."[2]

---

[1] I outline my understanding of the Bible as inspired Scripture in appendix 3 to my book *Blessed Are the Others: Jesus' Way in a Violent World* (Washington, DC: BitterSweet Collective, 2024).
[2] See Siobhan Marin and Andrew West, "What Is the Biblical Story of 'Amalek'? And Why Is It Being Used in South Africa's ICJ Case Against Israel?," ABC News, January 30, 2024, www.abc.net.au/news/2024-01-31/biblical-story-amalek-south-africa-icj-genocide-case-israel/103403552.

Netanyahu was invoking an othering biblical story. In this story, the indigenous people of Amalek ambush Israel as they seek to occupy Canaan after four hundred years of slavery in Egypt. In reaction, Moses others the Amalekites as enemies and commands Israel to totally exterminate them, what today is defined as genocide.[3] They were to be seen as totally unrelated, morally inferior, and unworthy of any compassion. It was an ominous biblical tradition to invoke amid Israel's war against its enemies. It was also another case of othering's irony: killing children in the name of protecting children.

As the war escalated, South Africans initiated an investigation with the International Court of Justice to determine whether the Israeli government was committing genocide against the people of Gaza. In many ways, they were continuing the prophetic legacy of Archbishop Desmond Tutu, who struggled against apartheid with a moral vision inspired by Hebrew Scripture. Tutu relentlessly reminded the world that all people are made in God's holy image and that each person is our precious neighbor. At the turn of the millennium, he wrote, "There are no ordinary people. . . . Each one of us is a very special person, a VSP far more important and far more universal than your normal VIP. . . . All, everyone, everything, belongs. None is an outsider, all are insiders, all belong."[4]

This is the complex tension we find in Hebrew Scripture. Its revelation can inspire a prophetic moral vision in which "none is an outsider, all are insiders, all belong." Its stories can also be weaponized to other neighbors as enemies and justify genocidal violence.

The Hebrew Bible or Christian Old Testament takes us to the origins of the neighbor-love movement in ancient Israel. It is a vast and complex library of books written in numerous genres across a thousand years. No

---

[3]As noted above, when I refer to genocide in this book, I have in mind the definition used by the United States Holocaust Memorial Museum: "Genocide is an internationally recognized crime where acts are committed with the intent to destroy, in whole or in part, a national, ethnic, racial, or religious group." See "What Is Genocide," United States Memorial Holocaust Museum, accessed January 19, 2025, www.ushmm.org/genocide-prevention/learn-about-genocide-and-other-mass-atrocities/what-is-genocide.

[4]Desmond Tutu, *No Future Without Forgiveness* (New York: Doubleday, 1999), 109, 265. Many Palestinians prophetically bear witness to neighbor love in the face of othering, hate, and genocide. From a Muslim perspective, see Izzeldin Abuelaish, *I Shall Not Hate: A Gaza Doctor's Journey on the Road to Peace and Human Dignity* (New York: Bloomsbury, 2012). From a Christian perspective, see Munther Isaac, *Christ in the Rubble: Faith, the Bible, and Genocide in Gaza* (Grand Rapids, MI: Eerdmans, 2025).

The Origins of Neighbor Love

summary can do this brilliant book full justice. I attempt to read it in the way I learned from my Jewish teacher Michael Fishbane: "The life-choices and situations embedded in the [biblical] text are not ignored or neutralized . . . but serve as pivots for moral reflection. Teaching is thus more than the transmission of information or even the deepening of the students' humanity. It may also bestow an example of freedom and responsibility."[5]

I hope to show in this chapter that the Hebrew Bible introduces us to an innovative vision of humanity and neighbor love. It breaks away from the violent creation myths we explored in the ancient world and casts a universal vision of human dignity. Still, it also contains deeply troubling limitations in who we see as neighbors and how others should be treated in light of Israel's painful conflicts and religious nationalism. These "life-choices" should not be "ignored or neutralized," as Fishbane writes.

This chapter will help us appreciate both the groundbreaking foundations on which Jesus builds and the innovations and expansions that he and the authors of New Testament make in their vision of neighbor love. One of the most sobering lessons of biblical wisdom is that it is possible for us to embrace the sacred command to love God and our neighbors as ourselves and still slip into othering and the justification of atrocious violence against those we see as enemies. We need to look patiently in the mirror of Scripture. Doing so helps us see ourselves more clearly and identify limits in our own vision of others and how we practice neighbor love today. As Fishbane writes, "It may also bestow an example of freedom and responsibility."

GENESIS 1: THE CREATION OF HUMANITY IN GOD'S IMAGE

The Bible begins with an astonishingly countercultural story. It claims that all people are made in God's holy image. It reads,

> Then God said, "Let us make humankind in our image, in our likeness, so that they may rule over the fish of the sea and the birds in the sky, over the livestock and all the wild animals, and over all the creatures that move along the ground."
> So God created humankind in God's own image,
>   in the image of God he created them;
>   male and female he created them. (Gen 1:26-27 NIV altered)

---

[5]Michael Fishbane, *The Garments of Torah: Essays in Biblical Hermeneutics* (Bloomington: Indiana University Press, 1989), 120.

The idea of the image of God was not new in the ancient cultures of Egypt and Mesopotamia. They saw their idols as the physical images and representatives of their gods on earth. On the social and political level, they sometimes saw their priests and kings as a god's image, bearing its exalted status and authority to rule over others on the god's behalf. Throughout, however, the image of god was exclusively reserved for powerful elites.[6]

Genesis 1 dared to break away from this dominant imperial culture and told a new story in which idols and elites don't image God. *All people*, including all women, image God. We are all made and marked by God to carry on the divine work of bringing presence, peace, and flourishing to the whole world. This preamble to the Bible is a groundbreaking vision of universal human dignity.[7]

In this vision, if we want to see God, we don't need to close our eyes in meditation, gaze upon idols, or bow before a priest or king. We need only to behold our neighbors. Each one is made in God's image with God's transcendent value and the creative responsibility to serve the world in all of its diversity. People are how God is primarily present on earth, even as the whole cosmos is celebrated as "very good" and suffused with primal blessing (Gen 1:31). Twelfth-century German mystic Hildegard of Bingen captured Genesis 1's beautiful vision: "Every creature is a glittering, glistening mirror of divinity."[8] Here goodness is original, primal, sovereign.

This vision is why Genesis 9:6 condemns murder as an attack on God Godself, "for in the image of God has God made humankind" (NIV altered). Here murder is not simply a violation of a human right. Murder is a violation of a divine right, God's inviolable gift of life to all people.[9]

Notice how radically different this is from the ancient myths we saw in chapter one. There the gods created the world and humanity through brutal murder. They then established an othering order and mandated the

---

[6] See J. Richard Middleton, *The Liberating Image: The Imago Dei in Genesis 1* (Grand Rapids, MI: Baker Academic, 2005).
[7] Studies that have influenced my interpretation of Genesis in addition to Middleton include Michael Fishbane, *Biblical Myth and Rabbinic Mythmaking* (New York: Oxford University Press, 2003); Leon Kass, *The Beginning of Wisdom: Reading Genesis* (Chicago: University of Chicago Press, 2006); Mark Smith, *The Priestly Vision of Genesis 1* (Minneapolis: Fortress, 2009); John Walton, *Genesis 1 as Ancient Cosmology* (University Park, PA: Eisenbrauns, 2009); and Ronald Hendel, *The Book of Genesis: A Biography* (Princeton, NJ: Princeton University Press, 2012).
[8] Quoted in Cynthia Overweg, "Hildegard of Bingen: The Nun Who Loved the Earth," *Quest* 105, no. 3 (Summer 2017): 21.
[9] Notice that Gen 9:6 still functions with a retributive ethic: killing is wrong, but the right response to it is more killing. Jesus will challenge this retributive justice in his vision of neighbor love.

enslavement of whole groups of people at the bottom of the hierarchy. By contrast, Genesis 1 envisions God making the world peacefully through God's creative communication and condemns murder as a violation of God's image embodied in all people, who bear equal value. In the beginning, creation is not a crime scene but a universal home in which all are beloved. God's world-making communication invites us into "belonging without othering."[10]

The claim that one God created the whole world and all humanity in God's image is a robust basis of moral universalism, the conviction that each and every person should be valued and treated equally without seeing others as unrelated or less than ourselves. It is the primal foundation of universal human rights and democratic governance. This moral circle encompasses and includes us all. According to ethicist David Gushee, this ancient biblical vision provides a foundation for human flourishing still today. It amounts to "the greatest moral contribution of the Christian tradition to world civilization."[11]

Read in its ancient context, then, Genesis 1 and its other-cherishing creation theology was a breakthrough in religion, ethics, culture, and politics. Rather than narrating warring gods ruling over othered factions of humanity, Genesis 1 invites us to see God as freely welcoming otherness and designing all people with sacred dignity and worldly responsibility. Each and every person is made in God's image, without privilege or prejudice. In the beginning, everyone is a priest and king in God's eyes. This, again, is why Desmond Tutu wrote, "There are no ordinary people. . . . All, everyone, everything, belongs. None is an outsider, all are insiders, all belong."[12]

When we look at any other in any place at any time, we're looking at a reflection of divine presence. We have never seen anyone who is not created by God—any other who is unrelated or less than ourselves. *All belong*. All are neighbors.

GENESIS 2–3: ORIGINAL HUMAN BELONGING AND THE ORIGINS OF OTHERING

Genesis 1 gives us a panoramic, big-picture view of creation. Genesis 2 gives us a zoomed-in, microscopic view of humanity. In the story of Genesis 2, humanity is pictured as being sculpted from the earth (*'adamah*) and then created

---

[10]See john powell and Stephen Menendian, *Belonging Without Othering: How We Save Ourselves and the World* (Stanford, CA: Stanford University Press, 2024).

[11]David Gushee, *The Sacredness of Human Life: Why an Ancient Biblical Vision Is Key to the World's Future* (Grand Rapids, MI: Eerdmans, 2013), 1.

[12]Tutu, *No Future Without Forgiveness*, 265.

from a single ancestor named *ha'adam*. Humans are made from the humus of the earth. With this story in mind, Paul tells the Greek philosophers in Athens, "From one human [God] made all the nations" (Acts 17:26 NIV altered).

Many other Christian thinkers across the ages then emphasized how Genesis 2 grounds humanity's original unity as one family. In the beginning, we are all human, all descended from a single ancestor, and thus all sacred siblings who belong in God's good creation. In this story, no human is a foreigner or alien to another.

Genesis 2 emphasizes another crucial insight into humanity: "It is not good for the human to be alone" (Gen 2:18 NIV altered). God created humans for relationship and life with others. We are fundamentally social creatures.

And thus God puts the man to sleep, removes a rib or side, and creates the woman. Eve is then introduced as Adam's "helper suitable for him." In English, *helper* could have a patriarchal overtone, like a servant or inferior. But the Hebrew word for "helper" (*kenegdo*) is often used in the Bible to describe God. Thus, Genesis 2 calls Eve Adam's *suitable* helper to clarify that they are equals to each other rather than Eve being Adam's superior.[13]

In this way, Genesis 2 gives us a picture of humanity's original unity and also our original need and desire to share relationship with other humans as we care for the earth from which we were made. In the Bible's primal vision of humanity, we are essentially relational creatures, dust of the earth's dust, bone of each other's bone, naked and shameless (Gen 2:25). Here again, the moral circle includes us all, and none is unrelated or less.

But this original belonging is soon shattered, and we encounter the origins of othering. In Genesis 3, the humans consume fruit from the one tree that God had marked as off-limits. In doing so, they assume that God has jealously withheld something from them to keep them inferior to God. Notice the competitive energy toward the other and insecure energy toward self. The voice of temptation promises that they will be "like God" if only they violate a limit and consume this fruit (Gen 3:5).

There is a profound irony in the text: God has already given them all creation as a good gift and freely made them in God's image, "like God." There was no competition between God and humanity but rather a relationship of welcoming, endowing with dignity, and blessing. Still, the

---

[13] J. Richard Middleton, "Reading Genesis 3 Attentive to Human Evolution," in *Evolution and the Fall*, ed. William Cavanaugh and James Smith (Grand Rapids, MI: Eerdmans, 2017), 93.

request to respect one small limit was interpreted through an inferiority complex and violated. Thus "the eyes of both of them were opened, and they realized that they were naked" (Gen 3:7).[14]

A first sign of the corruption of creation is the appearance of othering. The humans begin to feel shame, as if there were something wrong with themselves when they were really made *very good* in God's beloved image. They also perceive each other's God-imaging flesh with insecurity and enmity, as if they were threats to each other. They then cover themselves and blame each other for their loss of innocence. Rather than helping, they separate and attack each other.

Genesis 3 then observes that there will be struggle between us in light of our disordered desires. The fall did not simply rupture human relationship with God but also our relationship with the earth and other humans. From the beginning, our connection to God, ourselves, others, and all creation is inseparably woven together. Its rupture is rooted in our haunting sense of inferiority to someone else, the refusal to respect basic boundaries, and the feeling of shame. Now we feel as if the self needs to be hidden and the other needs to be distanced and blamed for our vulnerability.

In Genesis 4, the spread of othering is archetypally represented in the broken relationship of Adam and Eve's two sons. Like his parents with God, Cain is jealous of his brother, Abel. That is, he is afraid that Abel may have some superior status in the eyes of God that he doesn't possess. God warns Cain to master his temptation to soothe himself by attacking the other. But Cain's enraged sense of inferiority consumes him, and he kills his brother in a field.[15]

The story of the first murder in the Bible is dramatic: the ground itself cries out with the blood of Abel, shrieking against this act of murderous violation driven by the insecurity of perceived inferiority (Gen 4:10). The peaceful order of creation has been broken by the abuse of human freedom.

---

[14]For profound interpretations of this story and the wider biblical narrative through the lens of psychology and interpersonal neurobiology, see Curt Thompson, *The Soul of Shame: Retelling the Stories We Believe About Ourselves* (Downers Grove, IL: InterVarsity Press, 2015); Gena St. David, *The Brain and the Spirit: Unlocking the Transformative Potential of the Story of Christ* (Eugene, OR: Cascade Books, 2021).

[15]Note Vaclav Havel, *The Art of the Impossible: Politics as Morality in Practice* (New York: Knopf, 1997), 37: "It is said that those who hate suffer from an inferiority complex.... They are people with a complex based on the fatal perception that the world does not appreciate their true worth." See Aaron Beck, *Prisoners of Hate: The Cognitive Basis of Anger, Hostility, and Violence* (New York: Harper, 2000).

But here murder is not the origin of creation but a catastrophic consequence of its corruption. Genesis 4 offers an alternative origin story of othering in response to neighboring myths.

When the Lord asks Cain, "Where is your brother Abel?" Cain gives his famous reply, "Am I my brother's keeper?" (Gen 4:9). Insecure and arrogant, he denies having any real relationship with his own brother. Here we have shifted from shameless "bone of my bone and flesh of my flesh" to othering—to indifference and disowning the other. In this story, broken brotherhood marks the beginning of humanity's history of violence. When the other is no longer seen as related and equal in worth, killing becomes possible. Comparison, competition, and our desire for supremacy are at the roots of our war with one another.

Genesis 4 then notes that Cain's descendants became the makers of civilization, the musicians and metalworkers (Gen 4:21-22). This is a subtle but sobering warning: the soil of civilization is stained by blood, and its forefather killed his brother. Thus, the narrative of Genesis moves toward Egypt, an ancient superpower that enslaved others for its own power, prosperity, and prestige.

In the biblical imagination, we observe that empire finds its origins in the attitude that sees the other as unrelated and less than itself—as a thing to be used. There is a subtle critique of technology and civilization at work in Genesis, seeing their roots in one human othering his brother. Although othering does not go back to the beginning, whose core is good, its drive is deep within us. What we see as progress may easily unravel into a struggle for power. Vigilant, critical consciousness—the prophetic imagination—is crucially needed.[16]

In Genesis 4, our original belonging to one another, equally precious in worth, is ruptured. A new beginning for humanity is desperately needed.

GENESIS 11–12: ABRAHAM AND THE BLESSING FOR ALL OTHERS

A new beginning is what the story of Genesis gives us. In Genesis 11, we're introduced to Abraham, a Mesopotamian man from ancient Iraq. In the grief of his father's death, Abraham hears an unexpected call to embark on a journey to an unknown destination.

Abraham's call comes in the wake of othering, the splintering of humanity, and the rise of homogenizing empire. Genesis says that the earth was "full

---

[16]See Walter Brueggemann, *The Prophetic Imagination*, 2nd ed. (Minneapolis: Fortress, 2001).

The Origins of Neighbor Love

of violence" (Gen 6:11). In response, his new beginning would need to be radical: God tells Abraham to leave behind his people, his country, and his father's household. All that once defined his identity, security, and territory must be surrendered for this new odyssey.

God then makes a promise to Abraham: "I will make you into a great nation, and I will bless you. . . . All peoples on earth will be blessed through you. . . . To your offspring I will give this land" (Gen 12:2-3, 7). This promise looks far into the future, but it simultaneously reroots Abraham in God's primal intention for humanity. From the beginning, God blesses us and desires our full flourishing, alive with equal dignity, peace, and justice (Gen 1:28). I call this humane happiness.[17] Abraham is called to be part of restoring this primal, universal blessing.

In Genesis's story, Abraham thus becomes humanity's first heteronaut. Like an astronaut explores space, Abraham is called to explore otherness: a new God, a new home, and a new mission to bless all humanity. His vocation is to join his Creator in healing the human family.

Unless we've also experienced leaving home, it's difficult to appreciate how strange and even foolish he must have been seen in his time. But today almost half of humanity looks to Abraham as our spiritual parent.[18] This global movement started with Abraham's courageous willingness—his *faith*—to become vulnerable and go on an adventure with a mysterious God to an unknown land with new people for all of us (Gen 15:6; Rom 4:3).

Like creation, Abraham's covenant with God was universal in scope: *all people* of the earth would be blessed through him. None were to be left outside the circle of blessing. The New Testament will look back to this moment and see God's covenant with Abraham as the cornerstone of God's movement to redeem and reconcile all people, fulfilled in Jesus (Acts 3:25; Gal 3:8).

At heart, then, Abraham's daring decision to embark on this journey represented a new beginning of the neighbor-love movement that God initiated "in the beginning" with all creation. Abraham doesn't isolate and enrich himself with his own people like Plato's republic. He also doesn't go out to

---

[17] I explore Jesus' path of humane happiness in *Blessed Are the Others*. Notice that, like in Gen 9, Gen 12 also operates with a retributive, retaliatory imagination: those who curse Abraham will be cursed by his family (Gen 12:3). Jesus will challenge this mirroring, escalating retribution in his vision of neighbor love.

[18] See Jon Levenson, *Inheriting Abraham: The Legacy of the Patriarch in Judaism, Christianity, and Islam* (Princeton, NJ: Princeton University Press, 2014).

conquer the nations for an empire like Aristotle's student Alexander the Great. He embraces a mysterious call to leave home and become a vulnerable part of a universal movement to bless all humanity.

Wherever else Abraham's story and family may wander, this vocation to bless all people is the heart of God's desire and the trajectory of the biblical narrative as it looks toward future heteronauts who will dare to carry the movement forward.

GENESIS 9 AND DEUTERONOMY 7; 28: THE CURSE OF OTHERING

As we saw in Genesis 12, God's promise to Abraham is actually threefold: first, Abraham's people will have a special relationship or covenant with God; second, they will inherit the land of Canaan; third, they will be a blessing to all people. We can already feel the subtle tension inside this threefold promise. Are "others" also chosen by God? Is their need for home also to be respected?

The blessings of peoplehood and homeland can easily become part of an othering identity that sees itself as more chosen or superior to others and so muffles God's call to bless all others. The movement of neighbor love, conceptualized in and through the vision of the universal image of God in all people, could be overshadowed by Israel's understanding of itself as a special nation among many nations. We can call this religious nationalism.

We need to pay attention to the unfolding of Israel's story and how it envisions others. God's promise to Abraham is repeated around thirteen times in the Hebrew Bible (see Gen 12:7; 15:5-21; 17:4-8; 18:18-19; 22:17-18; 26:2-4; 28:13-15; 35:11-12; 46:4; Ex 3:6-8; 6:2-8; Neh 9:7-8; see also Ps 72:17; Mal 3:12). But the element of blessing others is only mentioned around five times (see Gen 18:18; 22:18; 26:4; 28:14). Midway through the Genesis story, Israel's calling to bless all people is never mentioned explicitly again in the Hebrew Bible (see Gen 28; Ps 72).

As Israel's story unfolds, we find a tensioned interest in the lives of others and an intensifying conflict between ethnic groups with complex histories, which increasingly favors the people of Israel. Going back to Israel's genealogical roots in Genesis 9, Noah's son Ham finds his father drunk and naked in his tent. Noah is enraged and brutally curses Ham with these fateful words: "Cursed be Canaan! The lowest of slaves will he be to his brothers. . . . May Canaan be the slave of Shem" (Gen 9:25-26). Thereafter, the Canaanites are to be seen as "low" and lesser in value, mere "slaves" to be used by the superior descendants of Shem (see 1 Chron 1:8, 13).

As we saw at the start of this chapter, the Canaanites came to be seen as Israel's "other," while Israel traced its ancestry back to Noah's favored son, Shem. So here we find yet another story of family conflict that justifies and fuels Israel's othering of the people of Canaan. Cain and Abel are recapitulated in Ham and Shem. This story would have massive implications for the future. Thousands of years later, White Christians in the United States claimed that Africans were the descendants of Ham to justify their enslavement by the "superior" children of Shem.[19] The ironies of othering abound across time and space.

This brief look at Genesis 9 indicates how the universalism of Genesis 1–12 and the blessing of Abraham may be decentered by othering as the Hebrew Bible's narrative unfolds. One way or another, Israel comes to see itself as superior to others and entitled to dominate, enslave, and kill whole groups of people. Religious nationalism—the claim to being exclusively chosen by God and above others—becomes Israel's idol.

We see this again with greater clarity a little later in the story. Deuteronomy, the Bible's fifth book, places repeated, intensifying emphasis on Israel's divine specialness. Here Moses gives a new, othering promise to Abraham's offspring. Moses tells them,

> You will be more blessed than any other people. (Deut 7:14)

> The LORD will establish you as his holy people, as he promised you on oath, if you keep the commands of the LORD your God and walk in obedience to him. Then all the peoples of the earth will see that you are called by the name of the LORD, and they will fear you. . . . The Lord will make you the head, not the tail. . . . You will always be at the top, never at the bottom. (Deut 28:9-10, 13)

> [God] will be an enemy to your enemies. (Ex 23:22)

Here the "other people" are not envisioned as being blessed by Israel but as *fearing* Israel, who is to be "more blessed." A competitive, hierarchical order is established, with Israel "on top" and others "at the bottom." The "head" represents dignity and agency, while the "tail" represents dirtiness and subservience.

---

[19]See David Goldenberg, *The Curse of Ham: Race and Slavery in Early Judaism, Christianity, and Islam* (New York: Oxford University Press, 2003).

In this image, Israel's identity gets tragically structured with othering: neighboring people are seen as unrelated or less, and Israel is exclusively chosen by God and above others, despite Israel's small size and rebellious heart (Deut 10:14-15). As in Plato's republic, this othering order is sanctified as the will of Israel's God, and Israel's enemies are marked as *God's* enemies. (They are not, however, described as "enemies by nature," as Plato and Aristotle imagined.)

If we are willing to be more honest, Moses calls Israel to fulfill its divine destiny through genocidal violence. Here the blessings of peoplehood and homeland seem to eclipse the call to bless all people. In Deuteronomy 7, Moses commands his community,

> You must destroy [the Canaanites] totally. Make no treaty with them, and show them no mercy. . . . You must destroy all the peoples the LORD your God gives over to you. Do not look on them with pity and do not serve their gods, for that will be a snare to you. . . . You will wipe out their names from under heaven. No one will be able to stand against you; you will destroy them. (Deut 7:2, 16, 24)

Texts such as this one are complex and should be interpreted with care. Scholars have read them in different ways, including as allegory and hyperbole.[20] Still, their potential to transfigure neighbors into others and to justify atrocious violence against them should not be ignored. Here again, we see the sad irony of othering: people being genocided as an act of faithfulness to the God who made them in God's image.

Many texts in the Hebrew Bible give gruesome accounts of Israel warring against its Canaanite neighbors and leaving "no survivors" and "utterly" destroying "men, women, and children" (Num 21:35; Deut 2:34; see also Deut 3:3-6; 6:10-11; Josh 6:21; 8:22-25; 24:12-13; 1 Sam 15:2; 27:9; 2 Sam 8:2). For example, in Numbers 31, Moses angrily asks his people after a battle, "Have you allowed all the women to live?" He then commands them to kill

---

[20]See Kate Common, *Undoing Conquest: Ancient Israel, the Bible, and the Future of Christianity* (Maryknoll, NY: Orbis Books, 2024); Eric Seibert, *Redeeming Violent Verses: A Guide for Using Troublesome Texts in Church and Ministry* (Louisville, KY: Westminster John Knox, 2023); Matthew Lynch, *Flood and Fury: Old Testament Violence and the Shalom of God* (Downers Grove, IL: IVP Academic, 2023); William Webb and Gordon Oeste, *Bloody, Brutal, and Barbaric? Wrestling with Troubling War Texts* (Downers Grove, IL: IVP Academic, 2019); Paul Copan, *Is God a Moral Monster? Making Sense of the Old Testament God* (Grand Rapids, MI: Baker Books, 2011); C. S. Cowles et al., *Show Them No Mercy: Four Views on God and the Canaanite Genocide* (Grand Rapids, MI: Zondervan, 2003); P. D. Stern, *The Biblical Herem: A Window on the Religious Experience of Israel* (Atlanta: Scholars Press, 1991).

all the surviving baby boys and nonvirgin women—a genocidal policy reminiscent of the one that Pharaoh had used against Israel in Egypt (Num 31:15-17; see Ex 1:15-22). Against the Canaanites, Moses instructs Israel, "Do not leave alive anything that breathes. Completely destroy them" (Deut 20:16-17; see also Deut 9:3; 20:3-4; 33:29).

Here othering borne of deep trauma and resentment seems to eclipse the vision of all people being made in God's image. It allows even noncombatant children and women to be targeted. Rather than rerooting itself in the primal blessing for all people, the community replays its painful historical trauma with others and enshrines a nationalistic promise of supremacy.

Israel's larger war policy against the Canaanites marked a specific group for focused annihilation: the Amalekites. Moses warns Israel to never forget how they ambushed Israel and to not let any Amalekites survive. Like a trail of tears, this mandate of genocide can be traced across the pages of the Hebrew Bible (see Ex 17:14-16; Num 24:20; Deut 25; 1 Sam 15; 2 Sam 1; Esther 8–9). In our time, we saw how Benjamin Netanyahu invoked this ancient tradition to justify Israel's devastating war against Gaza. Here Gazans are othered as Amalekites who are completely cut off from Israel and unworthy of any compassion.

The curse of othering is extremely powerful, especially when it is charged with religious significance. In this stretch of Israel's story, the image of God in all people, humanity as a single family, and Abraham's call to bless all people seem overshadowed, if not lost.[21] Israel doesn't imagine itself as one people among many, even if with a special calling from God to bless the rest. Israel is exalted as "the head" and the others reduced to "the tail," who fear Israel like Abel at the hands of Cain. With its new promise, Israel will always be at the top and the others at the bottom. Its identity becomes structured by othering, competitive and hierarchical, which it uses to justify violence and even genocide.

LEVITICUS 19: THE HEBREW COMMAND OF NEIGHBOR LOVE

While religious and ethnic othering is a real problem in Israel's biblical tradition, not to be ignored or neutralized, as Fishbane writes, Hebrew Scripture narrates how God called Israel to be a society of justice governed by law

---

[21] See Michael Walzer, *In God's Shadow: Politics in the Hebrew Bible* (New Haven, CT: Yale University Press, 2012).

rather than arbitrary force. Deuteronomy describes how the justice of Israel's laws and the intimacy of God to Israel's prayers would be a sign to the nations (Deut 4:6-8). At its best, Israel was meant to be a model society, and the command of neighbor love was woven into its moral fabric.

We find the command of neighbor love in Leviticus 19:18 among a collection of laws called the Holiness Code. This code was meant to define the community's character, action, and culture. The text reads, "Do not seek revenge or bear a grudge against anyone among your people, but love your neighbor as yourself. I am the LORD" (Lev 19:18).[22]

This command crystallizes some of Moses' most powerful moral teachings that uplift the dignity of others. In the verses before it, Moses commanded the community to leave some of its fields unharvested so the poor and foreigners could access food (Lev 19:9-10). He also required Israel to pay hired workers fairly (Lev 19:13), to refuse to exploit people with physical disabilities (Lev 19:14), and to treat the disadvantaged with the same justice as the more powerful (Lev 19:15). In the verses after the neighbor-love command, Moses teaches, "When a foreigner resides among you in your land, do not mistreat them. The foreigner residing among you must be treated as your native-born. Love them as yourself, for you were foreigners in Egypt. I am the LORD your God" (Lev 19:33-34). In context, then, the command to love our neighbor as ourselves seems to summarize Moses' teaching to respect and protect the well-being of the most vulnerable people in the community: the poor, workers, the physically disabled, and even foreigners. In terms of brute power, these others could be used and abused with little fear of repercussions to oneself, as we saw in Plato and Aristotle. But Moses demands love to overrule power. Rather than treating neighbors with revenge and grudges—potent factors in othering, as we saw in the case of Israel's conflict with the Amalekites—neighbors must be *loved*. Indeed, they must be loved as much as we love ourselves and our own people.[23]

---

[22]The Hebrew text is *we'ahabta lere'aka kamoka*. See 1 Sam 18:1, where "Jonathan became one in spirit with David, and he loved him as himself," and 1 Sam 20:17, "And Jonathan had David reaffirm his oath out of love for him, because he loved him as he loved himself [*be'ahbato 'oto ki-'ahabat naphsho*]." There is an interesting parallel to David and Jonathan's friendship in the Hittite "Treaty of Tudhaliya IV with Kurunta of Tarhuntassa on the Bronze Tablet Found in Hattusa" (2.18). There we read, "Already previously [before Tudhaliya's kingship] we were dear and good to each other. We even were parties to an oath: 'Each shall be loyal to the other.'" Quoted in William Hallo and K. Lawson Younger, eds., *Contexts of Scripture*, vol. 2, *Monumental Inscriptions from the Ancient World* (Leiden: Brill, 2000), 102.

[23]For studies of the ethics of neighbor love in Jewish tradition, see Kengo Akiyama, *The Love of Neighbour in Ancient Judaism: The Reception of Leviticus 19:18 in the Hebrew Bible, the*

Why, then, did the command of neighbor love not apply to the neighboring Amalekites and their children?

The Hebrew word for "neighbor" is *re'a*, and it appears 179 times in the Hebrew Bible. As we've seen, Israel attempted to live in a largely homogeneous community separated from others. So the common meaning of *neighbor* throughout the Hebrew Bible is usually restricted to "someone nearby," typically a fellow Israelite of the same ethnicity and religion. This is similar to the English word *neighbor*, which literally means a "near dweller" (*neah gebur*) or someone next door. The vast majority of uses of *re'a* in Hebrew Scripture have this local, limited meaning rather than the universal sense of human connectedness and equality of value.

In Leviticus 19:18, notice that "your neighbor" and "your people" are put in parallel: "Do not seek revenge or bear a grudge against anyone among *your people*, but love *your neighbor* as yourself." It seems that to love your neighbor primarily meant to have concern for your kin and to protect the solidarity of the group, not necessarily to open the boundaries of the group or to embrace a universal moral responsibility, at least when the term *neighbor* was used. We see this in that Leviticus needed to give two love commands: one for the neighbor and another for the foreigner (see also Deut 10:18-19).

This points to a troubling limit to neighbor love in the Hebrew Bible: in some cases, at least, it could be restricted to people *like us* and people *we like*, even as this limit was stretched by the command to love the foreigner. When certain groups were othered as enemies, such as the Amalekites, grudges could be held, and even their babies could seen without compassion and slaughtered. We observe how othering deactivates neighbor love and pushes othered people outside the moral circle of connection and protection. Jewish scholar James Kugel writes, "Thus, there were certainly grounds to claim that not all people are, in this sense, one's 'neighbor.' . . . Understood in this fashion, 'You shall not hate your *brother* . . . You shall love your *neighbor* as yourself' paradoxically became a summons to hate all those who were not in the category of 'brother' or 'neighbor'!"[24]

Septuagint, the Book of Jubilees, the Dead Sea Scrolls, and the New Testament (Leiden: Brill, 2018); Joseph Telushkin, *A Code of Jewish Ethics*, vol. 2, *Love Your Neighbor as Yourself* (New York: Harmony, 2009); Lenn Goodman, *Love Thy Neighbor as Thyself* (New York: Oxford University Press, 2008); Paul Mendes-Flohr, *Love, Accusative and Dative: Reflections on Leviticus 19:18* (Syracuse, NY: Syracuse University Press, 2007); Zelig Pliskin, *Love Your Neighbor: You and Your Fellow Man in the Light of the Torah* (Jerusalem: Aisha HaTorah, 1977).

[24]James Kugel, *Traditions of the Bible: A Guide to the Bible as It Was at the Start of the Common Era* (Cambridge, MA: Harvard University Press, 1999), 455-58. Kugel provides valuable

The Hebrew verb for love (*'ahab*) offers another clue into why love could be commanded but also deactivated. This word is more concerned with action than feeling. Like Erich Fromm points out in *The Art of Loving*, love is a *practice* rather than a preference. Jewish commentator Jacob Milgrom writes,

> How can love be commanded? The answer simply is that the verb *'ahab* signifies not only an emotion or attitude, but also deeds. This is especially true in Deuteronomy, which speaks of covenantal love [*hesed*]. The *ger* [foreigner] is to be "loved" by providing him with food and shelter (Deut 10:18-19). God is "loved" by observing his commandments (Deut 11:1; cf. 5:10; 7:5-6).... Thus *'ahab* also carries the meaning of "reach out, befriend"—a love that can be commanded.[25]

We find a deceptively similar-sounding command to love in the Succession Treaty of King Esarhaddon, the son of the great Sennacherib who later besieged Jerusalem. Esarhaddon reigned over the Neo-Assyrian Empire from 681 to 669 BC and called himself the king of the universe. As he prepared to hand power over to his son Ashurbanipal, he commanded his vassals, "You shall love Ashurbanipal, the great crown prince designate, son of Esarhaddon, king of Assyria, your lord, like your (own) lives."[26] Biblical scholar John Walton observes, "[Ancient Near Eastern] treaties are concerned about how people treat the king more than about how they treat one another.... [This command] is hardly talking about the same thing as Leviticus 19:18."[27] Esarhadon tells us to love the *king* "as our own life." Leviticus tells us to love our *neighbor* "as our self."

---

commentary on this verse and points out how later Jewish interpreters such as the Essenes read it in this more restricted sense. Kugel observes, "'Your neighbor' might not necessarily mean all human beings. This Hebrew word actually means something more like 'your friend,' and while it can simply mean 'your fellow,' it is basically used in this section of Leviticus interchangeably with 'your brother' and 'your kinsman.'"

[25]See Jacob Milgrom, *Leviticus 17–22*, Anchor Yale Bible Commentary (New Haven, CT: Yale University Press, 2000), 1653. See also 1 Kings 5:1; 2 Chron 19:2.

[26]Quoted in K. Lawson Younger, *Contexts of Scripture*, vol. 4, *Supplements* (Leiden: Brill, 2016), par. 24.

[27]Personal communication, April 5, 2019. Analyzing the Hebrew grammar of this historic command, John Walton wrote to me, "I am most persuaded by a translation such as, 'Show preference to your neighbor [who is] like you.'" He notes that the command to love the foreigner prevents the command of neighbor love from being exclusive or purely ethnocentric: "The direction in Leviticus 19 is to show equal preference to each [the neighbor/insider and the foreigner/outsider]. Treat them as insiders.... The point for us is that we are to actively work on the behalf of those around us with no regard to their outsider/insider status."

The Origins of Neighbor Love

The neighbor-love ethic had especially profound implications, then, in Israel's policies toward the poor. Recall that neighboring thinkers such as Plato and Aristotle saw the poor as inferior "by nature" and destined to remain trapped in poverty at the bottom of the social hierarchy. By contrast, Israel's law taught, "Give generously to [the poor] and do so without a grudging heart; then because of this the LORD your God will bless you in all your work and in everything you put your hand to" (Deut 15:10). In practice, the poor should receive interest-free loans, be protected from oppression, and be paid for their labor daily to strengthen their security. Every seven years, farmers should leave their fields completely unharvested, so the poor can gather food freely. The annual tithe to the Lord should be devoted to the poor every three years, meaning that Israel gave around 23 percent of its economy to the poor. Israelite debts should be canceled every seven years, and enslaved Israelites should be released from bondage every seven years. Moreover, the law taught that people who escaped from bondage should not be returned to their masters but given shelter from oppression (Deut 23:15-16).[28] Most importantly for a just society, Moses insists that the law and courts should rule equally over rich and poor, strong and weak neighbors. Again, this was very different from ancient philosophy and political order. It remains an inspiring, challenging moral vision for us today.

Like the image of God in Genesis 1, then, the command of neighbor love calls us to stretch our affection and service far beyond elite power to embrace the most vulnerable people in our community with love. In fact, God's name is repeated beside the neighbor-love command, as if it bears the personal signature of divine character. Ethicist Ronald Green notes that later Jewish commentary on this verse "emphasizes acts of kindness and respect.... To love the neighbor, says Maimonides, requires one to speak positively of him and 'have compassion upon his possessions.'" In this tradition, neighbor love is embodied in "acts of benevolence" such as "visiting the sick, consoling the bereaved, burying the dead, dowering the bride, and rejoicing for the bride and groom. All things that you want others to do for you, said Maimonides,

---

[28]Compare this to "The Agreement Between Ir-Addu and Niqmepa," dating from the Middle Babylonian period (1595–1155 BC), where these two kings agree that "fugitive slaves" must be imprisoned and returned to their owners (lines 22–25). Leaders who refused to return enslaved people were to be punished by having their hands cut off (line 31). See Hallo and Younger, *Contexts of Scripture*, 2:330.

'do them for your brother.'"²⁹ Rabbi Akiba (AD 50–135), who lived soon after Jesus, called neighbor love "the great general principle of Torah."³⁰

The prophet Jeremiah offers one of the most striking later invocations of neighbor in the story of Hebrew Scripture. In context, Jeremiah is calling the people of Israel to "reform [their] ways" and critiques their trust in empty religion centered on the temple (Jer 7:3). He urges them, "If you really change your ways and your actions and deal with your neighbor justly, if you do not oppress the foreigner, the fatherless or the widow and do not shed innocent blood in this place, and if you do not follow other gods to your own harm, then I will let you live in this place" (Jer 7:5-7). Like Leviticus, Jeremiah connects the way we treat our neighbor with the way we treat foreigners, orphans, and widows—representatives of the most vulnerable people in ancient society and often today. He makes Israel's belonging in the land contingent on its moral behavior. Moreover, Jeremiah daringly elevates our treatment of our neighbors over our religious piety in the temple. If we claim a religious identity but neglect treating our neighbor with justice, we're not actually worshiping God, Jeremiah insists. Jesus will pick up on Jeremiah's prophetic vision many centuries later.

Leviticus 19:18 is a diamond in the crown of the Hebrew Bible and a crucial moment in the history of the neighbor-love movement. Across our traditions, it challenges us to make love the very center of our lives and to choose to practice this love across othering boundaries of physical ability, economic class, and political power. As it does so, it also raises important questions for us to wrestle with today: Who do we see or not see as our neighbor? How might othering deactivate our love for some people? And what role does our faith play in whether we choose to love or other our neighbors?³¹

---

²⁹See Ronald Green, "Neighbor Love in the Jewish Tradition," in *Love and Christian Ethics: Tradition, Theory, and Society*, ed. Frederick Simmons and Brian Sorrels (Washington, DC: Georgetown University Press, 2016), 348. Like we saw in Genesis, Exodus and Leviticus teach an ethics of reciprocity and retribution: "Anyone who injures their neighbor is to be injured in the same manner" (Lev 24:19). Likewise, if your bull injures your neighbor's bull, you need to make restitution (Ex 21:35). Strikingly, the Mishnah (later Jewish commentary) says that if your bull gores a non-Israelite, you do not need to pay them back because a non-Israelite is not a neighbor. See Herbert Danby, trans., *The Mishnah* (Peabody, MA: Hendrickson, 2011), tractate Baba Kamma 37b.

³⁰Sifra Qodashim 4, quoted in Kugel, *Traditions of the Bible*, 459.

³¹In Ex 32, Moses commands the Israelites to kill their Israelite neighbors who worship gods other than the Lord. It appears that religious freedom of conscience was limited or not part of Moses'

Israel's Treatment of Others

The last section gave a snapshot of how Israel's God commanded the community to treat its fellow Israelite neighbors. But what about "others"? How were non-Israelite neighbors seen and treated in the Hebrew Bible?[32]

Once more, we find a tension between expansive ethical teachings and significant limitations. We need to observe this complexity with patience, humility, and an awareness of the tensions in our own moral visions today. As Fishbane writes, doing so may "bestow an example of freedom and responsibility."[33]

We've seen that Israel was twice commanded to love outsiders as themselves because God himself loves outsiders (Lev 19:34; Deut 10:18-19). Thus, non-Israelites living and working in Israel were to be treated as equals and not oppressed (Ex 22:21). This again was very different from the ethnocentric othering we saw in classical Greek philosophy.

Powerfully, Israel was required to make the communal declaration, "Cursed is anyone who withholds justice from the foreigner, the fatherless or the widow" (Deut 27:19). Here, allowing othering to corrupt the administration of justice is explicitly, collectively condemned. More specifically, Moses tells his community not to despise an Egyptian (Deut 23:7). After Israel suffered four hundred years of slavery in Egypt, this was a potent rejection of resentful othering against an easy target of traumatized aggression.

The Mosaic law also requires generosity toward impoverished foreigners (Lev 19:10; 23:22; 25:6, 35; Deut 24:14-22; 26:12). It commands, "The foreigners, the fatherless and the widows who live in your towns may come and eat and be satisfied, and so the LORD your God may bless you in all the work of your hands" (Deut 14:29). Thus, when the suffering Job defended his

---

vision of neighbor love. Again, this raises important questions for people who take Scripture seriously today: To what extent should we love our neighbors the way we want to be loved ourselves—that is, with the freedom to follow a faith that we happen to believe is valid? What temptations might religious believers face in seeking to control their society and make it more homogeneous according to their own vision of faithfulness?

[32]The Hebrew Bible uses various terms for "others," with various shades of meaning. Traditional translations include "alien" (*ger*), "alien" (*toshav*), "foreigner" (*zar*), "stranger" (*nakri*), "strange(r)" (*zar*), and "enemy" (*'oyeb*). See Reinhard Achenbach et al., eds., *The Foreigner and the Law: Perspectives from the Hebrew Bible and the Ancient Near East* (Wiesbaden: Harrassowitz, 2011); José E. Ramírez Kidd, *Alterity and Identity in Israel: The ger in the Old Testament* (New York: de Gruyter, 1999). More broadly, see M. C. Poo, *Enemies of Civilization: Attitudes Toward Foreigners in Ancient Mesopotamia, Egypt, and China* (Albany: State University of New York Press, 2005).

[33]Fishbane, *Garments of Torah*, 120.

innocence before God, he highlighted his commitment to care for others, declaring, "No stranger had to spend the night in the street, for my door was always open to the traveler" (Job 31:32).

The Hebrew Bible repeatedly insists that one law should rule over both the Israelite and the resident foreigner, and courts should not be biased (Lev 24:22; Num 9:14; 15:15). While the law does not abolish slavery altogether, it states that enslaved foreigners must be allowed to rest on the Sabbath like everyone else (Ex 20:10; 23:12; Lev 16:29; Deut 5:14). Foreign workers should also receive fair wages like Israelites, and they should not be mistreated or deprived of justice (Lev 19:34; Deut 24:14).

Foreigners are also included in some aspects of Israel's religious life. The law allows foreigners to bring offerings to the Lord (Num 15:14), and non-Israelite residents are allowed to celebrate the Passover if they are circumcised (Ex 12:48; Num 9:14; 2 Chron 30:25).[34] Later in the biblical story, King Solomon asks God to hear the prayers of foreigners when they come to visit the temple (1 Kings 8:41-43; 2 Chron 6:32). Here we hear echoes of the Bible's opening vision of one God creating all people.

We've also seen that the prophet Jeremiah makes not oppressing foreigners a condition for receiving God's favor and remaining in the land (Jer 7:6; 22:3). The prophets Ezekiel, Zechariah, and Malachi also condemn the mistreatment of foreigners (Ezek 22:7, 29; Zech 7:10; Mal 3:5). Indeed, Ezekiel prophesies that foreigners will be allowed to take land in Israel and be treated as "native-born Israelites" (Ezek 47:22).

Here the Hebrew Bible is profoundly inclusive and protective of its non-Israelite neighbors, to the point of commanding Israelites to love foreigners as themselves. This was unimaginable in Plato's republic, where non-Greeks were labeled "enemies by nature."

But there were also limitations to how Israel saw and treated its non-Israelite neighbors.

As we've seen, certain othered groups such as the Canaanites and the Amalekites in particular were supposed to be entirely annihilated. The circle of Israel's moral law against killing did not include them. Even their babies, children, and women were not to be shown mercy (Ex 17:14-16; Num 24:20; Deut 7:1-6, 14-26; 25:17-19; 1 Sam 15; 2 Sam 1:1-16; Esther 8–9).

---

[34] The guest or hired worker (*toshav*) may not, according to Lev 22:10.

The Origins of Neighbor Love

Moreover, othered groups such as the Moabites were supposed to be excluded from the Israelite community seemingly forever. Israelites were forbidden even to wish good for them or to be kind to them (Deut 23:3-6). The Moabites became so intensely othered that King David massacred them seemingly for fun (2 Sam 8:2).

In these cases, the Genesis 1 vision of all people being made in God's image, Abraham's calling to bless all people, and the command to release grudges and love the neighbor seem completely overshadowed. The othering that emerged out of bitter conflict and competition for land apparently deactivated this expansive moral vision.

Further, despite its demand for equality, Israelite law contains some significant double standards in how it treats foreigners. For example, while Israelites are required to cancel one another's debts every seven years to prevent entrenched poverty, foreigners' debts are not to be canceled (Deut 15:3). Likewise, while Israelites are to give one another interest-free loans to promote economic empowerment, they can charge foreigners interest on their loans (Deut 23:20). While Moses specifically teaches that enslaved Israelites should be released every seven years and given economic support to restart their lives, enslaved foreigners are to remain Israel's property until death, and their enslaved children are to be passed down as "inherited property" (Lev 25:44-46; see Deut 15:12). In fact, the Jerusalem temple itself, like most ancient monuments, was built by forced, foreign labor (2 Sam 20:24; 1 Chron 22:2). Even after the exile, Israel returned to the land with over seven thousand enslaved people, approximately one for every six Israelites (Ezra 2:64-65; Neh 7:64). These double standards seem to focus on preventing economic equity and full belonging for foreigners in Israel's community. The fear of universal equality is latent in the story.[35]

As the biblical story unfolds and Israel faces the vulnerability of returning from exile, we encounter openly othering sentiments and segregationist policies toward non-Israelites. For example, Israel's reformist leader Ezra refers to Jews as "the holy race" and seems to see mingling with non-Israelite blood as contaminating (Ezra 9:2). He then demands that mixed families be broken

---

[35]Note john powell and David Menendian, *Belonging Without Othering*, 116-18: "Some people may endorse the egalitarian principle in the abstract (appealing to their better angels) but oppose the implementation of the principle in practice or policy, or feel sadness, despair, or anger in its wake, and never notice the cognitive dissonance.... Simply the loss of dominance is felt as if the marginalized group is taking over. For members of a dominant group, equality can feel like a threat."

apart. To execute this policy, he requires the entire community to gather in Jerusalem within three days or forfeit their property and be expelled from the community. Then a list is made of Israelites who are married to foreigners, and the non-Israelite family members are systematically cast out (Ezra 10).

The leader Nehemiah continues this othering policy of complete separation from foreigners. He verbally curses and physically attacks Israelites who married non-Israelite women and have mixed children (Neh 13:25). Nehemiah's story ends with him "purifying" the community's leadership "of everything foreign" and praying, "Remember me with favor, my God" (Neh 13:30-31).[36]

Once again, we face a profound tension in how the moral circle was drawn in Israel's ethics. On the one hand, Israelites were explicitly commanded to love foreigners as themselves, to govern their society with equal justice for all, and to treat vulnerable foreigners with special care. Here the moral circle is incredibly expansive, especially when we compare it to neighboring societies. On the other hand, some non-Israelite others could be treated unequally, excluded, or even subjected to genocide. When Moses describes what life under God's curse would look like if Israel disobeyed God's law, he invokes a deep fear of non-Israelite others: "The foreigners who reside among you will rise above you higher and higher, and you will sink lower and lower. They will lend to you, but you will not lend to them. They will be the head, but you will be the tail" (Deut 28:43-44).

This othering identity and the xenophobic competition within it express themselves in deeply troubling ways toward the end of the Hebrew Bible's story: foreign blood being seen as contaminating to Israel's "holy seed," lists being made of integrated families, and a systematic campaign being executed to separate these families and "purify" Israel of "everything foreign." Here again the notion of purity plays a powerful role in othering. We also see the irony of othering once more: the claim to holiness justifies destroying families and treating women and children with cruelty.

Another challenging question confronts us in the mirror of Scripture: What does it mean to *love* people as ourselves who remain *othered*—disempowered and sometimes excluded and oppressed? This tension is not resolved in the Hebrew Bible, and we feel it intensely today in our own societies amid our age of othering.

---

[36] The prophet Zephaniah goes as far as condemning simply wearing foreign clothes (Zeph 1:8).

Israel's Treatment of Enemies

As we have seen, Israel was a people with "enemies" (*'oyeb*). As a nation at the crossroad of nations—crucially located between Egypt, Mesopotamia, the Arabian peninsula, and Greece—making and fighting enemies was part of Israel's core identity and common life. We see that when the other becomes the *enemy*, the moral circle seemingly closes completely.

Across its stories, we observe how Israel sought to dominate its enemies and claimed God's power in doing so. When Israel was in right relationship with God, it expected to dominate and destroy its enemies. As Moses promises, "[God] will be an enemy to your enemies" (Ex 23:22). Faithfulness to God and military power were linked in Israel's religious nationalism. Its sacred objects, such as the ark and the temple, were used as instruments for seeking God's favor in war against enemies (I Kings 8:44-45; 2 Chron 6:34).

There are approximately 234 references to enemies in the Hebrew Bible—55 more than the 179 references to neighbors. Among them, we do not find a command to love the enemy as we do the command to love the neighbor and foreigner. We also don't encounter much explicit teaching about how to reconcile with enemies or "defeat" them with nonviolent methods. After God called Abraham to be a blessing to "all people," we observe how enmity with others overshadows the vision, and peacemaking almost vanishes from the picture. Instead, Israel hated, dominated, and struggled to annihilate its enemies.

Some see the Hebrew Bible's view of enemies as its greatest weakness and most serious problem. Many verses could illustrate this concern, but Leviticus 26 is one troubling example: "You will pursue your enemies, and they will fall by the sword before you. Five of you will chase a hundred, and a hundred of you will chase ten thousand, and your enemies will fall by the sword before you" (Lev 26:7-8). Along with this image of chasing and mass-killing enemies, Israelite literature celebrates beheading enemies (Deut 32:42), crushing their faces in the mud (2 Sam 22:35-49), bathing in their blood and feeding their flesh to dogs (Ps 68:21-23), and killing their children (Ezek 9:5-7).

The book of Esther is among of the most famous in the Bible because of its inspiring story about the courageous Jewish heroine named Esther, who saves her people from the genocidal hatred of Haman. Christians have made many children's books and women's Bible studies from Esther's story. But what is often suppressed is that Esther ends with Israel turning this genocidal violence against its enemies. Between the lines, Esther unfolds as a story about Israel's ancient call to annihilate the Amalekites, since the villain Haman is a descendant of Amalek (Esther 3:10). When the tables turn, we read, "The Jews struck down all their enemies with the sword, killing and destroying them, and they did what they pleased to those who hated them.... They killed seventy-five thousand of them" (Esther 9:5, 16).

Here again we face a profound ethical tension. On the one hand, Esther is an exciting story of courage and deliverance in the face of persecution. But on the other, it is a story of brutal revenge bordering on gleeful genocidal violence. The Jews throw a feast after killing seventy-five thousand people. Strikingly, Esther is the only book in the Bible in which God's name is not mentioned. Between the lines, the text provokes the question: Has the nation idolized itself and taken the place of the God who created all people, including the Amalekites, in God's holy image?

Even so, the Hebrew Bible does contain traces of an ethic of love for enemies. We can briefly mention several here and then explore another example in more detail in the next section.

Significantly, God is the first practitioner of love for enemies in Hebrew Scripture. In Genesis 2, God commands the first humans to respect a basic boundary and warns them that refusing to do so will lead to certain death (Gen 2:17). But when they violate this boundary, God does not kill them; God calls out to them and covers their shame (Gen 3:9, 21). Similarly, in Genesis 4, God warns Cain to master his anger and to resist harming his brother Abel (Gen 4:6-7). But when Cain flouts God and murders Abel, God does not apply retributive justice and put him to death. Instead, God names the grave evil that Cain has committed and then marks him for protection against being murdered himself (Gen 4:10-12, 15-16). These foundational stories in Scripture simultaneously show that human violence has catastrophic consequences but also that God desires to respond with mercy.

In 1 Samuel 24, the persecuted David doesn't kill the vulnerable King Saul out of respect for his kingship. Saul finds this astonishing and says to David, "When a man finds his enemy, does he let him get away unharmed? May the LORD reward you well for the way you treated me today" (1 Sam 24:19; see 2 Kings 6:21-23; 2 Chron 28:15). Here kindness to an enemy is seen as behavior that God rewards.[37]

---

[37]See Ex 23:4, where Moses commands Israelites to return the lost property of their enemies.

The Origins of Neighbor Love

In Proverbs 16:7, the sage says, "When the LORD takes pleasure in anyone's way, he causes their enemies to make peace with them." Here God's favor is not manifested through destroying enemies but through making peace with them. What remains unclear is whether this peace is predicated on intimidating power or a genuine reconciliation of relationship.

In Proverbs 24:17, the sage says again, "Do not gloat when your enemy falls; when they stumble, do not let your heart rejoice." Echoing Leviticus 19:18's command to release grudges against neighbors, here celebrating an enemy's ruin is rejected. This text is in tension with Esther's story and other passages where the enemy's destruction is gleefully relished.

In Proverbs 25, the sage further says, "If your enemy is hungry, give him food to eat; if he is thirsty, give him water to drink. In doing this, you will heap burning goals on his head, and the LORD will reward you" (Prov 25:21-22). In ancient Egyptian literature, burning coals could represent purification rather than punishment.[38] Here practicing compassion toward enemies, like David did with Saul, is taught as behavior that God rewards. I will return to this text in chapter four.

Looking deeply into the mirror of Scripture is sobering: when *neighbors* are othered into enemies, the moral circle easily closes. In this exclusive space, atrocious evils that are otherwise condemned by God can be ironically celebrated in God's name or even eclipse God altogether. Othering that becomes enemy-making is the gateway to enslaving image-bearers of God, subjecting neighbors to segregationist policies, and gleefully perpetrating genocide that mocks our primal vocation to bless all people. We see this disturbing pattern across humanity's stories and our societies today. Thankfully, the Hebrew Bible also contains powerful stories that directly confront and challenge our impulse to see others as enemies. We turn to one of the most beautiful examples next.

RUTH: THE DIVINE LOVE THAT OVERCOMES OTHERING

The book of Ruth is one of the smallest in the Bible, but it narrates one of the Bible's most powerful stories of overcoming othering and loving the enemy. It's the story of Ruth and Boaz and their countercultural relationship.

As we've seen, the Moabites were othered as Israel's hated enemies. Moses commanded Israel never to allow Moabites to enter the community or even

---

[38]See William Klassen, "Coals of Fire: Symbol of Repentance or Revenge?," *New Testament Studies* 9 (1963): 337-50.

to show them kindness (Deut 23:3-6). Moabites were seen as descending from a dirty, incestuous ancestry, and they were resented for betraying Israel when it was journeying through the desert after escaping slavery in Egypt (Gen 19:36-38; Num 24).

This othering became so severe that King David brutally massacred and enslaved the Moabites (2 Sam 8:2). After the exile, the reformers Ezra and Nehemiah then reinforced Moses' law against the Moabites: they had all of them rounded up, separated from their Jewish families, and systematically excluded them (Ezra 10; Neh 13). Twenty passages in the Hebrew Bible have nasty, othering things to say about Moabites.[39]

This is the crucial background for understanding the radical ethics of the book of Ruth, because Ruth herself was a hated other: a Moabite.

In this seemingly innocent story, an Israelite woman named Naomi and her husband migrate to neighboring Moab in search of food during a famine in Israel. Soon enough, Naomi's husband dies. While still in Moab, her two sons marry Moabite wives, but the sons also die. It is likely that Israelite observers would have seen Naomi as cursed by God. After all, she voluntarily defied Moses' command and mixed with the despised Moabites. Her family is dead, and her life is falling apart.

After the famine ends, the bereaved Naomi decides to move back to Israel, and her widowed daughter-in-law Ruth insists on coming with her. Strikingly, Ruth is called a "Moabite" seven times in this story (Ruth 1:4, 22; 2:2, 6, 21; 4:5, 10). In the Bible, seven is the number of fullness, like the seven days of creation in Genesis 1. The author wants us to see Ruth as the total Moabite—as Moabite as it gets. Nevertheless, Naomi daringly welcomes Ruth to come home with her.

This is where the story becomes truly scandalous and subversive. Back in Israel, Naomi sends Ruth to work as a daily laborer in the field of a respected Israelite named Boaz. He is presented as a person of covenant love or *hesed* (Ruth 2:13, 20; 3:10; 4:13; see Ruth 4:15). This is extremely important because God names Godself as "abounding in *hesed*" when God reveals God's core character to Moses in perhaps the most significant divine revelation recorded in the Hebrew Bible (Ex 34:6). In fact, almost fifty verses in Hebrew

---

[39]See Ex 15:15; Num 25:1; Deut 23:3-6; Judg 3:12-14, 28-30; 1 Sam 14:47; 2 Kings 3; 2 Chron 20; 24:26-27; Neh 13:1-3, 23; Is 15:1; 25:10; Jer 25:21; 48; Ezek 25:8-11; Amos 2:1-2; Mic 6:5; Zeph 2:8-9.

The Origins of Neighbor Love

Scripture name *hesed* as God's essential attribute, which is alluded to in the first chapter of Ruth (Ruth 1:8).

So Boaz is a man of God, a human who embodies God's own loving character. How, then, will he respond to Ruth, the sevenfold Moabite? Will he exclude her as Moses commanded in the law and Ezra demanded in his "purified" community? Or will he do something different?

Against all expectations, Boaz proactively welcomes Ruth the Moabite to work in his field. In fact, he shows her special kindness. As if that weren't already too much, Boaz ends up fully embracing Ruth the Moabite and *marries* her. For Boaz, Ruth is "a woman of noble character" (Ruth 3:11), and her *character* matters to him far more than her othered *identity*.

Provocatively, then, Boaz is presented as the embodiment of God's covenant love precisely in his decision to break the Mosaic law and love an othered enemy as his own wife. In this story, love transcends law. Or, better said, Boaz's love for the other restretches the law back to its universal scope at the heart of creation and Abraham's calling to bless all people. Thus, the lawbreaker who should seemingly be condemned by God and expelled from the community becomes the archetype of God's own essential character and a crucial link in the community's ancient story. At the end of the book, we learn that Boaz and Ruth become the great-grandparents of King David (Ruth 4:22).

Even more shockingly, Ruth, the sevenfold Moabite, is listed as one of the great-grandmothers of Jesus in the first chapter of the New Testament (Mt 1:5). Boaz's practice of transcending biblical law with love for the enemy gives birth to the Messiah and participates in the fulfillment of God's promise to Abraham. The author thereby gives us an important clue into how we should set our expectations for who Jesus will become and how he will see others. The heteronautic Messiah will follow his great-great-grandparents' path and take it further than many imagined possible. Unsurprisingly, then, Christian interpreters have seen Boaz as a prototype of Jesus.

The book of Ruth is small but radical. It serves as a profound precedent for human character and divine love overcoming human othering and entrenched exclusion. In fact, Ruth gives an example of love abolishing othering even when that othering was justified by Scripture itself. Boaz's love for Ruth breaks out of the hardened pattern of othering *neighbors* into enemies and instead embraces them as family.

Once more, the universal image of God, the original belonging of humanity, God's own merciful response to human failure, and Abraham's call to bless all people come back to the center of the story.

The Prophets: The Future of Non-Israelite Others/Neighbors

Before we conclude this chapter, what is the fate of non-Israelite neighbors in the imagination of the Hebrew Bible? Should we hope for them or hope for their destruction? The way we envision others' future reveals a great deal about how we see them now.

Once again, the Hebrew prophets seem to offer a tensioned vision. As they look into the future, they are divided about God's ultimate intentions for the peoples of the world.

In some places, the prophets foresee that Israel will dominate, enslave, and even destroy others. For example, the prophet Isaiah says, "And the nations will take [Israel] and bring them to their place, and the house of Israel will possess the nations as male and female slaves in the Lord's land; they will take captive those who were their captors, and rule over those who oppressed them" (Is 14:1-2 NRSV; see Is 60:10-12; 61:5-6). Here the promises of peoplehood and land are repeated without the promise of blessing all people. The prophet Ezekiel offers a similar vision of the Hebrew Bible's eschatology of others or its view of their future: "I will display my glory among the nations, and all the nations will see the punishment I inflict and the hand I lay on them. From that day forward the people of Israel will know that I am the Lord their God" (Ezek 39:21-22).[40] Once more, the nations will be punished, Israel will be exalted, and everyone will know it. The othering of Israel's religious nationalism seems to be the end of the story.

But in other places, the prophets foresee that Israel and the other people of the world will be reconciled as God's one family. These visions seemingly take us back to Genesis 1–2 and imagine the fulfillment of God's promise to Abraham that all nations will be blessed. For example, Isaiah foresees the reconciliation of Egypt, Assyria, and Israel and says, "On that day Israel will be the third with Egypt and Assyria, a blessing in the midst of the earth, whom the Lord of hosts has blessed, saying, 'Blessed be Egypt my people, and Assyria the work of my

---

[40]In Ezek 37, the prophet pictures resurrected Israel as an army, which presumably wars against its enemies.

The Origins of Neighbor Love 57

hands, and Israel my heritage'" (Is 19:23-25 NRSV; see Is 49:6). This passage is extraordinary: Israel's historic enemies, Egypt and Assyria, are called God's own people and blessed by God along with Israel. In this vision, the prophet assures us that God's promise to Abraham of universal blessing will be fulfilled at last.

Later in his prophecy, Isaiah also declares that a new creation like Genesis 1 is our shared future. He says, "For as the new heavens and the new earth, which I will make, shall remain before me, says the LORD; so shall your descendants and your name remain. From new moon to new moon, and from sabbath to sabbath, all flesh shall come to worship before me, says the LORD" (Is 66:22-23 NRSV). In God's future, no one is othered or excluded. "All flesh" is embraced in God's presence. At last, the whole earth becomes a sacred temple filled with God's glory, as it was in the beginning (Is 11:9). Boaz's love for Ruth is universalized.

Several other prophecies dwell in this tension between final rejection and ultimate reconciliation. For example, Zechariah gives a provocatively inclusive prophecy and says, "Many nations will be joined with the LORD in that day and will become my people" (Zech 2:11). But this prophecy sits next to a prophecy about the Lord destroying others for Israel (Zech 2:8). In fact, Zechariah's book ends by resuscitating Israel's ancient othering: "And on that day there will no longer be a Canaanite in the house of the LORD Almighty" (Zech 14:21).

In short, then, the prophetic vision of Hebrew Scripture for others' future is complex and unclear. Some prophecies indicate a final, total reconciliation in which all nations will be blessed and embraced as God's family in a new creation. Other prophecies indicate a final, brutal rejection of non-Israelites, who will be dominated, enslaved, and killed. Some prophecies seem to say both.

Thus, until the end of the Hebrew Bible's story, the cross-pressures remain of God's threefold promise to Abraham of peoplehood, homeland, and being called to bless to all the people of the world.

CONCLUSION: A MIRROR FOR US TODAY

In this chapter, we've surveyed the Hebrew Bible's vision of humanity across its complex library of books. The story it tells is brilliant and groundbreaking. In the beginning, all people are pictured as being made in God's holy image and as belonging to a united human family with full belonging, unlike the othering myths of the ancient world. With Abraham, it launches a universal mission to bless all people. It also gives us the origin of the command to love our neighbors as ourselves within a larger vision of a just and generous society under law that welcomes and protects others. The Hebrew Bible introduces us to a profoundly expanded circle of moral consciousness and community, especially when we read it in the context of neighboring cultures. The story of Ruth and Boaz is an especially inspiring example of how neighbor love can transform enemies into family. In it, we encounter a powerful "example of freedom and responsibility."[41]

Still, the Hebrew Bible confronts us with significant limitations and examples of how powerful othering can be in the human imagination. As Fishbane writes, these are "pivots for moral reflection." When neighbors are othered into enemies, exclusion, enslavement, and genocide become possible—even against children like Eyob. The moral circle of our community closes and seemingly betrays its heart. The claim to a superior identity ironizes itself in appallingly evil behavior.

We saw the complexity of Hebrew Scripture's legacy today at the start of this chapter. Like Desmond Tutu did, its moral vision can be invoked to confront othering and remind us that "All, everyone, everything, belongs. None is an outsider, all are insiders, all belong." It can also be weaponized to other neighbors into enemies and justify devastating violence, as Benjamin Netanyahu did when he represented Gazans as Amalekites.

As I suggested at several points in this chapter, we need to look patiently and deeply into the mirror of Scripture. We need to wrestle with its complex reflections and catch glimpses of ourselves today. Who do we recognize as being made in God's holy image and worthy of love as our neighbors—people who are connected to us and equal in value? How does othering limit our vision and distort it into seeing some image-bearing neighbors as enemies who are unrelated or less than ourselves—perhaps to the point of excluding, oppressing, and even eliminating them? And what role does our faith play in how we form our identities and circle of belonging today? Does it lead us to see ourselves as above others in competitive relationships of insecurity, fear, jealousy, and aggression? Or does it invite us into an expansive vision in which we are all beloved neighbors who are called to recognize our shared value, surrender our insecurities and resentments, and bless one another?

In the next chapter, we'll continue wrestling with these questions as we explore Jesus of Nazareth and his universal vision of neighbor love.

---

[41] Fishbane, *Garments of Torah*, 120.

3

THE UNIVERSALIZATION OF NEIGHBOR LOVE AND THE ABOLITION OF OTHERING

Jesus of Nazareth

LIKE MEETING EYOB, MEETING Ferdosa changed my life.

In 2018, othering was rapidly escalating in Ethiopia. We witnessed a man get lynched naked and hung upside-down from a traffic light. Hundreds of people watched as he died. The photos of this public execution were horrifying and quickly circulated on social media. In another city south of Addis, another man was brutally beaten and left helpless in the street. A young woman poured kerosene on his body, lit him on fire, and raised her arms in triumph as he burned to death. The video that emerged was gruesome and also quickly spread online. Around this time, I received a desperate email from a senior Christian leader in the region. He told me that Christians were burning down one another's churches.

What was happening? As historic resentments intensified across the country, people increasingly saw their neighbors as others—as unrelated or less than themselves. Differences in ethnic, religious, and political identity were particularly potent. As others were transfigured into *enemies*, the moral circle closed, and we witnessed what othering can unleash: a public lynching, a man burned alive, Christians destroying one another's churches. In 2018, more people were being displaced from their homes in Ethiopia than anywhere else in the world. (Needless to say, this pattern is not unique to Ethiopia; I think of slavery, lynching, and the Great Migration of African Americans in the United States.[1])

---

[1]See Isabel Wilkerson, *The Warmth of Other Suns: The Epic Story of America's Great Migration* (New York: Vintage, 2011). In *Caste: The Origins of Our Discontents* (New York: Random House,

In eastern Ethiopia, not far from Somalia, youth went door-to-door in a city called Jijiga. They told their othered neighbors—ethnic minorities—to get out or expect to be killed. At the time, I was invited to give a talk at a city hall not far from Jijiga. As I drove from the airport into the city of Dire Dawa on October 17, I saw massive tents sheltering the people who had fled for their lives. When I arrived at city hall, the conference room was packed with about two hundred local youth. In light of this ethnic cleansing, I gave a passionate talk about why we should actively love our enemies.

As soon as the meeting ended, a young woman came up to me. Ferdosa was wearing a beautiful white hijab that circled her kind face. Her presence was gentle but fierce. I will never forget the passionate words she spoke to me: "Dr. Andrew, no one has ever told me to love my enemies before! Starting today, I will love my enemies and teach others to love their enemies!"

Ferdosa then held my hand and raised it up, like we were making an oath or covenant together. We took a selfie together—what I call an "otherie"—to symbolize our shared commitment to love our enemies. Years later, I asked Ferdosa what she considered her greatest strengths as she entered into adulthood. She told me, "I am a person who loves even my enemies."[2]

Ferdosa was living in one of the most ancient Christian and Muslim countries in the world. In fact, Ethiopia's national epic traces its story back to King Solomon, Moses, and the Garden of Eden itself. And yet, Ferdosa told me that she had never heard these three words before: *love your enemies.*

Still, as othering threatened to consume her society, this alternative invitation gave her hope. Rather than eliminating one another and expanding a spiral of othering, a new moral circle was possible: enemies could learn to see one another as neighbors, people who share relationship and equal worth. Together, they could seek a mutual dignity, security, and flourishing for all.

In this chapter, we turn to explore how Jesus introduced this radical moral vision of neighbor love to the world. Of course, as a descendant of Adam and Eve, Abraham and Sarah, and Ruth and Boaz, and as an interpreter of Moses' Torah, Jesus was building on the deep foundations of the Hebrew Bible (Mt 1:1-2, 5; Lk 3:38). But similar to Boaz's Scripture-stretching

---

2023), 95, Wilkerson documents the 1919 lynching of Will Brown, which was strikingly similar to the lynching in Ethiopia, though even more gruesome.
[2]Adapted from Andrew DeCort et. al., *Enemy, Stranger, Neighbor, & Friend: A Rough Guide on Religion and Othering* (Geneva: World Council of Churches, 2023), 34-35, www.oikoumene.org/resources/publications/enemy-stranger-neighbour-friend.

love for the othered enemy, Jesus stretched this moral vision even wider—to a fully universal scope. As Jesus himself said, "Every teacher of the law who has become a disciple in the kingdom of heaven is like the owner of a house who brings out of his storeroom new treasures as well as old" (Mt 13:52).

We'll find that for Jesus, *neighbor* means everyone without exclusion, including the enemy. And loving the neighbor as oneself becomes the pulsing heart of his countercultural movement, with love for the enemy as its distinctive signature.[3] Indeed, Jesus shifts the focus from identifying others as neighbors to asking whether *we ourselves* are neighbors to others, no matter who they are. He offers us the next chapter in the neighbor-love movement, bridging deep continuity with what came before and heteronautic courage for something new like Abraham.[4]

What I find especially inspiring about Jesus is that he universalized our vision of neighbor love in a society riven with othering, not unlike Ethiopia and much of our world still today. The Roman Empire had conquered and occupied Israel. Horrifying public executions bloodied the landscape of Jesus' everyday life. In fact, like the people from Jijiga, the New Testament records that Jesus himself narrowly escaped a political massacre as a child and became a refugee in Egypt. Violent resistance movements, apocalyptic religious sects, and a powerful establishment content with the status quo were all available to Jesus. But similar to Abraham and Boaz, he

---

[3] Peter Jackson, *Love Disconsoled: Meditations on Christian Charity* (New York: Cambridge University Press, 1999), 3. Works that have influenced my understanding of Jesus include N. T. Wright, *The New Testament and the People of God* (Minneapolis: Fortress, 1996); Wright, *Jesus and the Victory of God* (Minneapolis: Fortress, 1996); Wright, *The Resurrection of the Son of God* (Minneapolis: Fortress, 2003); Howard Thurman, *Jesus and the Disinherited* (Boston: Beacon, 1949); Richard Horsley, *Jesus and Empire: The Kingdom of God and the New World Disorder* (Minneapolis: Fortress, 2002); Walter Wink, *Jesus and Nonviolence: A Third Way* (Minneapolis: Fortress, 2003); and John Dominic Crossan, *God and Empire: Jesus Against Rome, Then and Now* (New York: HarperOne, 2008).

[4] Pheme Perkins examines these tensions and expansions in her "The Double Love Commandment" and "Love of Enemies," in *Love Commands in the New Testament* (New York: Paulist Press, 1982), 10-26 and 27-41. Perkins looks at Jewish gravestones and literature from Palestinian Judaism, including the Essenes at Qumran. Interestingly, representatives from Hellenistic Judaism indicate that the neighbor-love command began to be interpreted more broadly as Judaism interacted with Greek philosophy, for example, in Testament of the Twelve Patriarchs and Philo. See also Serge Ruzer, "The Double Love Precept: Between Pharisees, Jesus and Qumran Covenanters," in *Mapping the New Testament: Early Christian Writings as a Witness for Jewish Biblical Exegesis* (Leiden: Brill, 2007), 71-99; Robert Wall and Eugene Lemcio, "The Commands to Love God and Neighbor: History, Redaction, and Canon," in *The New Testament as Canon: A Reader in Canonical Criticism* (Sheffield: Sheffield Academic Press, 1992), 67-77; and Victor Furnish, *The Love Command in the New Testament* (Nashville: Abingdon, 1972).

chose another way—the path of neighbor love stretching as wide as the world and reaching back to the primal heart of God in creation.

Eleven passages in the New Testament directly discuss neighbor love, and five of them are found in Jesus' teaching in the Gospels (Mt 5:43; 19:19; 23:39; Mk 12:31, 33; Lk 10:27, 29, 36; Rom 13:9-10; 15:2; Gal 5:14; Eph 4:25; Jas 2:8; 4:12).[5] Four other teachings of Jesus touch on loving others.[6] We'll explore these nine texts one by one and reconstruct his prophetic vision, which so inspired Ferdosa as she struggled to find new hope for healing in her society amid othering.

MATTHEW 5–7: THE SERMON ON THE MOUNT

The Sermon on the Mount, narrated in Matthew 5–7, provides the first major teaching of Jesus where he addresses neighbor love and develops its ethical mandate. Importantly, Jesus gives this sermon soon after having a mystical experience of God in the desert. There Jesus saw heaven open, beheld God as the dove of peace, and heard God say, "You are my beloved son; I delight in you" (Mt 3:13-17, my translation). It seems that Jesus so accepted and internalized his own divine belovedness that he returned from the desert with an unprecedented vision of love for others that overflowed with healing.[7]

Before we dig deeper into the details, we need to notice three things about Jesus' groundbreaking sermon.

First, it's the first of five discourses that Jesus gives in the Gospel of Matthew. Subtly, Matthew wants us to see Jesus as a new Moses. Like Moses gave Israel five books of Torah, Jesus gives his movement five major teachings. And also like Moses taught his law from a mountainside, Jesus gives his first sermon from a mountainside.

This context is significant. Matthew wants us to see Jesus as giving new Scripture, an inspired vision that should define how followers of God love and live. What Jesus says is a revelation of God's will every bit as authoritative as God's revelation to Moses over a thousand years before.

Second, Jesus speaks to a more inclusive audience than Moses did. People from Syria, Greek-influenced cities, and the non-Jewish region east of the

---

[5]Acts 7:27 is a quotation from the Hebrew Bible that uses the generic meaning of "neighbor" (*plēsion*) which the NIV translates as "other."

[6]Mt 7:7-12 ("Do to others what you would have them do to you"); Lk 6:27-36 ("Love your enemies"); Jn 13:34-35 ("Love one another"); Jn 15:9-17 ("Love each other").

[7]I explore Jesus' mystical experience further in *Flourishing on the Edge of Faith: Seven Practices for a New We* (Washington, DC: BitterSweet Collective, 2022), chap. 1.

Jordan—people who were othered by Moses—are present together with Jews from the heartland of Israel (Mt 4:23-25). Jesus' message takes place within the embodiment of his universal theology of the neighbor, tangibly heightening and expanding Israel's neighbor-love tradition.

Third, Matthew tells us that Jesus addresses a "large crowd" of people who hang on his words. Many see his Sermon on the Mount as the manifesto for his public movement. It provides the crucial orientation and energy for Jesus' teaching and practice. It's his core agenda.

So what did Jesus actually say in this Scripture-making, boundary-expanding, movement-orienting sermon?

MATTHEW 5:38-42: THE PRACTICE OF CREATIVE NONVIOLENCE

In the early part of his sermon, Jesus gives a series of contrasts between traditional moral teaching and his own. He sets it up like this: "You have heard that it was said, but I tell you . . ." In some cases, Jesus intensifies and deepens Moses' law. But in other cases, Jesus stretches and goes far beyond it.

Jesus says, "You have heard that it was said, 'Eye for eye, and tooth for tooth'" (Mt 5:38). This is the standard moral teaching of reciprocity and retribution in the Hebrew Bible (see Gen 9:6; 12:3; Ex 21:24; Lev 24:17-21; Deut 19:21). In one sense, this law was meant to limit violence: if you knock out my teeth, I can't cut off your head. But this law also opened the door to a spiral of othering and revengeful violence like we saw with the Amalekites, Moabites, and Israel's other enemies.

Here Jesus goes beyond Moses. He teaches,

> But I tell you, do not resist an evil person. If anyone slaps you on the right check, turn to them the other cheek also. And if anyone wants to sue you and take your shirt, hand over your coat as well. If anyone forces you to go one mile, go with them two miles. Give to the one who asks you, and do not turn away from the one who wants to borrow from you. (Mt 5:39-42)

Here we encounter the reason Gandhi called Jesus "the most active resister known perhaps to history."[8] Jesus creatively rereads the biblical tradition in two important ways.

First, Jesus insists on practicing creative nonviolence and breaking the cycle of conflict. He doesn't accept the idea that we can solve our problems by

---

[8]Thomas Merton, *Gandhi: On Nonviolence* (New York: New Directions, 2007), 55.

mirroring the behaviors that started them. In Jesus' new way, the reactive violence we saw in the Hebrew Bible is surrendered. Here, we are not to relate to the other, the enemy, in and through an act of reciprocal aggression.[9]

But, second, Jesus doesn't teach passivity and submission to oppression. Instead, we should practice a *creative* agency that both asserts our own dignity and transforms othering behavior. For example, turning the other cheek is a defiant act of presence that faces the aggressor as an equal but without imitating their aggression. This act says, "I'm still here. You can't push me over or determine my behavior. I'm free and not governed by your violence." In fact, turning the other cheek is a powerful invitation to the aggressor to abandon their violence. It courageously gives them a second chance to reconsider and for a relationship to be created.

Similarly, if someone tries to sue you and you respond by voluntarily offering them the shirt off your back, this creative response breaks the cycle of retaliation. It simultaneously asserts your own agency and exposes the cruelty of greed. This action says, "If you want to hurt me, I'd rather be naked than hurt you back." Once again, it courageously challenges the aggressor and creates an opportunity for them to change their mind, while holding open the possibility of a new relationship.

Likewise, if a Roman soldier forces you to carry his gear for a mile and you insist on carrying it for two miles, the same pattern holds: you break the cycle of treating the other as less than yourself, nonviolently assert the dignity of your own agency, and give the oppressor an opportunity to rethink their actions. A door is opened to a new relationship and a recognition of mutual value.

Jesus' teaching of creative nonviolence was fresh, as inspiring as it was challenging. Each of Jesus' examples combines nonviolent courage with creative agency. Rather than giving us fixed responses, I believe Jesus is asking us to reimagine our moral action in the unique circumstances of our lives. How can we courageously break the cycle of othering while creatively asserting our agency, challenging oppression, and inviting a new relationship? As we'll see

---

[9] For studies of Jesus' teaching of nonviolence, see Walter Wink, *The Powers That Be: Theology for a New Millennium* (New York: Harmony, 1999), chap. 5, "Jesus's Third Way"; Wink, *Jesus and Nonviolence: A Third Way* (Minneapolis: Fortress, 2003). For a study of how Jesus' teaching of nonviolence was received and interpreted across Christian history, see Michael Long, ed., *Christian Peace and Nonviolence: A Documentary History* (Maryknoll, NY: Orbis Books, 2011). For a wider study of nonviolence across history, including in the teaching of Jesus, see Mark Kurlansky, *Non-violence: The History of a Dangerous Idea* (New York: Modern Library, 2008).

in chapter five, Martin Luther King Jr.'s nonviolent protest movement against institutionalized othering in America was profoundly inspired by Jesus.

In Jewish tradition at the time, some argued that you should show kindness to an enemy, because that would motivate God to punish them even more in the afterlife. Kindness was a kind of revenge, a delayed gratification of getting equal in the future. We find this attitude in the Dead Sea Scrolls and 2 Enoch.[10] Other Jewish thinkers, such as Aristeas and Josephus, encouraged nonretaliation as an attempt to convert nonbelievers to Judaism.[11]

In the Greek tradition at the time, Seneca and others argued that you should show magnanimity toward an enemy because it would demonstrate your own composure and virtue.[12] Greek philosophy highly valued controlling emotion and mastering the will. So showing kindness toward an enemy had an egocentric motivation: it showed your moral superiority to them.

In the Sermon on the Mount, Jesus teaches creative nonviolence simply because it embodies love for others. This practice both defies and transforms othering behavior, creating new relationships of moral equality and freedom. Jesus was also suggesting a method of social change that has proven to be robustly effective. Erica Chenoweth, professor of public policy at Harvard University, examined a data set of 627 cases of social upheaval from 1900 to 2019. Chenoweth demonstrated that nonviolent civil resistance is twice as effective as violent methods for bringing sustainable change. It's always successful when just 3.5 percent of a society's population commits to a nonviolent campaign.[13] As we'll see, Jesus is drawing on the moral universalism invoked by Genesis's creation theology but fleshes out its implications more expansively in his practice of creative nonviolence. Gandhi, King, and countless others have been inspired by Jesus' practice in their work to heal othering and transform society.

---

[10] See 1QS (Community Rule), column 10, lines 17-20, in Hugh Nibley, "From the Dead Sea Scrolls (1QS)," *Studies in the Bible and Antiquity* 2 (2010), article 5; and 2 Enoch 50:55.

[11] See Josephus, *Against Apion* 2.209-17, in *Josephus: The Life, Against Apion*, trans. H. St. John Thackeray (Cambridge, MA: Harvard University Press, 1929), 377-79.

[12] See Seneca, *On Benefits* 4.26, ed. Aubrey Stewart. Gutenberg ebook, 2010, www.gutenberg.org /files/3794/3794-h/3794-h.htm#link2H_4_0006; Seneca, *On Anger* 2.32, 3.42, ed. Aubrey Stewart (London: George Bell and Sons, 1900), https://en.wikisource.org/wiki/Of_Anger; and Seneca, *On the Firmness of the Wise Man* 4, trans. Aubrey Stewart, https://en.wikisource.org/wiki /On_the_Firmness_of_the_Wise_Man#IV.

[13] See Erica Chenoweth and Maria Stephan, *Why Civil Resistance Works: The Strategic Logic of Nonviolent Conflict* (New York: Columbia University Press, 2012); Erica Chenoweth, *Civil Resistance: What Everyone Needs to Know* (New York: Oxford University Press, 2021).

MATTHEW 5:43-48: LOVE YOUR ENEMIES

In the final contrast between one trajectory of traditional ethics and Jesus' innovative teaching, he begins, "You have heard that it was said, 'Love your neighbor and hate your enemy'" (Mt 5:43).

As we've seen, Moses teaches the command of neighbor love in Leviticus 19:18. Later in the Bible, the story of Ruth and Boaz powerfully illustrates how this love can overcome othering and enemies can become family. Other biblical texts name the wisdom of making peace with enemies and how God rewards this behavior.

Still, the Hebrew Bible doesn't give an explicit command to love our enemies and contains many examples of hatred, exclusion, and violence against them. In fact, the ability to dominate enemies is frequently associated with possessing God's favor. Moses has God say to Israel, "I will be an enemy to your enemies" (Ex 23:22; see Lev 26:8). In this spirit, King David prays, "If only you, God, would slay the wicked. . . . I have nothing but hatred for them; I count them my enemies" (Ps 139:19, 22). This is one of the strongest cases of othering's irony in Hebrew Scripture: David had just beautifully confessed his own precious value as God's creature, but then he turns with overflowing hatred toward other image-bearers of God.

In the Dead Sea Scrolls, the writings of the Essene community contemporary with Jesus, we find a similar sentiment of sacralized hate: "Love all the sons of light . . . but hate all the sons of darkness, each according to his guilt in the vengeance of God."[14] The Community Rule of the Essenes called "the wise" to hold "eternal hatred" against "the Men of the Pit."[15]

As we've seen, in the ancient Near Eastern myths and the philosophy of Plato and Aristotle, the enemy is similarly destined to be conquered, controlled, and often destroyed. Plato essentialized othering, referring to Greeks and non-Greeks as "enemies by nature."[16]

Jesus, then, is provocatively naming a pervasive and powerful attitude across cultures and his own community. When people heard Scripture and tradition being read, they expected the story of othering to be retold: the

---

[14]Thomas Ogletree, "Interpreting the Love Commands in Social Context," in *Love and Christian Ethics: Tradition, Theory, and Society*, ed. Frederick Simmons and Brian Sorrels (Washington, DC: Georgetown University Press, 2016), 30.
[15]See 1QS column 9, line 21.
[16]See Plato, *The Republic*, 2nd ed., trans. Allan Bloom (New York: Basic Books, 1991), 470c-d.

neighbor is a fellow community member, and they should be loved; but enemies are others, and they should be hated.

In response, Jesus teaches,

> But I tell you, love your enemies and pray for those who persecute you, that you may be children of your Father in heaven. He causes his sun to rise on the evil and the good, and sends rain on the righteous and the unrighteous. If you love those who love you, what reward will you get? Are not even the tax collectors doing that? And if you greet only your own people, what are you doing more than others? Do not even pagans do that? Be perfect, therefore, as your heavenly Father is perfect. (Mt 5:44-48)

In Jesus' world, this was unprecedented language: *love your enemies*.[17] But Jesus grounds this new teaching in the eternal character of God as our universal Creator, echoing Genesis 1. For Jesus, God's primal orientation toward humanity is kindness and care. Regardless of how we label people—good or evil, righteous or unrighteous—God made us good, blessed us from the beginning, and desires all of us to be well (Gen 1:28-31). God is "*our* Father," Jesus says, and so we are all God's beloved children. Brother Lawrence, a seventeenth-century French mystic, paraphrased Jesus' words like this: "God is what Love is, infinitely perfect, infinitely kind, infinitely far from all harming."[18]

Crucially, then, God's relationship with humanity is not defined by *our othering* character but by *God's unconditional* character. God doesn't love us

---

[17] For valuable studies on the ethics of enemy love in the New Testament and other ethical perspectives, see Hyung Jin Kim Sun, *Who Are Our Enemies and How Do We Love Them?* (Harrisonburg, VA: Herald, 2020); Arthur Brooks, *Love Your Enemies: How Decent People Can Save America from the Culture of Contempt* (New York: Broadside Books, 2019); Ronald Sider, *If Jesus Is Lord: Loving Our Enemies in an Age of Violence* (Grand Rapids, MI: Baker Academic, 2019); Jim Forest, *Loving Our Enemies: Reflections on the Hardest Commandment* (Maryknoll, NY: Orbis, 2014); Salim Munayer and Lisa Loden, *Through the Eyes of My Enemy: Envisioning Reconciliation in Israel-Palestine* (London: Paternoster, 2013); Gerard Vaderhaar, *Enemies and How to Love Them* (Eugene, OR: Wipf & Stock, 2013); Serge Ruzer, "From 'Love Your Neighbor' to 'Love Your Enemy,'" in *Mapping the New Testament: Early Christian Writings as a Witness for Jewish Biblical Exegesis* (Leiden: Brill, 2007), 35-70; William Swartley, ed., *The Love of Enemy and Nonretaliation in the New Testament* (Louisville, KY: Westminster John Knox, 1992); Lisa Cahill, *Love Your Enemies: Pacifism, Discipleship, and Just War* (Minneapolis: Fortress, 1994); William Klassen, *Love of Enemies: The Way to Peace* (Philadelphia: Fortress, 1984); John Piper, *Love Your Enemies: Jesus's Love Command in the Synoptic Gospels and Early Christian Parenesis* (Cambridge: Cambridge University Press, 1979).

[18] Brother Lawrence, *Practice of the Presence: A Revolutionary Translation*, trans. Carmen Acevedo Butcher (Minneapolis: Broadleaf Books, 2022), 50.

because we deserve love but because God is loving.[19] Thus, Jesus perceives the most essential elements that sustain our humanity like light and water as the tangible outpourings of this unconditional divine love. In essence, God is not retributive, reacting to the whim of human fallibility: God is *God*, "perfect" or completely whole in love (Mt 5:48). This is why Thomas Merton writes, "The only desire that is infallibly fulfilled is the desire to be loved by God."[20]

In this way, Jesus reconceptualizes the enemy within the moral scope of God's compassionate care and our responsibility. Jesus takes the ultimate other—the one we feel most justified to hate—and asks us to recalibrate our ethical vision. The enemy is to be seen and treated exactly as the neighbor: someone who is connected to us and equal in value as God's children. Our "enemy" siblings are *neighbors* to be loved.

Here Jesus cleverly names groups of people who were commonly othered in his society: tax collectors who collaborated with the hated Romans and "pagans" who didn't follow Jewish religion. Jesus then points out that even they practice a reciprocal, retributive ethic: loving and acknowledging only people in their own group. For Jesus, there's nothing different or divine in this pattern; it's the old beaten path of othering. If we want to live into the eternally innovative heart of God, unconditional love is the way.[21]

With this teaching, Jesus abolishes othering at its heart, or at least any moral justification for it. He calls us to *love* even those we are most conditioned to see as unrelated or less than ourselves, and this means that

---

[19]See Thomas Merton, *The Power and Meaning of Love* (London: SPCK, 2010), 29: "What we are asked to do is to love; and this love itself will render both ourselves and our neighbor worthy if anything can. Indeed, that is one of the most significant things about the power of love. There is no way under the sun to make a man worthy of love except by loving him. As soon as he realizes himself loved—if he is not so weak that he can longer bear to be loved—he will feel himself instantly becoming worthy of love. He will respond by drawing a mysterious spiritual value out of his own depths, a new identity called into being by the love that is addressed to him." See also Erich Fromm, *The Art of Loving* (New York: Open Road Media, 2013): "Infantile love follows the principle: 'I love because I am loved.' Mature love follows the principle: 'I am loved because I love.' Immature love says: 'I love you because I need you.' Mature love says: "I need you because I love you."' Jesus is calling us into the maturity of love.
[20]Thomas Merton, *No Man Is an Island* (New York: Houghton Mifflin, 1983), 17.
[21]See Jean-Luc Marion, *The Erotic Phenomenon*, trans. Stephen Lewis (Chicago: University of Chicago Press, 2007), 71: "The incomparable and unstoppable sovereignty of the act of loving draws all its power from the fact that reciprocity does not affect it any more than does the desire for a return on investment. . . . There is only one single proof of love—to give without return or chance of recovery, and thus to be able to lose and, eventually, to be lost in love. But love itself is never lost, because it is accomplished in loss."

othering can no longer limit the circle of our moral consciousness and care. On this path, the notion of "the enemy" can henceforth only function as a reminder to love even more radically, rather than triggering our enmity and aggression. God is an enemy lover, and lovers of God cannot legitimately hate any other, including our enemy-siblings.

Jesus points to this healing of our inner selves when he teaches, "And pray for those who persecute you" (Mt 5:44). Prayer emerges from the intimate place of the heart where our most basic desires develop and our decisions emerge. It's a kind of premeditation for action in which we name our deepest values and intentions for our life in the world with God.[22] It is also the place where othering can take root and hate festers. Recall David's prayer in Psalm 139 where he asked God to "slay the wicked" and confessed, "I have nothing but hatred for them." We often become answers to our prayers: David killed Moabites—kin of his grandmother Ruth—seemingly for sport (2 Sam 8:2). Jesus says to make this innermost place of prayer a sanctuary where we choose a new desire for our enemy-siblings. Rather than interceding for their condemnation and destruction, we open our hearts to ask God for their healing. This reorientation of our intention and action makes our practice of Jesus' creative nonviolence more natural and resilient. Our intimate prayer life becomes a prophecy of peacemaking.

Here in this inspired manifesto for his movement, Jesus abolishes othering and universalizes the circle of our moral community. In this vision, there are no longer any others. Even enemies are to be loved as neighbors. And prayer, our most basic practice of God's presence, becomes an exercise to heal our hearts and reroot ourselves in God's primal desire for all humanity's flourishing. In this way, creative nonviolence isn't passive submission, moralistic superiority, or even religious proselytizing. It's Jesus' invitation to imitate the divine character of our universal Parent. In fact, Jesus subtly names a profound paradox: we can't fully belong in God's family unless we surrender the othering that excludes our enemy-siblings from full belonging (Mt 5:44). In a sense, refusing to exclude others is the key to our own full inclusion. We'll see this paradox repeatedly in the pages to come.

---

[22]For further reflection on prayer as premeditation, see Andrew DeCort, *Flourishing on the Edge of Faith: Seven Practices for a New We* (Washington, DC: BitterSweet Collective, 2022), chap. 6, "Deliver Us from Evil: A Practice of Premeditated Nonviolence."

Matthew 7:12: The Golden Rule

In the final chapter of the Sermon on the Mount, Jesus gives the master key for overcoming othering and practicing neighbor love. Today we know it as the golden rule: "So in everything, do to others what you would have them do to you, for this sums up the Law and the Prophets" (Mt 7:12).[23]

According to Jesus, we can distill the entire moral teaching of Hebrew Scripture with its 613 laws into this one practice. He was likely innovating on the wisdom of the great Jewish sage Hillel a generation before him. Hillel was asked whether he could summarize the entire Bible while standing on one foot. He answered, "What is hateful to you, do not do to your neighbor. That is the whole Torah; the rest is commentary."[24] Jesus restates Hillel's principle in the positive, making our desire for ourselves the measure of how we see and treat others.

While this principle is familiar to us, we should not underestimate its ethical implications.

Once again, Jesus roots his ethics in the character of God and our equal preciousness to our divine Parent. Just before giving the golden rule, Jesus teaches about the generosity of God. He says that if fallible parents give their children food rather than stones when they are hungry, "How much more will your Father in heaven give good gifts to those who ask him!" (Mt 7:11). Based on this vision of God's kindness, Jesus continues, "So in everything, do to others what you would have them do to you" (Mt 7:12).

The clear meaning of Jesus' words is that we all want to be given good gifts. We want to be treated with kindness and care. Rather than being tricked with a stone when we are vulnerable, we long for our basic needs and desires to be met so that we can flourish. Jesus calls us to convert this elemental longing in ourselves into our desire for others. In this vision, others are no longer unrelated or less than ourselves; they are as intimately connected to us and equally precious as family. The divine desire of our universal Parent comes alive in us, and we become sacred siblings to one another.

The golden rule is powerful and challenging. As we've seen repeatedly in this book, we humans love privilege, prestige, and power over others. We

---

[23]For thorough studies of the golden rule in Jesus' teaching and across religious traditions, see Harry Gensler, *Ethics and the Gold Rule* (New York: Routledge, 2013); Jeffrey Wattles, *The Golden Rule* (New York: Oxford University Press, 1996).

[24]Recorded in the Talmud, Shabbat 31a, quoted in Shoshannah Brombacher, "On One Foot," Chabad, accessed January 18, 2025, www.chabad.org/library/article_cdo/aid/689306/jewish/On-One-Foot.htm.

often fight hard and pray piously to get ahead of others and have more—more access, more resources, more happiness, health, and success. Moses promises Israel that if they obeyed God, "You will be blessed more than any other people" (Deut 7:14). God is frequently invoked as the key to being "more blessed" and having a competitive advantage over others.

But Jesus' golden rule is an antidote to this othering. If we're living a life that aims to treat others the way we want to be treated, we will surrender seeking to get ahead of others. We won't want to be "above" them or "more blessed." Instead, we'll practice a life that aims at being *with* and *for* others with the generosity and care that God desires for all of us. The golden rule makes the other count just as much as ourselves. Like the command to love the enemy, it is the abolition of othering rooted in the heart.

We humans also easily slip into selective ethics. By this I mean values and practices that apply with some people but not with others, in some places but not in others. If it's a fellow Israelite, I must love him as myself. But if it's a Moabite, I must exclude her. And if it's an Amalekite, I must kill him.

To this tendency of human othering, Jesus says, "*In everything*, do to others what you would have them do to you." Like "love your enemies," Jesus' words "in everything" spell the end of a selective ethic that prioritizes our preferences and privileges. Those who want to follow Jesus and do God's will can't turn their ethics on and off. It's a full-time way of life rooted in the heart in which no people or place is left out of the circle of moral responsibility.

In sum, then, Jesus teaches that the moral principle summarizing everything of value in the Hebrew Bible is to live a life of generosity toward others that resists the othering temptations of self-privilege and selective responsibility. If we wouldn't want to be treated in a certain way, we shouldn't treat others that way. If we hope for others to treat us in a certain way, we should treat them just like that.

Jesus, the great-great-grandson of Boaz, introduces the world to an ethic of neighbor love that is universal and flows in the spirit of God's calling to Abraham to bless *all* people.

Matthew 7:21-24: God's Ultimate Desire

Jesus' Sermon on the Mount ultimately teaches that God's holy will is for us to embody the healing love God has for all people. At the end of the sermon,

Jesus repeats the paradox he mentioned in his teaching to love our enemies. Here Jesus warns,

> Not everyone who says to me, "Lord, Lord," will enter the kingdom of heaven, but only the one who does the will of my Father who is in heaven. Many will say to me on that day, "Lord, Lord, did we not prophesy in your name and in your name drive out demons and in your name perform many miracles?" Then I will tell them plainly, "I never knew you. Away from me, you evildoers!" (Mt 7:21-23)

With these sobering words, Jesus fiercely confronts othering religion disconnected from the practice of neighbor love. He names what religion often most highly prizes: invocations of God's name along with prophecies, exorcisms, and miracles.

Calling God "Lord" is often how we signal our belonging as religious insiders, the language that shows our membership in the group (see Deut 6:4; Rom 10:9). But Jesus is emphatically clear at the end of his movement's manifesto: simply calling God "Lord" and making a verbal confession of faith that attaches oneself to God is not enough. God wants a changed life that practices God's way of creative nonviolence, enemy love, and the golden rule.

Similarly, performing miraculous signs is commonly perceived as unmistakable proof of our authenticity and importance in God's kingdom. No signs would seem to be more impressive and unquestionably God's work than prophecy, driving out demons, and miracles. But Jesus repeats that we can do all of this and still be an "evildoer" whose way of life is unknown to God.

My mind returns to contexts in Israel, Ethiopia, and the United States where overwhelmingly religious populations confessed their faith in the Lord and defined their identities around religious performances. And still, othering was accepted and led to lynchings, bombings, mass displacement, and genocidal violence, terrible suffering.

According to Jesus, what God really wants is not religious words of loyalty or signs of power. God wants a new way of life that creatively overcomes othering and loves enemies as neighbors. Jesus says it like this: "Therefore everyone who hears these words of mine and puts them into practice is like a wise person who built their house on the rock" (Mt 7:24). Nothing can shake this life. It is rooted in God's own primal character and promised eternal life by our Father in heaven. Jesus warns that any other life, even an explicitly religious and impressively miraculous life, will ultimately fall apart.

The conclusion of Jesus' sermon takes us back to his command of enemy love: if we truly desire to belong in God's family, a new way of life with and for our othered siblings is not optional. Paradoxically, the universal kingdom of God is truly open only to those who practice their faith by loving beyond the traditional boundaries of our religion and culture. Ironically, what risks separating us from God is our othering, particularly as it is justified by religion. God is *our* Father, and we are *we*—sacred siblings in God's universal family.

Unsurprisingly, then, Matthew tells us, "When Jesus had finished saying these things, the crowds were amazed at his teaching, because he taught as one who had authority, and not as their teachers of the law" (Mt 7:28-29). In the wake of Jesus' manifesto, the othered neighbors from Syria, the Decapolis, and the east side of the Jordan were equals with everyone else. All who heard Jesus' words were given the same call to practice a new way of life embodied in creative nonviolence, love for enemies, and generously treating others the way they want to be treated. The moral circle was drawn around everyone, and any justification for othering was abolished.

This is the moral vision Jesus taught as he introduced his new Scripture at the beginning of his movement when the spotlight was on him and everyone was listening.

MATTHEW 19: THE WAY OF ETERNAL LIFE

Jesus' next teaching on neighbor love continues developing his moral vision and abolition of othering.

In context, Jesus has just declared that the kingdom of God belongs to little children (Mt 19:14). This was a challenging statement, because Jesus' disciples had been rebuking the people for bringing their children to Jesus for prayer. It seems that the disciples didn't consider children as equally important or worthy of Jesus' time as adults. In ancient cultures, as we saw in Aristotle, children were seen as the lowest members of society (see Deut 3:6; 12:31; 1 Sam 15:3). This attitude likely contributed to Eyob's neglect in Ethiopia.

To his disciples with their othering mindset, then, Jesus says, "Let the little children come to me, and do not hinder them, for the kingdom of God belongs to such as these" (Mt 19:14). For Jesus, children are not less important than adults. They are equally valuable and worthy of focused attention and care. The kingdom of God subverts our value hierarchies and extends full belonging to the "little" ones we may marginalize.

After this, a rich young man comes up to Jesus and asks him one of the ultimate questions of religion: "Teacher, what good thing must I do to get eternal life?" (Mt 19:16). This question makes sense in context; Jesus has just challenged the traditional order of societal value. At heart, this rich man wants to figure out what Jesus thinks is truly precious and enduringly valuable. What do you have to do to gain access to "eternal life," a life of full belonging and flourishing that outlives death itself?

Jesus provocatively pushes back. He asks the man why he wants to know "about what is good" and insists that only God is truly good. Subtly, Jesus is challenging the arbiter of othering that we saw in his teaching on enemy love: who is good versus who is evil and thus who is worthy of respect. Like he said there, Jesus says again, "If you want to enter life, keep the commandments" (Mt 19:17). The practice of God's love is itself the way of true life that never dies.

But the man isn't satisfied with Jesus' answer and asks Jesus *which* commands he's supposed to keep. As we might anticipate after his Sermon on the Mount, Jesus doesn't mention the theological commands to love and worship God. He focuses only on the commands involving human relationship: resisting murder, cheating, stealing, lying, and dishonoring parents. At the end of this list, Jesus says, "Love your neighbor as yourself" (Mt 19:19). Like the golden rule, Jesus understands neighbor love as the summary of all biblical revelation and God's will for human relationships.

The man replies, "All these I have kept. What do I still lack?" Jesus then responds more specifically: "If you want to be perfect, go, sell your possessions, and give to the poor, and you will have treasure in heaven. Then come, follow me" (Mt 19:21).

Recall that Jesus also used the word *perfect* in his teaching on enemy love. There it referred to the generosity of God, who gives life-sustaining gifts to all of us, regardless of whether we are good or evil (Mt 5:48). Here Jesus challenges this man to renounce his superiority as a rich person and to give all of his resources to the poor—people who are often marginalized from full participation in society like children. (Remember that Cicero, a Roman philosopher a generation before Jesus, called the poor "the scum" of the city.)

At heart, Jesus is interrogating this man's core identity: Does his worth reside in his superior wealth and status? Or is his worth found in simply being an equally beloved child of God among others whom God promises to provide for with perfect love?

Jesus' reply also indicates that in his cultural context it was possible to "love your neighbor" without sacrificially "giving to the poor." Once more, Jesus is challenging the group-centered, othering understanding of the neighbor and what it means to love them. If we think that our neighbor is simply "one of us"—someone in our economic class and social status—we've missed God's perfection and the everlasting life of heaven. Like his command of enemy love, then, Jesus challenges this man to go beyond conventional neighbor love to practice sacrificial love of the poor—people whom this rich, proud man may have seen as unrelated or less than himself.[25]

The kingdom of God embraces little children; eternal life opens to the poor and those who cherish them—this is Jesus' way of neighbor love. It lifts the belittled, welcomes the marginalized, and draws the moral circle around all of us. According to Jesus, this love is what is enduringly precious in life and worthy of giving everything to receive.

Finally, notice that Jesus makes this radical love the precondition for this rich man joining Jesus' movement: "Go, sell your possessions and give to the poor, and you will have treasure in heaven. *Then* come, follow me." This encounter began with one of the ultimate questions of religion: "What good thing must I do to get eternal life?" But Jesus continues articulating his vision from the Sermon on the Mount: a religious identity devoid of moral practice isn't recognizable to God. Once more, he prioritizes our relationships with others: "Give to the poor. . . . Then, come follow me." The paradox appears afresh: the only condition of our belonging is welcoming others to belong. Eternal life without the impoverished other isn't an option.

At the end of this episode, Jesus reiterates the subversive value system of his vision of belonging: "Many who are first will be last, and many who are last will be first" (Mt 19:30). This is very different from Deuteronomy's promise that Israel will be "always at the top" and others beneath them as "the tail." It's even more challenging to Plato's republic with its segregated gold, silver, and bronze classes supposedly willed by God. In Jesus' new teaching, the defenseless and devalued are the special citizens of God's kingdom, and only those who love them will feel at home in it.

---

[25]Jesus' teaching here is especially challenging in historical context. In the second century, a rabbinic council declared that pious Jews should not give more than 20 percent of their personal wealth to charity. The logic was to protect givers from being excessively generous and impoverishing themselves. But Jesus tells this man to give everything as an embodiment of neighbor love for the poor.

The old hierarchy with its competitive vision of people—adult versus child, good versus bad, rich versus poor—is dismantled in God's perfect love. Jesus abolishes othering.

MATTHEW 22: THE KEY TO DIVINE REVELATION

The command of neighbor love comes up yet again later in Matthew's Gospel. In context, Jesus has just been debating with religious leaders known as the Sadducees about the Bible's teaching on marriage and the resurrection. This connects back to Jesus' discussion with the rich man about how to access eternal life. Then a Pharisee wants to join the discussion and test what Jesus sees as the key for interpreting Scripture. The religious expert asks Jesus, "Which is the greatest commandment in the Law?" (Mt 22:36).

This was a crucial question that major Jewish teachers such as Shammai and Hillel had debated soon before Jesus. Rabbi Shammai argued that the greatest commandment was to love God and obey the Sabbath. As we've seen, Rabbi Hillel argued that the greatest commandment was to love God and our neighbor. The rest, he said, is "commentary."

Jesus follows Hillel's argument. He says, "'Love the Lord your God with all your heart and with all your soul and with all your mind' [Deut 6:5]. This is the first and greatest commandment. And the second is like it: 'Love your neighbor as yourself' [Lev 19:18]. All the Law and the Prophets hang on these two commandments" (Mt 22:37-40).[26] In light of Jesus' previous teaching on love for enemies, the golden rule, and love for the poor, we know that Jesus has his expansive, universal meaning of *neighbor* in mind here. For Jesus, loving God and loving our neighbors sums up everything Scripture has to teach us. In fact, Jesus says that "the Law and the Prophets"—the pillars of Scripture—"*hang* on these two commandments." By implication, Scripture falls apart when love for God and others doesn't define how we read it and live our lives. Here Jesus elevates neighbor love as the key to interpreting the Bible faithfully: if what we read doesn't lead us to love others as ourselves, we've missed the point.

---

[26]In Mt 7:12, Jesus says that the golden rule "sums up the Law and the Prophets," so it seems that Jesus understood "do to others what you would have them do to you" and "love your neighbor as yourself" to be essentially the same in meaning. See James Kugel, *Traditions of the Bible: A Guide to the Bible as It Was at the Start of the Common Era* (Cambridge, MA: Harvard University Press, 1999), 458: "Indeed, from an early period . . . Lev. 19:18 seems to have been exalted as a central principle and the epitome of all the Torah's laws concerning relations between human beings."

Moreover, Jesus says that love for God and love for our neighbor are "like" (*homoia*) one another. This Greek word can also be translated as "of the same nature" or "equal rank."[27] We can take Jesus as saying, then, that love for God and neighbor are fundamentally united and equal in importance. For a Jewish audience, the language of heart, soul, and mind invokes the whole sense of self; so loving God with "heart, soul, and mind" and loving our neighbor "as ourselves" are mirroring expressions. Thus, the early Christian theologian Clement of Alexandria (AD 150–211) wrote, "The second commandment [is] in no way less important than the first."[28]

According to Jesus, then, no part of a person is free from the responsibility to love both God and neighbor. We should love these divine and human others in exactly the same way: with all we are. This is "the greatest commandment of the law," the true meaning of Scripture rightly understood. As before, Jesus continues integrating his vision of divine and human relationship without separation. One without the other is incomplete.

MATTHEW 28: GLOBALIZING NEIGHBOR LOVE

In the first book of the New Testament, Jesus universalizes the meaning of the neighbor. Now *neighbor* no longer refers primarily to a blood relative, near dweller, or friend. *Neighbor* now explicitly refers to all "others," including our enemies, children, the poor, and everyone else. Jesus abolishes othering and any justification for it. Nonviolence, prayer, and generosity are crucial practices of this healing.

Moreover, in each of his teachings, Jesus repeats the paradox that we can't have an authentic belonging with God unless we embrace the belonging of all others. This is because of Jesus' Genesis-rooted theology: God is *our* Father, the Creator of *all* people. Thus, God's generous kindness extends to the entire human family regardless of whether we're "good" or "bad." To love *God*, then, without loving *others* is self-contradictory; it indicates that we love an idol of our own making rather than God. This hypocrisy is not a way of life that God recognizes (Mt 7:23). Thus, Jesus connects being children of God (Mt 5:45), inheriting eternal life (Mt 19:21), and rightly interpreting Scripture (Mt 22:40) with loving our neighbors as ourselves.

---

[27]See Johannes Schneider, "Homoia," in *Theological Dictionary of the New Testament*, ed. Gerhard Friedrich (Grand Rapids, MI: Eerdmans, 1967), 5:186-87.
[28]Clement of Alexandria, *The Rich Man's Salvation*, §29, quoted in Helen Rhee (ed.), *Wealth and Poverty in Early Christianity* (Minneapolis, MN: Fortress Press, 2017), 19.

Now, neighbor love has taken on not only a universal but an ultimate, everlasting scope. It is at the very center of Jesus' newly inspired Scripture and movement. Neighbor love is fundamental to Jesus' vision of how we can be fully human.

This integrated teaching of Jesus provides crucial insight into how we should interpret his last words in Matthew's Gospel. Here Jesus gives his Abrahamic calling to globalize the ethics of neighbor love beyond every boundary. In his final commission to his students, Jesus says, "All authority in heaven and on earth has been given to me. Therefore go and make disciples of all nations, baptizing them in the name of the Father and of the Son and of the Holy Spirit, and teaching them to obey everything I have commanded you" (Mt 28:18-20). Traditionally, Jesus' words have often been interpreted as a commission to proselytize others to become members of the Christian religion. But this misses the ethical core of Jesus' commission, which is calling for something much deeper.

Jesus says that his followers should make disciples, baptize, and teach "all nations" to "obey everything I commanded you." As we've seen above, the heart of what Jesus commanded was love for God and neighbors. This emerged out of his own baptism experience: "You are my beloved child; I delight in you" (Mt 3:17, my translation). It then stretched to include those we are most conditioned to other, such as our enemies, children, and the poor.

Thus, Jesus is calling his students to spread *this* way of being human beyond every boundary of othering. Now, rather than imagining the world as a battlefield for imperial subjugation, like Aristotle's student Alexander and the Roman emperors of Jesus' time did, the world is reimagined as a global neighborhood. The circle of our moral responsibility is universalized.[29]

In a profound sense, then, Jesus' Great Commission is an abolition movement against othering through the invitation to embody divine belovedness with all neighbors. This is the healing water that the descendant of the othered Ruth imagines "all nations" being baptized into. Here at last, the blessing of Abraham and the vision of the prophets are being fulfilled. Rather than calling the world to confess a religious "Lord, Lord" or conquering it with religious nationalism, Jesus sends his disciples out to teach obedience to his universal ethic of neighbor love. In the ancient world

---

[29]See Maureen O'Connell, *Compassion: Loving Our Neighbor in an Age of Globalization* (Maryknoll, NY: Orbis Books, 2009); James Walters, *Loving Your Neighbour in an Age of Religious Conflict: A New Agenda for Interfaith Relations* (London: Jessica Kingsley, 2019).

structured by othering, where the definition of neighbor was often limited and enclosed, Jesus offers what can be called a revolutionary global ethic.

MARK 12: THE GREATEST COMMANDMENT

In Mark's story of Jesus, the context for Jesus' discussion of neighbor love is equally significant. Jesus has entered Jerusalem as the messianic king. There he disrupts the religious trade in the temple to make space for the poor and outsiders. He tells a subversive parable and clarifies his views on paying taxes to Caesar and the resurrection. All of this touched the heart of religion and politics in Jesus' world: temple worship, loyalty to Caesar, and eternal hope.

Directly after this, Jesus is asked about his messianic identity. It's here that an expert in the law asks Jesus, "Of all the commandments, which is the most important?" (Mk 12:28). As in Matthew, Jesus replies, "The most important one is this: 'Hear, O Israel: The Lord our God, the Lord is one. Love the Lord your God with all your heart and with all your soul and with all your mind and with all your strength.' The second is this: 'Love your neighbor as yourself.' There is no commandment greater than these" (Mk 12:29-31). In Mark's Gospel, Jesus concludes, "There is no commandment greater than these" rather than "All the Law and the Prophets hang on these." Of course, the basic meaning is the same: the command to love God and our neighbors is what is most important in life. Once again, Jesus refuses to mention loving God without loving neighbors, even though the man asked for the *single* greatest commandment.

The legal expert then agrees with Jesus and says that this love is "more important than all burnt offerings and sacrifices" (Mk 12:33). Here he is alluding to Jeremiah's prophetic critique of practicing religion in the temple while neglecting love for foreigners, orphans, and widows (Jer 7:5-7; see also Is 1:13-18; Hos 6:6; Amos 5:21-24; Mic 6:6-8). His statement also subtly identifies the spirit of Jesus' prophetic disruption of the temple moments before. Like Jeremiah, Jesus refuses to comply with religion that excluded others from God's presence.

In response, Jesus says to the legal expert, "You are not far from the kingdom of God" (Mk 12:34). As we saw in Matthew 5; 7; 19, Jesus consistently connected neighbor love and eternal life. Is Jesus, then, telling this man that he has found the way to God's kingdom in his recognition that loving God and neighbor is more important than religion itself? Jesus' answer is pregnant and provocative.

What is clear is that Jesus himself repeatedly spends time with tax collectors, sex workers, the demon-possessed, and foreigners throughout Mark's Gospel.

These were among the most othered people in Jesus' society. Mark points out how scandalized the religious leaders were by Jesus' practice of belonging with "sinners" (Mk 2:13-17). Thus, when Jesus names neighbor love as the greatest commandment, united with loving God, he surely has in mind his expansive, universal vision. This is what brings us into proximity with God's kingdom.

For Jesus, loving God and our neighbors is "more important" than performing a religious identity. If our religion becomes organized around excluding others, Jesus prophetically models that we should disrupt it for the inclusive belonging God desires for everyone.

Luke 6: God Is Kind to the Ungrateful and Wicked

In Luke's story, Jesus gives his powerful Sermon on the Plain. Whereas Matthew's Sermon on the *Mount* emphasizes Jesus' authoritative height and his right to introduce new Scripture like Moses, Luke's Sermon on the *Plain* emphasizes Jesus' humility and his desire to teach on an equal footing with his listeners.

Here Jesus gives an expanded version of his command to love our enemies. He says, "But to you who are listening I say: Love your enemies, do good to those who hate you, bless those who curse you, pray for those who mistreat you" (Lk 6:27-28). In Matthew, Jesus told us to love our enemies and to pray for our persecutors. Here Jesus adds that we should do good to them and bless them. His emphasis on love's creative goodness in the face of othering becomes even more internalized and intense. Abraham's calling to bless others is fulfilled whenever we experience conflict in Jesus' way.

Jesus then repeats his teaching on creative nonviolence to break the cycle of othering: turn the other cheek, offer your coat, give freely. That is, assert your dignity and agency in a way that doesn't imitate and escalate othering. He also repeats his golden rule: "Do to others as you would have them do to you" (Lk 6:31). Likewise, Jesus re-articulates his critique of retributive ethics, which favor insiders and other outsiders. Jesus wants a love that abolishes a transactional, group-centered orientation to others.

Then Jesus declares for a second time, "But love your enemies, do good to them, and lend to them without expecting to get anything back. Then your reward will be great, and you will be children of the Most High, because he is kind to the ungrateful and wicked. Be merciful, just as your Father is merciful" (Lk 6:35-36). Notice again the beauty of Jesus' command to love our enemies and how it abolishes othering. He doesn't say to love our enemies so God will judge them more harshly in the future, to prove our moral superiority to them, or even to win them over to our religion. Jesus says to love our enemies and do good to them simply because this is how God loves and how *we* practice our belonging in God's universal family.

Here Jesus offers perhaps the only definition he ever gave of God: "God is kind to the ungrateful and wicked." There is a playful rhyme in the Greek text: God is *chrēstos* to the *akaristous*. In God's grammar, even human ingratitude and divine kindness find a way to rhyme. Why? Because God is overflowing, undeserved generosity—even to "the wicked."

Once more, we encounter the paradox of Jesus' spirituality and ethics: the only barrier to our full belonging in God's family is blocking others from full belonging. Our Father *is* merciful, and so Jesus says to *be* merciful. *Being* merciful goes far beyond extending kindness to those we prefer and withholding it from those we don't. It's a way of life that we become and thus can't turn on and off depending on who happens to need our mercy.

Jesus immediately turns to critique "judging others." He teaches, "Do not judge, and you will not be judged. Do not condemn, and you will not be condemned. Forgive, and you will be forgiven. Give, and it will be given to you. A good measure, pressed down, shaken together and running over, will be poured into your lap. For with the measure you use, it will be measured to you" (Lk 6:37-38). As we saw in Mathew 5, judgment easily becomes the justification of othering. When we bifurcate people into the binary of good versus evil, the condemned versus forgiven, we limit who we see as worthy of our love. Jesus says to surrender this othering mindset: condemn no one and forgive everyone. This is an ethic of abundance. If God is kind even to the ungrateful and wicked, then we don't have to fear that there won't be enough love for us.

Here I'm reminded of the first humans' insecurity that God had jealously withheld something from them and Cain's fear of having an inferior favor with God compared to Abel (Gen 3:1-7; 4:4-5). Jesus says to trust that the measure of God's love is so good that we can surrender these insecurities and comparisons. We hear echoes again of Jesus' baptism experience and how intimately he internalized it: "You are my beloved child; I delight in you" (Lk 3:22, my translation).

Jesus then comments, "Everyone who is fully trained will be like their teacher" (Lk 6:40). He doesn't expect us to magically convert to the way of neighbor love.

Instead, he expects us to make this love our *practice* and to see our lives as a process of *training*. The goal is to become "fully trained," precisely as we resist judging others who are in different places in their training. The paradox appears again: the more advanced we become in our practice of neighbor love, the less we need to see others in terms of how "advanced" or "backward" they are in theirs, at least not in any condescending or condemning sense.

Similar to Matthew, Jesus concludes his sermon in Luke by warning against religious hypocrisy (Lk 6:46-49). Jesus asks why his hearers would call him "Lord, Lord"—a confession of religious loyalty—and "not do what I say" (Lk 6:46). Once more, Jesus deprioritizes religious identity and centralizes the practice of neighbor love, including enemies. He says that the practitioner of his path is like a person of wisdom who builds their home on an unshakable foundation (Lk 6:47-48). On this rock, the torrents of life—presumably our volatile emotions within ourselves and the conflicts between us—no longer sweep us away. We remain regulated and integrated even amid the intensity of othering. By contrast, Jesus warns that religious affiliation without ethical practice will crumble in the flood (Lk 6:49).

More broadly, notice that Jesus likely gave his teaching on enemy love many times in diverse contexts. In Matthew, Jesus teaches enemy love on a mountainside and uses sunshine and rainfall to illustrate God's indiscriminate love for everyone. In Luke, Jesus teaches enemy love on a plain and uses metaphors from the marketplace to illustrate the same. The diversity in the Gospels' records suggest the repetition and richness of Jesus' teaching as he iterated and expanded it throughout his movement.

Across contexts, the implication is the same: Jesus universalized the moral circle of human responsibility and sought to abolish othering in the process.

Luke 10: The Parable of the Good Samaritan

Later in Luke's story, Jesus tells his famous parable of the good Samaritan. This may be the most radical story that Jesus told. It focuses on the meaning of neighbor love and how it can overcome some of the most intense othering in Jesus' culture.[30]

---

[30]For a study of how this parable has been (mis)interpreted across history, see Nick Spencer, *The Political Samaritan: How Power Hijacked a Parable* (New York: Bloomsbury, 2017). For its wider immediate context, see Claudio Gianotto, "The Lucan Parable of the Good Samaritan and Its Interpretations in Christian Antiquity," in *The Quest for a Common Humanity: Human Dignity*

Like the rich man in Matthew 19, a religious expert asks Jesus, "Teacher, what must I do to inherit eternal life?" (Lk 10:25). This is a question about ultimate happiness and how to overcome death, so we shouldn't be surprised that various people asked Jesus this question. All teachers are familiar with being asked the same important questions in different contexts.

As so often, Jesus answers with a counter-question: "What is written in the Law? How do you read it?" (Lk 10:26). The religious expert gives Jesus' own answer from Mark 12: love God completely and love your neighbor as yourself. Jesus then responds, "You have answered correctly. Do this and you will flourish" (Lk 10:28, my translation).[31] Once again, loving God and loving neighbors is true life: when we love, we flourish, and this life never dies. As bell hooks observed, "I know no one who has embraced a love ethic whose life has not become joyous and more fulfilling. The widespread assumption that ethical behavior takes the fun out of life is false."[32]

But like the rich man, the religious expert isn't satisfied. Instead, Luke tells us that he wants to "justify" himself and asks Jesus, "And who is my neighbor?" (Lk 10:29).

As we've seen in the Hebrew Bible and Matthew 19, many Jews in Jesus' context didn't see everyone as neighbors. Fellow Jews were certainly seen as neighbors, people who were connected and worthy of care. But outsiders and enemies were often not. They were "others" who, sometimes at least, could be excluded, condemned, and even attacked.

So, this man is asking Jesus to go on the record and confirm his adherence to the traditional interpretation of Scripture. He wants Jesus to declare that not all people are his neighbors and thus that he doesn't need to love all people in order to flourish with God forever. Some people can be left out—ignored or maybe even eliminated.

This question "Who is my neighbor?" cuts to the core of the othering of religious nationalism. Between the lines, we can hear the question, "Aren't I being biblical in believing that my people are special to God and that others are irrelevant to my flourishing?" In a sense, this man is asking Jesus to

---

and Otherness in the Religious Traditions of the Mediterranean, ed. Katell Berthelot and Matthias Morgenstern (Leiden: Brill, 2011), 125-38.

[31]The NIV translates Jesus' words as "Do this and you will *live*." But the Greek verb that is used here (*zēsē*) carries a richer sense of flourishing or being well, like recovering after an illness (see Mk 5:23).

[32]bell hooks, *All About Love: New Visions* (New York: HarperCollins, 2001), 88.

endorse the view that his own community is destined to be the head while others are reduced to the tail.

As we've seen, Jesus believed that everyone was our neighbor and that we must love even our enemies in order to inherit eternal life. So Jesus responds by telling a provocative story that centers on a Samaritan, an ultimate other in his society.

The context is essential to understand what Jesus is doing here. Many Jews fiercely hated and despised Samaritans. John tells us that some Jews wouldn't even touch a cup that a Samaritan had used (Jn 4:9). Here again we see the importance of purity in othering. Jews traveling between Jerusalem and Galilee would often travel around Samaria to avoid making contact with the dirty Samaritans and their defiling soil.

There were three primary reasons for this passionate hatred. First, the Samaritans mixed Jewish monotheism with pagan idolatry. They were religious heretics who abandoned the Jerusalem temple and built their own shrine. Second, the Samaritans had broken away from Judah and formed a separate state. They were political rivals. And, third, the Samaritans had mixed with non-Jewish people during the exile rather than preserving their purity as Ezra and Nehemiah insisted. They were ethnic others. Thus, the Samaritans embodied three of the most powerful triggers of othering in human history: religion, politics, and ethnic identity.[33]

Jesus also had a fourth reason to hate Samaritans. Just before this episode, Jesus had been personally rejected by a Samaritan village and sent away without food or shelter. Jesus' disciples were so furious that they asked Jesus whether they could burn down their village. This painful experience of being othered because of his Jewish identity was fresh in Jesus' memory (Lk 9:51-56).

Thus, against all expectations, when the religious expert asks Jesus, "Who is my neighbor?" Jesus responds by telling a story in which "even a despised Samaritan" is the neighbor—the one who does God's will and inherits eternal salvation.[34] In the story, a man is traveling the dangerous road from

---

[33]On the Samaritans mixing with foreigners who threatened "to replace the Israelites," see 2 Kings 17:24; on their religious syncretism, see 2 Kings 17:25-41; on their political rivalry with Israel, see 1 Kings 16:21-24. When the Samaritans offered to help rebuild the Jerusalem temple, the Jewish leaders responded, "You have no part with us in building a temple to our God" (Ezra 4:3). For a comprehensive study, see Gary Knoppers, *Jews and Samaritans: The Origins and History of Their Early Relations* (New York: Oxford University Press, 2013).

[34]Kugel, *Traditions of the Bible*, 456.

Jerusalem to Jericho. Eventually, he is attacked, stripped, and nearly killed by thieves. They leave him for dead on the roadside. Then a priest approaches, but "he passed by on the other side" (Lk 10:31). Another spiritual leader approaches, but he also "passed by on the other side" (Lk 10:32).

Jesus doesn't tell us why these religious leaders chose "the other side" and refused to help the suffering stranger. Interpreters have offered various speculations: Were they worried that the stranger might die and defile their religious purity, since ministers weren't supposed to touch dead bodies? Were they afraid that the thieves were waiting to attack the helpers of the original victim? Were they simply busy and on their way to an important religious function? Were they unsure about the man's ethnic and religious identity and thus whether he was worthy of their concern? Or did they simply not care at all? Jesus doesn't tell us. He simply says that they "passed by on the other side" and didn't help. With their behavior, they silently said to the suffering stranger, "It doesn't really matter to us whether you live or die."

Then a third man, a hated Samaritan, approaches the half-dead victim. But instead of passing by "on the other[ing] side," the Samaritan does four things. First, he sees the man: he gives him his attention (Lk 10:33). Second, he takes pity on him: he opens his heart with compassion to this stranger's suffering (Lk 10:33). Third, he comes close to the man: he doesn't stay at a safe distance with his pity (Lk 10:34). And, fourth, he bandages the man's wounds, takes him to a hospital, and personally pays for all of his expenses (Lk 10:35).

The Samaritan's actions embody authentic neighbor love. He crosses every boundary of religion, politics, and ethnicity to help a dying enemy—a man whose death many Samaritans probably would have celebrated. Indeed, he risks his own safety, his wealth, and his reputation to keep his enemy alive.

With his story told, Jesus turns to the religious expert and asks him, "Which of these three do you think was a neighbor to the man who fell into the hands of robbers?" (Lk 10:36). The man's limited concept of the neighbor has been exposed and exploded. He can only answer, "The one who had mercy on him" (Lk 10:37).

According to Luke, the religious expert doesn't identify "the one who did mercy" as "the Samaritan" like Jesus did. Why the absence here? Perhaps Luke is inviting the reader to consider how deep othering often goes in us. Was the man offended to name explicitly that a *Samaritan* could be an exemplary neighbor who inherits flourishing forever with God?

In any case, Jesus concludes the episode by saying, "Go and do likewise" (Lk 10:37).

Of course, Jesus didn't need to make a Samaritan his exemplar of neighbor love. He could have inserted anyone. But Jesus chose a Samaritan to make the powerful point that even our most hated enemy can be a neighbor and embody God's quality of love that flourishes forever.

In doing so, Jesus boldly challenges the religious nationalism of his audience. The other we are most tempted to hate, exclude, and leave for dead can show us that we have yet to enter into the full belonging of God's family. We need to stretch our moral circle and vision of flourishing wider—indeed, universally.

Jesus' final word to the religious expert is simple and subversive: "Go and act like the Samaritan. If you want eternal life, follow the example of your enemy who chose to love."

Luke 10: Insights from the Enemy

Before moving forward, I want to point out six insights from Jesus' famous parable.

First, this is the only place where we see Jesus reverse the logic of neighbor love. In this story, the real challenge is not to *identify* who the neighbor is but to *become* the neighbor who practices love. Between the lines, Jesus seems to suggest that when *we* are a neighbor to others, every *other* becomes a neighbor to us. The subtle question is raised, "Am I a neighbor?" For Jesus, what is important is *our* action for others, regardless of who they are or how they treat us. Neighbor love is a way of being in which moral responsibility is open to all.

Second, the practice of neighbor love embodies "pity" (Lk 10:33) and "mercy" (Lk 10:37). These are biblical words for compassion. Being a neighbor doesn't simply mean being nearby, having a blood relationship, or sharing a nationality. Those identity markers and boundaries don't matter. The practice of compassion is depicted in the way the Samaritan compassionately focused his attention on the other, came close to them amid possible danger, and actively responded to their needs. Neighbor love is far more than a kind sentiment; it is a choice and action.

Third, this means that anyone can be a neighbor, whether a political rival, ethnic minority, or religious heretic. As long as I am neighbor, everyone is a neighbor to me. According to ethicist Timothy Jackson, "The point of the story is not merely that *all* persons should *receive* love, as novel as that would seem to Jesus's listeners, but also that *all* persons should *give* love. Jesus is no sectarian with respect to either end of neighbor-love."[35]

Fourth, we see again that neighbor love was an issue of ultimate importance for Jesus. Remember the legal expert's original question: "What must I do to inherit eternal life?" When Jesus tells the parable of the good Samaritan, he's not simply defining the term *neighbor*. He's painting a picture of what eternal life looks like. So, once more, Jesus unites soteriology (what it means to flourish with God forever) and neighbor love (how we relate with others). Salvation looks like service for the suffering other. This connects with the paradox in Matthew 5 and Luke 6 where Jesus claims that being children of God requires loving others without limitation.

Fifth, Jesus reemphasizes the importance of action: "Go and do likewise." Jesus calls the religious expert to learn from a Samaritan and to follow his example. The most important thing is not defining terms and categorizing people but actively practicing neighbor love. *Go and do*. We're reminded of Jesus' challenge to the rich man to give his wealth to the poor and *then* come follow him.

Sixth, practicing this love is costly. In the Gospel of John, Jesus is labeled as a "Samaritan" himself and accused of being "demon-possessed" (Jn 8:48). We see that when we love the other, we ourselves may become the other. Many of our kin and comrades may feel betrayed by our practice of neighbor love and respond with rage. Nevertheless, this is Jesus' invitation, then and now: "Go and do likewise."

In this parable, then, Jesus provocatively imagines the enemy as a model of neighbor love. Here he offers a challenging ethic that the Christian tradition will develop, expand, and contradict across its history. With Jesus, even the most hated enemy is a neighbor.

Jesus' teaching was subversive in both Greek and Jewish cultures. Across contexts, he presents a new moral imagination in which the circle of our belonging is universalized to include all.

---

[35] Jackson, *Love Disconsoled*, 4.

The Gospel of John: For God So Loved the World

We've now looked at Jesus' teaching on neighbor love in the Gospels of Matthew, Mark, and Luke. In the Gospel of John, Jesus doesn't specifically refer to the command of neighbor love by name. But he centralizes love, and his teaching and practice match what we have seen in the other Gospels. For the author of John, as with the other Gospel writers, the *life* of neighbor love matters far more than the *language* of it. Whether we talk about "neighbor love," "enemy love," "love for all people," or "loving one another," self-giving concern and care for others is what matters in the ethics of Jesus.

As in the other Gospels, John roots love in the character of Godself. He writes, "For God so loved the world that he gave his one and only Son, that whoever believes in him shall not perish but have eternal life. For God did not send his Son into the world to condemn the world, but to save the world through him" (Jn 3:16-17). Here God is described as loving the whole world. John begins his Gospel with a mystical vision of Jesus as the Logos or energizing intelligence that was eternally present with God and participates with God in sustaining the entire universe (Jn 1:1-5). Rather than remaining exalted above creation, God wants to fully embrace it and become enfleshed within it (Jn 1:14). In John 3, then, John describes Jesus as God's ultimate gift of love for the world. As our Creator, God's intention in Jesus is not to condemn the world but to *save* it. Here again the paradox is suggested that we enter into this undying quality of life by receiving Jesus' gift and trusting in his "way" (see Jn 14:6).

As with God, Jesus' way of love is characterized by self-giving generosity with others. In John 10, Jesus says, "I am the good shepherd. The good shepherd lays down his life for the sheep. . . . The reason my Father loves me is that I lay down my life—only to take it up again. . . . This command I received from my Father" (Jn 10:11, 17-18). Jesus presents himself as humanity's faithful guide. But he doesn't drive and exploit his flock like many traditional religious leaders (Jn 10:1). He is "the good shepherd" who comes among us and sacrificially gives his own life for us. With intimacy, Jesus speaks of calling us "by name" and leading us into the freedom of an open pasture (Jn 10:3). His intention is for us "to have life, and have it to the full" (Jn 10:10), an ethic of abundance we saw in Luke. Jesus also names having "other sheep" that the traditional flock may not expect to be included. He says, "I must bring them also. They too will listen to my voice, and there will be one flock and one shepherd" (Jn 10:16). Here Jesus seems to allude to his universal vision in Matthew 28 of his "way" reaching out to all humanity. Jesus calls this work of self-giving love God's personal command (Jn 10:18).

A little later, Jesus embodies this love with a provocative act of service. John tells us, "Having loved his own who were in the world, he loved them to the end" (Jn 13:1). Jesus shares a final meal with his students before he is arrested. Despite the anguish of his coming suffering, we're told, "Jesus knew that the Father had put all things under his power" (Jn 13:3). But this power is the power of love, and so Jesus takes the often-othered position of the servant: he gets a towel, pours water in a basin, and washes his disciples' dirty feet (Jn 13:4-5). Jesus is unafraid of impurity.

Jesus then asks his disciples whether they understand the significance of what he did for them. Jesus explains,

> You call me "Teacher" and "Lord," and rightly so, for that is what I am. Now that I, your Lord and Teacher, have washed your feet, you also should wash one another's feet. I have set you an example that you should do as I have done for you. . . . A new command I give you: Love one another. As I have loved you, so you must love one another. By this everyone will know that you are my disciples, if you love one another. (Jn 13:14-15, 34-35)

In Jesus' way, the true teachers and lords are the ones who serve. They are not afraid of losing a superior power and exalted identity. Instead, their power and identity are embodied precisely in humble actions of connection and care for others. Something as simple and practical as washing feet is not beneath them or contaminating. It is the heart of their practice.[36]

Here Jesus himself intimately embodies the enemy love he taught in Matthew 5 and Luke 6. John tells us that Judas was around the table that night and had already decided to betray Jesus to a violent death. Jesus knows this agony is coming. But he stoops and washes Judas's feet with the rest of the disciples. Jesus doesn't exclude him or simply wait for him to leave. It's difficult to imagine a more intimate embodiment of Jesus' own words, "Love your enemies, do good to those who hate you" (Lk 6:27-28). Jesus gently washes the feet of the person he knows is going to hand him over to be murdered.

Having done this, Jesus tells his disciples to follow his example. He hasn't simply performed an eccentric act to inspire them. At the height of his power and with some of his final words, Jesus tells his students to embody

---

[36]This is a repeated theme in Jesus' teaching. See Mt 20:20-28; Mk 10:42-45.

this same love through practical acts of service that turn othering and its hierarchy upside-down. This is what the Teacher and Lord commands: "As I have loved you, you must love one another" (Jn 13:34).

Finally, Jesus says that his "new command" to love one another must be his disciples' identity in the world (Jn 13:34-35). This echoes Matthew 7 and Luke 6, where Jesus critiqued people calling him "Lord" and performing a religious identity but neglecting to practice neighbor love as their way of life. According to Jesus, the world won't be able to identify his disciples because of their religious vocabulary, gatherings, or rituals. The world will be able to recognize his disciples because of the way they love one another through action that upends the power hierarchies that keep some high and others low.

Jesus summarizes his teaching on love in John's Gospel like this: "As the Father has loved me, so have I loved you. Now remain in my love.... I have told you this so that my joy may be in you and that your joy may be complete. My command is this: Love each other as I have loved you. Greater love has no one than this: to lay down one's life for one's friends.... This is my command: Love each other" (Jn 15:9, 11-13, 17). From God to Jesus, from Jesus to his disciples, from his disciples to the whole world—Jesus' vision of love is an ever-expanding circle that embraces all creation. This is the way of complete joy. When we lay our lives down for one another, including the enemy who betrays us, othering is overcome and God's promise of blessing is fulfilled. Humane happiness is our destiny, even in the face of death.

Although Jesus doesn't use the language of neighbor love in John's Gospel, then, his teaching and practice of it is as boundary breaking and inclusive as it is in Matthew, Mark, and Luke. If anything, it becomes even simpler and more powerful: the Good Shepherd has "other sheep" and lays his life down for them. *Love one another.*

Luke 23: The Murder of Jesus and Unotherable Divine Love

We have now looked at all four of the Gospels and their passages related to neighbor love in Jesus' movement. Before concluding this chapter, we need to look briefly at the climax of each of their stories: the crucifixion of Jesus. In many ways, Jesus' violent death shows us the climax of neighbor love but also the ways in which this ethic is opposed by othering.

Why was Jesus arrested, tortured, and killed? Each Gospel tells us that Jesus' people found him to be too countercultural and dangerous to the traditional order of religion and society. In Luke's Gospel, Jesus' accusers say, "We have found this man subverting our nation" (Lk 23:2).

Jesus' teaching on neighbor love was central to this scandal. He was embracing all the othered people, breaking down barriers of exclusivist identity, and redefining what it means to have a relationship with God that flourishes forever. In this way, Jesus defied his community's expectations and desires for a messiah in the midst of Rome's violent imperial occupation. In reaction, many of the religious leaders conspired to execute him as a heretical criminal.

Luke tells us that the crowd who watched Jesus get executed on the cross tempted and insulted him. The religious leaders shouted, "He saved others; let him save himself if he is God's Messiah" (Lk 23:35). Then the Roman soldiers added, "If you are the king of the Jews, save yourself" (Lk 23:36). Finally, one of the criminals being executed next to Jesus screamed, "Aren't you the Messiah? Save yourself and us!" (Lk 23:39).

Here we discover perhaps the basic compulsion of othering, which ultimately crucifies neighbor love: "Save yourself!" In other words, value yourself above all; refuse to be vulnerable; use violence to survive. In this astonishing scene, all the witnesses—the religious, the political, and the criminal—assume that saving yourself is what is most important and what proves ultimate power.

In the final moment of his life, then, Jesus faces the greatest test of his love: Will he save himself? Or will he love God and his murderous neighbors to the point of his own death?

Jesus doesn't save himself; he gives himself. Each of the Gospels tells us that he suffered and died as an innocent victim. As he did so, Jesus practiced his way of neighbor love to the end.

With some of his final breaths, Jesus cries out to God, "Father, forgive them, for they do not know what they're doing" (Lk 23:34). Even in his agony, Jesus centers himself in the presence of our universal Father. As he prays, it seems that Jesus understands that othering has overtaken his executioners. They aren't acting in the conscious freedom of creative nonviolence; they are trapped in the reactive aggression of othering.

And so, rather than condemning them, Jesus cries out for their forgiveness. *God is kind to the ungrateful and wicked.* Jesus not only preached this love; he practiced it to the death—his own, not the others'.

Jesus' first followers then claimed that he rose from the dead three days later. They believed that the power of his self-giving love was so omnipotent that it overcame death itself and opened humanity to an everlasting quality of life. As Jesus himself promised when he was asked how to live forever, "[Love God and your neighbor], and you will flourish" (Lk 10:28, my translation).

Jesus' student Peter said something similar days later in Jerusalem: "God raised [Jesus] from the dead, freeing him from the agony of death, because it was impossible for death to keep its hold on him" (Acts 2:24). The moral claim of Jesus' resurrection is that the fear and force of othering ultimately can't kill the power of God's unconditional love. As a Hebrew poet wrote, "Love is as strong as death" (Song 8:6).

If this is true, then the "Save yourself!" compulsion of othering no longer needs to control us. Death is not the end of our story; it needn't be feared. As Jesus repeatedly taught, when we give ourselves with love, we don't lose anything at all. Instead, we enter into the divine life that created the world, shines like the sun, and never dies. "Unless a grain of wheat falls into the earth and dies, it remains alone," Jesus said. "But if it dies, it bears much fruit" (Jn 12:24 ESV).

After Jesus' resurrection, it is striking that he doesn't ask his disciples to seek retributive justice or to take revenge against his killers. In fact, Jesus doesn't even mention them. He is serious about creative nonviolence and its healing power. Instead, he says to his students, "Peace be with you! As the Father has sent me, I am sending you. . . . If you forgive anyone's sins, their sins are forgiven" (Jn 20:21, 23). Then he calls Peter to recommit himself to practicing love, even to the point of his own death (Jn 21:15-19).

Thus begins Jesus' global movement of neighbor love—a universal blessing for all people. If you forgive *anyone*'s sins, their sins are forgiven. This is a new story that shares healing with everyone (see Mt 28:18-20; Acts 3:24-26; Gal 3:7-9).

Conclusion: A Universal Hope in the Face of Othering

There are many other passages in the Gospels related to love in the life and teaching of Jesus. But what we have found in this survey leads me to the same conclusion as Hannah Arendt in her book *On Revolution*. In the face of the extreme othering of the twentieth century, Arendt wrote, "The only completely valid, completely convincing experience Western mankind ever had with active love of goodness as the inspiring principle of all actions . . . [was] the person of Jesus of Nazareth."[37]

---

[37]Hannah Arendt, *On Revolution* (New York: Viking, 1965), 76-77.

Jesus' teaching and embodiment of love are so beautiful, so powerful, and so practical.

Jesus teaches that every person we meet is our neighbor, someone who is related to us and equally worthy of love. The neighbor includes the enemy, the child, the poor, the foreigner, the Judas, the murderer, and every other human we encounter. In this universal vision, othering is abolished for good.

Moreover, the primary meaning of neighbor is subtly reversed and personalized: Am *I* a neighbor to others? Like the Samaritan, Jesus invites us to *become* people who see and treat others with compassion across every boundary of religion, ethnicity, and politics. He promises us, "Do this and you will flourish" (Lk 10:28, my translation).

Finally, Jesus sees neighbor love as ultimately important. All Scripture hangs on loving God and our neighbor. The greatest commandment is to embody this love with all we are and have. Indeed, our eternal life depends on loving our neighbor. This is the repeated paradox of Jesus' teaching: we can fully belong in God's family only when we overcome othering and embrace the full belonging of all people, including our enemies. This was Jesus' practice even to the point of being crucified for it.

In this way, Jesus universalizes the groundbreaking but limited vision of neighbor love in Hebrew Scripture. Here the holy image of God is rediscovered in all people, whoever they may be. We return to seeing one another as children of our primal parents, all members of one family created for belonging and sustained by God's creative generosity. And thus we reclaim the mission of Abraham to bless all people, including our enemy-siblings. This life transcends saving itself for the healing and wholeness of others, near and far. The moral circle surrounds us all. Othering is abolished.

This was Jesus' Great Commission, his call to globalize the vision and practice of neighbor love. Two thousand years later and almost three thousand miles away, this invitation would inspire new hope in Ferdosa as she faced a murderous crisis of othering in Ethiopia.

In the next chapter, we turn to look at how Jesus' neighbor-love movement spread among his first followers in their world and began reaching out to ours.

4

THE IMPROBABLE REVOLUTION OF NEIGHBOR LOVE

The New Testament

THE MAN WAS ENRAGED WITH OTHERING. He had zealously devoted his life to his community. But now a heretical movement threatened to corrupt it.

Observing this radicalized him. He found himself overseeing a public execution in the capital city. The offender, a leader of the movement, was brutally beaten to death with rocks. But he was unmoved as he watched him die.

In fact, this man made a plan to go door-to-door to arrest and root out these heretics. As his reputation spread, his name triggered terror. He was known for "breathing out murderous threats." But he embraced others' dread as a badge of honor. He believed that his devotion to God demanded this of him.

I'm not referring to an extremist in Ethiopia, America, or another modern context where we might observe nationalistic violence. I'm referring to the man we now know as Paul.

In first-century Israel, the movement Jesus started inspired people and, despite his execution, began to spread rapidly. In fact, they insisted that he had been resurrected to new life. In reaction, his followers were brutally othered and attacked like Jesus was. They were labeled "Christians" or "little christs": people who presumed to pattern their lives after Jesus' new way of being human.[1]

As a zealous religious nationalist, Paul was determined to stamp out this heretical movement. Like Ezra and Nehemiah before him, he wanted to

---

[1] Jesus' followers are first called "Christians" in Acts 11:26. They refer to Jesus' movement as "the way." See Acts 9:2; 19:9, 23; 22:4; 24:14, 22.

The Improbable Revolution of Neighbor Love

purify his community and protect its sacrosanct identity (Acts 22:3-5). He was willing to kill for it.

But against all odds, Paul himself had a mystical encounter with the post-execution Jesus. Jesus confronted Paul's othering and asked him, "Why do you persecute me?" (Acts 9:4). In the wake of this experience, Paul became a follower of the new way he once devoted his life to eliminating.

With time, the violent religious nationalist became known as a nonviolent apostle of love. He went on to devote his life to crossing the boundaries of the Roman Empire and spreading the movement started by the crucified-yet-alive Jesus who mysteriously met him in his enraged othering.[2]

This chapter takes us into the story of the earliest followers of Jesus. Starting with Paul, we'll explore how these little christs envisioned neighbor love and attempted to live it. What we'll find is far from perfect but profoundly inspiring.

The Earliest Movement of Jesus

The first Christians advanced Jesus' universal vision of neighbor love throughout their world. The moral circle became a global movement. They reaffirmed Jesus' teaching to love enemies, sought to abolish othering, and advocated for "one new humanity" as the movement spread across borders (Eph 2:15). As Paul wrote, "The goal is equality" (2 Cor 8:14).

In this way, the earliest Christians emerged as a countercultural, cosmopolitan community of hospitality, generosity, and liberation. They generously shared their resources with poor and oppressed neighbors. Luke tells us that the wealthy sold their homes and donated their savings, such that "there were no needy persons among them" (Acts 4:34).

Ethnic, religious, and political othering was also slowly overcome. After having his own mysterious vision, Peter, the movement's initial leader, confessed, "You are well aware that it is against our law for a Jew to associate with or visit a Gentile. But God has shown me that I should not call anyone impure or unclean" (Acts 10:28). Paul calls the escaped slave Onesimus a "dear brother" and "fellow human" rather than a piece of property to be repossessed like we saw in Plato and Aristotle (Philem 1:16 NIV altered).

In Paul's new vision of humanity, "There is neither Jew nor Gentile, neither slave nor free, nor is there male and female, for you are all one in

---

[2]For more of Paul's story, see N. T. Wright, *Paul: A Biography* (San Francisco: HarperOne, 2020).

Christ Jesus" (Gal 3:28; see also Rom 10:12; 1 Cor 12:13). The old identity markers of superiority or inferiority, inclusion or separation, are no longer relevant. Indeed, Paul dared to write, "Christ . . . is *in all*" (Col 3:11).

With this vision, women became apostles (Rom 16:7). The egalitarian values of Jesus' movement fueled other innovative movements to overthrow poverty, slavery, and patriarchy as othering evils that disgrace the image of God in all people (see Col 3:9-14). Liberation rippled widely.

Unsurprisingly, then, the first followers of Jesus were quickly othered themselves. In their native Jewish context, they were seen as heretics who had betrayed their "holy seed" by integrating with the Gentile others. In the wider Roman world, they were seen as atheists who no longer believed in the empire's gods and their hierarchy or "holy order."[3] Loving others led to the othering of the lovers. Addressing both audiences in his most famous letter, Paul delivers a passionate manifesto of Christian universalism to the heart of the empire in Rome. He declares, "God does not show favoritism" (Rom 2:11), "Abraham . . . is the father of us all" (Rom 4:16), "For there is no difference between Jew and Gentile—the same Lord [Jesus] is Lord of all and richly blesses all who call on him" (Rom 10:12).[4] Thus, the earliest Christians were often persecuted by religious nationalists and the imperial authorities like Jesus was. Ancient barriers between Jew and Gentile, men and women, slave and free, citizen and foreigner, rich and poor were being disregarded and dismantled. Christians were nonviolently subverting the established order and creating a new way from the ground up. Abraham's universal blessing was going global.

Paul, the religious nationalist turned apostle of love, describes it like this: "[Christ] has destroyed the barrier, the dividing wall of hostility. . . . His purpose was to create in himself one new humanity out of the two, thus making peace, and in one body to reconcile both of them to God through

---

[3]Polycarp (AD 69-155) was the first recorded Christian martyr. Justyn (AD 100-165) was the first Christian philosopher and was also a martyr. Both were condemned to death as atheists. See Justin Martyr, *First Apology*, in *The Ante-Nicene Fathers: Translations of the Writings of the Fathers down to A.D. 325*, ed. Alexander Roberts and James Donaldson (New York: Scribner's Sons, 1905), 1:165; and "The Martyrdom of Polycarp," 3.2, 8.2, in *The Apostolic Fathers*, trans. Kirsopp Lake (New York: Macmillan, 1923), 2:317, 329.

[4]See Alain Badiou, *Saint Paul: The Foundation of Universalism*, trans. Ray Brassier (Stanford, CA: Stanford University Press, 2003); and John Milbank, Slavoj Žižek, and Creston Davis, *Paul's New Moment: Continental Philosophy and the Future of Christian Theology* (Grand Rapids, MI: Brazos, 2010).

The Improbable Revolution of Neighbor Love   97

the cross" (Eph 2:14-16). We observe that Jesus had indeed started a movement to abolish othering and heal humanity. His divine purpose was to found not a new religion but a new way of being human. Stretching from holy Jerusalem to hated Samaria to the othered ends of the earth, these Christ-inspired innovators witnessed that God's promise to Abraham to bless all people had been fulfilled at last. A new creation was coming and with it "one new humanity." As James Baldwin observed, "The revolution which was begun by a disreputable Hebrew criminal" started challenging and transforming the Roman Empire that crucified him.[5]

The first followers of this revolution are the focus of this chapter. Their primary documents are found in the New Testament, which contains eleven passages on neighbor love (Mt 5:43; 19:19; 23:39; Mk 12:31, 33; Lk 10:27, 29, 36; Rom 13:9-10; 15:2; Gal 5:14; Eph 4:25; Jas 2:8; 4:12). We've already looked at five in Jesus' teaching in the Gospels. We'll now survey the remaining six and touch on several related passages on love.[6] What might these heretical, heteronautic "little christs" have to teach us?

ROMANS 12: PAUL'S ETHICS OF ENEMY LOVE

In his letter to the Jesus community in Rome, Paul takes us to the core of his ethics of love. It reads as a brief manual for the movement we saw emerging above. Paul writes, "Love must be sincere. Hate what is evil; cling to what is good. Be devoted to one another in love. Honor one another above yourselves. . . . Share with the Lord's people who are in need. Practice love for the other [*philoxenia*]" (Rom 12:9, 13 NIV altered). Earlier in his letter, Paul argued for his vision of humanity as a universal family (Rom 4:16). Here he makes the ethical implication explicit: "Love must be sincere." This love honors others above itself. It is free from othering's fear of vulnerability, which compulsively insists, "Save yourself!" Thus, those who love are willing to share and don't feel like

---

[5]James Baldwin, "White Racism or World Community?," in *James Baldwin: Collected Essays*, ed. Toni Morrison (New York: Library of America, 1998), 750.
[6]Rom 12:9-21 ("love must be sincere"); 1 Cor 13 ("Love never fails"); 1 Cor 16:14 ("Do everything in love"); Gal 6:1-5 ("Carry each other's burdens"); 1 Thess 4:9-12 ("you yourselves have been taught by God to love each other"); 1 Pet 1:22-23 ("love one another deeply"); 1 Pet 3:8-9 ("love one another"); 1 Pet 4:7-10 ("Above all, love each other deeply"); 1 Pet 5:14 ("Greet one another with a kiss of love"); 2 Pet 1:5-9 ("[add] to mutual affection, love"); 1 Jn 2:9-11 ("He who loves his brother and sister abides in the light"); 1 John 3:11 ("this is the message you heard from the beginning, that we should love one another"); 1 Jn 4:7-21 ("whoever does not love their brother or sister, whom they have seen, cannot love God, whom they have not seen"); 2 Jn 5-6 ("I ask that we love one another").

anything is lost in being generous with people in need. (Recall that the Roman Plautus said, "What is given to the poor is lost," and Cicero called the poor "the scum of the city.") Moreover, Paul says that sincere love gets embodied in *philoxenia*, which literally means "love for the other." This is the active practice of welcoming outsiders into belonging with warm hospitality.

Still, it might sound like Paul's focus is primarily on Christians loving other Christians. Notice the increasingly universal scope as Paul continues unpacking what sincere love looks like in practice:

> Bless *those who persecute you*; bless and do not curse. Rejoice with those who rejoice; mourn with those who mourn. Live in harmony with one another. Do not be proud, but be willing to associate with *people of low position*. Do not be conceited.
>
> Do not repay *anyone* evil for evil. Be careful to do what is right in the eyes of *everyone*. If it is possible, as far as it depends on you, live at peace with *everyone*. Do not take revenge, my dear friends, but leave room for God's wrath, for it is written: "It is mine to avenge; I will repay," says the Lord. On the contrary:
>
> "If your enemy is hungry, feed him;
>   if he is thirsty, give him something to drink.
> In doing this you will heap burning coals on his head."
>
> Do not be overcome with evil, but overcome evil with good. (Rom 12:14-21)

Paul echoes Jesus' teaching of creative nonviolence and calls the Christians in Rome to bless their persecutors. Rather than being reactive and mirroring aggression, they should exercise their dignity with a creative agency that transforms relationships by naming a new intention of well-being for all. This way of love abandons any sense of superiority to others and embraces all equally. "Peace with everyone" is the goal. Going all the way, Paul revoices Jesus' command to retire retributive justice and to practice enemy love instead. The way to overcome evil is not to imitate it but to embody goodness in the face of it. In action, this may look like feeding the hungry, giving water to the thirsty, and countless other forms.

Here Paul takes us far beyond the popular Stoic message of tolerance: don't hate, mind your own business, live and let live. Instead, Paul calls for an active, generous, full-hearted love for "everyone." Paul's message is clear and profound: if we have understood who Jesus is and the Abrahamic

The Improbable Revolution of Neighbor Love

movement he brought to fulfillment, we will love even our enemies, just like Christ loved us "while we were God's enemies" (see Rom 5:9).

Still, Paul's language about heaping burning coals on our enemy's head sounds arrogant and cruel. In fact, some interpreters insist that this is a place where Paul seems to view the enemy as the other, outside of our moral responsibility. But as we saw in chapter two, Paul is actually quoting from the book of Proverbs, which was heavily influenced by ancient Egyptian wisdom literature.

Ancient Egypt had a ritual in which a repentant person would carry a basin of burning coals over their head to symbolize their purification like gold in a fire. So Paul is not saying that when we love our enemies, we will punish and burn them. He's saying that when we love our enemies, our kindness has the power to help them change and embrace a new life in which hatred is melted away.[7]

The climax of Paul's universal manifesto in Romans is a call to practice sincere love. The climax of sincere love stretches to bless persecutors and show kindness to enemies. Paul has taken Jesus' Sermon on the Mount, given in rural Palestine, and transplanted it into the heart of the Roman Empire itself.

ROMANS 13: LOVE IS THE FULFILLMENT OF THE LAW

Paul doesn't stop talking about love in Romans 12. In the next chapter, he unpacks his ethics of love even further and articulates his most important statement on the command of neighbor love. He writes,

> Let no debt remain outstanding, except the continuing debt to love one another, for whoever loves others has fulfilled the law. The commandments, "You shall not commit adultery," "You shall not murder," "You shall not steal," "You shall not covet," and whatever other command there may be, are summed up in this one command: "Love your neighbor as yourself." Love does no harm to a neighbor. Therefore love is the fulfillment of the law. (Rom 13:8-10)

Once again, Paul is closely and explicitly following the teaching of Jesus on neighbor love. Like Jesus, Paul teaches that neighbor love is the summary and fulfillment of all the law. It's not just being nice or random kindness.

---

[7]See William Klassen, "Coals of Fire: Symbol of Repentance or Revenge?," *New Testament Studies* 9 (1963): 337-50.

Neighbor love is the core and culmination of God's will for humanity. When we have embraced seeing others as morally related to ourselves and equally worthy of love, the whole purpose of divine revelation has come to life in us. In short, there is nothing more important than neighbor love for Christian ethics, and everything else flows in and out of it. Jesus and Paul insist on this point.

We have already seen the "law" and the "greatest commandment" summarized as a double love command: to love God and love our neighbor. But Paul does something novel: he doesn't mention the love of God. Instead, he simply states that "this one command" of neighbor love, on its own, is the fulfillment of the law (Rom 13:9).

Of course, Paul thinks the love of God is extremely important. All of Romans and his other letters make that clear. But in this crucial passage, Paul is content to declare that neighbor love is the summary of every God-given commandment. This further emphasizes how truly important neighbor love was to Paul. It can stand on its own as a summary of God's law.

We can draw out the clear implication that Jesus emphasized: to claim to love God without loving one's neighbor is absurd and impossible. It is almost as if Paul thinks that the love of God is built into the love of neighbor, as we'll see many later Christians argue. When we learn to love that singular human other, whom God has created, the love of God is already included. In a sense, then, Paul may be suggesting that loving our neighbors is the primary way we love God. From this perspective, neighbor love is an accurate summary of the entire law. As Augustine, an African theologian sometimes referred to as "the second Paul," later wrote, "If God is love, whoever loves love loves God."[8]

Notice again that Paul understands the neighbor we are called to love in its universal, all-inclusive meaning, rather than only fellow Jews or Christians. This follows the heart of Paul's argument in Romans that God in Christ has reunited the entire human family. Moments earlier, Paul wrote, "There is no difference between Jew and Gentile—the same Lord [Jesus] is Lord of all and richly blesses all who call on him" (Rom 10:12-13).

Rather that ruling over a colonizing empire like Caesar, who called himself "Lord," this crucified Lord has freely given his life for his enemies

---

[8] Augustine, *Homilies on the First Epistle of John*, in *The Works of Saint Augustine* I/14, trans. Boniface Ramsey (Hyde Park, NY: New City, 2008), 43.

and desires to bless *all*. Thus, Paul repeats Jesus' ethic of nonviolence and teaches, "Love does no harm to a neighbor" (Rom 13:10).

The ancient idea that hurting others can help them or us has been abandoned for the creative agency of neighbor love: "Do not be overcome with evil, but overcome evil with good" (Rom 12:21). This is the only debt we owe to one another (Rom 13:8).

ROMANS 13: THE POLITICS OF LOVE

The context of Paul's teaching on neighbor love is his famous statement on political authority. He writes, "Let everyone be subject to the governing authorities, for there is no authority except that which God has established" (Rom 13:1). Paul goes on to mention three crucial criteria that identify authentic "governing authorities":

1. They cause no terror for those who do right (Rom 13:3).
2. They commend those who do right and serve the good (Rom 13:3-4).
3. They contain those who do evil (Rom 13:4).

Against common assumptions, then, Paul is not writing a blank check to authoritarian rulers in Romans 13. He's outlining basic Christian politics: all true authority comes from God, and all true authority will bear these three marks. Thus, politics for Paul isn't simply a matter of power and punishment. It's what he calls "a matter of conscience" (Rom 13:5), of seeking moral responsibility with and for others in the universal presence of God.

Immediately before this passage, Paul gave his teaching on loving enemies: "Do not be overcome with evil, but overcome evil with good" (Rom 12:21). Immediately after it, Paul summarizes his teaching of neighbor love (Rom 13:8-10). It makes sense, then, that Paul would address the question of how we should understand God's law at this precise point. What has God commanded, and what is God's law that must ultimately govern and critique human government?

Paul's answer points to a limited, justice-based political order. Modern Christian ethicists have argued that it is a basis for democratic society. First, Paul says we are commanded to love our neighbors as ourselves. Just relationships don't privilege or prejudice others but operate on the basis of universal, equal human value. Second, Paul says that "love does no harm to a neighbor." It overrides the traditional ethic of retribution and introduces a creative, healing vision of justice. For this reason Paul writes, "Love is the fulfillment of the law."

The clear implication is that any authority that can possibly claim God's legitimacy doesn't other or harm its neighbors. The limit of God-honoring action is the other's well-being. If our behavior disrespects, injures, or commits injustice against others, we have stepped outside God's will and rebelled against God's law. This is the basis of a claim that has been repeated across the centuries of Christian ethics: any law that fails to love the neighbor is no law at all. It is merely a human construction that tries to replace God's revealed will.[9]

It's worth noting here that John Stuart Mill's famous defense of democratic government in his book *On Liberty* (1859) is largely based on this principle: "Do no harm."[10] Mill argues that a government that institutionalizes harm against its people has violated its mandate. In doing so, it voids its claim to authority and should not be obeyed. It must be replaced by a new political order. This is the same text where Mill says neighbor love should be "fully, frequently, and fearlessly discussed" rather than becoming "a dead dogma" in "incrusted minds."[11] We see afresh why Mill included the word *fearlessly*.

Paul, then, is teasing out the political and social implications of legitimate authority grounded in neighbor love. No ruler or government can claim to be fulfilling God's will if they are causing harm to others. The reason couldn't be more fundamental: neighbor love is the fulfillment of God's law, and love does no harm to a neighbor.

In this way, Paul is sending a subtle but fierce message to the imperial authorities: if you want to have any real authority in the eyes of God, your politics must be governed by seeing and treating others as moral equals. This is the "debt"—the binding obligation—that God has placed on us all.

Neighbor love is the limit and litmus test of legitimate authority. Neighbor love is political.

ROMANS 13: LOVE AT THE END OF THE WORLD

Paul concludes Romans 13 by talking about the end of history. He writes, "And do this [love your neighbor] understanding the present time. The hour

---

[9]See Timothy Jackson, *Political Agape: Christian Love and Liberal Democracy* (Grand Rapids, MI: Eerdmans, 2015); Vincent Bacote, *The Political Disciple: A Theology of Public Life* (Grand Rapids, MI: Zondervan, 2015).
[10]See John Stuart Mill, *On Liberty* (New York: Penguin, 1974), 68-69, 141.
[11]See Mill, *On Liberty*, 96-97, 101-14.

has already come for you to wake up from your slumber.... The night is nearly over; the day is almost here" (Rom 13:11-12). As we saw in chapter two, the end of history was an important topic in the Hebrew Bible's prophetic literature. Some of the prophets heralded "the day" when Israel would finally triumph over her enemies and enslave the nations. Now Paul, who was himself once a religious nationalist, looks to the future and evokes the ultimate questions of human destiny: How should we get ready for the end of the world if God's will is really about to triumph? How do we prepare for the apocalypse?

Paul answers that we should love our neighbor, "understanding the present time." Neighbor love regulates egocentric desire and respects others, Paul writes. It is awake and sober, not compulsive and selfish. Paul specifically names how neighbor love overcomes jealousy, which we saw as a significant factor in humanity's fall into othering in Genesis 3–4 (Rom 13:13). Here he alludes to the shame the first humans felt in their nakedness and how they reacted by blaming and attacking one another. In response, Paul tells his community, "Clothe yourselves with the Lord Jesus Christ" (Rom 13:14)—a potent image of Jesus as the end of othering and the shame it runs on and fuels.

In this way, Paul envisions neighbor love like the first light of God's new creation that Isaiah foreshadowed. It is the practical sign that God is faithful to God's promises and that our ultimate healing is coming. This "one command," then, is not simply a matter of mere morality that doesn't touch our eternal life or God's final purpose. As Jesus repeatedly emphasized, it goes to the very heart of our origin and destiny in God's love. Similarly, in Romans 13, Paul sees the practice of neighbor love as proof that hope is near at hand. When we love our neighbor, heaven comes closer to earth, and God's kingdom is manifest for the world to see. The dark night of othering and the despair it produces is coming to an end.

In short, then, the vision and practice of neighbor love could not be more important for Paul's theology, ethics, and politics. But it is also equally important to his vision of hope for our ultimate future.

ROMANS 15: NONVIOLENT POWER AGAINST EMPIRE

There is one more passage about neighbors in Romans. It takes us into the brilliant irony of Paul's conclusion to his subversive manifesto to the empire.

Paul is writing to Rome, the capital of the empire that ruled Paul's world. Rome itself was a very violent place, and it presided over a violent empire. According to Tacitus, a Roman historian whose life overlapped with Paul's, Roman war policy created *deserts* and called them "peace." The Pax Romana (Roman peace) was often little more than domination, enslavement, and a scorched earth. Closer to home, Rome as a city was addicted to violent entertainment. The Coliseum famously exemplified this: over fifty thousand people could pack in to watch gladiators killing and being killed by one another. Rome was a city in which strength was everything; only the strong survived and received honor and glory for it. Machiavelli later captured the "natural principle" at the heart of Rome: "The man who makes another powerful ruins himself."[12]

Paul prophetically defied this principle. Rather than glory in Rome's culture of violence, Paul implores Christians in Rome to courageously resist it and prioritize the weak over the strong.[13] Paul writes,

> We who are strong ought to bear with the failings of the weak and not to please ourselves. Each of us should please our neighbors for their good, to build them up. For even Christ did not please himself. . . . May the God who gives endurance and encouragement give you the same attitude of mind toward each other that Christ Jesus had. . . . Accept one another, then, just as Christ accepted you. (Rom 15:1-3, 5, 7)

True strength is revealed in care for others, not in conquering them. For Paul, neighbor love reflects a new "mind" that is able to perceive the precious value of others. This mind not only transcends the Jew-Gentile boundary and overthrows the old restriction of loyalty to one's tribe (Rom 15:9). It also prioritizes the weak above the strong.

As *neighbors* now, those who were seen as losers to be left behind or enemies to be destroyed are equally valuable as oneself and worthy of special care. Here Paul challenges the foundation of Plato's politics, driven by eugenics and the isolation or elimination of the weak. The culmination of Paul's ethics of neighbor love places the "weak" in the center of the moral

---

[12]Niccolo Machiavelli, *The Prince*, 2nd ed., trans. Robert Adams (New York: Norton, 1992), 11.
[13]In *The Sacredness of Human Life: Why an Ancient Biblical Vision Is Key to the World's Future* (Grand Rapids, MI: Eerdmans, 2013), 127-28, David Gushee quotes early Christian thinkers like Tatian (AD 110-172), Tertullian (AD 160-225), and Cyprian of Carthage (ca. AD 250) who, following Paul, unanimously condemned the violence of Rome's entertainment.

circle. This is an ethic that undermines the violent othering at the heart of Greco-Roman society.

As we saw, Paul himself started off as a violent extremist. He's now writing a letter to the capital of an empire that worships violent power. And his closing message is a call to embrace the weakest among us with compassion and to practice mutual acceptance: "Accept one another, then, just as Christ accepted you" (Rom 15:7). This is the healing logic of Jesus' golden rule. We observe that Paul's conversion embodied what Audre Lorde called "the energy to pursue genuine change within our world, rather than merely settling for a shift of characters in the same weary drama."[14]

How, then, can Caesar be your hero after learning that love for even your weakest *neighbor* is God's will? How can you boast in the Roman military and its domination of weaker peoples? How can you be entertained in the stadium watching the strong destroy the weak? For Paul, Caesar cannot be your hero. For Paul, you cannot boast of military strength. For Paul, the violent entertainment of the Coliseum is a violation of God's command for a universal neighbor-love ethic.

As we'll see again in the next chapter, the early Christians didn't feel at home in the Greco-Roman social world. They were often othered and brutally persecuted, sometimes hung up on crosses like Jesus and then set on fire to serve as human torches. The Romans generally tolerated religious difference, so why did they attack these "little christs"?

A central reason was that they were seen as betrayers of the Roman order. They no longer gave their love and loyalty to othering gods, violent rulers, and their conquering empire with its dehumanizing entertainment. "Jesus is Lord," they confessed (Rom 10:9)—not as an identitarian religious slogan but as a call to a new way of being human. They had a new citizenship in a new kingdom where *everyone* was a neighbor, starting with the weakest. Any glory without that love was inglorious. Any authority without that love was authoritarian. Any victory without that love was loss.

Paul's letter to Rome, then, is rigorous in argument. It reorients the language of salvation and redemption toward an ethics revolving around loving the neighbor, loving the enemy, and loving the weak as the ultimate revelation of God's will. This was his moral universalism in the face of Roman

---

[14] Audre Lorde, *The Master's Tools Will Never Dismantle the Master's House* (London: Penguin, 2018), 15.

imperialism. Like Jesus' teaching, it is a nonviolent abolition of othering. This is the way of life that will take us to the end of our groaning world and into a new world of hope after human empires have crumbled. Paul confesses, "I am convinced that . . . [nothing] in all creation, will be able to separate us from the love of God in Christ Jesus our Lord" (Rom 8:39).

GALATIANS 2–3: HUMANITY REUNITED

In the last chapter, I pointed out that Jesus taught about neighbor love at different times in diverse contexts. This is why we have records of Jesus giving similar yet fascinatingly singular teachings on neighbor love. Likewise, Paul wrote about neighbor love in several of his letters. We turn next to his letter to the followers of Jesus in Galatia, another imperial city.

As is the case with Romans, many scholars believe that Galatians lays out Paul's most basic, fundamental theology. The Reformer Martin Luther called it "my epistle to which I have wedded myself" and compared it to his wife, Katie.[15] Christians today often return to Galatians to find essential vision for the Christian life. Also like Romans, the fact that Paul climaxes his teaching in this letter by discussing the command of neighbor love indicates again just how central this ethic was to Paul's life and vision. When he articulates his most basic theology, his mind ultimately returns to neighbor love.

In another similarity to Romans, Paul in Galatians discusses the basic meaning of Jesus' gospel or good news and what it means to live in a right relationship with God. This is what Paul calls "justification." Paul rejects the dominant assumption in his culture that religious, ethnic, and other identity markers such as circumcision have any importance in our relationship with God. Jesus has made these external, often othering "works of the law" irrelevant and obsolete. Paul argues, "A person is not justified by the works of the law, but by the faithfulness of Jesus Christ" (Gal 2:16, my translation).

What, then, is the heart of the gospel? What is the good news of Jesus that is worth celebrating? Paul writes, "I have been crucified with Christ and I no longer live, but Christ lives in me. The life I now live in the body, I live by faith in the Son of God, who loved me and gave himself for me" (Gal 2:20). For Paul, the good news of God is the life of Christ. And the core of Christ's life was self-giving love, even to his own death. Participating in this love,

---

[15]See Martin Luther, *What Luther Says: A Practical In-Home Anthology for the Active Christian*, ed. Edwald Plass (St. Louis: Concordia, 1959), 989.

then, means a new, self-transcendent life: our old self is dead, and now Christ lives in us. That is, Christ lives in the place of my self and overtakes what I previously guarded as my private property: my very own self. Similar to how Paul envisioned Christ as our clothes who covers our shame in Romans, Paul pictures Christ here as our very life that revives our dead humanity with his self-giving love.

Paul then underscores that this new life in Christ has made the old distinctions and exclusions of humanity irrelevant. He writes, "So in Christ Jesus you are all children of God through faith, for all of you who were baptized into Jesus Christ have clothed yourselves with Christ. There is neither Jew nor Gentile, neither slave nor free, nor is there male and female, for you are all one in Christ Jesus" (Gal 3:26-28). Galatians 3:28 is perhaps Paul's most radical expression of universal access to God and human equality: Christ has reunited humanity across all boundaries of identity and has called us into a new belonging. Abraham's promise has been fulfilled. Here Paul mentions ethnic, political, and sex distinctions. But his point seems to be that *every* aspect of our humanity—including anything that might lead us to see someone else as unrelated or less than ourselves—has been embraced "in Christ Jesus." "You are all one in Christ Jesus," he writes. The primal unity and original belonging of humanity narrated in Genesis 1–2 has been restored.

When Paul turns to discuss what this new life in Christ looks like with others, unsurprisingly, he zeroes in on the practice of neighbor-love.

GALATIANS 5–6: THE GARDEN OF LOVE

Galatians is complex. But toward the end of his letter, Paul makes crystal clear where he believes his theology leads: "The only thing that counts is faith expressing itself through love" (Gal 5:6).

This is an extraordinarily absolute statement: for Paul, the *only* thing in life with enduring value is faith (in Jesus) expressing itself through love (for others). Everything else, at its best, serves this faithful love. Anything else that diminishes or distracts from love is unimportant. This consciousness is where the new life in Christ leads. To put "faith" in Christ means to embrace a life of love for others, just as Christ did (Gal 2:20).

Paul then summarizes his ethical teaching on what truly "counts" and how we should live. He writes, "You, my brothers and sisters, were called to be free. But do not use your freedom to indulge the flesh; rather, serve one another humbly in love. For the entire law is fulfilled in keeping this one command: 'Love your neighbor as yourself.' If you bite and devour each other, watch out or you will be destroyed by each other" (Gal 5:13-15). Paul's teaching here is almost identical to Romans 13. He states that neighbor love is the fulfillment or fullness of God's law. It's the heart of God's desire for humanity. Learning to see and treat others as related to ourselves and equal in value sets us free. Neglecting or violating it leads us to self-destruction.

Also like in Romans 13, Paul doesn't feel the need to mention the love of God. He writes, "The *entire* law is fulfilled in keeping this *one* command: 'Love your neighbor as yourself'" (Gal 5:14). Once again, it seems that Paul understands loving our neighbors as the primary way that we love God, since this is who God is: a lover of others.

Here as well, the neighbor clearly means everyone, since Paul has already written that Christ has demolished all the othering barriers between people (Gal 3:28). In the next chapter, Paul will write, "Let us do good to *all people*" (Gal 6:10). Othering is abolished. The moral circle has become universal.

Moreover, Paul again sees love as an action far more than a feeling. For Paul, the synonym of *love* is *service* (Gal 5:13). When we are "in love," what we do is "serve one another humbly." After acknowledging conflict in the community (Gal 5:15), he writes, "Let us *do good* to all people" (Gal 6:10). As so often, Paul may be echoing Jesus, who taught, "Do good to those who hate you" (Lk 6:27). Love is a form of creative agency that nonviolently refuses to mirror conflict for something new.

Here the freedom of love also has a negative limit: "Do not use your freedom to indulge the flesh." Paul's language of "flesh" refers to our egocentric compulsions ("save yourself") that end up using others rather than loving them. Paul specifically mentions lust (compulsion for sex), greed (compulsion for money), pride (compulsion for status), hate (compulsion to destroy), and idolatry (compulsion to control God; see Gal 5:19-21). But Paul is not puritanically condemning human desire. He's pointing out the ways in which we slip into treating ourselves and others as if we don't share relationship and equal worth. When we do this, we've violated love and lost track of what truly counts. Freedom is very different from acting out of our compulsions; freedom is the exercise of love with and for others. This takes us back to Paul's claim in Romans 13:10: "Love does no harm to a neighbor."

Once more, Paul connects neighbor love to ultimate reality and God's final future for the world. At the end of his letter, he writes, "What counts is the new creation" (Gal 6:15). This comes after he wrote, "The only thing that counts is faith expressing itself through love" (Gal 5:6). It seems again that Paul is saying that love is the vanguard of new creation, the sign of God's promised new world. It's the only thing that matters now and lasts forever.

Finally, Paul teaches that love is the primary "fruit of the Spirit" (Gal 5:22). Love represents a new organizing center in the self. In Romans 13 and Philippians 2, Paul calls this the "mind" of Christ. Here in Galatians 5, Paul calls this the "Spirit" of Christ. The life of loving our neighbors as ourselves is a new life of feeling, thinking, desiring, willing, and acting. It is a new way of being human, inside and out.

When the Spirit of God makes us come alive, the first thing that will start bursting out of the soil of our lives is this love. With love, the moral gardens of our lives grow with "joy, peace, forbearance, kindness, goodness, faithfulness, gentleness and self-control" or regulated power (Gal 5:22-23). Paul says that this fruitfulness will protect us against pride and envy, powerful othering emotions that tempt us to feel above or below others rather than equal with them (Gal 5:26). With Paul's repeated linking of love and joy, I am reminded again of bell hooks's observation: "I know no one who has embraced a love ethic whose life has not become joyous and more fulfilling. The widespread assumption that ethical behavior takes the fun out of life is false."[16]

Just like in Romans, Paul's discussion of neighbor love ultimately points in a very practical direction. He writes in the last chapter of his letter, "Carry each other's burdens, and in this way you will fulfill the law of Christ. . . . Let us not become weary in doing good, for at the proper time we will reap a harvest if we do not give up. Therefore, as we have opportunity, let us do good to all people, especially to those who belong to the family of believers" (Gal 6:2, 9-10). At the end of Romans, neighbor love led to loving the weak. Here at the end of Galatians, neighbor love leads to carrying each other's burdens and "doing good for all people." This isn't works-righteousness or trying to earn God's acceptance. For Paul, doing *good* for others is the heart and soul of what it means to love God and follow Jesus. As in Romans, the newborn self doesn't exist for itself or a private relationship with God. The

---

[16]bell hooks, *All About Love: New Visions* (New York: HarperCollins, 2001), 88.

newborn self exists for others, both God and neighbor, and this leads to true joy and peace. Anything else, Paul insists, is religious self-deception that has missed the point (Gal 6:3).

Paul's theological ethics in Romans and Galatians are strikingly similar. The climax of both is a practical life of neighbor love for "all people." The othering hierarchy of Roman imperialism is discarded as the compulsive addictions of an "old self" that has be crucified and resurrected with Christ.

Ephesians 2–5: A New Way of Being Human

The last specific reference to the neighbor in Paul's writings is found in his letter to the Jesus community in Ephesus, yet another imperial city. Like Romans and Galatians, Ephesians unpacks his universal theology.

Here Paul writes that God has "torn down the dividing wall of hostility" between Jews and Gentiles. This was the sharpest, fiercest example of othering in Paul's home culture. Still, he writes, God has made "one new humanity out of the two" (Eph 2:15). Paul says that God has done this through Jesus, the mysterious revelation of "[God's] great love for us" (Eph 2:4). We can't control this or make it happen for ourselves: "It is the gift of God" (Eph 2:8). Having died for us, Christ was resurrected and raises us to new life with him. Paul writes, "Consequently, you are no longer foreigners and strangers, but fellow citizens with God's people" (Eph 2:19). Othering has been abolished, once and for all.

Paul writes that this new life is "rooted and established in love" (Eph 3:17). He calls it a divine love that "surpasses knowledge" (Eph 3:19). Like the universe itself, it reaches out in all directions—"wide and long and high and deep" (Eph 3:18). As he kneels in prayer, Paul rejoices that "every family in heaven and on earth derives its name" from our universal Father. (This again connects with Jesus' teaching in Mt 5 and Lk 6.) Overwhelmed with awe, Paul revels in "all the fullness of God" that wants to fill us and "do immeasurably more than all we ask or imagine" (Eph 3:19-20).[17] Love out-universes the impossible.

---

[17]See Jean-Luc Marion, *The Erotic Phenomenon*, trans. Stephen Lewis (Chicago: University of Chicago Press, 2007), 2, 222: "Philosophy defines itself as the 'love of wisdom' because it must in effect begin by loving before claiming to know. In order to comprehend, it is first necessary to desire to comprehend; put another way, one must be astonished at not comprehending (and this astonishment thus offers a beginning to wisdom). . . . Philosophy comprehends only to the extent that it loves. . . . God's highest transcendence, the only one that does not dishonor him,

The Improbable Revolution of Neighbor Love

What, then, are the ethical implications of this new life in Christ's universal love? Paul's answer is clear: "Live a life worthy of the calling you have received. Be completely humble and gentle; be patient, bearing with one another in love" (Eph 4:1-2).

In all his writings, Paul teaches that the authentic response to divine love is human love. Rather than competing for supremacy and control, this love is characterized by humility, patience, and "bearing with one another." Othering's separation of human existence into fractious factions has been healed in Christ and his new belonging of love. Paul pictures this belonging as a "whole body," which "grows and builds itself up in love, as each part does its work." Humanity is no longer imagined as an animal with an exalted head and a degraded tail. Humanity is an integrated body with Christ as its one head and all of us belonging to one another (Eph 4:15).

Similar again to Romans and Galatians, Paul writes, "Put off your old self, which is being corrupted by its deceitful desires; . . . be made new in the attitude of your minds; and . . . put on the new self, created to be like God in true righteousness and holiness" (Eph 4:22-23). The ethic of love is a new way of being human, a new mind and self alive with God's primal likeness in humanity.

Paul then writes, "Put off falsehood and speak truthfully to your neighbor, for we are all members of one body" (Eph 4:25). He challenges the community to overcome anger, refuse stealing, and stop using language that degrades others (Eph 4:25-31).

Notice that lies, anger, stealing, and insults all have a common core: they assume that the self is more valuable than the other. If am superior to you, I can trick you, abuse you, take from you, and degrade you with my words—the old irony of othering that claims superiority but then behaves shabbily. Paul writes, "That . . . is not the way of life you learned when you heard about Christ" (Eph 4:20-21).

Paul then calls followers of Jesus in Ephesus to work. The motivation isn't to stay busy, prove themselves, or accumulate wealth. Paul's logic for work is neighbor love: "doing something useful" and having "something to share with those in need" (Eph 4:28). Like Paul's vision of neighbor love in Romans 13, which prioritized the weak, and in Galatians 5, which emphasized carrying

---

belongs not to power, nor to wisdom, nor even to infinity, but to love. For love alone is enough to put all infinity, all wisdom, and all power to work."

one another's burdens, here Paul's love ethic leads to doing useful work and sharing with impoverished neighbors.

Indeed, Paul's entire moral vision is built around the precious value of others in the life of the self. His perspective is beautiful and challenging:

> Do not let any unwholesome talk come out of your mouths, but only what is helpful for building others up according to their needs, that it may benefit those who listen.... Be kind and compassionate to one another, forgiving each other, just as in Christ God forgave you. (Eph 4:29, 32)

> Be imitators of God, therefore, as dearly loved children and walk in the way of love, just as Christ loved us and gave himself up for us as a fragrant offering and sacrifice to God. (Eph 5:1-2 NIV adapted)

Notice that Paul doesn't say to avoid certain kinds of speech because they're bad or incur guilt. His logic is love: when talking, our intention should be to speak in a way that is helpful, elevating, and attentive to others' needs. Neighbor love leads to a healing speech therapy in which we learn to replace harmful words with helpful ones. This way of life imitates God's own example of kindness, compassion, and forgiveness—the divine qualities Jesus emphasized in his teaching about how God responds to enemies. Similar to Jesus' baptism in his divine belovedness, Paul writes that this "way of love" flows from internalizing our identity as "dearly loved children." The energy is delighting in our belovedness, not dutiful obligation.

Ephesians, then, powerfully synthesizes Paul's moral vision of neighbor love across his letters. In Christ, God has abolished othering, "the dividing wall of hostility." God now invites "one new humanity" to live in the healing circle of love as vast as the universe itself—high and wide and long and deep. As profoundly mystical as this vision truly is, its practice is equally down to earth: prioritizing the weak, carrying burdens, doing work, and sharing with others in need. "You are no longer foreigners and strangers, but fellow citizens with God's people," Paul writes (Eph 2:19). We are invited to live as if we truly belong to one another "as dearly loved children."

Paul's Love-Saturated Letters

Like Jesus in John's Gospel, Paul doesn't always use the language of neighbor love. But if we define neighbor love as the universalization of the neighbor—a way of life that sees every person as related to us and equal in value—then

The Improbable Revolution of Neighbor Love

the *life* of neighbor love is present throughout his letters even where its *language* is absent. We can briefly survey Paul's other writings on love.

Philippians 2 is a crucial example. Here Paul encourages his community to have "the same love" (Phil 2:2) and to abandon "selfish ambition" (Phil 2:3). This is how Paul envisions practicing this love:

> In humility value others above yourselves, not looking to your own interests but each of you to the interests of the others.
> In your relationships with one another, have the same mind as Christ Jesus:
> Who, being in very nature God,
> > did not consider equality with God something to be used to his
> > > own advantage;
> rather, he made himself nothing
> > by taking the very nature of a servant,
> > being made in human likeness. (Phil 2:3-7)

Here the spirit of othering—seeing others as unrelated or less than ourselves—is directly challenged. In fact, Paul says that love with Christ's mind "values others above" self. Even divinity is not a reason to assume superiority to others or to take advantage of them. As in John 13, Paul says that Jesus freely "takes the very nature of a servant" and "becomes nothing" by emptying himself on behalf of others.

Similar to Romans 15, in 1 Corinthians 8 Paul writes, "Knowledge puffs up while love builds up. . . . Be careful . . . that the exercise of your rights does not become a stumbling block to the weak" (1 Cor 8:1, 9). Speaking of the community as one body, Paul again argues that the weak must receive special care and honor (1 Cor 12:22-23). This leads into Paul's most unforgettable description of the life of following Jesus, what he calls "the most excellent way" (1 Cor 12:31):

> Love is patient; love is kind. It does not envy, it does not boast, it is not proud. It does not dishonor others, it is not self-seeking, it is not easily angered, it keeps no record of wrongs. Love does not delight in evil but rejoices with the truth. Love always protects, always trusts, always hopes, always perseveres. Love never fails. (1 Cor 13:4-8)

Once again, love overcomes the spirit of othering with its envy (inferiority) and pride (superiority). It creates new beginnings of hope and "never fails."

Ever practical, the mystic Paul concludes this letter by raising money for the poor. He signs off, "Do everything in love" (1 Cor 16:14).

In 2 Corinthians, Paul sums up Christian ethics like this: "Christ's love compels us. . . . He died for all, that those who live should no longer live for themselves but for him who died for them and was raised again" (2 Cor 5:14-15). The Christian life is a self-transcendent life with and for others. Thus, later in this letter, Paul writes, "See that you also excel in this grace of giving . . . that there might be equality. At the present time your plenty will supply what they need, so that in turn their plenty will supply what you need. The goal is equality" (2 Cor 8:7, 13-14). Remember how unthinkable this perspective was in the Greco-Roman context driven by the struggle for superior strength and status. But Paul sees giving as a *grace* and declares, "The goal is equality." This text will reverberate throughout the economics of the Christian movement. Indeed, Paul goes so far as to say, "We are glad whenever we are weak but you are strong" (2 Cor 13:9).

Like Galatians and Ephesians, in Colossians Paul declares that Christ has reunited humanity across all boundaries. With his universal vision, he writes,

> Therefore, as God's chosen people, holy and dearly loved, clothe yourselves with compassion, kindness, humility, gentleness and patience. Bear with each other and forgive one another if any of you has a grievance against someone. Forgive as the Lord forgave you. And over all these virtues put on love, which binds them all together in perfect unity. (Col 3:12-14)

In 1 Timothy, Paul writes that "the goal" of sound teaching "is love" (1 Tim 1:5). The reason is divine desire alive in us: "God our Savior . . . wants all people to be saved and to come to a knowledge of the truth" through Jesus' self-giving sacrifice (1 Tim 2:3-4). Echoing Jesus in Matthew 5 and Luke 6, Paul declares that God's desire is universal salvation. Against the hierarchical structure of his culture, Paul later writes that masters should be "devoted to the welfare of their slaves" (1 Tim 6:2).

Similar to his vision of work in Ephesians, Paul writes to Titus, "Our people must learn to devote themselves to doing what is good, in order to provide for urgent needs and not live unproductive lives" (Titus 3:14). Once more, the purpose of work is doing good and providing for others.

Although Paul does not always use the language of neighbor love, it saturates all his letters. The point of neighbor love is not slogans or words but how we actually think and live. Self-giving love in relationships of equal worth is always the focus for Paul.

James: Acceptable Religion and the Law That Liberates the Oppressed

The two remaining direct references to the neighbor in the New Testament are found in the letter of James. Ancient Christian tradition considered James to be the brother of Jesus. Whether this is the case or not, James's writing bears a striking resemblance to the teaching of Jesus in the Gospels. It has the mark of someone who was close to Jesus and wanted to advance his movement in his community.

In his first chapter, James writes, "Religion that God our Father accepts as pure and faultless is this: to look after orphans and widows in their distress and to keep oneself from being polluted by the world" (Jas 1:27). Like Jesus, his ethics is grounded in his theology. James writes, "Every good and perfect gift is from above, coming down from the Father of the heavenly lights" (Jas 1:17; see Matt 5:45; Lk 6:35-36). As our universal Parent is generous to us in creation, we too should be generous to one another in history. Life is God's gift, and so we never lose when we give ourselves for others, especially the most vulnerable. For James, this is "acceptable religion," which, like Jesus again, signals that much of our religion is unacceptable to God.

In his next chapter, James condemns favoring some above others, since we have all been equally created by God. He writes, "My brothers and sisters, believers in our glorious Lord Jesus Christ must not show favoritism" (Jas 2:1). James argues that favoring the rich and powerful rebels against the pattern of God's self-giving love for the poor and powerless. James continues, "Has not God chosen those who are poor in the eyes of the world to be rich in faith and to inherit the kingdom he promised those who love him? But you have dishonored the poor" (Jas 2:5-6). Here James echoes Jesus' Sermon on the Mount and reminds his community that God sees special value in those who are devalued by their society (see Mt 5:1-12). As we've seen, James is critiquing the dominant values of Greco-Roman culture.

James then grounds this ethical vision in the command of neighbor love. He writes, "If you really keep the royal law found in Scripture, 'Love your neighbor as yourself,' you are doing right. But if you show favoritism, you sin and are convicted by the law as lawbreakers" (Jas 2:8-9). Like Jesus, James sees human equality as the heart of neighbor love. When we love our neighbor as ourselves, we overcome othering the poor to win the favor of the rich and powerful. In fact, our attention and service are refocused on people who are culturally devalued and economically endangered.

As we've seen repeatedly throughout the ethics of the New Testament, James emphasizes that neighbor love overcomes othering and universalizes the moral circle. Our Creator gave us the gift of life when we had nothing to offer God in return. We too, then, ought to love the poor and powerless as our equally precious neighbors, even if they have nothing to offer in return other than themselves. This is "the royal law."

James next calls neighbor love "the law that gives freedom" (Jas 2:12). Neighbor love is the paradoxical limitation that liberates us. When we limit ourselves to loving people without favoring some over others, we ourselves enter into full belonging. He writes, "Speak and act as those who are going to be judged by the law that gives freedom, because judgment without mercy will be shown to anyone who has not been merciful. Mercy triumphs over judgment" (Jas 2:12-13). Here James names the paradox we found in Jesus' teaching on loving our enemies: the only barrier to our full belonging with God is blocking others from full belonging. When we practice mercy with others, we can trust that we ourselves will be treated with mercy. Judgment is not the end of our story. "Mercy triumphs."

Later in his letter, James writes, "There is only one Lawgiver and Judge, the one who is able to save and destroy. But you—who are you to judge your neighbor?" (Jas 4:12). Here again, James alludes to Jesus' teaching on loving our enemies. Recall that Jesus taught, "Do not judge, and you will not be judged" (Lk 6:37). Refusing to other people into the overly simple binary of good versus bad sets us free to be merciful toward all, including ourselves. God is the one true Judge, and God's "royal law" is mercy.

Still, James intensifies the paradox of neighbor love and God's judgment. He addresses "rich people" with great fierceness about the evil of exploiting the poor and their labor. His words inspired liberation theology in the twentieth century, as we'll see in chapter six. James writes,

> Now listen, you rich people, weep and wail because of the misery that is coming to you. . . . You have hoarded wealth in the last days. Look! The wages you failed to pay the workers who mowed your fields are crying out against you. . . . You have lived on earth in luxury and self-indulgence. . . . You have

condemned and murdered the innocent one, who was not opposing you. (Jas 5:1, 3-6)

Like Abel's blood crying out from the earth in Genesis 4, James imagines the unpaid wages of the poor as crying out to God. In God's eyes, the rich are not higher, nor the poor lower. We are one another's keepers. Thus, living in "luxury and self-indulgence" while others suffer under our power will not go unnoticed by God. In fact, James seems to see unfairly paying workers as a form of condemning and murdering them.[18]

For James, God sees how our often invisible, easily exploited neighbors are treated. There is no favoritism in God's moral economy. If we wish to live into "the law that gives freedom," practicing equal love for them is imperative. If we don't, James fiercely warns that we are in danger of excluding ourselves from God's future—a future that we've seen in Paul is signaled by neighbor love.

Once more, James's ethics significantly departs from the dominant ethos in Greco-Roman culture. He compresses Hebrew Scripture and the New Testament's moral vision of justice for our impoverished neighbors into one of its most prophetic expressions. Here the moral circle extends around us all. The rich and powerful hold no special favor in God's eyes; in fact, they are subjects of special scrutiny.

Authentic freedom is found in the equality of neighbor love and its attention to the most devalued and disadvantaged people in our world. This is the "the law that gives freedom." James' letter on "acceptable religion" marks a radical breakthrough toward equality and special care for the poor and oppressed.

Conclusion: An Abolition Movement for All People

Looking back to where we started, it's astonishing that Paul wrote most of the letters we've studied in this chapter. Paul began his journey as a violent religious nationalist. He ruthlessly arrested and executed othered Christians

---

[18]Critique of the wealthy and compassion for the poor was the moral consensus of the early Christians. More than a century after James, Tertullian (AD 160-240) wrote, "the Creator also [along with Jesus] disapproves of the rich.... He is the comforter of the poor." More fiercely, Basil the Great (300-379) wrote, "The person who can cure such an infirmity [poverty] and refuses one's medicine [resources] because of avarice, can with reason be condemned as a murderer." Quoted in Helen Rhee, ed., *Wealth and Poverty in Early Christianity* (Minneapolis, MN: Fortress Press, 2017), 34 and 67.

who followed a different way. Paul believed this lethal othering was actually being "zealous for God" (Acts 22:3).

But after he met Jesus himself, Paul became an apostle of love, a global ambassador of this universal movement for all neighbors. He was radicalized in a new way: to join Jesus in "[tearing] down the dividing wall of hostility" and bearing witness to "one new humanity" united in God's love for all people.

Paul's story is a provocative example of how the early Jesus movement began and what it spread. The writings of the first Christians are like a bass note of healing music that booms with the voice of Jesus to love all others as our precious neighbors across every boundary.[19] Beautifully, John names love as the home of God: "God is love. Whoever lives in love lives in God" (1 Jn 4:16).

In this new movement, love is the center of the moral circle, which radiates throughout the entire universe and includes all (Eph 3:18). To read the New Testament is to discover a new world within the old world, a world of hope that offers healing and a universal belonging.

The earliest way of Jesus, then, was truly an abolition movement against othering. Its mission was to bless all people as beloved neighbors. This moral vision slowly started revolutionizing the Roman Empire and the cultures where the movement spread beyond it. In the next chapter, we'll explore how this countercultural, cosmopolitan movement evolved and expanded up to the twentieth century.

---

[19]Many other passages resound with this healing music. See 1 Pet 1:22-23 ("love one another deeply"); 1 Pet 3:8-9 ("love one another"); 1 Pet 4:7-10 ("Above all, love each other deeply"); 1 Pet 5:14 ("Greet one another with a kiss of love"); 2 Pet 1:5-9 ("[add] to mutual affection, love"); 1 Jn 3:11 ("We should love one another"); 1 Jn 4:8 ("Whoever lives in love lives in God"); 2 Jn 5-6 ("I ask that we love one another").

5

THE RED THREAD

A Brief History of Jesus' Neighbor-Love Movement

When I met Ferdosa in eastern Ethiopia on October 17, 2018, I was in an Abrahamic moment in my own life. I had resigned from my job teaching Christian ethics at the Ethiopian Graduate School of Theology in Addis. I knew that I couldn't remain on a safe Christian island as othering escalated in Ethiopia, including in overwhelmingly Christian areas. But I wasn't sure what was next.

Ferdosa's words burned in my heart: "Dr. Andrew, no one has ever told me to love my enemies! Starting today, I will love my enemies and teach others to love their enemies!" As she held my hand up, it was like she was making a covenant of enemy love with me. In that moment, a question was born inside me: "How many other youth like Ferdosa are longing for hope beyond othering but have never been invited into the way of neighbor love?"

In the months that followed, my wife, Lily, and I, along with our partner Tekalign Nega, started the Neighbor-Love Movement. Our mission was simple: to invite the youth of Ethiopia to see their enemies as neighbors and to practice this love amid the crisis of othering. We wanted to revive the movement Jesus started in this ancient homeland of Christianity and Islam. We compressed the heart of this movement into a concise Neighbor-Love Covenant, with seven practices that embody this love in how we see, listen, and act with others.

Since 2019, thousands of youth have signed the Neighbor-Love Covenant, and over twenty million people have encountered our invitation to love others as neighbors. Our humble work continues today as Ethiopia is being devastated by the twenty-first century's deadliest civil war. Against odds, we believe with Ferdosa that this ancient movement can still bring healing and hope out of the despair of othering.[1]

---

[1] To learn more about the Neighbor-Love Movement, visit www.nlmglobal.org.

In this book, we've traveled a long way from the ancient world "without love" (Lindberg) governed by "natural inequality" (Siedentop). We've explored the expansive moral vision of Hebrew Scripture, the movement Jesus launched on its foundation, and the way his earliest followers sought to advance it in their world. What we've found is an ever-expanding movement of neighbor love that aims to abolish othering. Here the moral circle of our humanity is universalized for all people who are morally connected and equally precious in value.

In this chapter, we'll explore how this movement evolved over the next two thousand years in Western Christianity. Jesus' movement didn't start in the West and went far beyond it. But this is the tradition I've studied most thoroughly, and I hope this chapter can inspire further exploration of how Jesus' neighbor-love movement evolved in other contexts. We'll look at seven major figures across the centuries who have wrestled with neighbor love and see what lessons they can teach us today. While my reading of the tradition is far from exhaustive, I highlight Christians who made significant contributions to the story of neighbor love in the context of othering.

JESUS' EVER-EVOLVING NEIGHBOR-LOVE MOVEMENT

I take my lead from Larry Siedentop, the historian we met in chapter one. In his book *Inventing the Individual*, Siedentop asks how humanity went from the violent othering of the ancient world with its "natural inequality" to a modern moral order that strives to implement the Universal Declaration of Human Rights.[2] Siedentop argues, "A fundamental change in moral belief shaped the world we live in."[3]

This world-shaping moral belief revolved around the neighbor, who they are and how they should be treated. The early Jesus movement launched a moral revolution that saw all people as neighbors and thus people worthy of care and service, especially the previously ignored, excluded, and oppressed. This movement started identifying and undermining the ethnic and religious othering, economic hierarchy, and political militarism that dominated the ancient world. Though "a minority of a minority amidst the greatest power

---

[2]The declaration was ratified on December 10, 1945. Its first article paraphrases the biblical vision of neighbor love: "All human beings are born free and equal in dignity and rights. They are endowed with reason and conscience and should act towards one another in a spirit of brotherhood."
[3]Larry Siedentop, *Inventing the Individual: The Origins of Western Liberalism* (London: Penguin, 2015), 3.

the world had ever seen," it boldly pioneered an innovative path to a more egalitarian, compassionate, just society.[4]

To illustrate Siedentop's point, Gary Anderson's award-winning book *Charity: The Place of the Poor in the Biblical Tradition* offers helpful insight. Anderson asks us to imagine that we're flying in an airplane over "the ruins of a large Roman city." What we'd likely see is a "public theater, the baths, and various basilicas devoted to governmental functions" built by wealthy patrons. This was a world dominated by imperial religion, rich landowners, and powerful politicians.

Anderson then writes,

> If, on the other hand, we flew over a great medieval city, the picture changes considerably. Instead of theaters and baths, one sees the roofs of convents, hospices, orphanages, and soup kitchens for the poor. Charitable activity left an enormous and visible footprint on the design of the evolving Christian city. . . . What made the charitable works of the church distinctive was their religious grounding and singular focus on the abject poor. In contrast, Greco-Roman benefactors had little interest in helping the lower social classes and did not think of their donations as having a religious function. Homes for the elderly, orphanages, and hospitals . . . are institutions that appeared suddenly in the late Roman era and always in the wake of the expansion of the Christian church. New words, in fact, had to be invented in both Latin and Greek to identify these charitable organizations, a sure sign that they had no precedent; they were the fruits of this new religion.[5]

A "change in moral belief" led "this new religion" into an innovative love for previously overlooked and excluded neighbors. And this universal love led to new city planning and novel words to describe reality—the transformation of the physical and mental infrastructure of society. The Christian movement gave birth to orphanages, hospitals, nursing homes, soup kitchens, and schools, because it gave birth to a new love for the neighbors who needed them. Indeed, it gave birth to the moral vision to *see* these people *as neighbors* in the first place rather than as "the scum" that Cicero wanted to wipe away.

---

[4]David Gushee provides a robust survey of the ethics of the early Christian movement in *The Sacredness of Human Life: Why an Ancient Biblical Vision Is Key to the World's Future* (Grand Rapids, MI: Eerdmans, 2013), chap. 4 "The Sacredness of Life in Early Christianity" (143).
[5]Gary Anderson, *Charity: The Place of the Poor in the Biblical Tradition* (New Haven, CT: Yale University Press, 2013), 15-16.

Historians from Adolf von Harnack to Tom Holland have made the argument that this love is a primary reason why Christianity expanded so rapidly: it created an unprecedented belonging in which everyone had access, dignity, and care. Othered as it was, the Christian movement started off primarily at the bottom and margins of society and quickly grew because people felt alive and liberated within it. Historian Rodney Stark writes, "What Christianity gave to its converts was nothing less than their humanity."[6]

Ironically, the harshest critics of early Christianity confirm that this love is not a self-flattering illusion that Christians have projected into their past. It was real. For example, Celsus, a second-century philosopher who was one of the earliest attackers of Christianity, ridiculed the movement for attracting "slaves and women and children"—others he saw as unworthy of love.[7] Lucian, a second-century satirist who scoffed at Christianity, conceded that the early Christians were radically generous and loved in a new way.[8] In the fourth century, the Roman emperor Julian (332–363) urged his imperial priests to copy the Christians by caring for the poor, offering hospitality to strangers, and burying the dead. Julian hated Christianity, but he realized that these "little christs" were attracting many followers because they had embraced a new way of love for others beyond their own community. As he wrote, "the impious Galileans [Christians] support not only their poor, but ours as well."[9] This love was making Roman religion look inhumane and heartless.

Tertullian (AD 160–240), an influential Christian theologian from North Africa, captures how Christians got this reputation for countercultural love. He writes,

---

[6] Rodney Stark, *The Rise of Christianity: How the Obscure, Marginal Jesus Movement Became the Dominant Religious Force in the Western World in a Few Centuries* (San Francisco: Harper, 1997), 214-15. See also Tom Holland, *Dominion: How the Christian Revolution Remade the World* (New York: Basic Books, 2021); Bart Ehrman, *The Triumph of Christianity: How a Forbidden Religion Swept the World* (New York: Simon & Schuster, 2019); Alan Kreider, *The Patient Ferment of the Early Church: The Improbable Rise of Christianity in the Roman Empire* (Grand Rapids, MI: Baker Academic, 2016).

[7] See Henry Chadwick, trans., *Origen: Contra Celsum* (Cambridge: Cambridge University Press, 1980), 3.44. In a letter to Emperor Marcus Aurelius around AD 180, the Christian philosopher Athenagoras wrote that the Jesus movement was primarily made up of "uneducated persons, and artisans, and old women" who refuse to mirror violence and "love their neighbors as themselves." Quoted in Ronald Sider, *The Early Church on Killing: A Comprehensive Sourcebook on War, Abortion, and Capital Punishment* (Grand Rapids, MI: Baker Academic, 2012), 31.

[8] See Carter Lindberg, *Love: A Brief History Through Western Christianity* (London: Blackwell, 2008), 41.

[9] Quoted in Gushee, *Sacredness of Human Life*, 135.

> [Our monthly giving] supports and buries poor people, supplies the wants of boys and girls destitute of means and parents, and of old persons confined now to the house; [those who] have suffered shipwreck; and [people] in the mines, or banished to the islands, or shut up in the prisons.... It is mainly the deeds of love so noble that lead many to put a brand upon us. "See," they say, "how they love one another."... Our compassion spends more in the streets than you do in the temples.[10]

According to Tertullian, the first followers of Jesus focused on the poor, the parentless, the elderly, victims of tragedy, manual laborers, and the imprisoned because of their commitment to human equality: "We are the same to emperors and to our ordinary neighbors."[11] Historian Carter Lindberg provides a concise summary of what he is describing: "In the early church, worship, liturgy, and love for the neighbor were seen as inseparable."[12] This was the early Christian brand.

In fact, early Christian leaders such as bishops and deacons became the first social workers of ancient cities. As they sought to love their neighbors, they created systems of service and support for the suffering that were unprecedented in the ancient world. Stories of churches selling their property to support the poor, ransom prisoners, and care for refugees are surprisingly common in the early centuries of Christianity.[13]

---

[10] Quoted in Lindberg, *Love*, 42–43.

[11] Tertullian, *Apology*, in *The Ante-Nicene Fathers: Translations of the Writings of the Fathers down to A.D. 325*, ed. Alexander Roberts and James Donaldson (Buffalo, NY: Christian Literature, 1885), 3:45. In the early fourth century, Lactantius (250–325) articulated the Christian vision of human equality like this: "God who created human beings and gave them the breath of life wanted all to be equal.... With him, no one is a slave and no one is a master; for if he is the same father to all, we are his children with equal rights. No one is poor in God's eyes except the one lacking justice.... Therefore, neither the Romans nor the Greeks could possess justice because they kept people distinct in different levels from the poor to the rich, from the humble to the powerful, from common people to the highest authorities of kings.... The whole force of justice lies in the fact that it makes equal everyone who comes into this human condition on equal terms.... God has revealed to us what our true and just work is: we must live with our neighbors." Quoted in Helen Rhee, ed., *Wealth and Poverty in Early Christianity* (Minneapolis: Fortress, 2017), 49–51.

[12] Lindberg, *Love*, 41.

[13] See Helen Rhee, ed., *Wealth and Poverty in Early Christianity*; Peter Brown, *Through the Eye of a Needle: Wealth, the Fall of Rome, and the Making of the Modern West, 350–550 AD* (Princeton, NJ: University of Princeton Press, 2014). The Acts of Thomas from the early third century records the story of the Apostle Thomas being commissioned to build a palace for a king in India. When the king complained that he couldn't see the palace, Thomas replied that he had given all of the money to the poor and built an everlasting home in heaven. See Rhee, *Wealth and Poverty in Early Christianity*, 25.

Of course, the Christian movement's story isn't simple and is far from perfect, as I emphasized in chapter one. There have been many omissions and massive failures throughout the history of Christianity. We'll see this again below.[14] But the evidence indicates the soundness of Siedentop's claim: "A fundamental change in moral belief shaped the world we live in."

That belief was that all people are morally related to one another and equal in value: they are our *neighbors* and worthy of *love*. Irenaeus (130–202), whom some consider the founder of Christian theology, wrote that a follower of Jesus "counts no person his enemy but all his neighbors."[15] The world that resulted from this belief is one in which health care, education, political freedom, legal protection, and equal dignity have become human rights and ideals that nonreligious people also strive to advance. Christianity's neighbor-love movement revolutionized ancient culture and expanded the moral neighborhood in a way that was previously unimaginable and seemingly impossible. The moral circle became universal, and people found a new basis for living together with others, as Bonhoeffer wrote from his Nazi prison cell. Ironically, Friedrich Nietzsche was right when he angrily called Christianity "the vampire of the Roman Empire": it gave the empire's othering order "the kiss of death."[16]

What, then, does neighbor love look like as it develops in different times and places? How do Christians across the tradition clarify, expand, and attempt to embody the earlier vision of neighbor love first imagined by Jesus

---

[14]See Joanne Carlson Brown and Crole R. Bohn, eds., *Christianity, Patriarchy, and Abuse: A Feminist Critique* (New York: Pilgrim, 1990), on some of the failures and atrocities of Christianity throughout history. In this chapter, we'll look mainly at the writings of men. Gender and sexual identity are areas where neighbor love is still breaking down boundaries and empowering the voices of all people. As bell hooks writes in *All About Love: New Visions* (New York: HarperCollins, 2001), xx, "Visionary female thinking on the subject [of love] has yet to be taken as seriously as the thoughts and writing of men. Men theorize about love, but women are more often love's practitioners." Some of the female ethicists doing this important theorizing include Katie G. Canon, *Black Womanist Ethics* (Eugene, OR: Wipf & Stock, 1988), esp. part IV, on love in the ethics of Howard Thurman and Martin Luther King Jr.; Dolores Williams, *Sisters in the Wilderness: The Challenge of Womanist God-Talk* (Maryknoll, NY: Orbis Books, 1993); Barbara Hilkert Andolsen, "Agape in Feminist Ethics," in *Feminist Theological Ethics*, ed. Lois K. Daly (Louisville, KY: Westminster John Knox, 1994); Ada María Isasi-Díaz, "Solidarity: Love of Neighbor in the Twenty-First Century," in *Mujerista Theology: A Theology for the Twenty-First Century* (Maryknoll, NY: Orbis Books, 1996), 86-104. Isasi-Díaz argues for a vision of neighbor love as "solidarity," "liberative praxis," and "revolutionary politics."
[15]Irenaeus, Proof of the Apostolic Preaching, §96, quoted in Ronald Sider, *The Early Church on Killing*, 30.
[16]Friedrich Nietzsche, *The Antichrist*, in *The Portable Nietzsche*, ed. and trans. Walter Kaufmann (New York: Penguin, 1982), §58.

and his followers? This evolution is what we'll explore in this chapter. We'll find a universal moral vision of humanity that all-too-fallibly but powerfully sought to overcome othering for the flourishing of all neighbors. This is what the Neighbor-Love Movement seeks to continue today.

THE DIDACHE: NEIGHBOR LOVE AS THE WAY OF LIFE

The Didache, also known as the Teaching of the Twelve Apostles, is a likely first- or early second-century manual that lays out the basics of Christian teaching as Jesus' movement spread in the Roman Empire.[17] It gives us a window into what the earliest Christians beyond the New Testament were thinking about and prioritizing in their moral teaching and practice. What did they consider truly apostolic and foundational for the church?

The Didache starts by defining "two ways," the way of life and the way of death. It says that "there is a great difference" between them. The way of life is defined by the command to love God and our neighbors as ourselves: "The Way of Life is this: First, you shall love the God who made you, secondly, your neighbor as yourself; and whatever you would not have done to yourself do not do to another."[18] Here we see a continuation of what we found in Jesus and Paul's teaching. First, neighbor love is the way of life and inseparable from the love of God. Second, it has a positive, active meaning and demand. But, third, it also has a negative limit: don't do to others what you don't want them to do to you. Recall that Paul wrote in Romans 13:10, "Love does no harm to a neighbor."

Importantly, the meaning of *neighbor* is immediately clarified and has a universal scope. *Neighbor* includes enemies who curse us, persecute us, and hate us. The Didache here is building on Jesus' teaching in Matthew 5. In fact, it intensifies Jesus' requirement, saying that we should not only pray for our enemies but also fast for them. How should we get rid of enemies? It teaches, "'Love those that hate you,' and you will have no enemy."[19]

If we've heard a similar idea before, this statement may not astonish us in the way it should. Then and often now, as Ferdosa's story illustrates, enemies were eliminated by excluding or exterminating them. The Didache says that

---

[17]"The Didache," in *The Apostolic Fathers*, trans. Kirsopp Lake (Cambridge, MA: Harvard University Press, 1985), 1:305-33.
[18]Didache 1 (p. 309).
[19]Didache 1 (p. 309).

we eliminate our enemies by loving them. In this way, it was inheriting and extending the prophetic signature of Jesus' movement. After surveying the first 300 years of Christian thought after Jesus, Ronald Sider summarized:

> At least ten different writers in at least twenty-eight different places cite or refer to this biblical passage [love your enemies] and note that Christians love their enemies and turn the other cheek. Occasionally, they explicitly link this passage to a rejection of killing and war. . . . In at least nine cases, however, they link the passage to some statement about Christians being peaceable, ignorant of war, opposed to attacking others, and so on. From the earliest post-New Testament writing to the last pre-Constantianian writing, our authors cite Jesus's call to love our enemies.[20]

The Didache thus proceeds to articulate the early Christians' fierce commitment to practicing the creative nonviolence that Jesus himself taught: we should turn our cheek to those who hit us, go the second mile, give our extra clothing, and share our wealth with the poor. Its logic is based on God's generosity as Jesus taught in Matthew 5 and Luke 6: "The Father's will is that we give to all from the gifts we have received."[21] Since God is generous, we should be generous too, even to enemies. The neighbor-love ethic grounded the early Christians' unanimous rejection of violence, war, and capital punishment.[22]

The second section of the Didache affirms the Ten Commandments against murder, adultery, and stealing. But it adds commands against abortion and infanticide or killing children. These were common practices in Roman culture. They reached back to Plato's eugenicist *Republic* and amounted to killing off weak, sick, or disabled children. According to the Didache, the command of neighbor love requires that the weak, sick, and

---

[20]Ronald Sider, *The Early Church on Killing: A Comprehensive Sourcebook on War, Abortion, and Capital Punishment* (Grand Rapids, MI: Baker Academic, 2012), 171.

[21]Didache 1 (p. 311).

[22]In *The Early Church on Killing*, Ronald Sider collected every surviving Christian text with relevance to killing from the first three hundred years of the movement. He concluded, "What we can say with confidence is that every extant Christian statement on killing and war up to the time of Constantine says Christians must not kill, even in war" (194). In *The Sacredness of Human Life*, 128, David Gushee quotes Lactantius (240-317), who wrote, "it makes no difference whether you put a man to death by word [capital punishment], or rather by sword [war], since it is the act of putting to death itself which is prohibited. Therefore, with regard to this precept of God, there ought to be no exception at all; but that it is always unlawful to put to death a man, whom God willed to be a sacred animal."

disabled be respected and protected from harm. The Christian movement was uprooting traditional harmful practices against othered neighbors.[23]

Its moral instruction continues, "You shall make no evil plan against your neighbor. You shall hate no human; but some you should reprove, and for some you shall pray, and some you shall love more than your own life [*psychē*]."[24] "You shall hate no human": here is another one of the revolutionary imperatives that neighbor love introduced to the world. Again, there is a negative limit: make no evil plan and hate no one. Hatred is completely off-limits for authentic Christians. But within the command of neighbor love, there is a need for discernment: some people need confrontation; some need prayer; and some need such radical generosity that you love them even "more than your own life," which seems to suggest martyrdom. (The Didache is echoed in the Letter of Barnabas, a Christian letter written around AD 100: "You shall love your neighbor more than your own soul."[25]) Neighbor love is not like a hammer that only pounds nails. Instead, it is a complex tool whose application requires creative insight, innovation, and self-transcendence.

In section 11, the Didache explains how we can tell the difference between false and true prophets. A false prophet says, "Give me money." A true prophet tells you to give generously to the poor.[26] For the first Christians, the authenticity of a spiritual leader was not measured by their loud voice or impressive power. Their authenticity was measured by how they saw and treated the most vulnerable members of the community. This builds on Jesus' warning in Matthew 7 about not saying "Lord, Lord" but practicing his way, as well as James's liberative vision of neighbor love.

The Christian movement's earliest surviving manual for spiritual and moral practice presents neighbor love as the way of life that saves from death. It must extend to enemies and cancel hate. It must also become practical in the way we live, especially in our relationships with the most othered members of our society, such as children, the poor, and "those who hate us." In some cases, we shouldn't simply love our neighbors as ourselves but "love [them] more than [our] own life."

No room for othering remains. The universality of the moral circle is clear.

---

[23]In *The Sacredness of Human Life*, 124-26, David Gushee shows that this was the consensus of the early Christian movement. He writes: "The developing child is a 'neighbor' like any other neighbor and must be spared killing accordingly" (126).
[24]Didache 2 (p. 313).
[25]Letter of Barnabas 19.5.
[26]Didache 6 (pp. 325-27).

THE EPISTLE TO DIOGNETUS: EARLY CHRISTIAN COSMOPOLITANISM

This universality becomes even clearer in the Epistle to Diognetus, an anonymous early Christian letter. It was likely written in the third century and defends the Christian faith by explaining some of its basic teachings to a non-Christian audience.[27] It too develops an expansive theology of neighbor love that is universal in scope.

The letter is addressed to Diognetus, a man who wants to understand "the religion of the Christians" and has many questions about it. Thus, the writer seeks to unpack "the love which they have for one another, and why this new race [*genos*] or practice has come to life at this time." Before commencing, he challenges Diognetus and says, "Come then, clear yourself of all the prejudice which occupies your mind, and throw aside the custom which deceives you, and become as it were a new human from the beginning, as one who is about to listen to a new story."[28] In other words, Diognetus can only understand Christianity if he overcomes traditional othering. At heart, the Christian movement is about becoming "a new human" who surrenders the entrenched "prejudices" of our old humanity. It tells "a new story" that breaks out of the othering, nationalistic narratives we saw in chapter one.

The author then unpacks the meaning of all of this more thoroughly:

> The distinction between Christians and other people is neither in country nor language nor customs. For they do not dwell in cities in some place of their own, nor do they use any strange variety of language, nor practice any extraordinary kind of life . . . nor are they the advocates of any human doctrine as some men are. They live in Greek and barbarian cities. They follow the local customs, both in clothing and food and in the rest of life. Yet they show forth the wonderful and confessedly strange [*paradoxon*] character of the constitution of their own citizenship. They dwell in their own fatherlands but as if foreigners in them; they share all things as citizens, and suffer all things as strangers. Every foreign country is their fatherland, and every fatherland is a foreign country. They marry as all people, they bear children, but they do not kill their offspring. They offer free hospitality. . . . They obey the appointed laws, and they surpass the laws in their own lives. They love all people and are persecuted by all people. . . . To put it shortly, what the soul is

---

[27]"The Epistle to Diognetus," in *Apostolic Fathers*, 2:348-79.
[28]Epistle to Diognetus 1-2 (pp. 351-53).

in the body, that the Christians are in the world.... The soul loves the flesh which hates it and the limbs, and Christians love those that hate them.[29]

In brief, the Epistle to Diognetus argues that Christianity develops a way of being in the world that does not reinscribe ancient othering, ethnocentrism, and nationalism. Christians aren't different because they have their own country, language, or customs. They don't live in their own subcultures. Instead, they mix with everyone and embrace all different kinds of people. And this is what makes them "confessedly strange" and citizens of a new politics: "Every foreign country is their fatherland, and every fatherland is a foreign country."

The author's point is that Christians are brothers and sisters to all people. They see the entire human race as family—a vision Jesus, Paul, and James emphasized. Thus, they refuse to privilege any place or people as superior to others. Christians don't kill their disabled children, they offer hospitality to outsiders, and they go beyond local law with their moral values. In short, the author writes, "They love all people and are persecuted by all people."[30]

This is what makes Christians a "new race" with a "new story." Like Paul wrote in Galatians, they're neither Greeks nor Jews, neither Romans nor foreigners. They're ambassadors of a new humanity that crosses every border and overcomes every boundary with love. Indeed, Christians even love those who hate them. Paradoxically, this may be a primary reason why these countercultural Christians were hated and persecuted to begin with: they refused to accept the othering, nationalistic prejudices of their society in order to embrace all people. The early Christians were cosmopolitans, citizens of the whole world, which they celebrated as God's good creation. The author says they're like the soul in the body: with their love, they make humanity come truly alive and give it the energy to move and flourish.[31]

In the second half of his letter, the author continues this theme of radical love for others. Here he argues that this neighbor love is the key to true happiness. He writes,

> Happiness consists not in domination over neighbors, nor by seeking to hold the supremacy over those that are weaker, or by being rich, and showing violence towards those that are inferior.... But whoever takes up the burden of

---

[29]Epistle to Diognetus 5 (pp. 359-61).
[30]Epistle to Diognetus 5 (p. 361).
[31]Epistle to Diognetus 6 (p. 361).

his neighbor, and wishes to help another who is weaker where he is stronger, and by ministering to those in need the things which he has received and holds from God, becomes a god to those who receive them—this person is an imitator of God.[32]

The author is addressing perhaps the core question of Greco-Roman philosophy and culture: how to acquire *eudaimonia* or true happiness. Happiness was considered the highest, most important pursuit in life. It penetrated to the heart of how to live the genuinely good—indeed, godlike—life.

For this early Christian writer, happiness cannot be found in othering—what he calls "domination over neighbors" and "seeking to hold supremacy." Superiority in wealth, power, and status is ultimately unsatisfying. True happiness is found in carrying your neighbor's burden, helping the weak, and ministering to those in need. This is what *eudaimonia* or full flourishing looks like. The life of neighbor love embodies the divine life and makes you "an imitator of God."

This daring Christian is subverting the two pillars of Roman society. First, instead of defending a nationalistic homeland, Christians are at home in every society and see all people as family. And, second, instead of controlling superior wealth and power, Christians believe that true happiness is found in practicing neighbor love, which prioritizes the poor and powerless.

Home and happiness are two of the most fundamental questions and desires of the human heart. According to this early Christian, home is everywhere, and happiness is loving everyone. A nationalistic homeland and egocentric happiness are dead ends. To understand "the religion of the Christians," one must abandon traditional othering and join a new race that embodies a new humanity and tells a new story about loving the other as a neighbor.

Two hundred years after the Didache, the command of neighbor love remained central and constitutive in the early documents of the Christian movement. Seeking to abolish othering and advocate for a universal moral circle, Christians "love all people and are persecuted by all people." Paradoxically, this is how we come home and find true happiness.

---

[32] Epistle to Diognetus 10 (p. 373), translation modified.

AUGUSTINE: LOVE'S PURSUIT OF HAPPINESS

Augustine was a North African Christian and bishop who lived from AD 354 to 430. He is among the most influential theologians in Christian history.

Like so many in his world, Augustine sought to identify the source of true happiness. And like our previous author, he locates this happiness within the practice of neighbor love. Moreover, Augustine also does so within his critique of Rome's supremacist, violent culture.

As Rome came under increasing attack from "barbarians," many were blaming Christianity for its declining power. But Augustine sought to "strip off the deceptive veils, remove the whitewash of illusion, and subject the facts to strict inspection." As he examined Greco-Roman religion, culture, and politics, he found what he called "a lust for domination" throughout it. Rome was hell-bent on conquering, colonizing, and killing others, which Augustine calls "a blasphemous spectacle before the whole world." This, Augustine argues, is why the empire was crumbling: its foundations in violent othering were fundamentally rotten. True happiness is found elsewhere: in neighbor love.[33]

Augustine thinks that our entire lives are defined and driven by what we love. More than anything else, humans are creatures of love, and to know who we are, we must know what we love. This is why he focuses on love in his analysis of public life. In his critique of Rome, he argues that its love is really "self-love," a "lust for domination" that "lords it over" the others it "subjugates." By contrast, what Augustine calls "the Heavenly City" is created "by the love of God" and driven by "service for one another in love." He also calls it "a society of aliens" that speaks all languages and feels at home in all cultures. Here he makes a major claim: if we want to understand a people and its character, we need to "examine the objects of its love."[34] The quality of that love will show us the quality of the society, whether it leads to decay or true happiness.

Augustine unpacks his vision of what and how we rightly love in his book *On Christian Teaching* (AD 427). This is where he gives his primary teaching on neighbor love. Augustine's larger purpose in this book is to provide "rules"

---

[33] Augustine, *City of God*, trans. Henry Bettenson (New York: Penguin Books, 1973), 3.14 (pp. 104-5). See Eric Gregory, *Politics and the Order of Love: An Augustinian Ethic of Democratic Citizenship* (Chicago: University of Chicago Press, 2010).
[34] Augustine, *City of God* 14.28, 19.17, 19.24 (pp. 593, 878, 890).

by which all Christians can read the Bible with understanding. Like Jesus, he argues that if our reading of the Bible leads us to love God and our neighbor, then we've read the Bible well. If not, we've missed the point entirely. In fact, he claims that if we've learned to love God and our neighbor, then we no longer need the Bible, because we've learned everything that God wanted to teach us through it.[35]

In book 1, Augustine lays out how we should love God, our neighbors, and ourselves. Augustine's argument hangs on the question of whether, when we love something, we should "enjoy" (*frui*) it or only "use" (*uti*) it, or both. Augustine thinks we should truly *enjoy* something only when it promises us happiness and we can love it for its own sake.[36] By contrast, we should only *use* things that help us reach our happiness but don't give us happiness itself. Think of a journey: you love (*enjoy*) home as your final destination (happiness), so you love (*use*) your car to get there but don't love (*enjoy*) it for its own sake. Falling in love with your car would be to forget that it's just a vehicle to help you get home and thus miss the point.

This is how Augustine analyzes reality: we are all travelers trying to return to our true happiness. For him, there are only three possible options to find it: the destination (God), the road that takes us there (our neighbor), or bad roads that take us off the cliff (vices), such as the lust for domination. So Augustine thinks we should truly love (*enjoy*) only God, even as we should love (*use*) our neighbor as a means for loving God.

The reason is that Augustine thinks that only God is perfect and unchanging. In his argument, if we love anything other than the perfect and permanent, our happiness will be downgraded or disappointed. Neighbors aren't the objects of our love or joy; they're cars on our journey to come home to God.[37]

A valuable insight here is that it would be arrogant and even abusive to think that any one of us could make another completely happy.[38] Augustine urges a realism and humility about our finitude in his vision of love. In a sense, he is a first major Christian thinker of self-care when interpreting neighbor love. In a sermon, he preaches, "You can't love your neighbor as

---

[35]Augustine, *On Christian Teaching*, trans. R. P. H. Green (New York: Oxford University Press, 1997), 1.86, 1.89, 193 (pp. 27-28).
[36]Augustine, *On Christian Teaching* 1.7-8 (p. 9).
[37]Augustine, *On Christian Teaching* 1.15-16, 1.39-40, 1.42-43, 1.76 (pp. 11, 16-17, 25).
[38]Augustine, *On Christian Teaching* 1.77 (p. 25).

yourself, if you don't yet love yourself."³⁹ Since God is our true happiness, Augustine urges us to ground ourselves in loving and enjoying God first.

Still, Augustine sets up a new and troubling competition between loving God and loving our neighbors. Loving neighbors *more* seemingly equates with loving God *less*. But that's not what we found in the New Testament. There the two loves integrate and energize each other without competition. Paul even gives priority to loving our neighbors in Romans 13 and Galatians 5, calling it the summary of all of God's commands. Does Augustine subtly other the neighbor for God, as if humans are less valuable than their Creator who freely made them in God's own image?

Another concerning development in Augustine is that he seems to equate love with getting rather than mutual giving and receiving.⁴⁰ For Augustine, the point of love is possessing happiness for oneself. But in the New Testament, we found that the essence of love was self-giving care with and for others for a shared joy. In fact, the New Testament never sees neighbor love as a means to the end of earning God's favor. Neighbor love has intrinsic value. Jesus says, "Do this, and you will flourish" (Lk 10:28, my translation). Similarly, the Epistle to Diognetus shows that other early Christians thought that loving our neighbors was the key to true happiness. Is Augustine's love ultimately egocentric rather than truly egalitarian?⁴¹

What is clear is that Augustine continues the Christian movement's universalization of neighbor love. He writes, "All people should be loved equally. . . . That the commandment to love our neighbor excludes no human being is made clear by our Lord himself in the gospel and by the Apostle Paul."⁴² In fact, Augustine calls loving one group of humans more than another "totally wicked" and insists that neighbor love is so important that "even the Lord God himself wanted to be called our neighbor."⁴³ This

---

³⁹Augustine, "Sermon 90A," in *Sermons, III/11: Newly Discovered Sermons*, trans. Edmund Hill (Hyde Park, NY: New City, 2000), 80: "The first thing I want to know is whether you love yourself. The whole gist of the commandment lies here, the whole question turns on this point."

⁴⁰See Augustine, *Ten Homilies on the First Epistle of St. John*, trans. John Burnaby, Library of Christian Classics 8 (Philadelphia: Westminster, 1955), 5.4 (p. 78).

⁴¹See Oliver O'Donovan, *The Problem of Self-Love in St. Augustine* (New Haven, CT: Yale University Press, 1980).

⁴²Augustine, *On Christian Teaching* 1.67, 61 (pp. 21-22). See also "Letter 155 to Macedonius (413/414)," in *Augustine: Political Writings*, ed. E. M. Atkins and R. J. Dodaro (New York: Cambridge University Press, 2001), 97.

⁴³Augustine, *On Christian Teaching* 1.70-71 (p. 23). In "Letter 155," Augustine writes of a theater full of people who heard the words of the Stoic philosopher who said, "I am human, and I

is why he writes, "Love and do what you want."⁴⁴ When we truly love, our desire will be good, and our actions will be lifegiving for God, ourselves, and others. Like James saw, love is true freedom.

Likewise, Augustine explicitly affirms love for the enemy, the signature of Jesus' movement. He writes in a letter, "[Your enemy] is the same stuff as you are; you were both made together from the earth by the Lord, both quickened by him. He is exactly what you are too; look on him as your brother."⁴⁵ Augustine is so emphatic here that he calls "rejoicing at your enemy's death . . . something bad." He also continues the early Christian consensus of condemning the death penalty as an evil in the eyes of God and a betrayal of neighbor love.⁴⁶ Repeating its paradox, he insists that by not forgiving an offender, "you are deleting yourself from God's book."⁴⁷

Moreover, Augustine is brilliant in his critique of othering—"the lust for domination"—as the basic evil that corrupts and ultimately collapses human civilization. He writes, "You must want all human beings to be equal to you. . . . Woe to the man whose chariot is pride, for it will surely be wrecked."⁴⁸

Still, important questions persist in Augustine's theology around the apparent—perhaps even othering—competition he sets up between loving God (as enjoyment) and our neighbors (only as use). These questions had profound implications in the evolution of Christianity.

THOMAS AQUINAS: NEIGHBOR LOVE, CAPITAL PUNISHMENT, AND THE CRUSADES

In the eight hundred years after Augustine, many Christians wrote and worked on loving their neighbors. But none was as influential as Thomas Aquinas (1225–1274). Aquinas is especially famous for integrating Christian

---

consider nothing human alien to me." This caused the theater to explode with applause, to which Augustine responded, "Indeed, the fellowship of all human spirits naturally touched the heart of everyone, so much that everyone there thought of himself precisely as the neighbor of every other human being."

⁴⁴Augustine, *Ten Homilies on First John* 7.7 (p. 110).

⁴⁵Augustine, "Sermon 56," in *Sermons: III (51-94) on the New Testament*, trans. Edmund Hill (New York: New City, 1992), 103.

⁴⁶Augustine, *On Christian Teaching* 1.9 (pp. 30-31). On the death penalty, see Augustine, "Letter 13," in *Political Writings*, 124-25. As we saw with Ronald Sider in footnote 22 above, opposing the death penalty was the traditional Christian position.

⁴⁷Augustine, "Sermon 56," 104. Note Augustine, *Ten Homilies* 5.7 (p. 82): "Love alone, then, distinguishes between the children of God and the children of the devil."

⁴⁸Augustine, *Ten Homilies* 8.8 (p. 122).

theology with Aristotle's philosophy, which was rediscovered through Arabic translations. With Aquinas, we see an increasingly systematic or scholastic approach to learning across academic disciplines, including theology and ethics. The mixing of urban development, international trade, human migration, textual translation, and growing universities naturally led to an explosion in critical questions and the reconsideration of tradition.

By this point, Christianity had entirely taken over or Christianized the Roman Empire. But Aquinas's vision of neighbor love raises the question of whether the Roman Empire had also transformed or Romanized Christianity as it now went to war against its "enemies" in the Crusades (1095–1291).

In his five-volume masterwork *Summa Theologica*, Aquinas understands love as a virtue infused in us by God that enables us to obey divine law. It fulfills our human nature and empowers us to rise up to God. Similar to Augustine's vision, love is the divine energy or "life of the soul" we need to be fully alive as moral agents on our journey toward heaven.[49]

More specifically, Aquinas defines *love* as "friendship." By this he understands an act of "benevolence" in which we "love someone so as to wish good to him." In other words, love is goodwill for the well-being of others. Here Aquinas follows Augustine and argues that we should truly love only God, while loving our neighbors for the sake of God.[50] For a second time now, the neighbor is seen as a stepping stone in our journey to return to God and possess our perfect happiness.

Whatever we make of Aquinas's Augustinian understanding of love, we might ask whether his view limits love to friends. To the contrary, Aquinas cleverly argues that friendship makes us friends of friends. And if God loves enemies and strangers, and if love is ultimately "friendship with God," then we must love enemies and strangers based on our love for God. To use another example, Aquinas says that even if your friend's kids don't like you, you'll love them anyway because they're your *friend's* kids. Here Aquinas reaffirms the Christian movement's universal vision of neighbor love, which includes everyone in the circle of moral responsibility, even enemies.

However, Aquinas revises Jesus' teaching on neighbor love and argues that we are not required to have "a special movement of love" toward our enemy. To be sure, we should be prepared to love them. But we don't need

---

[49] Thomas Aquinas, *Summa Theologica* (New York: Benziger, 1948), IIaIIae, question 23, article 2.
[50] Aquinas, *Summa Theologica*, question 23, article 1; question 25, article 1.

to go out of our way to do so. In fact, Aquinas argues that enemy love is "perfect" love and thus isn't necessary for our salvation or a healing relationship with God.[51]

This is a subtle but significant revision. As we saw in chapters three and four, Jesus and his first followers taught that loving our enemies is inseparable from entering into eternal life. I've been calling this the paradox of neighbor love: the only thing that blocks our belonging with God is blocking the belonging of others. Similarly, Augustine wrote that when we refuse to fully love our enemies, we "erase [our] name from the book of life." Aquinas, then, is making a major innovation—or deviation—here in the path of the neighbor-love movement.

Aquinas gives more detail about loving our enemies later in his *Summa*. He writes, "Augustine says that *when it is said: 'You shall love your neighbor,' it is evident that we ought to look upon every man as our neighbor*. Now sinners do not cease to be men, for sin does not destroy nature. Therefore we ought to love sinners out of charity."[52] Aquinas is making an important argument. Since every human being is created good by God, no human can be fully evil by "nature." Here he rejects the essentializing of othering we saw in Plato and Aristotle. And thus Aquinas argues that we are never justified to hate humans. While humans can abuse their freedom and commit terrible evils, no person ever ceases to be human. This is a powerful theological argument against othering, especially when it opens the door to dehumanizing and demonizing others. As we saw in Genesis 1, goodness is original and sovereign.

Still, Aquinas continues his argument and writes, "Now hatred of a person's evil is equivalent to love of his good. Hence also this perfect hatred belongs to charity."[53] One worries that Aquinas is splitting hairs and opening a loophole to hate "sinners" in our practice. Here Aquinas makes another important break with the Christian movement of neighbor love: he parts with its consensus up to Augustine and builds an argument for the death penalty. In short, Aquinas sees a limit to love: when someone's sin becomes "incurable, we ought no longer to show them friendliness," and the death penalty gets justified.

---

[51] Aquinas, *Summa Theologica*, question 25, articles 8-9.
[52] Aquinas, *Summa Theologica*, question 25, article 6; see also article 8.
[53] Aquinas, *Summa Theologica*, question 25, article 6.

Aquinas gives three reasons why he thinks capital punishment can be coherent with Christian neighbor love. First, killing the wrongdoer prevents them from further harming others, and thus it promotes "the public good." Second, Aquinas thinks that the fear of death can motivate the wrongdoer to repent and convert, which would lead to their ultimate peace with God despite a temporary death. Third, even if the wrongdoer doesn't repent, Aquinas thinks that they will be prevented from sinning any more, and thus their judgment before God will be less severe in the afterlife.[54]

Aquinas has made two moves here with major consequences for the history of Christianity and the trajectory of its neighbor-love movement. First, he argues that loving our enemies isn't mandatory for Christians or truly at the heart of being children of God, as Jesus and his followers taught at least up to the fifth century. Rather, it's an expression of "perfect" love. Second, he argues that it is possible to love our neighbors to death by killing them.

Understanding Aquinas's historical and cultural context is vital as we consider his vision of neighbor love. Aquinas was living during the time of the Crusades, and he supported them. In fact, Aquinas held public discussions in which he defended the Crusades and argued that Christian warriors would receive special favor from God by going to fight their "enemies." Thus, Aquinas's logic provided a justification for Christian soldiers from Europe to travel to Jerusalem and slaughter their Muslim neighbors without sensing that they had done anything wrong. Indeed, they thought they had done something pious that God would reward in heaven.[55]

Here we see again that moral beliefs can have massive implications for the real world. Aquinas took Jesus' clear teaching, which rejects hatred and requires nonviolent enemy love, and opened large loopholes for hating sinners and killing enemies. In the process, he ironically justified some of the most infamous violence in the Christian tradition.

There are other limits to Aquinas's vision of neighbor love. Later in his *Summa*, he asks whether we should love one neighbor more than another. He answers affirmatively and calls this "the order of charity."[56] Of course, Aquinas was living in an intensely hierarchical society in which special

---

[54] Aquinas, *Summa Theologica*, question 25, article 6.
[55] Soon before Aquinas, the famous mystic Bernard of Clairvaux said, "The Christian glories in the death of the pagan, because Christ is glorified." Quoted in David Gushee, *The Sacredness of Human Life: Why an Ancient Biblical Vision Is Key to the World's Future* (Grand Rapids, MI: Eerdmans, 2013), 177.
[56] Aquinas, *Summa Theologica*, question 26, article 6.

loyalty to lords, priests, and family was taken for granted. As we've seen, Aquinas was also reviving Aristotle, who believed hierarchy was built into the structure of the universe with God on top, then men representing divine rationality, and then women and children beneath them. It's no surprise that Aquinas asks this question.

He answers that we should have goodwill for all but that it is "natural" for us to have special commitments toward some more than others. Thus, Aquinas argues that we should love blood relations more than strangers, fathers more than children and mothers, a benefactor more than a beneficiary, and people who are "closer" to God more than people who are "farther away" from God.[57]

As with the Crusades, we see that Aquinas builds into his vision of neighbor love a theological justification for the patriarchal, feudalistic, hierarchical structure of his medieval society. One worries that Aquinas also justifies preferential, if not openly othering, "loves," which Jesus, the apostles, and the writer of the Letter to Diognetus explicitly condemned. Alas, those who already had the power in this Christianized empire—men, the wealthy, and the religious—now receive theologically justified privilege. Forms of othering begin to be naturalized again.

It is easy to imagine where medieval Christians could take Aquinas's theology: (1) they should love Christian neighbors more than non-Christian, especially Muslim neighbors; (2) they could excuse themselves for not loving their enemies because they're not "perfect"; and (3) violence against "sinners" can be an act of "love" and a stepping stone to heaven.

In this way, devastating campaigns such as the Crusades were justified. The moral circle narrows here, and othering seemingly creeps back in with its atrocious irony.

JULIAN OF NORWICH: *REVELATIONS OF DIVINE LOVE*

Mysticism is ambient throughout the unfolding of the neighbor-love movement. By *mysticism*, I mean the experience of "a direct and transformative presence of God," as Bernard McGinn describes it.[58]

Abraham hears an unexpected voice after his father dies. This divine voice calls him to leave home for an unknown destination that will ultimately bless

---

[57] Aquinas, *Summa Theologica*, question 26, articles 8-12.
[58] Bernard McGinn, *The Essential Writings of Christian Mysticism* (New York: Modern Library, 2006), xiv.

all people (Gen 12:1-3). Jesus journeys into the desert, where he is immersed in the Jordan River before giving his Sermon on the Mount. There he sees heaven open, and God appears as the dove of peace. Then Jesus hears God call him "beloved" (Mt 3:17). When he returns from the desert and gives his movement's manifesto, Jesus envisions sunlight and rain as the outpouring of God's love for all humanity, including our enemies (Mt 5:43-48). Paul encounters the resurrected Jesus on his way to arrest his heretical followers in Damascus. Paul falls to the ground and is temporarily blinded (Acts 9:1-6). After this mystical experience, he travels the Roman Empire proclaiming "how wide and long and high and deep is the love of Christ"—a universing love that "surpasses knowledge" (Eph 3:18-19). Even the scholastic Thomas Aquinas had a mystical vision at the end of his life. After it, he said that all of his writings were "like straw." Neighbor love unfolds every bit as much in the heart as in the head, as much in the ensouled body as in the abstract intellect.

With Julian of Norwich (1342–after 1416), mystical vision comes to the center of the neighbor-love movement. An English recluse, Julian is the first woman whose writings can be identified in the English language. Not much is known about her personal life. But she endures as one of the most inspiring mystics in Christian history. The visions she saw, which she described in her *Revelations of Divine Love*, are deeply moving.[59]

Julian had sixteen visions, but all of them focus on the love of God embodied in Jesus. At thirty years old and stricken with illness, she believed she was dying and gazed upon a crucifix. She writes, "In the image of the cross there remained a light for all mankind." In this healing light, Julian beholds "how intimately he loves us. . . . I saw that he is everything that is good and comforting and helpful to us." She pictures God in Christ as "our clothing that enwraps us and enfolds us, embraces us and wholly encloses us, surrounding us out of tender love."[60]

Julian then sees the entire universe as a tiny hazelnut in the palm of her hand. She is puzzled by how something so small and fragile could endure. She observes, "Man's soul is made of nothing." But then she hears, "It lasts, and always will, because God loves it; and in the same way, everything has its being through the love of God. . . . God has made everything that is made

---

[59]Julian of Norwich, *Revelations of Divine Love*, trans. Barry Windeatt (New York: Oxford University Press, 2015).
[60]Julian, *Revelations of Divine Love*, 5-7.

for love." Similar to Jesus and Paul, Julian beholds the whole universe as suffused and sustained with divine love. Creation itself is God's act of loving us into being, of cherishing us into life when we were nothing at all. "In this love we have our beginning," she beholds.[61]

This mystical vision of God's act of creation is perhaps the most radical grounding of humanity's unconditional value. When we were nothing, when we had nothing, when we could offer God nothing—God loved us into life. Julian writes, "For before he made, he loved us." Whatever else happens in history and our own stories, this is our absolute prehistory, our identity, and thus our destiny. "Whether we are unclean or pure, his love for us is the same."[62]

We saw glimpses of this vision of creation in Jesus, Paul, and many others in their invocation of God as our universal Father who parents us with love into life and is kind to us even when we are "ungrateful and wicked." This led Paul to conclude, "I am convinced that . . . [nothing] in all creation, will be able to separate us from the love of God that is in Christ Jesus our Lord" (Rom 8:38-39). This mystical vision will ground Simone Weil's ethics of neighbor love, as we'll see in the next chapter.

Thus, Julian's mystical visions repeatedly refocus her attention on humanity as a universal family united in love. She writes, "In this oneness of love depends the life of all humanity. . . . We are all as one in love." With daring beauty, Julian beholds Jesus as the mother of the human family; (s)he holds all of us and all things with healing compassion. She writes, "Jesus is our true mother. . . . He says, 'All shall be well; and you shall see for yourself that all manner of things shall be well.' And then the bliss of our motherhood in Christ will begin anew in the joy of our God; a new beginning which will last without end, always beginning anew." With Jesus as "our true mother" who embraces our flesh, we ourselves enter into "the bliss of our motherhood in Christ." The othering and aggression of humanity are healed. We are enlivened to begin anew with "the wisdom and the kindness of motherhood."[63] Trust is born in us to hear the sacred promise, "All shall be well."

The destiny of our humanity, then, is not disintegration. Like the tiny hazelnut in her hand, we are being held by the mysterious presence of divine

---

[61]Julian, *Revelations of Divine Love*, 119, 7-8, 165.
[62]Julian, *Revelations of Divine Love*, 119, 153.
[63]Julian, *Revelations of Divine Love*, 9, 51, 129, 136, 128.

love. Our destiny is universal hope: "You shall be filled full of love and of bliss," for "God is the goodness that cannot be angry."[64] After our bodies fall dead on the earth, "suddenly out of this body [will spring] a very beautiful creature, a little child perfectly shaped and formed, swift and full of life." God's mothering love is "our everlasting friend"—"our medicine"—who brings what we thought was lost back to life.[65]

It is important to note that Julian did not have a naive view of humanity. She describes how we are "weak and foolish" and often "overwhelmed." We suffer "sorrow and misery." Julian herself had a severe illness that caused her acute pain; in fact, it was so severe that she was expecting to die as she saw these visions. Still, she writes, "Our failing is full of fear, our falling is full of shame, and our dying is full of sorrow; but throughout all this the sweet eye of pity and love never looks away from us." We are being perceived by God. Our true Mother sees us and "is nearer to us than our own soul."[66]

Like John, Julian doesn't use the *language* of neighbor love. But its *life* suffuses her visions. Jesus is our universal Mother. We exist because God loved us into being when we were nothing, and nothing we can do in history can degrade this precious value. Thus, humanity is "all as one in love." This is "the light for all mankind." Her mystical visions do not lead to a prideful sense of superiority to others; instead, Julian writes, "The soul is highest, noblest, and worthiest when it is lowest, humblest, and gentlest."[67] There could hardly be a more universal moral circle or healing vision for human othering, which seeks to secure value through separation and superiority. Here humility and gentleness are cherished.

Julian's mystical visions speak to the soul still today. They are precious gifts of love across the ages for all neighbors. She summarizes them like this: "Love was [God's] meaning. Who showed you this? Love. What did he show you? Love. Why did he show it? For love. Hold fast to this, and you will know and understand more of the same. . . . Before God made us he loved us, and this love has never abated nor ever shall."[68]

---

[64]Julian, *Revelations of Divine Love*, 136, 110. Rather than sloppy sentimentalism, Julian is developing Jesus' vision of God in Lk 6 as "kind to the ungrateful and wicked."
[65]Julian, *Revelations of Divine Love*, 137, 154-55, 161.
[66]Julian, *Revelations of Divine Love*, 101-2, 123.
[67]Julian, *Revelations of Divine Love*, 129.
[68]Julian, *Revelations of Divine Love*, 164.

Martin Luther: Reform and Radical Contradiction

Not long after Julian, we meet Martin Luther (1483–1546), the fiery German Catholic priest who became known as a Protestant reformer. Many scholars see him as a founding figure of the modern world. Energized by his own mystical visions, Luther launched a powerful reform movement that reaffirmed Paul's vision that every individual can have an immediate relationship with God through Jesus Christ. Luther's theology celebrated personal conscience, exalted everyday life, and dignified marriage, sex, and family.[69] He also vehemently critiqued the corruption he witnessed in the Roman Catholic Church that had raised him. His sentiments are expressed well by his contemporary Martin Bucer in his beautiful little book *Instruction in Christian Love*:

> It cannot be denied that most churchmen ... now everywhere seek their own interest and not the benefit and blessedness of those under them, except in the measure in which the others' benefit and blessedness bring them natural advantages and subserve their prestige.... *Churchmen have fallen*.... From all this it is evident that at present there is no more dangerous, more disquieting, and more condemnable condition than that of churchmen, popes, bishops, clergymen, and monks.[70]

In short, Bucer believed the Christian church had been infested with othering. Its leaders' Christianized imperial hierarchy sought their own "interest," "advantages," and "prestige" above those "under them." This othering state of the church couldn't be "more dangerous" and "condemnable." Luther entirely agreed, though his critique of this corruption often ironically slipped into reinscribing othering. Luther was brash and reveled in using insults against his opponents.

Throughout his voluminous writings, Luther saw what Paul called "sincere love" as the solution to the crisis in the church. Luther didn't write a single work devoted exclusively to neighbor love, but he discusses it throughout his sermons and essays. Luther thought that, like the shadow follows the body, love should follow true faith in God. In his famous essay

---

[69] See Katie Barklay, *Caritas: Neighbourly Love and the Early Modern Self* (New York: Oxford University Press, 2021); Charles Taylor, *A Secular Age* (Cambridge, MA: Harvard University Press, 2018), part 1, "The Work of Reform"; Sheldon Wolin, *Politics and Vision: Continuity and Innovation in Western Political Thought* (Princeton, NJ: Princeton University Press, 2016), chap. 5, "Luther: The Theological and the Political."

[70] Martin Bucer, *Instruction in Christian Love*, trans. Paul Fuhrmann (Eugene, OR: Wipf & Stock, 2008), 33–34.

"The Freedom of the Christian," Luther argues that the Christian "lives in Christ and the neighbor." Similar to the writer of the Letter to Diognetus, Luther saw the neighbor as the Christian's home.

Luther summarizes his view of neighbor love in his *Confession Concerning Christ's Supper*. He writes, "[Christian love] serves every needy person in general with all kinds of benevolent deeds, such as feeding the hungry, giving drink to the thirsty, forgiving enemies, praying for all people on earth, and suffering all kinds of evil on earth."[71] He offers a more specific account of his vision of neighbor love in two of his most provocative essays.

In 1527, ten years after he purportedly nailed his Ninety-Five Theses to the church door in Wittenberg, Luther wrote a short essay titled "Whether One May Flee from a Deadly Plague." Like our world's renewed familiarity with a pandemic, this question was very real and practical in sixteenth-century Europe.[72] A few generations before, the bubonic plague had killed nearly two hundred million people. Luther's question was poignant: Are Christians permitted to run for their lives when a deadly plague strikes their city?

To the prevailing mindset we explored at the beginning of this book, Luther's question might not even seem like a *real* question: *of course, run away; protect yourself*. But for this Christian fifteen hundred years into Jesus' neighbor-love movement, the precious value of the other had made this question fundamental and urgent. Through the lens of neighbor love, what is most concerning about the city is not that it has a dangerous plague but that it has suffering *neighbors* who need help. If we are commanded to love them, is leaving a legitimate response?

Luther answers resolutely: "No one should dare leave his neighbor unless there are others who will take care of the sick in their place and nurse them."[73] Unless we are certain that there are enough people to help the sick and dying, a Christian has no right to flee from the danger.

For Luther, this policy proceeds directly out of Jesus' teaching of neighbor love. He writes, "We must give hospital care and be nurses for one another in any extremity or risk the loss of salvation and the grace of God. Thus it is written in God's word and command, 'Love your neighbor as yourself,' and

---

[71] Quoted in Lindberg, *Love*, 123.
[72] For an account of neighbor love during Covid-19, see Jason Mahn, *Neighbor Love Through Fearful Days: Finding Purpose and Meaning in a Time of Crisis* (Minneapolis: Fortress, 2021).
[73] Martin Luther, "Whether One May Flee from a Deadly Plague," in *Martin Luther's Basic Theological Writings*, 2nd ed., ed. Timothy F. Lull (Minneapolis: Fortress, 2005), 481.

in Matthew 7:12, 'So whatever you wish that people would do to you, do so to them.'"[74] Luther's exposition of neighbor love is striking, because he is most famous for insisting that human salvation comes only by the grace of God through our faith, not through our works. And still, Luther repeats the paradox of neighbor love: if we flee from our endangered neighbors, we risk "the loss of salvation and the grace of God."

Luther then unpacks three additional reasons Christians should embrace the real risks of neighbor love. First, he says that if we're not willing to take risks for our neighbors, we probably don't really love them to begin with. Real love is risky and requires personal cost. Luther writes, "If I see that [my neighbor] is hungry and thirsty, I cannot ignore him but must offer food and drink, not considering whether I would risk impoverishing myself by doing so. A person who will not help or support others unless he can do so without affecting his safety or his property will never help his neighbor."[75]

Second, Luther says that Jesus loved us so much that he accepted a brutal execution with terrible suffering. If Christ is our Lord and example, who are we to run away from the suffering required to love our neighbors? With his signature style, Luther writes,

> If Christ shed his blood for me and died for me, why should I not expose myself to some small dangers for his sake and disregard feeble plague? If you can terrorize, Christ can strengthen me. If you can kill, Christ can give life. . . . Are not these glorious and mighty promises of God heaped up upon those who minister to the needy . . . even though he might have as many contagious boils on him as hairs on his body?[76]

Neighbor love is ultimately unkillable. It is the way of eternal life. Even if loving our neighbors entails our bodies being afflicted with "many contagious boils," Christ can strengthen us amid this terror. In this love, even plague is "feeble."

Third, Jesus said in Matthew 25 that we serve Christ himself when we serve "the least" of our neighbors. This is the echo I heard when I met Eyob: "If you say no to him, you've said no to me." Luther argues, then, that turning away from people with plague means turning away from Jesus himself. His commentary is worth quoting at length:

---

[74] "Whether One May Flee," 484.
[75] "Whether One May Flee," 483.
[76] "Whether One May Flee," 485.

> This I well know, that if it were Christ or his mother who were laid low by illness everybody [would] . . . gladly become a servant or helper. Everyone would want to be bold and fearless; nobody would flee but everyone would come running. And yet they don't hear what Christ himself says, "As you did to one of the least you did it to me" [Mt 25:40]. When he speaks of the greatest commandment, he says, "The other commandment is like unto it, you shall love your neighbor as yourself" [Mt 22:39]. There you hear that the command to love your neighbor is equal to the greatest commandment to love God, and that what you do or fail to do for your neighbor means doing the same to God. If you wish to serve Christ and to wait on him, very well, you have your sick neighbor close at hand. Go to him and serve him, and you will surely find Christ in him. . . . But if you do not wish or care to serve your neighbor, you can be sure that if Christ lay there instead, you would not do so either and would let him lie there.[77]

These are challenging words. Luther insists that if we aren't willing to serve our neighbor who has the plague, we shouldn't fool ourselves into thinking that we would serve Jesus himself if he had the plague. We "surely find Christ" in our endangered neighbor. Again, real love requires risk.

Overall, then, Luther sees serving victims of plague, running hospitals, caring for the dead, and organizing cemeteries as activities that embody Christ's command of neighbor love. Even a dangerous epidemic is no justification for othering. As in the early church, here again in the early modern world, we see neighbor love providing the lens for social vision and public policy. It demands that no one be treated as less or left behind.

Now, if we read only Luther's essay on how to respond to a deadly plague, it would seem that he held an extremely radical, all-inclusive vision of neighbor love. In many ways, he did. But unfortunately, the story is not so simple.

Sixteen years later, in 1543, Luther wrote a bitterly antisemitic tract titled "On the Jews and Their Lies." In this essay, Luther others the Jews as "miserable and accursed people." Thus, he asks another question: "What should Christians do with this rejected and condemned people?"[78]

Sadly, Luther gives four, atrociously othering answers. He says that Christians should (1) burn down Jews' synagogues, (2) confiscate all of their books,

---

[77]"Whether One May Flee," 486.
[78]Martin Luther, "On the Jews and Their Lies," in Lull, *Martin Luther's Basic Theological Writings*, 25, 30.

(3) ban their worship, and (4) forbid them from mentioning the name of God in the hearing of Christians. In fact, Luther insists that any Christian who hears a Jew mention the name of God should report them to the police, throw pig dung on them, or chase them away. To justify his hate, Luther alludes to Hebrew Scripture's genocidal vision in Deuteronomy 7 and insists, "May no one be merciful and kind" to them.[79]

With bitter irony, here we see the afterlife of othering texts against Israel's enemies in the Hebrew Bible inflaming violence against Jews in Europe. For a second time, Luther tells his Christian readers to "burn down their synagogues" and impose forced labor on them. In his final paragraph, Luther completely demonizes Jewish people. They become the other against which this Christian reformer offers an account of a superior Christian identity. Thus again we observe the irony of othering: a claim of superiority justifies appalling evil. The moral circle violently closes.

Of course, we cannot simplistically blame Luther for the German Holocaust five hundred years later. Still, Luther's antisemitic writing was used in Nazi Germany as religious propaganda to justify and fuel the flames of genocide against six million Jewish neighbors. Luther himself fell into the othering that Bucer said couldn't be "more dangerous, more disquieting, and more condemnable."

If Luther had, at minimum, called for nonviolent neighbor love for the Jewish people, perhaps German Christians would have responded differently than they did to Hitler's othering, genocidal vision. We observe again with great sobriety how moral beliefs can in fact change the world—both for better and for worse.

Søren Kierkegaard: *Works of Love*

Three centuries later, Søren Kierkegaard (1813–1855) was deeply inspired by the better insights of Luther's work. In the forty-two years of his life in Copenhagen, Kierkegaard produced some of the most influential works of modern philosophy. Ludwig Wittgenstein called Kierkegaard "by far the most profound thinker of the nineteenth century."[80] In this final section, we turn to look at Kierkegaard's remarkable book *Works of Love*.

---

[79]Luther, "On the Jews," 31.
[80]Quoted on the back cover of Søren Kierkegaard, *Works of Love*, trans. Howard and Edna Hong (New York: HarperCollins, 2009).

On its first page, Kierkegaard writes about the person who, because of his "conceited shrewdness proud of not being deceived," will "believe in nothing which he cannot see by means of his physical eyes."[81] Here Kierkegaard is responding to the increasingly materialistic worldview of modernity. He argues that when we take such a reductive view of reality, "then first and foremost one ought to give up believing in love."

For Kierkegaard, this loss of love presents us with an ultimate irony: "If one did this and did it out of fear of being deceived, would not one then be deceived?" He acknowledges that deception is real and that we are right to be careful and critical in what we believe. But Kierkegaard argues that we can "also be deceived by the superficiality of shrewdness, by the flattering conceit which is absolutely certain that it cannot be deceived." Here othering is intellectualized, assuming superiority over the mysterious vulnerability of love that Paul said "surpasses knowledge." Kierkegaard argues, "To cheat oneself out of love is the most terrible deception; it is an eternal loss for which there is no reparation."[82]

In *Works of Love*, then, Kierkegaard is trying to call the modern, disenchanted individual back into a larger, more complex and expansive vision of existence. Like in Julian, this vision can perceive invisible realities such as God, love, and the neighbor itself throughout our experience. Kierkegaard writes, "It is in fact Christian love which discovers and knows that one's neighbor exists and that . . . everyone is one's neighbor. If it were not a duty to love, then there would be no concept of neighbor at all. But only when one loves his neighbor, only then is the selfishness of preferential love rooted out and the equality of the eternal preserved."[83] Like his contemporary John Stuart Mill, Kierkegaard is asking his readers to break out of an "incrusted mind" that observes neighbor love as a "dead dogma."

In his heavily Christianized culture in Denmark, seeing others as neighbors might seem obvious. But Kierkegaard argues that, without Christ's command to love our neighbors as ourselves, there would be "no concept of neighbor at all." Instead, "preferential" or othering "love" would prevail. When we recall what we found in the ancient world, this is not a self-flattering exaggeration of a Christian philosopher. Kierkegaard insists, "No

---

[81] Kierkegaard, *Works of Love*, 23.
[82] Kierkegaard, *Works of Love*, 23.
[83] Kierkegaard, *Works of Love*, 58.

one in paganism loved his neighbor—no one suspected that there was such a being. . . . You see, the times are past when the powerful and prominent alone were men, and the others—human slaves and serfs. We are indebted to Christianity for this."[84] Without the biblical vision of neighbor love, Kierkegaard observes that we would still be stuck in the ancient world's "natural inequality," which othered neighbors into "slaves and serfs." Our moral perception would remain limited to the familiar lenses of family, friends, strangers, and enemies. Friedrich Nietzsche made Kierkegaard's point as he sought to revive classical culture's ethic against neighbor love. Nietzsche insisted, "You shall always be the first and excel all others: your jealous soul shall love no one, unless it be the friend."[85]

Kierkegaard reminds us that Christian love discovers that the neighbor even *exists*, that they are *everyone*, and that we have a divine *imperative* to see and treat them with *love*. For Kierkegaard, this is the miracle of existence unlocked in Christian revelation.[86] If "cheating oneself out of love is the most terrible deception," discovering that we live in a world full of neighbors is the most wondrous awakening to reality. It transforms how we see and feel and act in all of our relations, as Julian perceived with great beauty.

Kierkegaard's vision of neighbor love weaves together several threads we've traced throughout the earlier Christian movement's ethic.

First, like Jesus and Julian, Kierkegaard thinks that love is fundamentally rooted in God's character, which is revealed in the gift of creation and the sacrifice of Christ. We are not the first lovers; we are born and embedded in a much more ancient and absolute divine love. While trusting this eternal Lover requires the ultimate courage of faith, it also awakens us to reality as if for the first time. Kierkegaard writes, "Love is the origin of everything, and spiritually understood love is the deepest ground of the life of the spirit." When we are freed from reductive self-deceptions, the eyes of our hearts are opened. We begin to perceive love mysteriously flowing in everything, like a spring whose source disappears into the ground and like the sun, which blinds us when we look directly into its face.[87]

---

[84]Kierkegaard, *Works of Love*, 66, 84.
[85]Friedrich Nietzsche, *Thus Spoke Zarathustra*, in *The Portable Nietzsche*, ed. and trans. Walter Kaufmann (New York: Penguin, 1982), 172.
[86]Kierkegaard, *Works of Love*, 41, 138.
[87]Kierkegaard, *Works of Love*, 20, 26, 205, 27.

Second, Kierkegaard emphasizes that true love is practical: it is a decision and action for the well-being of others. This is why Kierkegaard's book is titled *Works of Love*. Love is not merely romantic emotions or poetic words. Love is *work*. Its authenticity is proven by fruit far more than feelings.[88] Kierkegaard underscores that God *commands* us to love, not as an imperious dictate but as a call that activates our agency and then gets practically embodied in our relationships with others.

Third, Kierkegaard argues that neighbor love is universal: every singular person we meet is our neighbor, someone who is morally related to us and equal in value. Alluding to Jesus' parable of the good Samaritan, Kierkegaard claims that the other is not our neighbor because we know them or like them or even happen to feel pity for them. The other is our neighbor because God commands us to *be* neighbors. When *we* are neighbors, every *other* becomes a *neighbor* to us with God's love connecting us.[89]

This is the basis of Kierkegaard's affirmation of Jesus' command to love our enemies. He observes that Jesus never commanded us to love others because they've done something to deserve our love. Like Jesus highlighted, Kierkegaard repeats that such love wouldn't be love at all but only a self-serving transaction that reinscribes othering. We are commanded to *be* lovers and thus *to* love, regardless of whether our love is deserved and returned or rejected and opposed. Kierkegaard calls this "Christianity's blessed equality," which relentlessly overcomes the othering hierarchies we invent.[90] It is love that creates the neighbor, not the neighbor that creates the love.

On this basis, Kierkegaard offers one of the most powerful articulations of the universality of neighbor love in the movement Jesus started. He writes,

> Christian love teaches love of all people, unconditionally all. . . . Christianity never suffers a person to go in vain, not even a single step, for when you open the door which you shut in order to pray to God, the first person you meet as you go out is your neighbor whom you shall love. . . . Christianity has made it forever impossible to make a mistake about him. There is in the whole world not a single person who can be recognized with such ease and certainty as one's neighbor. You can never confuse him with anyone else, for indeed all people are your neighbor.[91]

---

[88] Kierkegaard, *Works of Love*, 106, 20.
[89] Kierkegaard, *Works of Love*, 38, 112.
[90] Kierkegaard, *Works of Love*, 77, 79, 81, 71; see also 92.
[91] Kierkegaard, *Works of Love*, 63-65.

Whomever we encounter, in whatever condition, in whichever context, the other is our neighbor. There is no one with whom we don't share moral connection and equal worth. Whenever we open our door, we come in contact with neighbors. Playfully, Kierkegaard observes that finding a friend or lover may be "a long, hard job," but "one's neighbor is easy to recognize, easy to find—if one himself will only recognize his duty."[92]

Fourth, Kierkegaard thus argues that neighbor love overcomes the core of othering. He may be the clearest thinker we've encountered so far on this point. When Jesus commands, "Love your neighbor *as yourself*," Kierkegaard says that he "wrenches open the lock of self-love and thereby wrests it away from humanity."[93] He writes,

> [The neighbor] is just as near or ought to be just as near to you as you are to yourself. The concept of *neighbor* really means a duplicating of one's own self. *Neighbor* is what philosophers would call the *other*, that by which the selfishness in self-love is tested. . . . What selfishness absolutely cannot endure is duplication, and the words of the command *as yourself* are simply duplication. . . . In this way *one's neighbor* is as close to the life of self-love as possible.[94]

Throughout this book, we've observed that the core of othering is seeing oneself or one's group as separated from or superior to others. But loving our neighbor *as ourselves* makes the other as close to us as we are to ourselves. In this way, it tests us: Are we willing to love the other as if they were a "duplicate" of ourselves, that is, as fully connected and equally precious to ourselves? Moreover, are we willing to love *ourselves* in the same way we love *others*, whether this implies a transformation or expansion of our self-love?

For Kierkegaard, Christian neighbor love is the abolition of othering in the heart of the self. As such, it presents us with this test.[95] In practical terms, if I love for myself to be valued, protected, and empowered to flourish, I must love for my neighbor to be valued, protected, and empowered to flourish too. Anything less is othering.

---

[92]Kierkegaard, *Works of Love*, 39.
[93]Kierkegaard, *Works of Love*, 34. In the final chapter, I will clarify that neighbor love rejects *selfishness* but affirms *self-love*.
[94]Kierkegaard, *Works of Love*, 37-38. See John Lippitt, *Kierkegaard and the Problem of Self-Love* (New York: Cambridge University Press, 2013).
[95]Kierkegaard, *Works of Love*, 39: "The law is, therefore: you shall love yourself in the same way as you love your neighbor when you love him as yourself."

Finally, like Jesus, Paul, and several others we've studied, Kierkegaard writes that love endures for eternity.[96] It never fails and is never truly deceived. He imagines someone, inspired by love, giving money to a beggar who doesn't need it or wastes it. But the love of this act will endure for eternity and thus prove to be wise, Kierkegaard argues. Lovers have nothing to lose, for in love nothing is lost.[97] The truly impoverished person is not the one without money but the one without love. Similarly, the truly rich person is not the one who owns the whole world but the one who has chosen the love that never changes. While "life without loving is not worth living," the one who loves is "eternally and happily secured against despair."[98] Love leads to everlasting joy.

This is the hopeful challenge that one of the most brilliant philosophers of the nineteenth century presented to a wave of modern thinkers who increasingly argued that they had unmasked love and found something more powerful, whether money (Marx), power (Nietzsche), sex (Freud), or something else. Eighteen centuries after Jesus, Kierkegaard argues that there is nothing more powerful or precious than neighbor love. It universalizes the moral circle, establishes "a blessed equality," and overcomes despair for everlasting joy.

Conclusion: The Globalization of Neighbor Love

We started this chapter with the historian Larry Siedentop's claim, "A fundamental change in moral belief shaped the world we live in." As we look at the movement of neighbor love across Christian history, I believe this claim illuminates the evidence we find. We have seen it from the Didache's ancient declaration that neighbor love is "the way of life" that calls us to love others "even more than ourselves," to Kierkegaard's modern critique of othering and call to embrace the "blessed equality" of seeing all people as beloved neighbors. Again and again, the "fundamental change in moral belief" across the centuries follows the shape of Jesus' othering-abolishing ethics of neighbor love in the Gospels.

---

[96]Kierkegaard, *Works of Love*, 76.
[97]See Jean-Luc Marion, *The Erotic Phenomenon*, trans. Stephen Lewis (Chicago: University of Chicago Press, 2007), 71: "There is only one single proof of love—to give without return or chance of recovery, and thus to be able to lose and, eventually, to be lost in love. But love itself is never lost, because it is accomplished in loss."
[98]Kierkegaard, *Works of Love*, 28, 44, 46, 52.

The neighbor is now everyone—not just family members, friends, one's ethnic group, or fellow religionists. To love these neighbors means to embrace an active commitment to their flourishing—not just fuzzy feelings or random niceness. And neighbor love necessarily stretches to include love for our enemy-siblings—those we are most tempted to other, hate, or destroy. In fact, the reaffirmation of Jesus' call to love our enemies has been one of the signature innovations throughout our study.

In this historic movement at its best, no one is excluded from the ethical neighborhood. The moral circle is drawn around us all. There are no people who can be othered or eliminated if we want to follow Jesus. This is the paradox of neighbor love: we only exclude ourselves from full belonging with God if we exclude others.

Throughout this movement, we have seen a return to Genesis's primal vision: each person is made in God's image, we are part of our Father's single human family, and Abraham's children are called to be a blessing to all nations of the earth. In a sense, we have seen a partial fulfillment of Jesus' Great Commission in Matthew 28:19-20 to go into all the world and teach everyone to practice his commands—commands that center on loving all people as ourselves.

But we have also seen subtle corruptions and massive failures of neighbor love throughout Christian history. These atrocities should never be suppressed or minimized. In this chapter, we briefly touched on the justification of hierarchy, the violence of the Crusades, and the demonization of the Jews, which pointed ahead to the horror of the Holocaust. Many other problems should be examined, including European colonialism and American genocide and slavery.[99] We observe that neighbor love can be twisted into self-justifying violence or simply silenced and overridden. In these important cases, Christians themselves participate in the othering that the tradition has tried to overcome. Modern critics of Christianity such as Friedrich Nietzsche and Sigmund Freud rightly help us become more self-aware and honest in our practice today.[100]

---

[99]See Nicole Delia Legnani, *The Business of Conquest: Empire, Love, and Law in the Atlantic World* (Notre Dame, IN: University of Notre Dame Press, 2020).

[100]Nietzsche repeatedly attacked Christian neighbor love. See Friedrich Nietzsche, *Beyond Good and Evil*, trans. Judith Norman (New York: Cambridge University Press, 2005), §§33, 43, 60, 175, 201-2, 262; Nietzsche, *Thus Spoke Zarathustra*, 170-73; Nietzsche, *On the Genealogy of Morals*, ed. and trans. Walter Kaufmann (New York: Vintage, 1969), I §14; III §18. Sigmund Freud's most direct critique of neighbor love is found in *Civilization and Its Discontents*, trans. Joan Riviere (New York: Doubleday, 1958), 58-59, 65, 104-5.

There have also been disturbing omissions. As just one example, we find few women like Julian of Norwich who are given significant voice in the mainstream canon of Western Christian thought, which has greatly impoverished it. These failures and omissions give credence to modern critics of Christian neighbor love. As I wrote in chapter one, neighbor love is an ethic of solidarity rather than superiority, and so I believe these critics should be seen as collaborators rather than competitors in our calling to love our neighbors as ourselves.

Still, the neighbor-love movement Jesus launched brought massive transformations for human flourishing and points to how we ended up codifying a Universal Declaration of Human Rights. It also contains within itself the moral resources to critique and reform itself. This is a primary intention of this book. We have come a long way from the ancient world's "natural inequality" and found an expansive basis for living together with other people—if, that is, we are willing to wake up from what John Stuart Mill calls "the deep slumber of a decided opinion" and "frequently, fully, and fearlessly" revive neighbor love. Ferdosa bears witness that this ancient movement can still bring healing and hope for our world in the face of othering today. The Neighbor-Love Movement presses on in this hope.

In the next chapter, we turn to explore neighbor love in the twentieth century. This was a time with many catastrophic examples of othering. But it also witnessed some of the most inspiring exemplars of neighbor love in the ever-evolving movement Jesus started.

6

TWENTIETH-CENTURY EXEMPLARS OF NEIGHBOR LOVE

Bonhoeffer, Weil, King, Romero, and Teresa

Growing up outside Chicago in my evangelical family, I had no idea that neighbor love would lead me to Ethiopia and work amid civil war. That wasn't on my radar.

My family traveled extensively in the United States, but we never really crossed the border. I still remember hearing racist jokes about our Black and Mexican neighbors. I'm grateful for the way my parents taught me to love my neighbors next door and to see value in all people. But I wasn't taught that neighbor love originated as a prophetic response to othering and mobilized a revolutionary movement to heal it. We mowed our neighbor's lawn, picketed the abortion clinic, stuffed letters for local politicians, and cheered for the American military in Iraq after 9/11. Neighbor love didn't disrupt our safe suburban lifestyle or our American Christian nationalism.

Still, I did something as a teenager that changed my life: I took the Bible seriously. I spent countless hours studying the Hebrew prophets, Jesus' teaching in the Gospels, and how the first Christians practiced their universal vision of neighbor love. In college, this study inspired me to leave home and do an internship at a social center for impoverished women and children in Addis Ababa called the Mercy Center.

Thereafter, neighbor love rapidly evolved for me. It shifted from being "a dead dogma" into an othering-abolishing vision of hope that I was "frequently, fully, and fearlessly" discussing with my friends and students. I met Eyob, married Lily, did a PhD in Christian ethics, met Ferdosa, and then the Neighbor-Love Movement was born on the brink of Ethiopia's civil war.

Twentieth-Century Exemplars of Neighbor Love

When we designed the Neighbor-Love Movement's messaging, we wanted to introduce Ethiopia's youth to inspiring exemplars who had practiced neighbor love in the face of othering. The public lynchings, mass displacements, and rumors of civil war were rapidly escalating. Othering was tearing Ethiopia apart. How, then, had seeing others as neighbors brought healing and hope in different contexts with similar crises?

In this book, we've followed neighbor love from its ancient origins in Israel, through the movement Jesus started, and across its history to the nineteenth century. In this chapter, we turn to look at five inspiring exemplars of neighbor love in the twentieth century. Happily, there are countless others we could explore. But these five have been particularly inspiring for me in my work with the Neighbor-Love Movement: Dietrich Bonhoeffer, Simone Weil, Martin Luther King Jr., Óscar Romero, and Mother Teresa.

Each of them practiced Jesus' universal vision of neighbor love in particular contexts and did so with great courage in the face of extreme othering. They worked amid antisemitic genocide, racial segregation, and the oppression of impoverished laborers and orphans in subordinated castes. Women and men, they represent diverse traditions in the Christian movement. Their locations included Europe, the United States, Latin America, and India. Some of them died young martyrs; some lived to old age.

None of them was without limitation and failure, as none of us is. But each of them uniquely practiced what they preached. Their life and love, words and work were powerfully integrated. In his poem "The Garrison," W. H. Auden writes, "To serve as a paradigm now of what a plausible Future might be is what we're here for."[1] These people present a paradigm of a plausible future for us today in the twenty-first century—a future in which all others are loved as neighbors, a future in which we have a basis for living together as one human family.

DIETRICH BONHOEFFER: BECOMING CHRISTS FOR OTHERS

Dietrich Bonhoeffer (1906–1945) grew up in a large German family with a rich history of academic scholarship, pastoral ministry, and public service.[2]

---

[1] W. H. Auden, "The Garrison," in *W. H. Auden: Collected Poems*, ed. Edward Mendelson (New York: Random House, 1976), 633-34.

[2] For a brief biography of Bonhoeffer through the lens of moral leadership, see David Gushee and Colin Holtz, *Moral Leadership for a Divided Age: Fourteen People Who Dared to Change Our World* (Grand Rapids, MI: Brazos, 2018), 155-78.

He was a Lutheran theologian, university professor, dissident pastor, beloved friend, and Nazi resister. In the wake of World War I, he started his career amid Adolf Hitler's rise to power.

Othering fueled Hitler. He saw it as the key to his power and what he called a "Greater Germany." In 1933, Hitler made his vision clear:

> My program for educating youth is hard. Weakness must be hammered away. In my castles of the Teutonic Order [a Christian military society], a young generation will grow up before which the world will tremble. I want the young to be violent, domineering, fearless, cruel. . . . The free, splendid beast of prey must once again flash from its eyes. . . . That is how I will eradicate thousands of years of human domestication.[3]

For Hitler, neighbor love wasn't an inspiring movement of human liberation. It was "thousands of years of human domestication." He wanted to "eradicate" it, resuscitate the predatory ethic of ancient culture, and create what he called "the New Order."

To do so, Hitler sought to unify White Germans by othering Jews into their enemies. He dehumanized them as "rats" and insisted that Jews were fundamentally "alien" to Germany's "Aryan" race. He blamed them for impoverishing its power and eventually mobilized his "final solution" to annihilate them.

Sadly, most German Christians, raised in the church that Luther established, were intoxicated by Hitler's vision. In Bonhoeffer's home region, 89 percent of Christian leaders pledged their loyalty to Hitler.[4] The outcome of this extreme othering was one of the most atrocious genocides in history. Over six million Jews and other minorities like Black and queer people were murdered.

But also in 1933, Dietrich Bonhoeffer became the first Christian to publicly oppose Hitler's othering vision. Bonhoeffer was only twenty-seven years old, but he soon became a founder of the Confessing Church, which broke away from Nazified German Christianity. In 1935, Bonhoeffer opened an underground seminary to train dissident pastors who would courageously practice Jesus' vision of neighbor love against Hitler's genocidal othering. In 1943, after joining the resistance movement to overthrow Hitler, Bonhoeffer was arrested by the Gestapo and jailed in Berlin's notorious Tegel

---

[3]Quoted in Jonathan Glover, *Humanity: A Moral History of the Twentieth Century*, 2nd ed. (New Haven, CT: Yale University Press, 2012), 337.

[4]See Eberhard Bethge, *Dietrich Bonhoeffer: A Biography*, rev. ed. (Minneapolis: Fortress, 2000), 601.

Prison. From his cell in 1944, Bonhoeffer summarized the vision of neighbor love that had inspired his subversive work:

> Our relationship to God is no "religious" relationship to some highest, most powerful, and best being imaginable—that is no genuine transcendence. Instead, our relationship to God is a new life in "being there for others," through participation in the being of Jesus. The transcendent is not the infinite, unattainable task, but the neighbor within reach in any given situation.[5]

Bonhoeffer continued developing his vision of this "new life in being there for others" in prison to his last breath. With his final recorded words before his execution in the Flossenbürg concentration camp in 1945, Bonhoeffer confessed, "This is for me the end, but also the beginning. . . . I believe in the principle of our Universal Christian brotherhood which rises above all national hatreds and that our victory is certain."[6]

Against Hitler, Bonhoeffer didn't see the thousands of years of neighbor love that came before him as "human domestication." Instead, its universal vision of the human family laid "the foundations for a meaningful human life." In fact, in a time of genocidal othering, it endured as "a basis for living together with other people"—what Bonhoeffer soon before his execution called "the most important question for the future."[7]

Bonhoeffer spoke and wrote incessantly about neighbor love. But we can summarize his ethics as a christological vision of others and an integrated practice of sharing life with them. At heart, it's "a new life in being there for others."

Throughout his short career, Bonhoeffer wrote about how we meet Jesus Christ—"God himself"—in the others we encounter in everyday life, especially the poor, powerless, and oppressed. Like Luther but liberated from his othering limitations, Bonhoeffer found this conviction in Matthew 25:40. There Jesus teaches, "Whatever you did for one of the least of these brothers and sisters of mine, you did for me." That is, Jesus claims that he himself is personally present in the hungry, the thirsty, the naked, the foreigner, the sick, and the prisoner—a striking summary of the victims Hitler mass-produced.

---

[5]Dietrich Bonhoeffer, "Outline for a Book," in *Letters and Papers from Prison*, ed. John de Gruchy (Minneapolis: Fortress, 2010), 501. I reconstruct Bonhoeffer's ethical vision in my book *Bonhoeffer's New Beginning: Ethics After Devastation* (Lanham, MD: Fortress Academic, 2018).

[6]Quoted in Andrew DeCort, "Appendix: Bonhoeffer's Last Words," in *Bonhoeffer's New Beginning*, 225-27.

[7]Dietrich Bonhoeffer, "Letter to Hans-Walter Schleicher on June 2, 1944," in *Letters and Papers from Prison*, 409.

Bonhoeffer took this teaching of Jesus extremely seriously and repeatedly returned to it. For example, in 1928, when Bonhoeffer was just twenty-two years old and training to become a pastor in Barcelona, he preached,

> Jesus Christ, God himself, speaks to us from every human being; the other person, this enigmatic impenetrable You, is God's claim on us, indeed, it is the holy God in person whom we encounter. God's claim is made on us in the wanderer on the street, the beggar at the door, the sick person at the door of the church, though certainly no less in every person near to us, in every person with whom we are together today. "Just as you did it to one of the least of these, you did it to me," Jesus says. I am for you, and you are for me God's claim, God himself; in this recognition, our gaze opens to the fullness of divine life in the world.[8]

As C. S. Lewis and Desmond Tutu would later say, there are no ordinary people. For Bonhoeffer, every human other is "the holy God in person," starting with the most vulnerable. When we learn to see people this way, "our gaze opens to the fullness of divine life in the world." In this vision, we behold our neighbor's face "as if [we] were seeing God's face."

As Hitler gained popularity, Bonhoeffer developed this vision further and repeated the paradox of neighbor love. He preached, "Whoever does not find his brother [in the other] also does not find God. It is for this reason that God himself became our brother in Christ, so that behind every brother and sister we see him again. . . . Each shall become a Christ for the other."[9] On the brink of the Holocaust, this paradox—that we only exclude ourselves from full belonging with God when we exclude others from it—takes on greater gravity. Bonhoeffer was opposing a cultural Christianity that called Jesus "Lord" but ended up participating in another lord's (*Führer*) annihilation of six million neighbors. From before it started, Bonhoeffer resisted this "cheap grace" that claims a religious identity while othering neighbors and reclaimed Jesus' "costly discipleship." To the end, he insisted, "The transcendent is not the infinite, unattainable task, but the neighbor within reach in any given situation."

---

[8] Dietrich Bonhoeffer, "Sermon on Matthew 28:20 from Barcelona on April 15, 1928," in *Barcelona, Berlin, New York: 1928–1931*, ed. Clifford Green (Minneapolis: Fortress, 2008), 492, 494-95.
[9] Dietrich Bonhoeffer, "Sermon on Genesis 32:25-32; 33:10 from March 13, 1932," in *Ecumenical, Academic & Pastoral Work: 1931–1932*, ed. Victoria Barnett et al. (Minneapolis: Fortress, 2012), 432.

Bonhoeffer's vision of neighbor love transfigures how we see others. Whenever we see anyone, including ourselves, we glimpse God's face. And this face cries out for our reverence and responsibility. Bonhoeffer writes, "You who give yourself completely to your neighbor are giving yourself to God; through your neighbor, you will be redeemed by God."[10] Here again Bonhoeffer alludes to his vision of "each becoming a christ for the other." What heals us is not a religious identity but becoming an embodiment of Christ's love with and for others. The love—not the label—redeems us.

Bonhoeffer's vision of the other as a neighbor thus enabled him to see through Hitler's othering delusion, which dehumanized Jews into "rats" to be "exterminated." It also made actively assisting or passively ignoring their arrest and execution impossible. Like Paul and the Didache, Bonhoeffer insisted, "The honor of the other is more important than my own."[11]

Bonhoeffer's spiritual classic *Life Together* grew out of his underground seminary in Finkenwalde, where he trained dissident pastors. In it he describes forms of service in community that embody this prophetic vision of neighbor love and make it real in practice. We can briefly summarize them.

First, Bonhoeffer writes that listening to others is the primary and most important practice of neighbor love. We love God by listening to God's Word; similarly, we love people by listening to their words. Bonhoeffer writes, "We do God's work for our brothers and sisters when we learn to listen to them." Here he critiques our tendency to preach at others or offer cheap answers to their questions. He insists,

> Listening can be a greater service than speaking. Many people seek a sympathetic ear and do not find it among Christians, because these Christians are talking even when they should be listening. But Christians who can no longer listen to one another will soon no longer be listening to God either; they will always be talking even in the presence of God. The death of the spiritual life starts here, and in the end there is nothing left but empty spiritual chatter and clerical condescension which chokes on pious words. Those who cannot listen long and patiently will always be talking past others, and finally no longer will even notice it. Those who think their time is too precious to spend listening

---

[10] Dietrich Bonhoeffer, "Sermon on Luke 17:33 from October 21, 1928," in Green, *Barcelona, Berlin, New York*, 535.
[11] See Dietrich Bonhoeffer, *Life Together*, ed. Geffrey Kelly (Minneapolis: Fortress, 1996), 96-97.

will never really have time for God and others, but only for themselves and for their own words and plans.[12]

Here Bonhoeffer diagnoses how his Christian culture collapsed into othering. Rather than empathically listening to others, including othered Jewish neighbors, Christians had fallen prey to Hitler's "empty spiritual chatter" and their church leaders' "clerical condescension." For Bonhoeffer, "The death of the spiritual life starts here." When we no longer listen to others and the realities of their lived experience, we also stop listening to God.

But like Julian saw Jesus as "our true mother" who sees us, Bonhoeffer saw God as the great listener who hears us. Neighbor love calls us to imitate God and become empathetic listeners who hear others' voices and respond to them. This is the only way we can learn to speak a truly "liberating and healing word."[13]

Second, then, Bonhoeffer teaches that neighbor love leads to "active helpfulness" with others. He writes, "Nobody is too good for the lowest service. Those who worry about the loss of time entailed by such small, external acts of helpfulness are usually taking their own work too seriously."[14]

Here Bonhoeffer attacks othering idols such as status and busyness—idols that ultimately enabled the Holocaust to emerge and escalate. When we see others as neighbors, we no longer see ourselves as above them and so too important or busy to help them. Bonhoeffer warns us to be ready for God's interruption, lest we become like the priest who passed by the suffering man on the roadside. Neighbor love grows in what Bonhoeffer calls "the school of humility," where we learn "not to spare our hand where it can perform a service."[15]

Bonhoeffer himself helped Jews escape from Germany to Switzerland. Unless our hands are actively serving our neighbors, Bonhoeffer teaches that our mouths should remain silent about God and our religion. Like Bucer, he asks, "What is more perilous than speaking God's word superfluously?"[16]

Third, Bonhoeffer writes that when we listen to others and become active in serving them, we must be willing to suffer for them. Recall that Bonhoeffer taught this vision in his underground seminary for dissident pastors

---

[12]Bonhoeffer, *Life Together*, 98.
[13]Bonhoeffer, *Life Together*, 103.
[14]Bonhoeffer, *Life Together*, 99.
[15]Bonhoeffer, *Life Together*, 100.
[16]Bonhoeffer, *Life Together*, 100.

as Nazi terror escalated. The Gestapo would eventually close his school and ban Bonhoeffer from writing. His words are beautiful and challenging:

> The law of Christ is a law of forbearance. Forbearance means enduring and suffering. The other person is a burden to the Christian, in fact for the Christian most of all. The other person never becomes a burden at all for the pagans. They simply stay clear of every burden the other person may create for them. However, Christians must bear the burden of one another. They must suffer and endure one another. Only as a burden is the other really a brother or sister and not just an object to be controlled. The burden of human beings was even for God so heavy that God had to go to the cross suffering under it. God truly suffered and endured human beings in the body of Jesus Christ. But in so doing, God more than as a mother carries her child.[17]

Here Bonhoeffer alludes to Julian's mystical vision of God's mothering love and Kierkegaard's claim that Christian love discovers "the other" as a *neighbor* to begin with. He also echoes Kierkegaard's insight that the test of authentic neighbor love is whether we are willing to love others *as ourselves* to the point of suffering for them.

Bonhoeffer writes that this love drove Jesus to surrender the othering "save yourself" attitude and willingly endure an agonizing execution for our healing. In Bonhoeffer's context, where millions of Jews would soon be atrociously executed, his teaching that neighbor love must willingly embrace suffering for others was especially challenging. It explains why Bonhoeffer courageously chose to critique Hitler's ideology, participate in rescuing Jewish neighbors, and give his life to resisting Nazi genocide. For Bonhoeffer, "The church is church only when it is there for others," and genuinely being there for others requires suffering with them.[18]

Bonhoeffer's universal vision of neighbor love with its integrated practice of listening, service, and suffering penetrated through the delusions of Hitler's othering genocide. In its wreckage, it also pointed to an answer to the "ultimate question" of "how we can find a basis for living together with other people." When we learn to see others as Christ himself and thus hear their voices, help them, and suffer with them, we are not "domesticated," as Hitler insisted in his propagandistic "program for educating youth." We become what Bonhoeffer

---

[17]Bonhoeffer, *Life Together*, 100.
[18]Bonhoeffer, *Letters and Papers from Prison*, 503.

calls "the most revolutionary human being[s] on earth."[19] Alluding to Paul's letter to the Romans, this was his manifesto in the face of Hitler's madness:

> Christianity stands or falls with its revolutionary protest against violence, arbitrariness and pride of power and with its defense of the weak. I feel that Christianity is rather doing too little in showing these points than doing too much. Christianity has adjusted itself much too easily to the worship of power. It should give much more offense, more shock to the world, than it is doing. Christianity should take a more definite stand for the weak than to consider the potential moral right of the strong.[20]

Bonhoeffer's Christian community in Germany catastrophically failed in this calling and fell into extreme othering with its worship of power. But Bonhoeffer remained defiantly hopeful to the end. With his final words, he confessed the universal moral circle at the heart of the neighbor-love movement amid one of the most seemingly hopeless episodes of othering in human history: "I believe in the principle of our Universal Christian brotherhood which rises above all national hatreds and that our victory is certain."

SIMONE WEIL: A VOCATION BEYOND AN OTHERING CHURCH

A contemporary of Bonhoeffer, Simone Weil (1909–1943) was a French philosopher, political activist, and Christian mystic. In addition to her writing, Weil worked as a high school teacher, farmhand, and factory worker. Her passionate moral vision drove her to oppose fascism in Europe and its colonialism across the earth. She devoted her short life to advocating for a universal vision of human dignity, social justice, and global responsibility.[21]

Weil may seem like an unlikely choice to include among explicitly Christian exemplars of neighbor love. While she was deeply influenced and inspired by Christianity, she chose not to be baptized in her native Catholic Church and had an uneasy relationship with Christianity. (Weil was also not

---

[19]Dietrich Bonhoeffer, "Sermon on John 8:32 from 1932," in Barnett et al., *Ecumenical, Academic & Pastoral Work*, 471.
[20]Dietrich Bonhoeffer, "Sermon on 2 Corinthians 12:9 from London in 1934," in *London: 1933–1935*, ed. Keith Clements (Minneapolis: Fortress, 2007), 402. See Andrew DeCort, "Protest: Love's Primal Vocation," *Offensis: An Online Magazine for Theology* (Germany), February 10, 2022, https://offensis.de/protest-loves-primal-vocation-%EF%BF%BC/.
[21]Weil developed this vision in her posthumously published works *The Need for Roots: A Prelude Toward a Declaration of Duties to Mankind* (New York: Routledge, 2001) and *Oppression and Liberty* (New York: Routledge, 2001).

a formal member of any political party.) The cultural Christianity of Europe, which we glimpsed in Bonhoeffer's Germany, repulsed her. She didn't want to be part of a Catholic Church that wasn't truly *catholic* or universal.[22]

Weil wrote to antifascist priest Joseph-Marie Perrin that she had chosen to remain unbaptized in solidarity with others who had no home in the church. Her letter is worth quoting at length:

> If it were conceivable that in obeying God one should bring about one's own damnation while in disobeying him one should be saved, I should still choose the way of obedience. . . . I cannot help still wondering whether in these days when so large a proportion of humanity is submerged in materialism, God does not want there to be some men and women who have given themselves to him and to Christ and who yet remain outside the Church. . . . Nothing gives me more pain than the idea of separating myself from the immense and unfortunate multitude of unbelievers. I have the essential need, and I think I can say the vocation, to move among men of every class and complexion, mixing with them and sharing their life . . . merging into the crowd and disappearing among them, so that they show themselves as they are, putting off all disguises with me. It is because I long to know them so as to love them just as they are. For if I do not love them as they are, it will not be they whom I love, and my love will be unreal.[23]

As she articulates her "vocation" to "remain outside the Church" and "move among men of every class and complexion," Weil reverses the paradox of neighbor love: she excludes herself from an othering Christian church in order to recognize the belonging of all people in God's love—even if this should lead to her own "damnation." She says that "nothing gives [her] more pain" than separating herself from others. A love that remains distant from others is "unreal." Real love embraces others "just as they are." Here Weil does what her French contemporary Albert Camus claimed "Christianity never did: be concerned with the damned."[24]

---

[22]See Simone Weil, *Waiting for God* (New York: HarperPerennial, 2009), 31-32.
[23]Weil, *Waiting for God*, 6-7. Weil's Catholic contemporary Thomas Merton articulated a similar vocation. See Merton, *A Life in Letters: The Essential Collection* (New York: HarperOne, 2008), 345: "I believe my vocation is essentially that of a pilgrim and exile in life, that I have no proper place in this world but for that reason I am in some sense to be the friend and brother of people everywhere, especially those who are exiles and pilgrims like myself."
[24]Quoted in Patricia Munhall et al., *The Emergence of Man into the 21st Century* (Sudbury, MA: Jones and Bartlett, 2002), 401. Camus's critique of Christianity amid the horrors of the twentieth century is valid, but he was wrong that Christians haven't been deeply concerned for the damned

In another letter, she further unpacks for Father Perrin the motivation of her vocation. The heart of it is her opposition to religious othering. She writes,

> I am afraid of the Church patriotism existing in Catholic circles. By patriotism I mean the feeling one has for a terrestrial country. . . . I do not want any feeling of such a kind in myself. . . any feeling of this kind, whatever its object, would be fatal to me. There were some saints who endorsed the Crusades or the Inquisition. I cannot help thinking they were in the wrong. I cannot go against the light of conscience. . . . They were blinded by an exceptionally potent force. . . . I do not want to be adopted into a circle, to live among people who say "we" and to be part of an "us," to find I am "at home" in any human milieu whatever it may be.[25]

This "force" is another name for othering. She notes how "exceptionally potent" it becomes when it is justified by religion. A subtle philosopher herself, Weil was unpersuaded by Aquinas's loopholes in neighbor love, which allowed him to endorse the violence of the Crusades. She believed this violence worshiped "an *ersatz* divinity" rather than God.[26] In her quest to obey *God*, she understood that any "circle," any "we," any "home" that doesn't include everyone is ultimately "fatal."

Writing amid World War II, Weil's critique of Christian patriotism was not hyperbolic. We saw above how Hitler justified the horror of the Holocaust in the name of a greater Germany. In her spiritual autobiography, she quips that "a few sheep should remain outside the fold in order to bear witness that the love of Christ is essentially something different." Echoing the Epistle to Diognetus, she continues, "The children of God should not have any other country here below but the universe itself. . . . That is the native city to which we owe our love."[27]

Bonhoeffer, himself a Lutheran pastor, expressed the same conviction as Weil based on his vision of neighbor love. Commenting on Paul's letter to

---

across history. Paul himself writes in Rom 9:3 that he would rather be "accursed" than saved without the Jewish people. Based on Paul, Martin Bucer wrote in the sixteenth century, "[The Christian] commits no sin, therefore, who loves God and desires to please Him to such an extent that he is ready to forfeit his own salvation in order to obtain this blessedness for his neighbors." See Bucer, *Instruction in Christian Love*, trans. Paul Fuhrmann (Eugene, OR: Wipf & Stock, 2008), 32.

[25]Weil, *Waiting for God*, 12-13. See Martha Nussbaum et al., *For Love of Country: Debating the Limits of Patriotism* (Boston: Beacon, 1996).

[26]Weil, *Waiting for God*, 12.

[27]Weil, *Waiting for God*, 32, 49.

the Romans, Bonhoeffer writes, "[Paul in Romans 9:3] curses himself out of community with God and from his people to the place of damnation, where they are, precisely because he truly loves both community with God and his people, which means he is obedient to the command that we should unreservedly surrender ourselves to the neighbor."[28] Mother Teresa, a Catholic nun we'll explore below, expressed a similar vision of giving up her own salvation if others were still damned: "I will be continually absent from Heaven—to light the light of those in darkness on earth."[29]

With this moral vocation, Weil was deeply committed to entering into the lived experience of others. She wasn't content with abstract ideals and detached advocacy. She wanted an embodied solidarity, what she called "a truly incarnated Christianity," especially with oppressed neighbors. She was committed to feeling the "reality and presence of God through all external things" and people.[30]

We see this embodied solidarity in her decision to take a leave of absence from her teaching and work as a farmhand at a French vineyard and as a factory worker in Paris. Weil wanted to experience firsthand what it felt like to do underpaid labor in harsh conditions. This radical empathy also led to her death. Although her exact motivations are not documented, many believe that Weil went on a hunger strike to protest World War II and share the suffering of its victims who had little to eat. Eventually, she died of malnutrition in England at thirty-four.[31]

What drove Weil to her vocation of radical empathy and embodied activism? It was her mystical vision of neighbor love harking back to Julian of Norwich and Jesus himself.

In her spiritual autobiography, Weil writes, "I always had the Christian idea of love for one's neighbor, to which I gave the name justice—a name it bears in many passages of the Gospel and which is so beautiful."[32] As her

---

[28]Dietrich Bonhoeffer, *Sanctorum Communio: A Theological Study of the Sociology of the Church*, ed. Clifford Green (Minneapolis: Fortress, 1998), 185
[29]Mother Teresa, *Come Be My Light: The Private Writings of the "Saint of Calcutta,"* ed. Brian Kolodiejchuk (New York: Doubleday, 2007), 230.
[30]Weil, *Waiting for God*, 32, 3-4. I'm grateful to Alicia Hawkins for the term "embodied solidarity."
[31]See Katie Tobin, "The Enigma of Simone Weil," *Verso Books*, February 28, 2024, www.versobooks.com/blogs/news/the-enigma-of-simone-weil.
[32]Weil, *Waiting for God*, 24. See bell hooks, *All About Love: New Visions* (New York: HarperCollins, 2001), 30, 33, "Without justice there can be no love. . . . The heart of justice is truth telling, seeing ourselves and the world the way it is rather than the way we want it to be."

childhood faith matured, Weil said that, even in her suffering, she experienced the presence of God like "the smile of a beloved face." She writes that as she labored in the vineyards, she prayed Jesus' prayer to "our Father" "each morning with absolute attention." This prayer with its universal "we" ushered her into an ever-expanding vision of divine love.[33]

Similar to Julian's vision of the whole universe contained in a chestnut, Weil envisions all of creation as an egg. She writes,

> Every existing thing is equally upheld in its existence by God's creative love. The friends of God should love him to the point of merging their love with his with regard to all things here below. When a soul has attained a love filling the whole universe, indiscriminately, this love becomes the bird with golden wings that pierces an opening in the egg of the world. After that, such a soul loves the universe, not from within but from without; from the dwelling place of the Wisdom of God, our first-born brother.[34]

Julian's mystical vision led her to see Jesus as "our true mother," who guides us into "the wisdom and the kindness of motherhood." Weil's vision leads her to see Jesus as "our first-born brother," who incarnates "the Wisdom of God." This divine wisdom guides us into "a love filling the whole universe."

In her essays, Weil develops her vision of God's act of creation as God's own primal act of neighbor love. She writes,

> God created through love and for love. God did not create anything except love itself, and the means to love. . . . Because no other could do it, he himself went to the greatest possible distance, the infinite distance. This infinite distance between God and God, this supreme tearing apart, this agony beyond all others, this marvel of love, is the crucifixion. . . . This tearing apart, over which supreme love places the bond of supreme union, echoes perpetually across the universe in the midst of the silence, like two notes, separate yet melting into one, like a pure and heart-rending harmony. This is the Word of God. The whole creation is nothing but its vibration. . . . Those who persevere in love hear this note from the very lowest depths into which affliction has thrust them.[35]

---

[33]Weil, *Waiting for God*, 27, 29.
[34]Weil, *Waiting for God*, 50.
[35]Weil, *Waiting for God*, 72. I hear echoes of this "heart-rending harmony" in the music of Jon Guerra and Emile Mosseri.

Weil's mystical vision is complex but compelling. If God alone has existed from eternity, then God's act of creation was a radical new beginning in the life of God. In a sense, God had to accept a "supreme tearing apart" in order to make room for others. Weil calls this "the infinite distance between God and God."

The "and" is where otherness exists, what she names the "voluntary effacement of God," in which God is apparently absent but secretly present. "On God's part," she observes, "creation is not an act of self-expansion but of restraint and renunciation."[36] Before creation, God was All. But after it, God became One among others. Reality itself became a neighborhood in which God lives with others, including all space, matter, and people. For Weil, all of reality is thus the vibration of this world-creating love.

From this perspective, God's act of creation and Jesus' acceptance of crucifixion are really one and the same event: love embracing the other. Weil calls this "supreme union" vibrating with "heart-rending harmony." For her, this mystical vision should saturate our material experience. She writes, "This universe where we are living, and of which we form a tiny particle, is the distance put by Love between God and God." Thus, alluding to her time working in the factories of Paris, she observes, that when we finish our "apprenticeship" in divine love, we can recognize "things and events, everywhere and always, as vibrations of the same divine and infinitely sweet word [of love]."[37]

This mystical vision of creation led to Weil's universal understanding of neighbor love, which disestablishes and seeks to abolish all othering. Writing about Jesus' imperative to love our neighbors in the parable of the Good Samaritan, she points out that "the neighbor is a being of whom nothing is known, lying naked, bleeding, and unconscious on the road. It is a question of completely anonymous, and for that reason, completely universal love." Weil describes this love as opening to "a miraculous newness," indeed, "a new revelation of the universe and of human destiny." "Here," she writes, "we must love absolutely everything"—not just our human neighbors but all our neighbors in the material reality we share, including the earth itself.[38]

Like Bonhoeffer's practice of listening, Weil taught that neighbor love gets embodied in the practice of attention. As a teacher at a girls' secondary

---

[36]Weil, *Waiting for God*, 89.
[37]Weil, *Waiting for God*, 75, 78.
[38]Weil, *Waiting for God*, 50-51, 3.

school, she writes, "the development of the faculty of attention forms the real object and almost the sole interest of studies." For Weil, the "right use of school studies" is thus training our attention. Using the challenge of learning geometry as her example, she observes that "twenty minutes of concentrated, untiring attention is infinitely better than three hours of the kind of frowning application that leads us to say with a sense of duty done: 'I have worked well!'"[39]

Weil understands our everyday lack of attention as an existential expression of othering at work within us. She writes, "Something in our soul has a far more violent repugnance for true attention than the flesh has for bodily fatigue. This something is much more closely connected with evil than is the flesh. That is why every time we really concentrate our attention, we destroy the evil in ourselves." The reason we feel "repugnance" for attention, Weil argues, is that it requires us to empty ourselves like God in creation. It is an act of self-restraint and opening to otherness. She writes, "Attention consists of suspending our thought, leaving it detached, empty, and ready to be penetrated by the object." In short, it is an act of intentional "waiting" on what is other than ourselves, like God did when God created the world. Thus, when we practice attention, "we destroy the evil in ourselves" that wants to diminish or destroy the otherness God has created in love.[40]

Weil then immediately applies this practice of attention to loving our neighbors. She writes,

> The love of our neighbor, which we know to be the same love [as the love of God], is made of this same substance [of attention]. Those who are unhappy have no need for anything in this world but people capable of giving them their attention. The capacity to give one's attention to a sufferer is a very rare and difficult thing; it is almost a miracle; it *is* a miracle. Nearly all those who think they have this capacity do not possess it. Warmth of heart, inquisitiveness, pity are not enough. . . . The love of our neighbor in all its fullness simply means being able to say to him: "What are you going through?" It is a recognition that the sufferer exists, not only as a unit of collection, or a specimen from the social laboratory labeled "unfortunate," but as a human, exactly like us, who was one day stamped with a special mark of affliction.[41]

---

[39] Weil, *Waiting for God*, 58, 61.
[40] Weil, *Waiting for God*, 61-62.
[41] Weil, *Waiting for God*, 64.

Writing soon before the Holocaust, Weil's vision of neighbor love as attention and the ability to ask a suffering person, "What are you going through?" is extremely profound. In a time when the moral circle, including the *Christian* moral circle, was rapidly closing, Weil calls her students to open themselves and wait on others in pain with focused attention. She calls this a "way of looking" that "empties itself of all its own contents in order to receive into itself the being it is looking at, just as he is, in all his truth."[42]

An essential aspect of what made the Holocaust possible was precisely the othering unwillingness to look at a suffering neighbor "stamped with a special mark of affliction" "in all of his truth." This core practice of neighbor love, then, is indeed "a very rare and difficult thing" in our apprenticeship of neighbor love. It is like God embracing an "agony beyond all others" and creating the world when we were nothing. In a Christianized Europe that was literally reducing millions of people to nothing, Weil's vision was prophetic and invited very practical transformation.

Weil concludes then, "Every school exercise, thought of in this way, is like a sacrament."[43] We see that, remaining outside an othering church, Weil's radical activism and embodied solidarity with excluded and oppressed neighbors was really her sacramental practice of neighbor love through focused attention. Like Bonhoeffer and Jesus himself, this practice ultimately led to her death as she protested the violence of extreme othering and voluntarily entered into the suffering of the countless neighbors it was starving to death. Her Christian vocation offers hope to many people today who also feel like they can have no home in an othering church.

MARTIN LUTHER KING JR.: THE SALVATION OF OUR CIVILIZATION

Bitterly, the othering that Bonhoeffer and Weil opposed in Europe had been engineered in America. The Nazis studied the ideology and institutionalization of racialized segregation that White Americans had used against African Americans for centuries. James Baldwin calls this "the myth of white supremacy."[44] The Germans then applied it to Jews and other minorities in Germany, as well as the other countries it conquered for Hitler's "Greater

---

[42] Weil, *Waiting for God*, 65.
[43] Weil, *Waiting for God*, 63.
[44] James Baldwin, "The Dangerous Road Before Martin Luther King," in *James Baldwin: Collected Essays*, ed. Toni Morrison (New York: Library of America, 1998), 657.

Germany."⁴⁵ Alas, neighbor love truly became "a dead dogma" in white supremacist America.⁴⁶

Like Bonhoeffer, Martin Luther King Jr. (1929–1968) only lived to the age of thirty-nine. His vision and practice of neighbor love were so countercultural and challenging to the status quo in America that he was ridiculed, jailed, and eventually assassinated in Memphis.⁴⁷ In the United States, this status quo had been cemented by centuries of genocidal violence against Native Americans since Columbus landed in the New World in 1492, the enslavement of Africans from 1619 to 1863, and then the segregation of African Americans after 1863 until 1965. Throughout American history, non-White "others" have been seen as fundamentally unrelated and less than White Americans.

Raised amid segregation in the South, King was the son of a Baptist minister. His mother also had a deep lineage of Black preachers in America. King himself went on to become an eloquent Baptist minister and was deeply inspired by the moral vision of Black theology that developed amid centuries of suffering.⁴⁸ In 1955, King earned his PhD in theology, just a few months before a series of lynchings that drove Rosa Parks to stay in her seat in a segregated bus in Alabama. Parks was arrested.

In his book *Strength to Love*, King writes, "The end of life is not to be happy nor to achieve pleasure and avoid pain but to do the will of God, come what may."⁴⁹ This is what King attempted to do in the neighbor-love movement he led in America, which we know as the civil rights movement.

King led the 381-day Montgomery bus boycott in 1955 soon after Park's arrest. In 1957 he became the founding president of the Southern Christian Leadership Conference at age twenty-seven. Deeply influenced by the creative nonviolence of Jesus and Gandhi, King and his colleagues led marches,

---

⁴⁵Isabel Wilkerson documents this extensively in *Caste: The Origin of Our Discontents* (New York: Random House, 2023), 78-88. She notes, "Hitler especially marveled at the American 'knack for maintaining an air of robust innocence in the wake of mass death'" (81). Wilkerson uses *caste* as her word for othering and the hierarchical order it creates. See also Jan Gross, *Neighbors: The Destruction of the Jewish Community in Jedwabne, Poland* (New York: Penguin, 2002).
⁴⁶See John Compton, *The End of Empathy: Why White Protestants Stopped Loving Their Neighbors* (New York: Oxford University Press, 2020).
⁴⁷For a brief biography of King through the lens of moral leadership, see Gushee and Holtz, *Moral Leadership for a Divided Age*, 297-319.
⁴⁸See James Cone, *God of the Oppressed*, rev. ed. (Maryknoll, NY: Orbis, 1997).
⁴⁹Martin Luther King Jr., *Strength to Love* (Minneapolis: Fortress, 2010), 151.

sit-ins, and other forms of civil disobedience in protest of the racialized, institutionalized othering in America.

For his work, King won the Nobel Peace Prize in 1964, just four years before being assassinated by a White nationalist in 1968. King was one among many others, both in his struggle for civil rights and in the price that he paid for it. Medgar Evers (1963), Malcolm X (1965), and Fred Hampton (1969) were also assassinated, to name just a few. James Baldwin called this mournful elegy, "which no American is prepared to hear," "many thousands gone."[50]

Still, King's sacrificial love for othered neighbors in America was ultimately, if still incompletely, victorious. Legal segregation was overthrown in 1965. The cancer of racial othering was brought to the center of consciousness in American society. After his death, King was awarded the Presidential Medal of Freedom. With it, he was named "the conscience of his generation," who, as Paul pictured Jesus two thousand years before, tore down the dividing wall of segregation with the power of love. Millions of people around the world continue to be inspired by his example to practice nonviolent love in the face of othering today.

King was a prolific preacher and writer. Baldwin says that King penetrated into the American heart unlike any Black author before him. Again and again, King's prophetic witness focused on Jesus' ethic of neighbor love. Baldwin calls him "a man solidly anchored in those spiritual realities concerning which he can be so eloquent."[51]

King was careful to define what love really means. In a speech given at the University of California in 1957, King defined love as "understanding, creative, redemptive good will for all [people]." He clarified that *loving* is not the same thing as *liking*. As Jesus taught, King said that love is not motivated "because [people] are likable, not because they do things that attract us, but because God loves" all people, despite our hateful actions. And thus, while love does not affirm injustice or evil—in fact, it hates injustice and evil— "[love is] a willingness to go to any length to restore community" following the redemptive will of God.[52]

---

[50] James Baldwin, "Many Thousands Gone," in *Collected Essays*, 18.
[51] James Baldwin, "The Dangerous Road Before Martin Luther King," in *Collected Essays*, 639.
[52] Martin Luther King Jr., *A Testament of Hope: The Essential Writings and Speeches of Martin Luther King Jr.*, ed. James Washington (New York: HarperCollins, 1986), 13, 16. King's contemporary Dorothy Day, who also taught and practiced nonviolence, writes, "We must love to the

King was serious about going to any length to restore community. In a fierce Christmas sermon, he confronted the persecution he was facing and declared, "We shall match your capacity to inflict suffering by our capacity to endure suffering. We will meet your physical force with soul force. Do to us what you will and we will still love you."[53] This was the moral center of King's practice of nonviolent neighbor love. He clarifies its universal vision in a sermon titled "On Being a Good Neighbor," based on Jesus' parable of the good Samaritan. Here again, King challenges othering in America and across cultures. He preaches, "[A neighbor is] anyone who lies in need at life's roadside. He is neither Jew nor Gentile; he is neither Russian nor American; he is neither Negro nor white. He is 'a certain man'—any needy man—on one of the numerous Jericho roads of life."[54] King then expounds three requirements of practicing this nonviolent neighbor love.

The first is "universal altruism." King describes this as "regard for and devotion to the interests of others." Such universal love goes beyond the accidents of "race, religion, and nationality." It overcomes the mindset that "does not really mind what happens to the people outside [one's] group," which sees others merely as things and not as people. King writes, "The good neighbor looks beyond the external accidents and discerns those inner qualities that make men human and, therefore, brothers."[55]

Like Bonhoeffer's call to embrace suffering, the second requirement of authentic neighbor love is "dangerous altruism." Reminding us of Martin Luther's argument about how Christians should respond to a deadly plague, King argues that neighbor love that isn't willing to take risks for others and face real danger isn't love at all. Appealing to the example of Abraham Lincoln on the brink of the Civil War, he writes, "The ultimate measure of a man is not where he stands in moments of comfort and convenience but where he stands at times of challenge and controversy. The true neighbor will risk his position, his prestige, and even his life for the welfare of others."[56] This commitment to dangerous altruism is what energized King to remain unwavering even in the face of arrest, the bombing of his home, and his eventual assassination.

---

point of folly." See Day, *By Little and by Little: The Selected Writings of Dorothy Day*, ed. Robert Ellsberg (New York: Knopf, 1984), 99.
[53]King, *Testament to Hope*, 256.
[54]King, *Strength to Love*, 22.
[55]King, *Strength to Love*, 22-25.
[56]King, *Strength to Love*, 26-27.

The third requirement of neighbor love is what he calls "excessive altruism." This love not only cares for all people and is committed to making personal risks for them. True neighbors open their soul to others and have deep empathy for them. Here we are reminded of Bonhoeffer's call to practice listening and Weil's call to attention. Rather than simply doing things for people, King writes that loving neighbors want to be *with* people—to share their life in all of its celebration and suffering. He insists, "True neighborliness requires personal concern" that goes "far beyond the call of duty" and into our "inner attitudes" and "person-to-person relations."[57]

Still, King also realized that some of our neighbors may also be our enemies. Like the other followers of Jesus we've studied in this book, King didn't have a naive understanding of our humanity. The extreme othering, exclusion, and violence that he and his community suffered in America made this impossible.

Inspired by Jesus, King saw nonviolent neighbor love as a creative response to enemies rather than a reactive conformity to the conflict they cause. Like his vision of neighbor love, he taught three practical ways to love our enemies. Rather than "a pious injunction," he called this practice "an absolute necessity for our survival."[58]

First, King argues, "We must develop and maintain the capacity to forgive." He is clear that forgiveness does not mean "ignoring what has been done" or acting like it wasn't wrong. Forgiveness means releasing the other's failure and removing the "barrier to relationship," which allows a new beginning. King is blunt in saying that if we can't forgive our enemies, loving them will be impossible.[59]

Second, King argues that we need to realize that our enemies' evil actions don't express the totality of who they are or their nature. We saw this idea in Thomas Aquinas. King insists that there is some good "even in our worst enemy," as well as some evil in ourselves. Here King resists essentializing enmity and calls us to wrestle with the "persistent civil war" that rages inside each one of us. Doing so interrupts our temptation to other our enemies or to see ourselves as totally innocent. Even our enemies bear the image of God, which calls for our respect and restraint. None of us is totally evil or totally good. We are all complex and need mercy.

---

[57]King, *Strength to Love*, 28.
[58]King, *Strength to Love*, 44.
[59]King, *Strength to Love*, 44-45.

Third, loving the enemy requires understanding them and "winning their friendship" rather than trying to defeat or humiliate them. This is where King's definition of love becomes extremely important and practical. King is not calling for fuzzy feelings or to "like" enemies who try to kill us. He's calling for "creative, redemptive goodwill." This will refuses to give up and does everything it can to restore community.[60] Here neighbor love becomes curious and asks questions such as, "How did our conflict begin? How might I have contributed to it? What can I do to build a bridge, even if the other should go first?" Astonishingly, King refers explicitly to the people who bombed his home and tried to kill his children. And yet, he still challenges himself to try to understand them and win their friendship.

Even after two thousand years of Christian history and White America's claim to be a "Christian nation," King realized that many people would still think that loving our enemies didn't make sense and wasn't worth the sacrifice. In response, he offers several reasons why we should embrace this countercultural practice of neighbor love.

King begins by pointing out that hating others who hate us only produces more hate. It's a dead end that escalates othering and initiates a race for domination. Everyone becomes poorer in the process. Courageous love is the only way to break the spiral of conflict. This is why King calls Jesus a "practical realist" when he commands us to love our enemies.[61]

King then argues that we must love our enemies because "hate scars the soul and distorts the personality."[62] Hate is like an acid that eats us alive and leaves us empty.[63] Even if we don't want to love others for their own sake, we should still love them for our own, lest we damage and divide ourselves with our hatred. Here King reminds us, "All men are caught in an inescapable network of mutuality, tied in a single garment of destiny. . . . I can never be what I ought to be until you are what you ought to be, and you can never be what you ought to be until I am what I ought to be. This is the interrelated structure of reality."[64] Or, as Baldwin writes, "Salvation, humanly speaking, is a two-way street."[65]

---

[60]King, *Strength to Love*, 46.
[61]King, *Strength to Love*, 44.
[62]King, *Strength to Love*, 47.
[63]See Aaron Beck, *Prisoners of Hate: The Cognitive Basis of Anger, Hostility, and Violence* (New York: Harper, 2000).
[64]King, *Strength to Love*, ix.
[65]Baldwin, "Dangerous Road," 647.

Moreover, love is the only way to transform an enemy into a friend. King understands that we can dominate and defeat our enemy, but they're still an enemy, even if they're dead. In fact, in doing so, we become like the one we hate. As the Didache teaches, if we really want to eliminate an enemy, the only way to do so is to eliminate our enmity or the hatred that mutilates us into enemies to begin with. Here King refers to Abraham Lincoln again, who appointed his archrival Edwin Stanton to serve in his cabinet. According to King, Lincoln said to people who thought he was crazy, "Yes, I know Mr. Stanton. I am aware of all the terrible things he has said about me. But after looking over the nation, I find he is the best man for the job."[66] In doing so, Lincoln overcame his hatred, made a friend of an enemy, and did what was best for the unity of the country in a time of bitter conflict.

King gives a final, specifically Christian reason to love our enemies: God commands it. Here he repeats Jesus' paradox of neighbor love: we exclude ourselves from full belonging with God if we hold on to our hatred and exclude others from this love. As a Christian preacher, King took Jesus' command and its warning seriously.

King's ethics of neighbor love even for enemies powered his method of nonviolent resistance to institutionalized othering. Like Baldwin saw, this love amounts to "creat[ing] ourselves without finding it necessary to create an enemy."[67] Similarly, Audre Lorde calls this "the energy to pursue genuine change within our world, rather than merely settling for a shift of characters in the same weary drama."[68] King outlines this energizing method's core practices in his famous "Letter from Birmingham Jail."[69] According to King, when there is injustice in our society, we should follow four steps:

1. Research the facts to confirm that the injustice is real.
2. If it is, approach the perpetrator and ask them to negotiate for a non-violent resolution of the injustice.
3. If they refuse, purify ourselves of all othering and its reactive energy.[70]

---

[66] King, *Strength to Love*, 49.
[67] James Baldwin, *The Cross of Redemption: Uncollected Writings*, ed. Randall Kenan (New York: Vintage Books, 2010), 251.
[68] Audre Lorde, *The Master's Tools Will Never Dismantle the Master's House* (London: Penguin, 2018), 15.
[69] Martin Luther King Jr., "Letter from Birmingham Jail," in *Why We Can't Wait* (New York: HarperCollins, 1964), 78. See Michael Nagler, *The Nonviolence Handbook: A Guide for Practical Action* (San Francisco: Berrett-Koehler, 2014).
[70] For example, King and his movement held trainings in which each member would be put in the middle of a circle and subjected to cursing, screaming, and threats. These simulations were

4. Finally, engage in direct action to protest the injustice and awaken the conscience of society, even at personal cost.

King's creative, nonviolent method for transforming othering with neighbor love takes us back to his call for "dangerous altruism." He rejects what he called "easy answers" and "half-baked solutions." If othering is to be genuinely overcome and not reinscribed in our very resistance to it, we must embrace "a toughness of mind and tenderness of heart"—what King calls "a creative synthesis of opposites in fruitful harmony."[71] This requires doing our research, seeking negotiation, purifying ourselves, and taking the risks of nonviolence to transform the conflict of othering into "the beloved community"—what Baldwin more pointedly calls "the growing up of this dangerously adolescent country."[72]

Looking back, we can see that, in both Germany and America, neighbor love had become "a dead dogma" in "incrusted minds." Like Bonhoeffer wrote from prison to his church in Germany, which had adopted America's institutionalized othering, King challenged the church in America to examine itself and wake up from its slumber. He writes,

> If the church does not recapture its prophetic zeal, it will become an irrelevant social club without moral and spiritual authority.... A religion that professes a concern for the souls of men and is not equally concerned about the slums that damn them, the economic conditions that strangle them, and the social conditions that cripple them is a spiritually moribund religion.[73]

With relentless courage, King's prophetic call was for Christians everywhere to practice neighbor love beyond every boundary of race, religion, and nationalism. The moral circle is universal and includes us all. Each of us is morally connected to the other and equally precious in value. For King, like Weil, the stakes of recognizing this could not be higher: "This love might well be the salvation of our civilization.... Love is ultimately the only answer to mankind's problems.... He who has love has the key that unlocks the door to the meaning of ultimate reality."[74]

---

meant to prepare them to peacefully respond to psychological and physical violence. These trainings are depicted in the 2014 film *Selma*, directed by Ava DuVernay.
[71] King, *Strength to Love*, 1.
[72] Baldwin, "Dangerous Road," 641.
[73] King, *Strength to Love*, 92.
[74] King, *Testament to Hope*, 140, 250.

ÓSCAR ROMERO: A VOICE FOR THE VOICELESS

King critiqued "religion that professes a concern for the souls of men and is not equally concerned about the slums that damn them" and "the economic conditions that strangle them." Óscar Romero (1917–1980) gradually came to share King's prophetic vision. Similar to Weil, he then made social justice for impoverished farmers central to his work as San Salvador's archbishop.[75]

At the time, the Revolutionary Government Junta ruled El Salvador. This regime was infamous for its repression of impoverished farmers (*campesinos*) and brutal violence against any expression of dissent. With time, Romero discovered the integral implications of neighbor love in the face of this entrenched injustice. He then courageously devoted his life to Salvadoran liberation. Throughout his sermons in the capital city, he spoke to a Christian upper class that was othering guerrilla fighters and trying to make farmers out to be villains, even as the government that protected these elites was spreading terror for the most vulnerable. Romero's core message became that "the church has no enemies," which inspired him to call for reconciliation and restorative justice.[76]

Romero was a pastor with humble beginnings. He started training to become a carpenter, but when he was fourteen he left carpentry and entered seminary. Eventually he traveled to Rome to train to become a Catholic priest, and then he served as a pastor in San Miguel for twenty years.

In 1967, the fifty-year-old Romero moved to the capital city of San Salvador to work as the secretary of El Salvador's bishops. There he became friends with a fellow priest named Rutilio Grande. This passionate man ended up changing Romero's life.

A few years later, Romero himself became a bishop. At this time, he was a conservative church leader who criticized other Christian leaders for "mixing" the gospel with a passion for justice and freedom for the poor. He gained a reputation for being stubborn, unsympathetic, and even reactionary. But his conscience was pricked in 1975 when five peasants were massacred by the Revolutionary Government's security forces in his church

---

[75]For a brief biography of Romero through the lens of moral leadership, see Gushee and Holtz, *Moral Leadership for a Divided Age*, 203-26.

[76]I am particularly grateful for the insight of Colton Bernasol in this section. See his brilliant master's thesis, "Theology After Symbolic Devastation: Method in the Liberation Theologies of Juan Luis Segundo, Jon Sobrino, and M. Shawn Copeland" (MTS thesis, Garret-Evangelical Theological Seminary, 2022).

community. This violence provoked Romero to write a letter to El Salvador's president and opened him to a more radical liberation theology.

Two years later, Romero was elected to serve as the archbishop of San Salvador. This was a dark time of terrible violence in the country. The presidential election had been stolen, and protesters were massacred by the police as death squads terrorized El Salvador's impoverished farmers. Some think that Romero was chosen to become archbishop because this bookish, humble man was seen as a conservative who would keep quiet and not challenge the status quo.

But a month later, Romero's dear friend and fellow priest Rutilio Grande was also murdered by a death squad as he drove to minister at a rural church in the countryside. Once again, Romero's conscience was overwhelmed by the terrible violence in his society. But this time, the violence had become intensely personal in the killing of his friend.

In protest, Romero responded by closing the churches and canceling mass on the following Sunday in San Salvador. Instead, he led a single service in front of the central cathedral, which was attended by one hundred thousand people. Romero's funeral sermon for his martyred friend was titled "Dedicated Love." In it, he declared,

> Dear people of El Salvador, at this crossroad in our history it can seem that there is no other solution but to seek violence. I tell you, my sisters and brothers: Blessed be God who through the death of Father Grande is telling the Church: Yes, there is a solution. The solution is love. The solution is faith. The solution is found in the fact that the Church has no enemies. The solution is based on the reality that the Church is a circle in which God hopes to encounter all people.[77]

In his devastated grief, Archbishop Romero had finally, truly discovered the universality of neighbor love's moral circle for all people. It was no longer intellectual but existential. Romero declared to his one hundred thousand listeners that Father Grande had embodied the sacrificial death of Jesus and pointed the way to El Salvador's healing: "The Church has no enemies. . . . The Church is a circle in which God hopes to encounter all people."

---

[77] Óscar Romero, "Dedicated Love," homily, March 17, 1977, Romero Trust, www.romerotrust.org.uk/sites/default/files/homilies/dedicated_love.pdf.

Nevertheless, in the following months, the national crisis intensified. More church leaders were assassinated by the regime, and its army desecrated churches. A group called the White Warrior Union threatened to kill all Jesuit priests if they didn't exit the country within thirty days. Amid the terrible suffering of *campesinos* who were being exploited and oppressed on the land, and the systematic violence spreading throughout the country, Romero courageously rose up as a voice of the voiceless.

Romero's message centered on Christ's "preferential option for the poor," the maxim of the first generation of liberation theologians led by Gustavo Gutiérrez (1928–2024), whom Romero had initially held in suspicion. In *A Theology of Liberation*, Gutiérrez wrote, "The purpose of those who participate in the process of liberation is to create a new man. . . . We meet God in our encounter with men. . . . We love God by loving our neighbor. . . . To know God is to do justice."[78] This maxim echoed the biblical teaching that God loves all people but has a special concern for our poor and oppressed neighbors as Jesus said in Matthew 25:31-46.[79]

On February 5, 1978, Romero invoked Jesus' teaching in Matthew 25 and preached, "There is one rule by which to judge if God is near us or is far away. . . . Everyone concerned for the hungry, the naked, the poor, for those who have vanished in police custody, for the tortured, for prisoners, for all flesh that suffers, has God close at hand."[80] With this vision of God's presence among the suffering, Romero started using his Sunday sermons to condemn the regime's violence and to unpack the ethical implications of Christ's neighbor love. He would specifically name and talk about neighbors who had been abducted, tortured, or murdered in the country. In these sermons, he would ask the community for information about the victims and call them to comfort those who were grieving. He refused for the church to be silent or distant from the suffering. Thus, Romero's sermons and his faithful presence among the poor became a prophetic microphone of God's demand for justice, protection of the weak, and love for the stranger and enemy.

---

[78] Gustavo Gutiérrez, *A Theology of Liberation*, trans. Caridad Inda and John Eagleson (Maryknoll, NY: Orbis Books, 1973), 189, 194, 196, 199. See also 201: "We find the Lord in our encounters with men, especially the poor, marginalized, and exploited ones. An act of love towards them is an act of love towards God."

[79] Óscar Romero, *Voice of the Voiceless: The Four Pastoral Letters and Other Statements*, trans. Michael Walsh (Maryknoll, NY: Orbis Books, 1985), 171.

[80] Óscar Romero, *The Violence of Love*, compiled and trans. James Brockman (Maryknoll, NY: Orbis Books, 2004), 34.

Later in 1978, Romero was nominated for a Nobel Peace Prize for his courageous moral leadership. Still, the abduction, torture, and killing in El Salvador continued. In the face of these severe challenges, Romero remained relentlessly committed to serving the suffering, comforting the mourning, and prophetically declaring God's condemnation of murder and command of neighbor love.

On March 23, 1980, after a series of military coups, Romero boldly called on soldiers to stop killing their neighbors who had been othered into powerless "peasants." He declared, "The peasants you kill are your own brothers and sisters. When a man tells you to kill, remember God's words: 'Thou shalt not kill.' In the name of God and in the name of this suffering people, I beg you, I beseech you, I order you in the name of God, stop the repression!"[81]

The next day, like King, Romero paid the ultimate price for loving his suffering neighbors as himself. While he was preaching a sermon in the chapel of the cancer hospital where he lived, an assassin shot and killed him with a single bullet. The next Sunday, government forces threw bombs into the crowd at Romero's funeral, and forty more people died. It was soon discovered that a wealthy major in the military had funded and ordered Romero's murder.

In the final years of his ministry before being assassinated, Romero's countless sermons and pastoral letters to his churches resound with the teaching of Jesus and incessantly focus on God's command to love all people. Like Paul indicated in Romans 13, he insisted that Christian neighbor love had political implications. Romero preached this integral vision in a sermon from 1978:

> If there were love of neighbor there would be no terrorism, no repression, no selfishness, none of the cruel inequalities in our society, no abductions and no crimes. Love sums up the law. Not only that, love gives Christian meaning to all human relations. Even those who call themselves atheists, when they are humane, they fulfill the essence of the relationship that God wants among human beings: love. Love gives plenitude to all human duties, and without love, justice is only the sword. With love, justice becomes a brother's embrace.[82]

---

[81] Óscar Romero, "The Final Homily," homily, March 24, 1980, Romero Trust, www.romerotrust.org.uk/homilies-and-writings/homilies/final-homily-archbishop-romero.

[82] Óscar Romero, "A Prophetic, Sacramental, Loving Church," homily, September 10, 1978, Romero Trust, http://www.romerotrust.org.uk/homilies/116/116_pdf.pdf.

For Romero, neighbor love is not merely a private feeling or personal practice. Neighbor love is God's sovereign law, which stands again terrorism, repression, inequality, abduction, torture, and murder. Like Genesis 9 suggests, this law reveals that these evils are not merely crimes but an insurrection against God's will, which Christians cannot silently accept or blindly overlook.

This vision of neighbor love enabled Romero to understand that sin is not merely personal but also social and political. He insists that sin begins in each of our failures to love God and our neighbor as ourselves; the root of sin is selfishness. But when that selfishness is systematized—when it becomes the ruling law between people in society—it turns into structural evil that destroys human life and devastates the moral neighborhood. Romero called this "institutionalized sin."

From this biblical perspective, Romero came to understand that analyzing and exposing injustice was not a sign of Marxism. It is the consistent practice of Jesus and all of his followers in the Bible. The command to love our neighbors demands a social order in which citizens are not harmed and limits are respected. When political violence destroys these bonds and boundaries, sin has become institutionalized. In response, it is the obligation of God's people to do what must always be done in the face of sin: call for repentance and conversion in the name of Jesus.

In this way, Romero embraced the prophetic calling to denounce social and political evil. In another sermon in 1978 reminiscent of Weil, Romero preached,

> In light of the gospel the Church has an obligation and the right to denounce injustice, evil, and sin that might be found in any organization, even those organizations that call themselves Christian. The Church is not committed to any one organization in order to be able to speak to all organizations and tell them: This is an evil act! This is sinful! I must denounce this action! I repudiate that action! . . . The Church cannot be silent in front of these injustices. Your pastors have to speak. We must all be a prophetic people and cry out.

Later in this sermon, Romero continued with compassionate courage:

> I want to console the victims of atrocities, of injustice and with courage I also want to denounce the atrocities, the tortures, the disappearances of prisoners, and the social injustice. This is not engaging in politics; this is building up the

Church and carrying out the Church's duty as imposed by the Church's identity. My conscience is undisturbed, and I call on all of you—Let us build up the true Church![83]

In his sermon "Christ Saves All People," Romero described this prophetic calling to "uproot" sin in individual hearts, the economy, and the political order as central to Christian evangelism.[84] How can people hear the gospel, repent, and be transformed if they do not face their sin? And how can people face their sin unless the church is willing to confront the evils and injustices that reject God and destroy human life?

Romero calls this "integral evangelization," which embraces the fullness of Christ's gospel and original Great Commission. He repeatedly insists that denouncing violence and evil is not "political." It is the basic requirement of obeying Christ, loving our neighbors as ourselves, and spreading the gospel. The goal is always what he calls "conversion," the new beginning of a changed life by the grace of God.[85]

But Romero didn't stop with denouncing evil. Like King, he believed that neighbor love always moves toward reconciliation and healed community. Thus, he called his congregation to refuse to hate the people who had killed his dear friend Rutilio Grande. In his funeral sermon for Grande, Romero movingly addressed the unknown killers and extended belonging even to them. He said,

> My dear criminals, we want to tell you that we love you and we ask God to pour forth repentance into your hearts. The Church is incapable of hatred. The Church has no enemies. Its only enemies are those who declare themselves as such. But even these she loves and dies for like Jesus, saying to them: Father, forgive them, they know not what they do.[86]

In chapter five above, we noted historian Gary Anderson's observation that the early Christian movement innovated linguistic expressions in the culture of its time. Here we see this again in the twentieth century with Romero: "My dear criminals." The power of Christ's love empowered him to speak

---

[83]Romero, "Prophetic, Sacramental, Loving Church."
[84]Óscar Romero, "Christ Saves All People," homily, January 15, 1978, Romero Trust, www.romerotrust.org.uk/homilies-and-writings/homilies/christ-saves-all-people-people.
[85]Romero, *Voice of the Voiceless*, 172, 125.
[86]Óscar Romero, "Motivation of Love," homily, March 14, 1977, Romero Trust, www.romerotrust.org.uk/homilies-and-writings/homilies/motivation-love.

with striking tenderness and tenacity to those who callously slaughtered his beloved friend. This love "has no enemies" and sees even "criminals" as "dear," despite their despicable violence. Here we are reminded of King's vision of love as "universal altruism" and "a willingness to go to any length to restore community." Like his fellow archbishop in South Africa, Desmond Tutu, Romero understood that there is no future without forgiveness.

Romero's response to the civil war in El Salvador offers a remarkable vision of neighbor love. Death squads terrorized his country, Romero's colleagues were being killed left and right, Romero himself was getting death threats, and then he had to bury his beloved friend. And still he refused to speak an othering word against these "dear criminals." In fact, he insisted that it was impossible for him to have enemies. Jesus' three words—"love your enemy"—had changed his life. He writes, "Love wants to make all men and women truly human." This is what Romero called "the civilization of love."[87]

After his humble beginnings as a carpenter and early reactionary views as a priest, Romero came to understand that self-sacrificial neighbor love is the pastor's calling in the face of othering and violence. It is impossible to claim to love one's neighbor and remain silent while they are being terrorized, abducted, tortured, and murdered. Thus, Romero's prophetic preaching each Sunday became the practical embodiment of what neighbor love required for the *campesinos* and all Salvadorans.

In his final sermon, during which he was assassinated, Romero echoed Bonhoeffer and King's vision and prophetically proclaimed,

> One must not love oneself so much as to avoid getting involved in the risks of life that history demands of us. . . . Those who try to fend off the danger will lose their lives, while those who out of love for Christ give themselves to the service of others, will live, live like the grain of wheat that dies, but only apparently. . . . Only by undoing itself does it produce the harvest.[88]

Romero got involved in the risks of life to the point of his own assassination. But the seed of his life, like "Jesus's long-term moral revolution," as he called it, continues to produce a harvest of neighbor love in El Salvador and around

---

[87]Romero, *Voice of the Voiceless*, 77.
[88]Romero, "Final Homily." See Karl Rahner, "Epilogue: The Mystery of Unselfish Communion," in *The Love of Jesus and the Love of Neighbor* (New York: Crossroad, 1983), 99-104.

the world.[89] In 2015, Romero was recognized as an official martyr of the church. In 2018, he was named a saint.

But far more than a martyr or saint, Romero was a courageous pastor who made practical love for his oppressed neighbors the passion of his ministry. His preaching continues to echo today as a voice for the voiceless. As he insisted, "We must all be a prophetic people and cry out" with this healing vision: "The Church is a circle in which God hopes to encounter all people."[90]

Mother Teresa: I Belong to the Whole World

Agnes, who later became known as Mother Teresa (1910–1997), was a Catholic nun who embodied the mystical, integral vision of Weil and Romero. In many ways, she lived Julian's vision of Jesus as "our true mother" who teaches us "the kindness and the wisdom of love."[91]

When she was eighteen, Mother Teresa moved to Ireland to train with the Sisters of Loreto. A year later, she moved to India to become a missionary and a teacher at St. Mary's high school. She formally became a nun in 1931. Like Weil, Teresa loved teaching, and she was popular among her students. She remained a teacher at the Catholic girls school in Calcutta for fifteen years. Nevertheless, she was troubled by the extreme poverty that surrounded her comfortable fortress. This poverty was cemented by the othering of India's caste system. This system represented subordinated, suffering people as unworthy of love and destined to remain trapped in misery. As in ancient Greece and white supremacist America, othering had been essentialized.[92]

Then, on September 10, 1946, when she was thirty-six, Mother Teresa received what she called her "call within a call"—a second calling after already being called to India as a teacher. It came during a time of "quiet, intimate prayer with our Lord." Later she recalled, "The message was clear: I was to leave the convent and help the poor while living among them. It was an order. I knew where I belonged, but I did not know how to get there."[93]

---

[89]Romero, *Violence of Love*, 34.
[90]See Óscar Romero, *The Church Cannot Remain Silent: Unpublished Letters and Other Writings* (Maryknoll, NY: Orbis Books, 2016).
[91]For a brief biography of Mother Teresa through the lens of moral leadership, see Gushee and Holtz, *Moral Leadership for a Divided Age*, 179-201.
[92]See Wilkerson, *Caste*, 73-77, 101-2.
[93]Mother Teresa, *Mother Teresa: Essential Writings*, ed. Jean Maalouf (Maryknoll, NY: Orbis Books, 2001), 12.

This call echoes Bonhoeffer's vision of neighbor love as a life *with* others. It came to Mother Teresa while she was riding on a train, not in a chapel or on a spiritual retreat. But it took Mother Teresa two years to receive permission to leave the school and start her new mission in 1948. She refused to give up, and her call to the poor ended up bringing profound healing to the world.

Mother Teresa then began to dedicate her life to living with the poor and serving them. Later in 1948, she took a short training in hygiene, nutrition, and nursing. Her work started small: she taught children the alphabet and hygiene under a tree, which connected her to their families and their desperate needs at home. At that time, she didn't have any money to give, so she simply gave herself and her love. Eventually she received a large donation, and she started a two-room schoolhouse and medical center for children.

In 1950, Teresa established the Missionaries of Charity with nine other sisters, some of them her former students. This was when she became known as Mother Teresa. Together, their mission was to give "compassion and love to the poorest of the poor." Like the earliest followers of Jesus, their essential activities included "seeking out in towns and villages all over the world even amid squalid surroundings the poorest, the abandoned, the sick, the infirm, the leprosy patients, the dying, the desperate, the lost, the outcasts; taking care of them, rendering help to them, visiting them assiduously, living Christ's love for them, and awakening their response to his great love."[94]

In 1952, Mother Teresa opened her first Home for the Dying. This was a place of medical care and compassion intended to give dignity and relief to the dying and impoverished people in subordinated castes. Her work incrementally increased and expanded beyond India. Today her Missionaries of Charity has over five hundred organizations around the world, serving the poorest of the poor in over 130 countries. Prior to the spread of neighbor love, such a movement was virtually unimaginable.

Due to her relentless service, Mother Teresa was awarded the Nobel Peace Prize in 1979, two years after Romero was nominated for it. Still, she maintained a modest view of herself. She told a journalist, "By blood and origin, I am Albanian. My citizenship is India. I am a Catholic nun. As to my calling, I belong to the whole world. As to my heart, I belong entirely to Jesus."[95] The

---

[94] Mother Teresa, *Essential Writings*, 14.
[95] Mother Teresa, *Essential Writings*, 15.

revolutionary teachings of Jesus continued to change the world through this humble woman who confessed, like Weil, "I belong to the whole world." Mother Teresa died on September 5, 1997, at eighty-seven. Her last words were, "Jesus, I love you." She received a state funeral in India, the first of its kind since Gandhi's. She was named a Catholic saint in 2016.

Several aspects of Mother Teresa's story are inspiring and challenging as we trace her practice of neighbor love. Like Romero, her core ministry started relatively late in her life. She was thirty-six when she left the convent school, just three years younger than when Bonhoeffer and King died. Even so, her call to serve the poor built on the work she was already doing as a teacher; it wasn't completely new. Moreover, she received her call in an ordinary place: riding in a train. Yes, she was praying, but she was also just going about her business. Then she started small, under a tree with just nine other women. For decades afterward, she sustained her work among the most othered people in India; she was not a flashy trendsetter but a faithful servant in the trenches. As she did so, she lived for nearly fifty years with a gnawing sense of God's absence and silence. She did not feel like a spiritual giant changing the world but she refused to give up on her calling.[96]

Looking back on her life, what is perhaps most inspiring about Mother Teresa's love for her neighbors is that there was nothing superhuman about it. She simply loved people in the ways she knew how and never abandoned her calling. Mother Teresa beautifully describes this love in her book *No Greater Love*:

> What we need is to love without getting tired. How does a lamp burn? Through the continuous input of small drops of oil. What are these drops of oil in our lamps? They are the small things of daily life: faithfulness, small words of kindness, a thought for others, our way of being silent, of looking, of speaking, and of acting. Do not look for Jesus away from yourselves. He is not out there; He is in you. Keep your lamp burning, and you will recognize Him.[97]

Mother Teresa's writings on love are especially beautiful because of their simplicity, honesty, and practicality. All throughout them, her imagination

---

[96]Mother Teresa, *Come Be My Light*.
[97]Mother Teresa, *No Greater Love*, ed. Becky Benenate and Joseph Durepos (Novato, CA: New World Library, 1989), 22.

and the mission she describes are radically energized by Jesus. She summarizes her way of life as "with Jesus, for Jesus, to Jesus."[98] Today Mother Teresa is perhaps the most famous example of the revolutionary power of meeting and loving the Jesus of the Gospels, who calls us to love our neighbors. The universalizing, boundary-crossing, other-embracing neighbor love of Jesus was powerfully alive in Mother Teresa.

Unsurprisingly, then, Mother Teresa incessantly emphasized that we meet Jesus in our neighbors, especially the poor and suffering. Often alluding to Matthew 25, like so many others in this book, Mother Teresa perceived that Jesus gives his divine dignity to every neighbor who suffers.[99] Thus, we can see no one who should not be looked on with love and given practical care. Those the world sees as valueless or repulsive others are especially worthy of reverence. Mother Teresa writes,

> Who is Jesus to me?
> Jesus is—God. . . .
> The hungry I feed
> The naked I clothe
> The homeless I take in
> The sick I nurse
> The child I teach
> The lonely I console
> The unwanted I want
> The mentally ill I befriend
> Jesus is—The Helpless—I help
> The beggar—I welcome
> The leper—I wash
> The drunkard—I guide.[100]

This vision simultaneously shattered and healed India's caste system. God's holy dignity is embodied in the impoverished, suffering neighbor whom others overlook or discard. We are all morally connected and equally precious. Like so many others we've studied, she repeated the paradox

---

[98]Mother Teresa, *Essential Writings*, 25.
[99]For an insightful study of how Mt 25 has been interpreted across Christian history, see Sherman Gray, *The Least of My Brothers: Matthew 25:31-46: A History of Interpretation* (Atlanta: Scholars Press, 1989).
[100]Mother Teresa, *Where There Is Love, There Is God*, ed. Brian Kolodiejchuk (New York: Doubleday, 2010), 361-62.

of neighbor love and confessed that God will judge us by how we serve our most vulnerable neighbors—not by our caste, wealth, education, or accomplishments.[101]

This is why Teresa thought prayer was so important, as Jesus taught. She writes, "We need to pray—for prayer gives a clean heart and a clean heart can see God in each person. If we see God in others, naturally, we will love one another as God loves each one of us."[102] With this sacred vision reminiscent of Bonhoeffer's, Teresa asked a simple but profound question: "If everyone were capable of discovering the image of God in their neighbors, do you think that we would still need tanks and generals?"[103]

Even with this daring vision, Mother Teresa repeatedly taught that our task is not to do great things but to do little things with great love. She said, "To show great love for God and our neighbor we need not do great things. It is how much love we put in the doing that makes our offering Something Beautiful for God."[104] Lest we look off into the horizon and ignore one another here and now, she asks, "How can you find Jesus hidden under the distressing appearance of the poor if you cannot see him in each other?"[105]

Thus, Teresa didn't challenge people to become missionaries in other parts of the world like herself. She encouraged them to play with their children, to visit lonely neighbors, to embrace others in their anguish, to read the newspaper to the blind, to spend time with the rich who are starved for love.[106] She understood that poverty is much more than economic deprivation; its core is being unloved. She writes,

---

[101] Mother Teresa, *Essential Writings*, 20.

[102] Mother Teresa, *Where There Is Love*, 16. See Henri Nouwen, *The Wounded Healer* (New York: Image Books, 1979), 52: "People of prayer are, in the final analysis, people who are able to recognize in others the face of the Messiah. They are people who make visible what was hidden, who make touchable what was unreachable."

[103] Mother Teresa, *No Greater Love*, 47-48.

[104] Mother Teresa, *Essential Writings*, 78. This is a beautiful theme throughout the history of Christian mysticism. For example, seventeenth-century French mystic Brother Lawrence taught, "Love accomplishes everything. It's also not necessary to have great things to do. I flip my little omelette in the frying pan for the love of God. When it's done, if I have nothing to do, I prostrate myself on the floor and love my God who gave me the grace to do it. After that, I get up happier than a king. When I can do nothing else, it is enough for me to pick up a straw from the ground for the love of God. . . . The love of God and the love of neighbor are one and the same practice." See Brother Lawrence, *Practice of the Presence: A Revolutionary Translation*, trans. Carmen Acevedo Butcher (Minneapolis: Broadleaf Books, 2022), 156, 188.

[105] Mother Teresa, *Essential Writings*, 98.

[106] Mother Teresa, *Essential Writings*, 78.

> The poor we seek may live near us or far away. They can be materially or spiritually poor. They may be hungry for bread or hungry for friendship. They may need clothing, or they may need the sense of wealth that God's love for them represents. They may need the shelter of a house made of bricks and cement or the shelter of having a place in our hearts.[107]

For Teresa, these needs were equally valid and worthy of love. In fact, she argues that it's easier to love people who are far away but harder to love people "right next to us."

With this vision, Mother Teresa warns against love becoming a form of escapism from our daily lived experiences and responsibilities. She repeatedly emphasizes that "love begins at home." There is no task that is so small or simple that it is unworthy of being done with love.[108] For a Nobel Prize winner who was called "the most powerful woman in the world," this is a countercultural and refreshing perspective—"the kindness and the wisdom of a mother." She praises simple things such as smiling at others and shaking hands. Like Julian, she renounces othering's hunger for greatness and insists,

> Always be faithful in little things, for in them our strength lies. To God nothing is little. He cannot make anything small; they are infinite. . . . Do not pursue spectacular deeds. We must deliberately renounce all desires to see the fruit of our labor, doing all we can as best we can, leaving the rest in the hands of God. What matters is the gift of your self, the degree of love that you put into each one of your actions.[109]

To her critics who said that she had not done enough to change social structures, she answered that she was called to serve one individual person at a time rather than crowds. She said that if she was thinking of crowds, she would never have actually started her work: "I believe in the personal touch of one to one. . . . Just begin . . . one, one, one," she said.[110] Every individual neighbor matters and matters equally.

---

[107] Mother Teresa, *Essential Writings*, 80.
[108] Mother Teresa, *Essential Writings*, 93, 87.
[109] Mother Teresa, *No Greater Love*, 30. Dorothy Day, Teresa's contemporary who served with the poor in New York City, called this "the sacrament of the present moment—of the little way." Day, *By Little and by Little*, 104. See bell hooks, *All About Love: New Visions* (New York: HarperCollins, 2001), 144: "We can begin by sharing a smile, a warm greeting, a bit of conversation; by doing a kind deed or by acknowledging kindness offered to us."
[110] Mother Teresa, *No Greater Love*, 20, 80.

Even so, Mother Teresa called for radical generosity as the essence of love. An interviewer once asked Mother Teresa, "Can you sum up what love really is?" Quoting John 3:16, she answered, "Love is giving. God loved the world so much that He gave his Son. Jesus loved the world so much, loved you, loved me so much that He gave His life. And He wants us to love as He loved. And so now we have also to give until it hurts. True love is giving and giving until it hurts."[111] This vision of giving until it hurts echoes Bonhoeffer's call to accept suffering, King's call for dangerous altruism, and Romero's call to embrace the risks of life when loving our neighbors. For Mother Teresa, neighbor love is universal in its embrace—the circle of our moral responsibility expanded because of the God who gives God's love to all of us.

And like the Epistle to Diognetus and Simone Weil, Mother Teresa thought this self-giving love for others was the key to true happiness. She writes, "It is through love of God and of neighbor that one arrives at complete happiness, at total service without limits, thus giving God to others, a God of peace, a living God, a God of love."[112]

This points to another important aspect of Mother Teresa's vision of neighbor love, which echoes Bonhoeffer's practice of listening, Weil's attention, and King's excessive altruism. It is not enough merely to give food to others. They must also be given happiness, joy, celebration—the cherishing of their humanity. Rather than simply giving the sick a cure, Teresa says we must also give them our hearts.

Neighbor love, then, is much more than impersonal government aid. Again, she understood that the most radical form of poverty is not a lack of wealth; "the deepest poverty is not being loved."[113] Thus, a true, self-giving love of our neighbors is a love that brings them joy—a shared joy that illuminates our share in God's divine image regardless of race, class, caste, nationality, religion, or any other boundary. The moral circle of neighbor love is universal. As Mother Teresa confessed, "I belong to the whole world."

According to Mother Teresa, "The world has never had such a need for love as it has today."[114] In the face of the devastating forms of othering we've seen in this chapter—from genocide to segregation to the oppression of

---

[111] Mother Teresa, *Where There Is Love*, 4.
[112] Mother Teresa, *Essential Writings*, 75.
[113] Mother Teresa, *Essential Writings*, 77, 80.
[114] Mother Teresa, *Essential Writings*, 26.

impoverished factory workers, farmers, and low-caste orphans—her words ring true. When we love our neighbors as ourselves, we become "Something Beautiful for God" and the world. As Julian, an earlier mother of the church, witnessed, "And then the bliss of our motherhood in Christ will begin anew in the joy of our God; a new beginning which will last without end, always beginning anew."[115]

Conclusion: Stars in the Darkness

Ethicist William Schweiker, my PhD adviser at the University of Chicago, calls the twentieth century the "barbaric century."[116] Nearly a hundred million people were slaughtered in war. A hundred million women were killed or disappeared. Hannah Arendt, herself a Jewish woman who survived Hitler's Holocaust, ominously called the late twentieth century "the time after all hopes have died."[117]

Nevertheless, all throughout this barbaric time, there were shining stars in the terrible darkness—courageous witnesses to the power of Jesus' love and "paradigms of a plausible future." As everything was seemingly falling apart, the five exemplars of neighbor love we've explored in this chapter—and countless others—were embodying "a basis for living together with other people" across every boundary and barrier that othering could erect. They modeled a vision of neighbor love that was so much more expansive and transformative than the American Christianity that raised me.

We've seen incredible diversity among our exemplars. Bonhoeffer, Weil, King, and Romero directly engaged public life through political resistance, social protest, and public ministry. Teresa worked primarily with individuals in the interpersonal sphere, even as the other exemplars also emphasized practices of listening, attention, excessive altruism, and grieving with the suffering. Various approaches are valid and needed. There is no single formula for neighbor love. All the fullness of human creativity and responsibility is needed to love our neighbors as ourselves. Each of them in their own ways demonstrated that Jesus' movement of neighbor love can endure the worst of human evil, overcome othering (including Christianized

---

[115]Julian, *Revelations*, 136.
[116]William Schweiker, "Loose Morals," *The Christian Century* 120, no. 10 (May 17, 2003): 36-38, www.christiancentury.org/reviews/2003-05/loose-morals.
[117]Hannah Arendt, *The Origins of Totalitarianism* (New York: Schocken Books, 2004), xxvi.

othering), and bring healing in seemingly hopeless situations. Like Julian, out of this century's crucifix, we witness "a light for all mankind."

These paradigmatic people have given us too much wisdom to summarize in a few words. I hope you might go back through this chapter and note what you think is most relevant and useful for your life and practice of neighbor love in your own context. I am inspired by the fact that, in a time when human life was so radically cheapened and destroyed by extreme othering, each of these people witnessed the precious value in others, especially the most impoverished, oppressed, and powerless—the damned. Bonhoeffer gave his life for genocided Jews and other antifascist resisters. Weil gave her life for underpaid workers and starving victims of World War II. King gave his life for racial minorities and second-class citizens. Romero gave his life for impoverished farmers and targets of state terrorism. Mother Teresa gave her life for the extremely poor and suffering in India's subordinated-caste slums.

In each case, these exemplars bore witness to the universal moral circle of neighbor love for all people, including our enemy-siblings. In this golden circle, othering is abolished. As Bonhoeffer beheld, "in this recognition, our gaze opens to the fullness of divine life in the world." We learn to perceive unkillable divine love in our neighbors, even amid the extreme othering and extraordinary suffering we witness in our world today.

7

NEIGHBOR LOVE NOW

The Abolition of Othering and a New Beginning for Humanity

WHEN I FIRST LEFT HOME for Ethiopia twenty years ago, I had no idea that I would meet Eyob, marry Lily, and root my life in Ethiopia. When I quit my job at the Ethiopian Graduate School of Theology and met Ferdosa fourteen years later, I didn't know we were going to start the Neighbor-Love Movement. And when we did that, I didn't know it would lead to work amid civil war, death threats, and exile. As Abraham glimpsed, the heteronautic journey that leads to the blessing of neighbor love is an adventure accompanied by many life-changing surprises—what Julian calls "a new beginning which will last without end, always beginning anew."[1]

The Neighbor-Love Movement focused on inviting Ethiopia's youth and people of all identities to see others as *neighbors*, humans who are morally related to us and equally precious in value. We designed our logo as a diamond to represent the complex preciousness of every other. This diamond is surrounded by a compass to symbolize how this moral vision guides us into human flourishing. At the center of our movement was and remains the Neighbor-Love Covenant. It's a simple statement of everyday commitment to orient our life and love: "Today I covenant to love my neighbor as myself. Every woman, man, and child is my neighbor across every boundary and identity. I choose to see and treat my neighbors with value, respect, and practical compassion. Today I say Yes: I am an ambassador of neighbor love." We invite our ambassadors to embody this covenant with seven practices that seek to compress the wisdom we've discovered throughout the history

---

[1] Julian of Norwich, *Revelations of Divine Love*, trans. Barry Windeatt (New York: Oxford University Press, 2015), 136.

of neighbor love. These practices are rooted in our bodies and don't require any special status, wealth, or technology. They require only the courageous willingness of daily practice with others:

Figure 7.1a. Covenant and Practices of Neighbor-Love Movement

 1. **Eyes:** See others as your neighbors—people with precious value—and smile at them. Resist overlooking, labeling, or dehumanizing others.

 2. **Ears:** Listen to your neighbors with patience and empathy, even when you disagree. Resist closing your ears to others.

 3. **Mouth:** Speak to your neighbors with truth, respect, and kindness, even when you disagree. Resist speaking words of insult, generalization, or hatred. Ask for forgiveness when you make mistakes.

 4. **Hands:** Serve your neighbors with justice and compassion in little and big ways. Resist using your power to exploit or hurt others.

 5. **Heart:** Open your heart to your neighbors' joy and pain. Pray for others and bless them. Release envy, grudges, curses, and desire for revenge.

6. Feet: Move toward outsiders and enemies and build relationship. Walk with people who are different than you. Resist staying in your own circle.

 7. Brain: Understand your vocation as an act of neighbor love. Resist separating your work and values. Live an integrated life.

We didn't know where this covenant and its practice would lead. But once we launched the Neighbor-Love Movement and started traveling Ethiopia with this invitation, thousands of youth were inspired and signed our covenant. Today over twenty million people have encountered our invitation online.

Starting with Ferdosa, we discovered that millions of people were longing for hope beyond othering as rumors of civil war escalated. Ethiopia's incoming attorney general signed our covenant and told me, "This is as timely and important as it gets." The chief commissioner of Ethiopia's Human Rights Commission also signed our covenant and said, "This could not be more important work. You should go with full force."

That's what we attempted to do. With a small grant from the European Institute of Peace, we started traveling to Ethiopia's regional universities and inviting thousands of students to become ambassadors of neighbor love in their communities. We produced a video curriculum for all forty-five of Ethiopia's public universities on what neighbor love is and how to practice it amid the escalating othering and polarization online. We published local and global articles and *Balinjeraye*, the first book in an Ethiopian language on the ethics of neighbor love.[2] We also started producing a TV show on how to creatively practice neighbor love with the most othered people in Ethiopia, such as house maids, daily laborers, and political enemies.[3]

---

[2] See Andrew DeCort, "Ethics During Crisis: From Missed Chances to Neighbor-Love," *The Ethiopian Herald*, February 20, 2018; DeCort, "Public Theology in Ethiopia: State, Church, and Neighbor-Love," in *What Does Theology Do, Actually?* eds. Matthew Ryan Robinson and Inja Inderst (Leipzig, Germany: Evangelische Verlagsanstalt GmbH, 2020), 209-224; DeCort, "Othering: A Virus More Dangerous Than COVID-19," *Addis Fortune*, February 23, 2020, https://andrew-decort.com/essays/othering/; DeCort, "Balinjeraye: Unity and Diversity Are Neighbors, and So Are We," *Ethiopia Insight*, April 26, 2020; DeCort, "Neighbor-Love Week for National Reconciliation," *Ethiopia Insight*, April 14, 2021, https://andrew-decort.com/essays/the-neighbor-love-week-for-national-reconciliation/; DeCort, "Christian Nationalism Is Tearing Ethiopia Apart," *Foreign Policy*, June 17, 2022, https://foreignpolicy.com/2022/06/18/ethiopia-pentecostal-evangelical-abiy-ahmed-christian-nationalism/; Tekalign Nega, *Balinjeraye [My Neighbor]* (Addis Ababa, Ethiopia: Faith and Flourishing Books, 2020).

[3] The Neighbor-Love Movement's covenant and practices, the Neighbor Love Course (Amharic), and other resources are available at www.nlmglobal.org and YouTube at www.youtube.com/@nlmnow.

All throughout, we met with Ethiopia's senior religious and political leaders to ask them to embody and advocate for neighbor love in the face of the crisis of othering. I didn't know it at the time, but this was the decisive and most dangerous step in our movement. In many ways, these leaders embodied othering in Ethiopia. Some saw them as heroes and saviors. Others saw them as villains and enemies. As we crossed the lines of othering and invited these leaders to meet with one another, people became confused and angry. Again, othering is powerful: it locks us into identities of good versus evil, us versus them, neighbors versus enemies. When it becomes severe, othering locks us into identities of humans and monsters, the grievable and ungrievable, angels and demons. We defied these divisions, met with everyone, and invited them into public dialogue. I began with two iconic opposition leaders, Eskinder Nega and Jawar Mohammed, who were both eventually imprisoned on charges of terrorism.

Ironically enough, on Good Friday 2020, I started getting death threats. Then a "documentary" began circulating about me online, insisting that I was a foreign agent (notice the othering) hell-bent on overthrowing the Ethiopian government and destroying Ethiopia's ancient church. Powerful media personalities made TV shows about me that spread similar propaganda. As I became an increasingly public "other" in Ethiopia, many people—primarily Christians—sent me messages saying that they would throw me off a bridge, run me over with their cars, or butcher my body like an animal. I got over fifty pages of death threats. The rage of othering is ruthless.[4]

In the process, I learned a profound but painful lesson: when you *love* the other, you often *become* the other. Philosopher Nicholas Wolterstorff offers sobering insight here. Like Bonhoeffer, he writes, "Love in our world is suffering love. Some do not suffer much, though, for they do not love much. Suffering is for the loving. This, said Jesus, is the command of the Holy One: 'You shall love your neighbor as yourself.' In commanding us to love, God invites us to suffer."[5] After Ethiopia's civil war erupted in November 2020, I started wearing a tracking device in case I was abducted.

---

[4] I tell more of this story in *Blessed Are the Others: Jesus' Way in a Violent World* (Washington, DC: BitterSweet Collective, 2024) and *Flourishing on the Edge of Faith: Seven Practices for a New We* (Washington, DC: BitterSweet Collective, 2022).

[5] Nicholas Wolterstorff, *Lament for a Son* (Grand Rapids, MI: Eerdmans, 1987), 89.

Neighbor Love Now

Lily and I sheltered in a safe house. Eventually, the threats became so severe that we needed to leave Ethiopia. Like so many othered Ethiopians, we became personae non gratae and went into exile. Exile is where I write today.

Suffering love that it is, we've seen from the start that neighbor love isn't fuzzy feelings or random kindness limited to one's personal life. Neighbor love is an embodied movement that seeks to heal our humanity and transform our world. As such, it nonviolently confronts the othering that so powerfully defines so much of our human identity and worldly structures. As it does so, as we saw in the Roman Empire, people often feel threatened. When othering makes us feel safe and like ourselves, being asked to overcome it can feel like an attack. Othering functions like an addiction: even though it enslaves and impoverishes us, we come to depend on it, even enjoy it, and sometimes violently defend it. In a sense, neighbor love is a sobriety journey for the whole human family. And we addicts—all of us—often don't take kindly to its medicine. The withdrawals can be brutal.

The stakes are high. Othering left Eyob to wander in the streets of Addis as he was dying of a hideous head wound. It found Ferdosa wearing her beautiful hijab but never having heard the invitation to love her enemies. It fueled Paul's violent religious nationalism in first-century Palestine and the devastation of the Israel-Palestine conflict today. Tragically, Ethiopia's civil war has become one of the saddest examples of what extreme othering produces: 1.2 million neighbors killed, 5 million neighbors displaced from their homes, and 20 million neighbors afflicted with hunger. Ethiopia's attorney general was right, even as he tragically went on to defend this unjust and unjustifiable war: "[Neighbor love] is as timely and important as it gets"—in Ethiopia, in America, and across the world.

In this final chapter, we turn to synthesize some of what we've discovered in this ever-timely adventure of neighbor love. In an attempt to revive this "dead dogma," as Mill called it, we started with the emergence of neighbor love in ancient Israel, studied its universalization in the movement Jesus started, and then traced some of its evolution across history into the twentieth century. Now in our century, what can we learn from this ancient neighbor-love movement, and how might it help heal our world? What does it mean to love our neighbors as ourselves today?

The Meaning of Love

Again and again throughout our journey, we've observed that neighbor love isn't fuzzy feelings and random kindness limited to one's personal life. Neighbor love is passionate will and practical work for others and our integrated well-being. It's a conscious choice and embodied commitment to our mutual flourishing as people who are morally related to one another and equally precious in value.

Thus, Martin Luther King Jr. emphasized that neighbor love isn't limited to liking others. Following Jesus' teaching, he and many others clarified that real love doesn't depend on others deserving our positive regard and practical care. Neighbor love depends on *us* and who *we* are. Are we neighbors who love? Simone Weil writes, "If I do not love [others] as they are, it will not be they whom I love, and my love will be unreal."

Love has so often been belittled into fickle feelings and flickering acts. The love we encounter in the neighbor-love movement is fierce and fulsome. Neighbor love wants to infiltrate our core identity, all of our relationships, and the structures of our world that we cocreate as moral agents. Weil notes that "neighbor love" is another term for *justice*, which seeks right relationships of mutual flourishing. Thus Cornel West writes, "Justice is what love looks like in public."[6] Óscar Romero calls this "the civilization of love."

Neighbor love, then, is a liberating love. Yes, "love starts at home," as Mother Teresa so beautifully observed. It must begin within ourselves and between our selves in our intimate personal relationships if it is to have integrity and endurance. Jesus' movement started with his mystical vision of the divine dove of peace and hearing God speak to his core identity: "You are my beloved child; I delight in you." This belovedness is where we all must begin our individual neighbor-love journey. But neighbor love stretches out from this and seeks to transform society itself in the cultures we create, the economies we develop, and the political orders we govern.

We saw this in Jesus' ministry and the early Christian movement as it gave the "kiss of death" to the Roman Empire. Rome's othering order produced a hierarchical culture of violence and imperial domination. In the face of it, the early Christians innovated novel expressions like Romero's "dear criminals" and new institutions such as public schools, hospitals, orphanages,

---

[6]Cornel West has made this statement many times in numerous places.

nursing homes, and more equitable economic relationships. Neighbor love is what inspired and energized their innovative work.

In the process, "a world without love" governed by "natural inequality" was slowly overcome, and othering was incrementally disestablished, however much Christians have failed in this abolitionist vocation and reproduced the evil of othering themselves. Thomas Aquinas, Martin Luther, and the othering churches in Bonhoeffer, Weil, and King's societies are sobering examples that can help cultivate self-awareness and honest self-critique in us today.

Jesus promises, "Do this"—love your othered neighbor—"and you will flourish." The Didache calls this "the way of life." The Epistle to Diognetus describes this love as the source of our true happiness and ultimate home. As the movement spread, Tertullian said that love for all people, especially the poorest and most oppressed, had become Christianity's "brand."

Against Hitler's delusions, then, neighbor love is not "the domestication of humanity." It is what Bonhoeffer calls "the basis of a meaningful life" and an unshakable foundation for "living together with other people." Still today, neighbor love offers a compelling answer to what Bonhoeffer calls "the ultimate question" of "how we can find a basis for living together with other people." Thus, Dr. King prophetically declared, "This love might well be the salvation of our civilization. . . . Love is ultimately the only answer to mankind's problems. . . . He who has love has the key that unlocks the door to the meaning of ultimate reality."[7]

THE IDENTITY OF THE NEIGHBOR

Neighbor love universalizes the identity of the neighbor. We began our journey in the countercultural story of Hebrew Scripture and Moses' groundbreaking command, "Love your neighbor as yourself" (Lev 19:18). We observed how this command sought to energize a society of justice and gave birth to Boaz's othering-overcoming love for Ruth. Still, we also observed troubling limitations in the moral circle of the Hebrew command of neighbor love. Israel's religious nationalism justified othering the Amalekites and other indigenous people into enemies for genocide. It preserved a society with inequitable laws and produced apocalyptic visions of enslaving and eliminating others.

---

[7]Martin Luther King Jr., *A Testament of Hope: The Essential Writings and Speeches of Martin Luther King Jr.*, ed. James Washington (New York: HarperCollins, 1986), 140, 250.

But eighteen hundred years after Jesus, Søren Kierkegaard quipped that the neighbor is the easiest person to identify. He writes, "Christian love teaches love of all people, unconditionally all. . . . There is in the whole world not a single person who can be recognized with such ease and certainty as one's neighbor. You can never confuse him with anyone else, for indeed all people are your neighbor."[8] Jesus abolished othering at its heart with his unprecedented command, "Love your enemies" (Mt 5:44; Lk 6:27). Now, even the ultimate others are equally our *neighbors*—the signature thread of Jesus' movement. In his teaching, Jesus insists that neighbor love doesn't depend on others deserving it. It is grounded in God's own identity and unconditional love.

Jesus taught that God is our universal and universally loving Parent. He says, "[Your Father] is kind to the ungrateful and wicked" (Lk 6:35). As such, God indiscriminately pours out divine love in the essential elements of our existence such as light and water. This love flows equally to those we label as good and evil, righteous and unrighteous. In this infinite love, there is no ground for seeing any other as morally unrelated or less than ourselves.

The Didache, the earliest Christian manual for Christian faith, extends and absolutizes Jesus' teaching of neighbor love. It says, "'Love those that hate you,' and you will have no enemy. . . . You shall hate no human."[9] Desmond Tutu summarizes this teaching in his declaration, "All, everyone, everything, belongs. None is an outsider, all are insiders, all belong."[10]

This has been one of the signature themes in our study of neighbor love: God is our Father and Mother, our universal Parent. And thus, as Genesis 1–2 primally envisioned, we are one family who belong to one another. When Jesus taught us to prayer to "*Our* Father," he gave us a spiritual practice to uproot othering and make this universal divine identity the center of our conscious attention and way of belonging with one another.[11] As Simone Weil practiced Jesus' prayer, she developed Jesus' universal vision of God's love for every person and all creation with rare insight. She writes, "God created through love and for love. . . . The whole creation is nothing but its vibration. . . . Those who persevere in love hear this note from the very

---

[8]Søren Kierkegaard, *Works of Love*, trans. Howard and Edna Hong (New York: HarperCollins, 2009), 63-65.
[9]Didache 2, in *The Apostolic Fathers*, trans. Kirsopp Lake (Cambridge, MA: Harvard University Press, 1985), 1:309, 313.
[10]Desmond Tutu, *No Future Without Forgiveness* (New York: Doubleday, 1999), 265.
[11]I develop this interpretation of Jesus' "Our Father" or Lord's Prayer in in *Flourishing on the Edge*.

Neighbor Love Now

lowest depths into which affliction has thrust them."[12] Weil envisions the love that inspired God to create the world and the love that inspired Jesus to give his life for his enemies in his crucifixion as one and the same love. As all true love is at heart, this love makes room and embraces the other—whether the other who had no existence of its own in the beginning or the other who had betrayed its existence with hate amid history. The neighbor, including the enemy, is a vibration of this cosmic divine love.

We see, then, that neighbor love is truly a revolutionary movement to abolish othering, overcome dehumanization, and heal our humanity. It spells the end of what Judith Butler calls "ungrievability," the way othering hardens us to the suffering of others and makes our enemy's pain pleasurable to us. Paul wrote to the followers of Jesus in Rome that "love must be sincere" (Rom 12:9). This sincere love "rejoice[s] with those who rejoice and weep[s] with those who weep" (Rom 12:15). It embodies hospitable "other-love" (*philoxenia*) even with our enemy-siblings (Rom 12:9-21). Now no one can be seen as morally unrelated or less than ourselves.

With this vision, Paul writes, "[Jesus] himself is our peace, who has made the two groups one and has destroyed the barrier, the dividing wall of hostility. . . . His purpose was to create in himself one new humanity out of the two, thus making peace" (Eph 2:14-15). Paul calls Jesus' self-giving love on the cross for his enemies "the death" of our "hostility" (Eph 2:16). This love ends othering: "Consequently, you are no longer foreigners and strangers, but fellow citizens with God's people and also members of his household" (Eph 2:19).

Like Jesus and the tradition after him, Paul then names that "every family in heaven and on earth derives its name" from one "Father" (Eph 3:14-16). He prays "that you, being rooted and established in love, may have power, together with all the Lord's holy people, to grasp how wide and long and high and deep is the love of Christ, and to know this love that surpasses knowledge—that you may be filled to the measure of all the fullness of God" (Eph 3:17-19). In awe of this fullness, Paul declares that God's love "is able to do immeasurably more than all we ask or imagine . . . throughout all generations, for ever and ever" (Eph 3:20-21).[13] This is the inestimable power of neighbor love for all people.

---

[12]Simone Weil, *Waiting for God* (New York: HarperPerennial, 2009), 72.

[13]Richard Rohr seeks to develop this primal biblical vision in *The Universal Christ: How a Forgotten Reality Can Change Everything We See, Hope For, and Believe* (New York: Convergent Books, 2019).

Across the generations, neighbor love then gave birth to the cosmopolitanism or global citizenship of Jesus' movement. Defying loyalty to Rome, Paul wrote, "Our citizenship is in heaven" (Phil 3:20).[14] Early in the Christian movement, the Epistle to Diognetus then explained,

> The distinction between Christians and other people is neither in country nor language nor customs. . . . [Christians] show forth the wonderful and confessedly strange character of the constitution of their own citizenship. They dwell in their own fatherlands but as if foreigners in them; they share all things as citizens, and suffer all things as strangers. Every foreign country is their fatherland, and every fatherland is a foreign country. . . . They love all people and are persecuted by all people. . . . Christians love those that hate them.[15]

Almost two millennia later, Dietrich Bonhoeffer made "the principle of our Universal Christian brotherhood which rises above all national hatreds" his final confession.[16]

Simone Weil also revoiced the cosmopolitan vision of neighbor love. She wrote to her spiritual director, "The children of God should not have any other country here below but the universe itself. . . . That is the native city to which we owe our love." Denouncing any Christian justification for violence like the Crusades, she confesses, "I do not want to be adopted into a circle, to live among people who say 'we' and to be part of an 'us,' to find I am 'at home' in any human milieu whatever it may be." The universal moral circle of neighbor love—its all-inclusive *we*—is what inspired Weil's countercultural vocation beyond the church. She writes, "I have the essential need, and I think I can say the vocation, to move among men of every class and complexion, mixing with them and sharing their life. . . . It is because I long to know them so as to love them just as they are. For if I do not love them as they are, it will not be they whom I love, and my love will be unreal."[17] Weil's vocation beyond an othering church resonates with many post-Christians today who feel like Christianity has become an imperious institution infested with othering.

---

[14]See Andrew DeCort, "Paul's Politics: Notes on a Letter from Prison," *The Other Journal*, no. 30 (March 2021): 42-52.
[15]Epistle to Diognetus 5, in *Apostolic Fathers*, 2:359-61.
[16]Quoted in Andrew DeCort, *Bonhoeffer's New Beginning: Ethics After Devastation* (Lanham, MD: Fortress Academic, 2018), 225-27.
[17]Weil, *Waiting for God*, 32, 49, 12-13, 6-7.

A few decades later, Martin Luther King Jr. similarly warned about the American church becoming "an irrelevant social club." His universal vision of neighbor love drove him to articulate a global, cosmopolitan vision of human belonging and responsibility. In the face of America's racialized, segregating othering, he preached, "All men are caught in an inescapable network of mutuality, tied in a single garment of destiny.... I can never be what I ought to be until you are what you ought to be, and you can never be what you ought to be until I am what I ought to be. This is the interrelated structure of reality."[18]

Kierkegaard, Bonhoeffer, Weil, King, and countless others in the neighbor-love movement came to the same conclusion as Henri Nouwen: "Every human face is the face of a neighbor." The bedrock is Jesus' command "Love your enemies," based on his vision of God as our universal Parent. In this "inescapable network of mutuality," they rejected Christian nationalism for a cosmopolitan Christian identity. The moral circle surrounds us all. Thus, they did what the earliest followers of Jesus urged to their Roman audience to do: "clear yourself of all the prejudice which occupies your mind ... and become as it were a new human from the beginning, as one who is about to listen to a new story."[19]

LOVING OUR NEIGHBORS *AS OURSELVES*: THE TEST OF SELFISHNESS

In this new story, we are commanded to love our neighbors *as ourselves*. Kierkegaard writes that doing so "wrenches open the lock of self-love and thereby wrests it away from humanity."[20] In unlocking our selfishness, neighbor love again goes to the heart of othering with its drive to see itself as separated from or superior to others. Kierkegaard explains,

> [The neighbor] is just as near or ought to be just as near to you as you are to yourself. The concept of *neighbor* really means a duplicating of one's own self. *Neighbor* is what philosophers would call the *other*, that by which the selfishness in self-love is tested.... What selfishness absolutely cannot endure is duplication, and the words of the command *as yourself* are simply

---

[18] Martin Luther King Jr., *Strength to Love* (Minneapolis: Fortress, 2010), ix.
[19] Henri Nouwen, *Ministry and Spirituality* (New York: Continuum, 1996), 134; Epistle to Diognetus 2 (pp. 351-53).
[20] Kierkegaard, *Works of Love*, 34.

duplication.... In this way *one's neighbor* is as close to the life of self-love as possible.[21]

As I'll emphasize in the next section, our self-love rightly motivates us to care for ourselves with intentionality, excellence, and urgency. When we are hungry, we eat; when we are ill or injured, we seek medical care; when we are in danger, we desire security. Kierkegaard writes that this self-love is the "test" of neighbor love: Are we willing to love others in the same way?

Jesus' willingness to be executed by his enemies endures as one of the most powerful examples of how he loved his neighbors *as himself*. It was for this reason that Hannah Arendt, herself a secular Jew, described Jesus as "the only completely valid, completely convincing experience Western mankind ever had with active love of goodness as the inspiring principle of all actions."[22] Rather than damning his executioners to hell, Jesus practiced his own preaching of "pray[ing] for those who persecute you" and cried out to God, "Father, forgive them, for they do not know what they are doing" (Lk 23:34). He continued to love the neighbors who killed him.

Martin Luther, at his best at least, powerfully articulated what loving our neighbors *as ourselves* requires in practice. He writes, "If I see that [my neighbor] is hungry and thirsty, I cannot ignore him but must offer food and drink, not considering whether I would risk impoverishing myself by doing so. A person who will not help or support others unless he can do so without affecting his safety or his property will never help his neighbor."[23] Luther extended this practical ethic to situations of public health epidemics in which personal safety was a real concern. In fact, Luther, the icon of salvation by grace through faith alone, declared, "We must give hospital care and be nurses for one another in any extremity or risk the loss of salvation and the grace of God. Thus it is written in God's word and command, 'Love your neighbor as yourself.'"[24]

---

[21]Kierkegaard, *Works of Love*, 37-38. In *Civilization and Its Discontents*, Sigmund Freud says that he could accept Jesus' command if he had said, "Love your neighbor the way they love you." Freud thought this law of reciprocity was more "rational." Jesus, Kierkegaard, and the entire tradition of neighbor love challenge this limited, reactive vision of love.

[22]Hannah Arendt, *On Revolution* (New York: Viking, 1965), 76-77.

[23]Martin Luther, *Martin Luther's Basic Theological Writings*, 2nd ed., ed. Timothy F. Lull (Minneapolis: Fortress, 2005), 483.

[24]Luther, *Basic Theological Writings*, 484.

Neighbor Love Now

As we've seen, Luther's vision of neighbor love was rooted in Matthew 25 and Jesus' teaching that he himself is embodied in our most vulnerable neighbors. Thus, Luther writes,

> What you do or fail to do for your neighbor means doing the same to God. If you wish to serve Christ and to wait on him, very well, you have your sick neighbor close at hand. Go to him and serve him, and you will surely find Christ in him. . . . But if you do not wish or care to serve your neighbor, you can be sure that if Christ lay there instead, you would not do so either and would let him lie there.[25]

This is the call that echoed in me after I said no to Eyob and heard Jesus say, "If you say no to him, you've said no to me." Luther challenges us: if we aren't willing to give our attention, time, and treasure to the most vulnerable neighbor, we shouldn't fool ourselves into thinking that we would care if it were Christ himself. In the eyes of neighbor love, the neighbor is Christ, and so Bonhoeffer calls us to "become Christs for one another."[26]

The challenge to love our neighbors *as ourselves* has echoed across the Christian movement. It was especially resonant in our twentieth-century exemplars in the face of extreme othering. In *Life Together*, Bonhoeffer writes, "Only as a burden is the other really a brother or sister and not just an object to be controlled." He saw listening as an essential practice here, which he says "can be a greater service than speaking." As othering escalated in Germany, Bonhoeffer observed, "Many people seek a sympathetic ear and do not find it among Christians, because these Christians are talking even when they should be listening." He warns, "The death of the spiritual life starts here."[27]

Similarly, Weil emphasizes attention as the core practice of loving our neighbors *as ourselves*.[28] She calls this a "way of looking" that "empties itself of all its own contents in order to receive into itself the being it is looking at, just as he is, in all his truth." When we look and listen to others like this, "we

---

[25] Luther, *Martin Luther's Basic Theological Writings*, 486.
[26] Dietrich Bonhoeffer, "Sermon on Genesis 32:25-32; 33:10 from March 13, 1932," in *Ecumenical, Academic & Pastoral Work: 1931-1932*, ed. Victoria Barnett et al. (Minneapolis: Fortress, 2012), 432.
[27] Dietrich Bonhoeffer, *Life Together*, ed. Geffrey Kelly (Minneapolis: Fortress, 1996), 100, 98.
[28] See Andrew DeCort, "Seeds of Contemplation and Revolution amid War: The Subversive Power of Attentive Presence," *Comment*, Winter 2023, https://comment.org/seeds-of-contemplation-and-revolution-amid-war/.

destroy the evil in ourselves." Such love is practiced in asking others simple questions such as, "What are you going through?"[29]

In the face of the othering inflicted on African Americans simply because of their skin color, Martin Luther King Jr. called for "dangerous altruism." Like his namesake, Martin Luther, King preached that neighbor love that isn't willing to take risks for others and face real danger isn't love at all. Amid bombings and death threats for his struggle to secure civil rights for all, King declared, "The ultimate measure of a man is not where he stands in moments of comfort and convenience but where he stands at times of challenge and controversy. The true neighbor will risk his position, his prestige, and even his life for the welfare of others."[30]

Loving our neighbors *as ourselves* is further reflected in Óscar Romero, yet another victim of othering's violence. He extended King's dangerous altruism even to the killers of his beloved friend Father Grande, whom he addressed as "Dear Criminals." In his final sermon, he declared,

> One must not love oneself so much as to avoid getting involved in the risks of life that history demands of us. . . . Those who try to fend off the danger will lose their lives, while those who out of love for Christ give themselves to the service of others, will live, live like the grain of wheat that dies, but only apparently. . . . Only by undoing itself does it produce the harvest.[31]

Loving our neighbors *as ourselves* is indeed a challenging test of our love's authenticity. Mother Teresa calls this "giving until it hurts."[32] As Toni Morrison observes, "Anything coming back to life hurts."[33] Loving our neighbors *as ourselves* enlivens us by allowing others to enter into the intimacy of our souls and to receive the same quality of attention and care we give to ourselves.

Still, like Weil, Mother Teresa reminds us that neighbor love needn't be grand. It is often embodied in the most ordinary of ways, such as smiling at others or offering them a hug. She writes,

---

[29]Weil, *Waiting for God*, 65, 61-62, 64.
[30]King, *Strength to Love*, 26-27.
[31]Óscar Romero, "The Final Homily," homily, March 24, 1980, Romero Trust, www.romerotrust.org.uk/homilies-and-writings/homilies/final-homily-archbishop-romero.
[32]Mother Teresa, *Where There Is Love, There Is God*, ed. Brian Kolodiejchuk (New York: Doubleday, 2010), 4.
[33]Toni Morrison, *Beloved* (New York: Knopf, 2019), 35.

> Always be faithful in little things, for in them our strength lies. To God nothing is little.... Do not pursue spectacular deeds. We must deliberately renounce all desires to see the fruit of our labor, doing all we can as best we can, leaving the rest in the hands of God. What matters is the gift of yourself, the degree of love that you put into each one of your actions.[34]

Mother Teresa calls this "Something Beautiful for God" and the way that we "arrive at complete happiness."[35]

Loving our neighbors as ourselves, then, calls us to love others with the same quality of intentionality, excellence, and urgency with which we love ourselves. This part of the command challenges our apathy and othering's compulsion of "Save yourself!" against others. Neighbor love is a revolution within the self in which others now matter just as much to us as we do. Our heart and mind are no longer private property. They are now open and inhabited by our neighbors—a shared neighborhood of hospitality, generosity, and practical care. Others' pain isn't less important than our own. Others' needs aren't less pressing than our own. Others' hopes and dreams aren't less valuable than our own.

The ethical vision of the neighbor-love tradition is clear: neighbor love must permeate all our senses, our thinking, our desiring, our willing, and our vocation. We must learn to love others with all we are—a love that, if given earlier, could have saved Eyob's life, like Belay saved the wounded girl at the door of the church while worshipers streamed by her.

Loving *Ourselves* as Neighbors: The Affirmation of Self-Love

While neighbor love rightly challenges our *selfishness*, it simultaneously affirms our *self-love*. The two are not the same; one is vicious, the other virtuous. Before anyone else, each of us is a neighbor to our self. Thus, the command to love our neighbor *as our self* is also a command to *love our self* as a neighbor. As seventeenth-century mystic Brother Lawrence taught, "Respect Love present within."[36]

---

[34] Mother Teresa, *No Greater Love*, ed. Becky Benenate and Joseph Durepos (Novato, CA: New World Library, 1989), 30.
[35] Mother Teresa, *Mother Teresa: Essential Writings* (Maryknoll, NY: Orbis Books, 2001), 75.
[36] Brother Lawrence, *Practice of the Presence: A Revolutionary Translation*, trans. Carmen Acevedo Butcher (Minneapolis: Broadleaf Books, 2022), 48.

This simple insight is often overlooked: we too are one of God's children vibrating with divine love. Neighbor love is not self-loathing or even self-*less*ness. Both are really just forms of othering ourselves. It is essential to remember that neighbor love means seeing and treating others as morally *related* and *equally* precious in value—not superior.

There may be times when neighbor love in the face of extreme othering calls us to sacrifice ourselves for others as Bonhoeffer, Weil, King, Romero, and countless others have. But the God of neighbor love calls each one of us beloved and a cause for delight. Augustine crucially reminds us, "You can't love your neighbor as yourself, if you don't yet love yourself. The first thing I want to know is whether you love yourself. The whole gist of the commandment lies here, the whole question turns on this point."[37]

As we've seen, Jesus himself began his movement in the wake of hearing God say to him, "You are my beloved child; I delight in you" (see Mt 3:17, my translation; Mk 1:11; Lk 3:22). In fact, this is the singular message we hear God revoice to Jesus throughout his life recorded in the Gospels (see Mt 17:5; Mk 9:7; Lk 9:35; 2 Pet 1:17). It seems that Jesus so entirely internalized his own divine belovedness that he then returned from the desert with his revolutionary vision of neighbor love even for enemies. Thereafter, Jesus' presence overflowed with healing for others.

Jesus himself often retreated in silence, protected time for rest, celebrated with merrymakers at banquets, and allowed himself space to grieve his suffering.[38] Before his death, Jesus was overwhelmed with anguish; he was fully human like we are and didn't *want* to die but *live*. While he ultimately accepted the call to love his neighbors *as himself* to the point of his own death, it is clear that Jesus *loved himself*. His unkillable love for his enemies started here.

Again, then, neighbor love doesn't mean loving others *more* than ourselves, as if they were superior to us. It also doesn't mean loving ourselves *less*, as if we were inferior to others. It means loving one another as equally precious in value, starting with ourselves. Neighbor love *abolishes* othering's competitive vision of humanity rather than *internalizing* it and targeting it

---

[37]Augustine, "Sermon 90A," in *Sermons, III/11: Newly Discovered Sermons*, trans. Edmund Hill (Hyde Park, NY: New City, 2000), 80. See Thomas Merton, *No Man Is an Island* (New York: Houghton Mifflin, 1983), xvii: "We cannot love others unless we love ourselves."

[38]See Tricia Hersey, *Rest Is Resistance: A Manifesto* (New York: Little Brown Spark, 2022).

at the self. Self-loathing and striving to be sel*fless* only perpetuate othering and inevitably act out against others.[39]

As Augustine made clear, loving others well flows out of loving ourselves well. If we're able to ask ourselves, "What are you going through?" there's a better chance we'll be ready to ask others this important question. If we know how to see ourselves with compassion when we're hurting, there's a better chance we'll know how to extend compassion to others when they're in pain. When we practice speaking words of kindness to ourselves when we make mistakes, we're cultivating the muscle memory to forgive others when they make mistakes. When we pay attention to our needs, know our limits, and tend to our own rest, we're apprenticing in how to see and serve the needs of our neighbors. bell hooks observes, "One of the best guides to how to be self-loving is to give ourselves the love we are often dreaming about receiving from others."[40]

The opposite is also true. If we've normalized being hardhearted toward ourselves, speaking insulting words to ourselves, and ignoring our needs, there's a better chance that we'll replicate these harmful habits in our behavior with others. In fact, we might neglect or hurt our neighbors and be totally unaware that we're even doing it, because we do these things to ourselves. How many of our failures to love our neighbors *as ourselves* originate in our neglect to *love ourselves*?[41]

Here we encounter a more delightful paradox of neighbor love: loving our neighbors *as ourselves* begins with *loving ourselves*. When we accept our divine belovedness and internalize it through practices of self-love, we're not actually becoming more selfish. We're learning how to love others *well*—the way we ourselves want to be loved. We're becoming healthier, holier, happier people who can bring happiness to God by accepting God's love and who can share happiness with others by learning the art of love.

This is why the Neighbor-Love Movement designed seven practices of self-love that complement our other seven practices that embody our covenant. We invite our ambassadors not only to dare to do these practices but to dare to *enjoy* doing them:

---

[39]See Andrew DeCort, "Pain, Neighbor-Love, Intimacy," *Pace: The Art of Living Slowly* (Singapore), June 2022.
[40]bell hooks, *All About Love: New Visions* (New York: HarperCollins, 2001), 67.
[41]Henri Nouwen offered a beautiful vision of self-love in his book *The Inner Voice of Love: A Journey Through Anguish to Freedom* (New York: Doubleday, 1998).

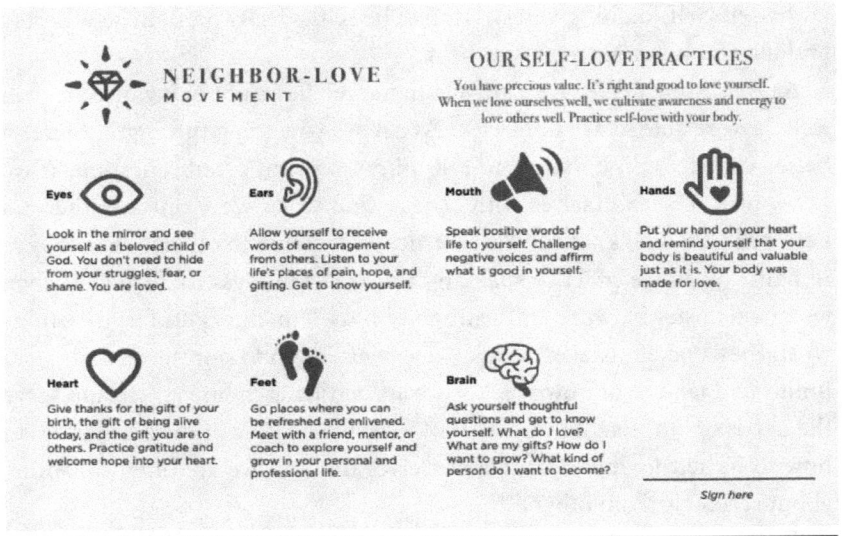

Figure 7.2a. Self-Love Practices of Neighbor-Love Movement

 1. **Eyes:** Look in the mirror and see yourself as a beloved child of God. You don't need to hide from your struggles, fear, or shame. You are loved.

 2. **Ears:** Allow yourself to receive words of encouragement from others. Listen to your life's places of pain, hope, and gifting. Get to know yourself.

 3. **Mouth:** Speak positive words of life to yourself. Challenge negative voices and affirm what is good in yourself.

 4. **Hands:** Put your hands on your heart and remind yourself that your body is beautiful and valuable just as it is. Your body was made for love.

 5. **Heart:** Give thanks for the gift of your birth, the gift of being alive today, and the gift you are to others. Practice gratitude and welcome hope into your heart.

 6. **Feet:** Go places where you can be refreshed and enlivened. Meet with a friend, mentor, or coach to explore yourself and grow in your personal and professional life.

 7. **Brain:** Ask yourself thoughtful questions and get to know yourself. What do I love? What are my gifts? How do I want to grow? What kind of person do I want to become?

Toni Morrison's novel *Beloved* inspired us to design these practices of self-love. There Baby Suggs, a woman who narrowly escaped the extreme othering of American slavery, gathers her community in a forest. As they wait on divine presence, Baby Suggs tells these survivors,

> Here in this here place, we flesh, flesh that weeps, laughs; flesh that dances on bare feet in grass. Love it. Love it hard. Yonder they do not love your flesh. They despise it. . . . Love your hands! Raise them up and kiss them. Touch others with them, pat them together, stroke them on your face 'cause they don't love that either. *You got to love it*, you! . . . Love your neck; put a hand on it, grace it, stroke it and hold it up. And all your inside parts that they'd just as soon slop for hogs, you got to love. The dark, dark liver—love it, love it, and the beat and beating heart, love that too. More than eyes or feet. More than lungs that have yet to draw free air. More than your life-holding womb and your life-giving private parts. Hear me now, love your heart. For this is the prize.[42]

Practicing self-love powerfully resists the all-too-easy internalization of the othering we suffer and sometimes inflict. In the vision of neighbor love, each neighbor—including our self—is created by God, loved by God, and thus invited by God to love our self. "This is the prize." When we love ourselves, our love for others becomes enlivened, insightful, and exquisite.

Love your neighbor *as yourself*.

THE PERENNIAL WISDOM OF THE NEIGHBOR-LOVE MOVEMENT

Before concluding this book, we can summarize some of the perennial wisdom we've observed across the neighbor-love movement's millennial history. This summary is far from exhaustive. There is much more wisdom to glean in this verdant, abundant garden. But these fifteen insights linger with me as I survey the ground we've covered.

1. **Othering is ironic.** At heart, othering drives us to separate ourselves from others or to claim superiority over them. But in doing so, othering always leads to cheap or even atrocious behavior. It often imitates the behavior it self-righteously condemns. We've seen this throughout the ancient world, in the Bible itself, and in compromised moments in Christian history

---

[42]Morrison, *Beloved*, 88-89. See Jean-Luc Marion, *The Erotic Phenomenon*, trans. Stephen Lewis (Chicago: University of Chicago Press, 2007), 21: "I could not be, nor accept to endure being, without at least the open possibility that at one moment or another someone is loving me. For me, to be signifies nothing less than to be-loved."

such as Aquinas's support for the Crusades and Luther's vicious othering of the Jews.

Thankfully, there is no universal other across human history. And thus there is nothing inevitable about othering itself. When Jesus commanded, "Do not judge others," he cut the root of this tragically perennial weed, which may be the only true enemy of humanity.

2. **Neighbor love is paradoxical.** This is the repeated paradox in Jesus' teaching of neighbor love and those who extend it: we only exclude ourselves from full belonging with God when we exclude others from full belonging. The reason isn't that God harbors any trace of othering in Godself. Jesus defined God as "kind to the ungrateful and wicked," one whose love is given indiscriminately to all God's children. The reason is that God *is* love (1 Jn 4:8, 16). If we ourselves don't love *love*, then we won't feel at home with God or desire the full belonging that God desires for all of us. Dorothy Day, who devoted her life to living with impoverished neighbors in New York, captures this paradox: "[Christ] made heaven hinge on the way we act toward Him in His disguise of commonplace, frail, ordinary humanity."[43]

3. **Neighbor love is humane happiness.** Again and again, we've seen that neighbor love is a source of joy, both in ourselves and with others. It is not a self-loathing obligation or stoic duty. Jesus promises, "Do this, and you will *flourish*" (Lk 10:28, my translation). Many figures we've studied—from the author of the Epistle to Diognetus all the way to Mother Teresa—called it the key to our true happiness. I note bell hooks's wisdom once more: "I know no one who has embraced a love ethic whose life has not become joyous and more fulfilling. The widespread assumption that ethical behavior takes the fun out of life is false."[44]

4. **Neighbor love is self-reforming.** In the Sermon on the Mount, Jesus prophetically warns that many who call him "Lord," conjure miracles, and otherwise perform a religious identity but don't obey his commands are unrecognizable to him. Thereafter, prophetic Christians have used neighbor love as the decisive standard by which to critique Christian corruption and hypocrisy. We've seen that Jesus and many others primarily focused this critique on religious leaders who use their position for their own prestige,

---

[43]Dorothy Day, *By Little and by Little: The Selected Writings of Dorothy Day*, ed. Robert Ellsberg (New York: Knopf, 1984), 97.
[44]hooks, *All About Love*, 88.

privilege, and power. But we've also seen neighbor love marshaled to critique wider corruption in Christianized cultures, like Bonhoeffer did in Germany, Weil in France, King in America, and Romero in El Salvador. Simone Weil is an especially striking example in our study. In the twentieth century, she reversed the paradox of neighbor love and excluded herself from being baptized in the Catholic Church to embody solidarity with the nonbelievers that the church has othered.

5. **Neighbor love is mystical.** What kind of mystical experience may Boaz have had? With his great-great-grandson Jesus, mysticism—"the direct and transformative presence of God"—starts suffusing the neighbor-love story.[45] Jesus sees heaven open and hears God call him *beloved*. Thereafter, Jesus teaches that the essential elements of our existence, such as light and water, are the outpouring of our Parent's love for all of us, including our enemy-siblings.

Julian of Norwich, with her vision of the universe as a tiny hazelnut sustained by Jesus "our true mother," is a special moment in neighbor love's mystical unfolding. She writes, "In this oneness of love depends the life of all humanity. . . . We are all as one in love."[46] Similarly, Simone Weil sees the universe as a golden egg that cracks open and overflows with divine love. In this vision, God's act of creation and Jesus' death on the cross are essentially the same event: God's loving embrace of others. Weil writes, "This universe where we are living, and of which we form a tiny particle is the distance put by Love between God and God." This she calls a "supreme union" that vibrates not only in every human but the earth and everything that exists.[47]

In the mysticism of neighbor love, then, we learn to experience our neighbor's presence as a vibration of divine love, whether they love us back or not. The tradition repeatedly roots this vision in Jesus' teaching in Matthew 25:31-46. Dorothy Day concisely captures it again: "Our neighbors are Christ, appealing to [us]."[48]

Mystical neighbor love extends to a fearless embrace of death itself. If we are commanded to love our enemies and if death is "the last enemy," as Paul writes, we may even love death as it delivers us into our next heteronautic adventure with God and our neighbors. Here the fear of self-loss at the heart

---

[45]Bernard McGinn, *The Essential Writings of Christian Mysticism* (New York: Modern Library, 2006), xix.
[46]Julian, *Revelations of Divine Love*, 9, 51.
[47]Weil, *Waiting for God*, 75, 72.
[48]Day, *By Little and by Little*, 94.

of othering is surrendered, and the self-sacrifice that may be required in neighbor love is suffused with hope. As J. K. Rowling writes at the end of the Harry Potter story, in many ways a story about othering and how neighbor love ultimately overcomes it: "Do not pity the dead, Harry. Pity the living and, above all, those who live without love."[49]

6. ***Neighbor love positively others enemies into neighbors.*** Jesus teaches, "You have heard that it was said, 'Love your neighbor and hate your enemy.' But I tell you, love your enemy and pray for those who persecute you that you may be children of your Father in heaven" (Mt 5:43-45). It seems that Jesus was attempting to revive the heart of Moses' original command, which begins, "Do not seek revenge or bear a grudge against anyone among your people" (Lev 19:18)—but Jesus universalizes who counts as "your people." In his vision, "our people" are now *everyone*, including our enemy-siblings.

This teaching has been one of the most consistent threads across the history of the neighbor-love movement. The ones we are most tempted and feel most justified to other—our enemies—are also our *neighbors*. They are people who are morally related to us and equally precious in value. Here again, neighbor love fundamentally uproots othering. We are one another's people. We are *we* and commanded to love one another.

7. ***Neighbor love is cosmopolitan.*** From Genesis 1's vision of all people being created in God's holy image, to Abraham's call to bless all people, to Jesus' global Great Commission, to the Epistle to Diognetus, to Simone Weil and well beyond, neighbor love calls us to see ourselves as citizens of the whole universe. This connects with neighbor love's mysticism but also its prophetic, self-reforming energy.

We saw that religious nationalism was a crucial factor that prevented ancient Israel from fully abolishing othering and universalizing neighbor love. We've also seen how potent notions of ethnic, racial, and national identity were in fueling some of the most atrocious expressions of othering in the twentieth century, including racialized segregation and genocide. Neighbor love defies all nationalism as one of the most lethal forms of othering.

Near or far, all people are our neighbors and thus morally connected to us and equal in value. The other's citizenship, lack thereof, or any other

---

[49]J. K. Rowling, *Harry Potter and the Deathly Hallows* (New York: Scholastic, 2009), 722. See Andrew DeCort, "The Ethics of Harry Potter," andrew-decort.com on March 28, 2022 at https://andrew-decort.com/essays/harry-potter/.

marker of identity does not make them any less worthy of our love. Our world is one human neighborhood, a universal moral circle, and we are commanded to love our neighbors as ourselves across every border and boundary. As Mother Teresa says, "I belong to the whole world."

8. **Neighbor love is liberating.** From the Hebrew prophets, to Jesus' movement, to the earliest embodiments of it in primal Christianity, neighbor love has prioritized the poor, oppressed, and powerless. James calls neighbor love "the law that gives freedom" (Jas 2:12). This is what energized Jesus' followers to innovate public schools, hospitals, nursing homes, and other institutions that overcame systemic injustice.

Of course, neighbor love enshrines the moral equality of all people. But it repeatedly focuses special concern on victims of othering, especially our culturally marginalized, economically impoverished, and/or politically oppressed neighbors. Thus, it led to groundbreaking reforms and unprecedented innovations in society for human flourishing. Romero, following the liberation theology he once held in suspicion, called this "God's preferential option for the poor." Simone Weil writes that neighbor love is another name for justice—"a name it bears in many passages of the Gospel and which is so beautiful."[50]

Thankfully, neighbor love's journey of human flourishing continues today. In recent centuries, poverty has dramatically fallen. Basic health and life expectancy have skyrocketed. Many diseases have been eradicated, cured, or contained. Access to education and opportunities for learning are at unprecedented levels. Laws have been passed to protect the dignity of women, children, and the marginalized in most societies.

The ethic of neighbor love must be passionately committed to the liberating work of justice in all its forms in the face of our contemporary crises of othering I mentioned in chapter one. It should build on and expand its ancient precedents of imagining, advocating, and implementing innovative, sometimes revolutionary transformations in the structures of human society.[51]

9. **Neighbor love is creative nonviolent power.** Creative nonviolence was one of Jesus' most innovative teachings and has endured as a signature, if often smudged, sign of the neighbor-love movement. Jesus taught that

---

[50]Weil, *Waiting for God*, 24.
[51]See Maureen O'Connell, *Compassion: Loving Our Neighbor in an Age of Globalization* (Maryknoll, NY: Orbis Books, 2009); Eric Gregory, "Agape and Global Economy," in *Global Neighbors: Christian Faith and Moral Obligation in Today's Economy*, ed. Douglas Hicks and Mark Valeri (Grand Rapids, MI: Eerdmans, 2010), 16-42.

neighbor love creatively transforms injustice rather than reactively transferring it. Its justice is not retaliatory or retributive, nor its nonviolence weak or ineffective. It is the powerful embodiment of our moral agency and prophetic defiance in the face of othering, refusing to imitate othering in the name of overcoming it. As Paul taught his Roman audience amid its culture of violence, "Love does no harm to a neighbor" (Rom 13:10).

After analyzing all of Christianity's surviving literature from its first three hundred years, Ronald Sider concluded, "What we can say with confidence is that every extant Christian statement on killing and war up to the time of Constantine says Christians must not kill, even in war."[52] Martin Luther King Jr. endures as one of the most inspiring teachers and practitioners of the nonviolent neighbor love Jesus taught. He writes, "The way of violence leads to bitterness in the survivors and brutality in the destroyers. But the way of nonviolence leads to redemption and the creation of the beloved community."[53]

Today Erica Chenoweth has demonstrated that nonviolence is twice as effective as violence at bringing sustainable change in situations of conflict. It always works when just 3.5 percent of a society's population organizes around a nonviolent campaign.[54] This social-scientific research offers fresh fuel for the neighbor-love movement's creative nonviolence today.

10. *Neighbor love is intimately personal and immediately practical.* Amid all its cosmopolitan energy rightly invested in liberation and nonviolence, neighbor love is grounded in our personal relationships, including with ourselves. Jesus was famous for relating to every kind of neighbor in his society, asking them curious questions, and listening to them. Bonhoeffer also emphasized being *with* others and listening to them as crucial practices of neighbor love. Weil similarly grounded her vision of neighbor love in giving our attention to others and inviting them to be "exactly as they are, in all of their truth."

The Neighbor-Love Movement has sought to distill these practices of neighbor love in our practices that embody our covenant's other-love and self-love. When this practice becomes our life's work, we start with ourselves and "at home," as Mother Teresa said—whether with a smile, a gentle touch, or another expression of humanity. Then, neighbor love ripples out of our

---

[52]Ronald Sider, *The Early Church on Killing: A Comprehensive Sourcebook on War, Abortion, and Capital Punishment* (Grand Rapids, MI: Baker Academic, 2012), 194.
[53]King, *Testament to Hope*, 25.
[54]Erica Chenoweth, *Civil Resistance: What Everyone Needs to Know* (New York: Oxford University Press, 2021).

selves and personal relationships into our wider social, political, and economic structures with authenticity, integrity, and resilience.

11. **Neighbor love is an interfaith ethic for all people.** We started our study of neighbor love by examining its expression in the Jewish ethics of Hebrew Scripture. We then explored Jesus' universalization of the neighbor-love ethic on this Jewish foundation and how it evolved across Christian history.

Again and again, we've seen that neighbor love is an ethic of solidarity rather than supremacy—an ethic of cooperation rather than competition. As my partner in the Neighbor-Love Movement, Dr. Tekalign Nega, often says, "Love is a multiplier." Neighbor love is not the monopoly of any one faith tradition. Jesus himself praises the "faith" of the Canaanite woman whom Moses had marked for genocide (Mt 15:21-28). Weil calls neighbor love "completely universal love."[55]

In a future project, I hope to explore neighbor love across non-Christian traditions. For example, the Holy Qur'an teaches, "Be good to neighbors, near and far" (4:36). The Prophet Muhammad is quoted in the Hadiths as teaching, "None of you has faith until you love for your neighbor what you love for yourself." Repeating the paradox of neighbor love, he says, "He will not enter paradise whose neighbor is not secure from his wrongful conduct."[56]

Buddha taught, "Let a man overcome anger by love. . . . For hatred does not cease by hatred at any time; hatred ceases by love; this is an old rule." A medieval Buddhist scripture calls this "work for the liberation of all beings."[57] Echoing Weil's statement of not wanting to belong to

---

[55] Weil, *Waiting for God*, 50-51, 3.
[56] Muslim: *Kitab al-iman* [*Book of Faith*], book 1, #72 and #74, quoted in *A Common Word: Muslims and Christians on Loving God and Neighbor*, ed. Miroslav Volf, Ghazi bin Muhammad, and Melissa Yarrington (Grand Rapids, MI: Eerdmans, 2010). For important studies of Islamic ethics, see Oddbjørn Leirvik, "Aw qāla: 'Li-jārihi': Some Observations on Brotherhood and Neighborly Love in Islamic Tradition," *Islam and Christian-Muslim Relations* 21, no. 4 (2010): 357-72; Abdulaziz Sachendina, *The Islamic Roots of Democratic Pluralism* (New York: Oxford University Press, 2001); and Yaser Ellethy, *Islam, Context, Pluralism and Democracy: Classical and Modern Interpretations* (New York: Routledge, 2014). On the relationship of Judaism, Christianity, and Islam, see David Nirenberg, *Neighboring Faiths: Christianity, Islam, and Judaism in the Middle Ages and Today* (Chicago: University of Chicago Press, 2014); Kelly James Clark, Aziz Abu Sarah, and Nancy Fuchs, *Strangers, Neighbors, Friends: Muslim-Christian-Jewish Reflections on Compassion and Peace* (Eugene, OR: Cascade Books, 2018); Leonard Grob and John K. Roth, eds., *Encountering the Stranger: A Jewish-Christian-Muslim Trialogue* (Seattle: University of Washington Press, 2012). Jordan Duffner, *Islamophobia: What Christians Should Know (and Do) About Anti-Muslim Discrimination* (Maryknoll, NY: Orbis Books, 2021), discusses neighbor love in chap. 10.
[57] Buddha, "Overcome Anger by Love," in *The Power of Nonviolence* (Boston: Beacon Press, 2002), 3; Donald Lopez Jr., ed., *Buddhist Scriptures* (New York: Penguin Classics, 2004), 524-25.

any *we* that excludes others, the beloved Buddhist monk Thich Nhat Hanh writes more simply, "We are they."[58]

Strikingly similar to Jesus' teaching in Matthew 25, Hindu scripture teaches, "Be one for whom a stranger is God."[59] Hindu poet Balkrishna Sama, known as Nepal's Shakespeare, then writes, "I see God with my eyes wide open in the dear sight of every person."[60]

Vaclav Havel, an agnostic playwright, anti-authoritarian dissident, and the first president of the Czech Republic, said, "Identity is not a prison; it is an appeal for dialogue with others. Love for one's fellow humans is the central commandment of all our contending cultures."[61] The fact that our diverse, sometimes "contending" religious traditions share an overlapping ethic of neighbor love does not mean that they are all the same. That itself would be a violation of neighbor love by denying the uniqueness of the other, both in their treasures and challenges. But it does mean that neighbor love is a truly universal, interfaith ethic with shared values and practices that can help heal our othering and bridge our differences, real and imagined.[62]

12. **Neighbor love is a revolutionary abolition movement against othering.** In the moral vision of neighbor love, no justification remains for seeing any other as morally unrelated or less than ourselves—as anything other than a *neighbor*. As Paul writes, Christ has "destroyed the barrier," "put to death [our] hostility," and "create[d] in himself one new humanity" (Eph 2:14-16).

Whether others are righteous or unrighteous, whether they are a citizen or a foreigner, whether they are a stranger or an enemy, they remain our *neighbor*—morally related to us and equal in precious value. The Didache teaches, "You shall hate no human." Past resentments, present conflicts, and future ambitions offer no justification for othering.

The neighbor-love movement should continue in its revolutionary vocation of disestablishing and abolishing othering in all its forms across the earth today. Audre Lorde calls this "the energy to pursue genuine change

---

[58] Thich Nhat Hanh, *Essential Writings* (Maryknoll, NY: Orbis Books, 2001), 130.
[59] *Taittiriya Upanishad* 1.11.1-2, Shlokam (2024), https://shlokam.org/texts/taittiriya-1-11-2/.
[60] I'm grateful to my friend Nikhil Mandalaparthy for sharing Sama's quote.
[61] Vaclav Havel, *The Art of the Impossible: Politics as Morality in Practice* (New York: Knopf, 1997), 202. See Amartya Sen, *Identity and Violence: The Illusion of Destiny* (New York: Norton, 2006).
[62] See James Walters, *Loving Your Neighbour in an Age of Religious Conflict: A New Agenda for Interfaith Relations* (London: Jessica Kingsley, 2019). For a Sikh perspective, see Valarie Kaur, *See No Stranger: A Memoir and Manifesto of Revolutionary Love* (New York: One World, 2021).

within our world, rather than merely settling for a shift of characters in the same weary drama."[63]

13. **Neighbor love witnesses a hopeful universalism.** In his command to love our enemies, Jesus teaches, "[Your Father] is kind to the ungrateful and wicked" (Lk 6:35). With some of his final breaths, Jesus prays for his killers, "Father, forgive them" (Lk 23:34). In his famous poem, Paul writes, "Love always protects, always trusts, always hopes, always perseveres. Love never fails" (1 Cor 13:7-8). In his manifesto to Rome, he insists further, "I am convinced that . . . [nothing] in all creation, will be able to separate us from the love of God that is in Christ Jesus our Lord" (Rom 8:38-39). Likewise, Paul tells his mentee Timothy that "God our Savior . . . wants all people to be saved" (1 Tim 2:3-4).

With this primal Christian teaching, many of the people we've studied across the history of neighbor love believed that God would ultimately save all people in the final resurrection of the dead. Indeed, Paul, Bucer, Bonhoeffer, Weil, Mother Teresa, and others across the neighbor-love movement insisted they would rather be damned if others were not saved.

Of course, God alone knows our future; it would be presumptuous to make dogmatic statements of certainty. But, at the very least, neighbor love leads to a *hopeful* universalism. What could be more aligned with the spirit of neighbor love than for all of us neighbors to *hope* for one another's ultimate healing in the presence of God? Indeed, what could be a more ironic, ultimate expression of othering than to hope for our own salvation without hoping for the salvation of other sinners just like ourselves? As Jesus promises, "Do not judge, and you will not be judged" (Lk 6:37; see Mt 7:1).

Here the othering in our apocalyptic visions is offered healing and hope.

14. **When we love the other, we often become the other.** Neighbor love is costly. As Nicholas Wolterstorff writes, "In commanding us to love, God invites us to suffer."[64]

When Jesus loved his Samaritan neighbors, he was othered as a Samaritan itself. This painful pattern persists across the neighbor-love movement into my own experience in Ethiopia amid civil war.

---

[63]Audre Lorde, *The Master's Tools Will Never Dismantle the Master's House* (London: Penguin, 2018), 15. See Letha Scanzoni and Virginia Mollenknott, *Is the Homosexual My Neighbor? A Positive Christian Response* (San Francisco: Harper, 1994).
[64]Wolterstorff, *Lament for a Son*, 89.

Othering presents as a superior identity, but it is intensely insecure. It feels threatened when others are included and equalized. Like an addiction, it enslaves and impoverishes us, but we may come to enjoy it and feel safe within it.

As I wrote at the start of this chapter, neighbor love is a sobriety journey for the whole human family. But we addicts can be ruthless amid the withdrawals of othering. When we love others as *neighbors*, we shouldn't be surprised to be marked as others ourselves. Anticipating this can make us more centered, compassionate, creative, and resilient in the face of othering.

15. **Neighbor love heals us.** The fundamental desire of every person is to feel worthy and like we belong. Worth and belonging are what neighbor love invites us to experience. Othering hopelessly attempts to secure our desire *at the expense of* others and ironically reproduces the very things we so intimately hate: exclusion and inferiority. Neighbor love promises us equal worth and full belonging by sharing them *with* others.

In neighbor love, we no longer need to *compete* against one another, terrified of scarcity and exhausted to keep up. We can *cooperate* with one another. We no longer need to struggle for *superiority*, afraid of losing our place and being humiliated. We can share solidarity in the inexhaustible abundance of our divine belovedness. We are we—neighbors—morally related and equally precious.

Ironically, humbly facing our tendency to other can unify us: we all want the same thing—to feel worthy and like we belong. The addiction points to authentic desire. As Baldwin writes, "Our humanity is our burden, our life; we need not battle for it; we need only to do what is infinitely more difficult—that is, to accept it."[65]

Two thousand years ago, Jesus promised, "Do this, and you will flourish" (Lk 10:28, my translation). This promise resounds across the centuries to us today. Othering is not the end of our story. Neighbor love heals and never fails.

Conclusion: The Global Abolition Movement of Neighbor Love Today

Neighbor love is a way of life that joins God in healing our world. Loving our neighbors, loving our enemies, loving one another, loving ourselves—that is

---

[65]James Baldwin, "Many Thousands Gone," in *James Baldwin: Collected Essays*, ed. Toni Morrison (New York: Library of America, 1998), 18.

this ancient movement's universal invitation and enduring response to the crisis of othering.

Here at the end, I return to Jesus' original vision and final commission for his neighbor-love movement: "All authority in heaven and on earth has been given to me. Therefore go and make disciples of all nations, baptizing them in the name of the Father and of the Son and of the Holy Spirit, and teaching them to obey everything I have commanded you. And surely I am with you always, to the very end of the age" (Mt 28:18-20). Alluding to his own baptism in divine belovedness, Jesus invited his movement to immerse all humanity in this belovedness and to apprentice all humanity in the practice of neighbor love. His Great Commission was and remains a call to globalize his *great commandment* of neighbor love—and, with it, to abolish othering across the earth. Jesus promised to be with us in it to the very end.

This is what his movement, at its best, has done for the last two thousand years and continues to do today, as we've now seen. Loving our neighbors as ourselves is how we can continue to fulfill Jesus' ultimate commission in our world. It's how we can embody God's promise to Abraham to bless all people. It's how we can heal the one human family that we are, who descend from shared ancestors and belong together. It's how we can return to the beginning and see the image of God in each person—"every creature" as "a glittering, glistening mirror of divinity."[66] It's how we come home to the universal golden circle of God's eternal, everlasting love.

Love your neighbor as yourself: when we revive this "dead dogma" and "frequently, fully, and fearlessly" reroot ourselves in it, we find the answer to that "most important question for the future" that Dietrich Bonhoeffer asked in his Nazi prison cell: "How are we going to find a basis for living together with other people?"

Three months after the assassination of Dr. King, James Baldwin addressed the World Council of Churches. He surveyed "the dangerous place we find ourselves in today." Then he named his hope in this dark age: "The revolution which was begun two thousand years ago by a disreputable Hebrew criminal may now have to be begun again by people equally disreputable and equally improbable."[67]

---

[66] Hildegard of Bingen, quoted in Cynthia Overweg, "Hildegard of Bingen: The Nun Who Loved the Earth," *Quest* 105, no. 3 (Summer 2017): 21.
[67] James Baldwin, "White Racism or World Community?," in *Collected Essays*, 750.

That revolution continues. Jesus began a healing movement of neighbor love that remains alive today. Will we join Jesus in beginning it afresh, even if doing so seems improbable and disreputable in our time of escalating othering? Julian of Norwich called this movement of divine love "a new beginning which will last without end, always beginning anew," until "All shall be well."[68]

All shall be well. Even for Eyob, the victims of Ethiopia's civil war, and all of us others in the Mexico Square of our world. All shall be well.

---

[68]Julian, *Revelations of Divine Love*, 129, 136.

AN INVITATION TO THE NEIGHBOR-LOVE MOVEMENT

In 2019, I cofounded the Neighbor-Love Movement (NLM) in Ethiopia with my wife, Lily, and our partner, Dr. Tekalign Nega. Our desire was and remains to mainstream the ancient-yet-emerging vision of neighbor love in the face of contemporary othering. Since then, thousands of people have signed our covenant and committed to embodying its practices. Over twenty million others have encountered our invitation to nonviolent spirituality. I warmly invite you to learn more about NLM, digitally sign our covenant, and partner in our work at www.nlmglobal.org. I also invite you to physically sign the covenant below as a small but tangible act of commitment to practice neighbor love today. Please join us in promoting love, justice, and flourishing for all neighbors in our world.

STUDY GUIDE

Questions for Reflection and Discussion

Chapter 1: Neighbor Love: The Crisis of Othering and the Hope of Humanity

1. What thoughts, emotions, or experiences surfaced in you as you read Andrew's story about meeting Eyob and wrestling with the pain of othering?

2. Othering can be defined as seeing others as unrelated or less than ourselves. As you read Andrew's survey of othering across human storytelling, philosophy, and society, can you think of additional examples of othering in your life and world?

3. Who is your neighbor? Which others have you been conditioned to see as unrelated or less than yourself? When you are fully honest, who does your moral circle include and exclude?

4. J. S. Mill wrote that neighbor love easily becomes a "dead dogma" slumbering in "incrusted minds." As you think about your life and context, is neighbor love a dead dogma, a living truth, or something else?

5. Neighbor love can be defined as seeing others as morally related and equally precious in value to ourselves. It's passionate will and practical work for our shared well-being, which Andrew describes as a movement that can overcome othering and heal our world. How would you describe neighbor love in your own words? What might begin to grow or change in your life and world if you fully, frequently, and fearlessly engaged neighbor love in this way?

Chapter 2: The Origins of Neighbor Love: The Hebrew Bible

1. Desmond Tutu and Benjamin Netanyahu's words illustrate how Scripture can be used in very different ways, whether to dignify or dehumanize

others. Michael Fishbane wrote that Scripture presents "pivots for moral reflection" that should not be "ignored or neutralized" but actively engaged for our "freedom and responsibility." How does this way of reading Scripture deepen or disturb the way you currently read it?

2. Have you ever tried reading Scripture as if you were an othered Canaanite or Moabite rather than as a favored Israelite? How might this change in perspective enlarge your reading and faith?

3. What did you find particularly inspiring in the Hebrew Bible's moral vision of humanity and call to love our neighbors as ourselves? Describe specific examples and their practical implications for how we can learn to see and treat others today.

4. What was particularly troubling to you in the way the Hebrew Bible may limit who we see as neighbors or even mark some others for unequal status, exclusion, or extermination?

5. As you look into the mirror of Scripture, how might your own community simultaneously promote neighbor love but also reinscribe othering? Does religious nationalism play a role in your group's identity and circle of belonging—perhaps seeing itself as the head and some others as the tail? Who is your Canaanite/enemy, and how should these image-bearing neighbors be treated? As you reflect on these questions, pay attention to how your body experiences emotions like insecurity, fear, disgust, jealousy, resentment, anger, and aggression, as well as empathy, trust, curiosity, appreciation, gentleness, and hope.

CHAPTER 3: THE UNIVERSALIZATION OF NEIGHBOR LOVE AND THE ABOLITION OF OTHERING: JESUS OF NAZARETH

1. Before Jesus began his public movement, he went into the wilderness and heard God say to him, "You are my beloved child; I delight in you" (Mt 3:13-17, my translation). How do you think this mystical experience of God's love influenced how Jesus understood and practiced neighbor love? How might internalizing our own divine belovedness intersect with loving our neighbors today?

2. In his movement's manifesto known as the Sermon on the Mount, Jesus universalized neighbor love and taught, "You have heard that it was said, 'Love your neighbor and hate your enemy.' But I tell you, love your

enemy and pray for those who persecute you, that you may be children of your Father in heaven" (Matt 5:43-35). After reading this chapter, how does Jesus' groundbreaking teaching strike you differently than it may have before? What is freshly inspiring or challenging to you? Be sure to comment on Jesus' teaching of creative nonviolence.

3. Jesus had a very high view of neighbor love: he taught that it is the key to interpreting Scripture (Mt 22:36-40), the heart of God's will (Mt 7:12; 19:17-19; Mk 12:28-34), and the way of eternal life (Lk 10:28). Do you observe the communities that claim Jesus' name today giving neighbor the same centrality that Jesus did, or has something changed?

4. Jesus provocatively chose an othered Samaritan to serve as the exemplar of neighbor love in his famous parable in Luke 10. If you retold his story today, which contemporary others might substitute for the role of the Samaritan? How does it make you feel to name *them* as exemplars of God's will and promise of eternal life? How might this exercise help us re-access the radical potency of Jesus' original vision of neighbor love today?

5. Andrew interpreted Jesus' death as his ultimate embodiment of neighbor love and the "unotherability" or unconditionality of God's love for all people, including his murderers. Have you understood Jesus' death like this before? How does this interpretation deepen or disturb your current interpretation of Jesus' death?

6. Andrew interpreted Jesus' Great Commission in Matthew 28 as Jesus' call to universalize our moral circle, globalize neighbor love, and abolish othering across the earth. Have you ever interpreted Jesus' commission for his movement this way before? What do you see as the practical implications for us today?

Chapter 4: The Improbable Revolution of Neighbor Love: The New Testament

1. In the section titled "The Earliest Movement of Jesus," Andrew surveyed how Jesus' first followers sought to practice neighbor love and overcome othering in their world. What surprised or inspired you?

2. Paul repeatedly writes that "Love your neighbor as yourself" is the "fulfillment" or "summary" of God's will for us (see Rom 13:8-10;

Gal 5:13-15). Strikingly, Paul doesn't mention the command to love God in these passages. How might this singular focus indicate the fundamental importance of neighbor love in Paul's vision of God and how we are meant to love God?

3. In his discussion of Romans 13 and 15, Andrew described how Paul's focus on love "doing no harm to a neighbor" and prioritizing our "weak" neighbors was a direct challenge to Rome's idolization of power and violent entertainment. How might neighbor love challenge othering values in politics, culture, and entertainment today?

4. When Paul summarizes the life of Jesus and neighbor love, he often names core identities in his society like "male and female," "Jew and Gentile," "slave and free" (Gal 3:28; Col 3:11; Eph 2:11-20). He then declares that these (often othering) identities are no longer definitive "in Christ," because Jesus "tore down the dividing wall of hostility" and "created one new humanity in himself" (Eph 2:14-15). What identities might Paul name if he were writing today? How might neighbor love help us reimagine our identities and heal othering in our contexts?

5. James called neighbor love "the law that gives freedom" (Jas 2:12). He then applied it to critique the religious hypocrisy and economic inequality in his context. How might neighbor love critique our religion and economics today?

Chapter 5: The Red Thread: A Brief History of Jesus' Neighbor-Love Movement

1. When Ferdosa first heard the invitation "Love your enemy" amid ethnic cleansing in her community, she was astonished and committed her life to this way of love. Have you had a similar experience that awakened you to the radical challenge and hope of neighbor love?

2. The earliest critics of Jesus' movement attacked it for attracting "slaves and women and children." Tertullian wrote that Christianity was "branded" for loving the most othered people in society. Compare and contrast how Christianity might be attacked and "branded" today. What do you observe, and what does this indicate about how Jesus' movement has deepened or deviated from its roots?

3. Andrew wrote that the spread of Jesus' neighbor-love movement helps explain "how humanity went from the violent othering of the ancient world with its 'natural inequality' to a modern moral order that strives to implement the Universal Declaration of Human Rights." How did this chapter help you reimagine Christianity not merely as a religion or belief system but as an embodied movement of neighbor love to abolish othering?
4. This chapter explored seven snapshots of neighbor love across the Christian movement: the Didache, the Epistle to Diognetus, Augustine, Thomas Aquinas, Julian of Norwich, Martin Luther, and Søren Kierkegaard. The call to love our enemies and resist nationalistic identities were common threads in the story. What did you find most inspiring and worth reviving today? Be sure to comment on Julian of Norwich's "revelations of divine love" and how they empowered her to confess, "All will be well."
5. This chapter also looked at sobering cases like Thomas Aquinas and Martin Luther where influential Christians made loopholes for othering, dehumanized groups of people, and justified terrible violence. What can we learn from honestly confronting the othering in our histories? Where do you see similar perversions of faith today?

Chapter 6: Twentieth-Century Exemplars of Neighbor Love: Bonhoeffer, Weil, King, Romero, and Teresa

1. Andrew began this chapter by describing how his Christian upbringing introduced him to neighbor love but "didn't disrupt our safe suburban lifestyle or our American Christian nationalism." How did your upbringing influence who you saw as a neighbor and how you treated others? How has your vision and practice of neighbor love evolved since then?
2. Dietrich Bonhoeffer, Simone Weil, Martin Luther King Jr., Óscar Romero, and Mother Teresa each modeled various practices of neighbor love like listening, attention, service, grieving with victims, organizing nonviolent protest, prophetic critique of injustice, doing small things with much love, and the willingness to suffer for others. Which of these practices are most challenging and useful for your life and practice of neighbor love?

3. Each of the exemplars in this chapter directly confronted extreme forms of othering: antisemitism in Europe, racism and white supremacy in America, the oppression of impoverished factory workers and farmers in Europe and El Salvador, the caste system in India. How is othering manifested in your society, and how do these exemplars of neighbor love encourage you to resist it?

4. Dietrich Bonhoeffer wrote, "Jesus Christ, God himself, speaks to us from every human being." With her mystical vision of creation, Simone Weil wrote that all of reality is a "vibration" of divine love. Mother Teresa asked, "Who is Jesus to me?" and then listed many of the others in her society. Each of our exemplars practiced an expanded perception of God's presence alive in the other and the material world. Have you ever experienced God in another person or creature? How might your life change if you cultivated this sacred attention to others?

5. Nonviolence has been a significant presence throughout the neighbor-love movement. Jesus introduced the practice of creative nonviolence in his teaching of neighbor love. Inspired by Jesus and Gandhi, Martin Luther King Jr. became a global icon of nonviolent resistance to injustice through his practice of neighbor love. Do you believe that neighbor love requires nonviolence? How do you want to practice nonviolence today?

6. Throughout this book, Andrew has traced what he calls "the paradox of neighbor": we only exclude ourselves from full belonging with God when we exclude others from it. What do you think of Simone Weil's decision to refuse baptism and remain an outsider to her church as an act of protest to its exclusion of others? How might forms of religious protest like this embody a deeper faithfulness to the God of neighbor love?

Chapter 7: Neighbor Love Now: The Abolition of Othering and a New Beginning for Humanity

1. The Neighbor-Love Movement created and promoted its Neighbor-Love Covenant and Practices as a response to the crisis of othering in Ethiopia. What do you think about this simple document, and how might it be usefully adapted in your context?

2. After reading this book, who is your neighbor, and how do you want to practice loving them?
3. Andrew wrote, "While neighbor love rightly challenges our *selfishness*, it simultaneously affirms our *self-love*." Where are you in your journey of learning to actively love yourself? How might NLM's Self-Love Practices be helpful for you in cultivating a deeper self-love that can overflow with and for others?
4. Andrew highlighted fifteen insights from the perennial wisdom of the neighbor-love movement. Which two or three insights are particularly energizing or challenging to you?
5. How do you want to actively participate in continuing and expanding the global abolition movement of othering today in our world? Jesus promised, "Do this, and you will flourish" (Lk 10:28).

RECOMMENDED READINGS IN NEIGHBOR LOVE

DeCort, Andrew, Lani Mireya Anaya Jiménez, Ikenna Paschal Okpaleke, and Matthew Ryan Robinson. *Enemy, Stranger, Neighbor, and Friend: A Rough Guide on Religion and Othering*. Geneva: World Council of Churches, 2023. www.oikoumene.org/resources/publications/enemy-stranger-neighbour-friend.

This accessible rough guide offers short meditations and group exercises that foster religious literacy on how faith can overcome othering and heal our humanity. It is designed for small group use and includes many helpful resources.

Weil, Simone. "Reflections on the Right Use of School Studies with a View to the Love of God." In *Waiting for God*, 105-16. New York: Putnam's Sons, 1951.

This short essay insightfully describes how even the most tedious tasks in our daily lives, by exercising our attention, can be embraced as practices of learning how to love God and our neighbors as ourselves. Weil shows us how *everything* can be done and valued as training in neighbor love.

King, Martin Luther, Jr. *Strength to Love*. Minneapolis: Fortress, 2010. Chapters 3-5.

These three sermons from Dr. King briefly encapsulate an enormous amount of the wisdom and passion of neighbor love throughout Christian history. They can be fruitfully read and reread as a primer in neighbor love.

Gordon, Wayne. *Who Is My Neighbor? Lessons Learned from a Man Left for Dead*. Grand Rapids, MI: Baker Books, 2010.

This beautiful book offers forty meditations on who our neighbors really are and what it means to practically love them as ourselves. Accessible and compelling, this book comes directly out of Wayne Gordon's decades of pastoral ministry in Chicago. It's perfect for a personal or small group journey focused on neighbor love.

Lindberg, Carter. *Love: A Brief History Through Western Christianity*. Malden, MA: Blackwell, 2008.

This book doesn't focus specifically on neighbor love but love more generally in Christian history. It provides an accessible, eye-opening introduction to how Christians have thought about love and transformed culture across the centuries.

Hallett, Garth L. *Christian Neighbor-Love: An Assessment of Six Rival Versions.* Washington, DC: Georgetown University Press, 1989.

This academic study analyzes "six rival versions" of how neighbor love has been interpreted in Christian ethics. Though a bit dry and abstract, it attempts to define what neighbor love truly means and requires. This is a good place to start going deeper into the theory of neighbor love.

Simmons, Frederick, and Brian Sorrels. *Love and Christian Ethics: Tradition, Theory, and Society.* Washington, DC: Georgetown University Press, 2016.

As I write, this is the most up-to-date academic resource on the Christian ethics of love. This volume includes chapters on some of the major thinkers in Christian history, as well as some of the fundamental issues intersecting the ethics of love. These essays are intended for a scholarly audience and may be difficult for the general reader.

NEIGHBOR LOVE

An Extensive Bibliography for an
Ancient-yet-Emerging Field of Study and Practice

I BROADLY DEFINE NEIGHBOR LOVE as seeing and treating others as morally related and equally precious in value to oneself and one's group(s). (This also includes the other that we are to ourselves.) The following texts significantly engage with neighbor love, love more broadly, human dignity and equality, and/ or belonging without othering. They range from popular books to scholarly works. They are primarily Christian in perspective but also include Jewish, Islamic, Buddhist, Hindu, Sikh, nonreligious, and other perspectives.

Expertise in neighbor love is ultimately and most importantly a matter of practice, that is, how we actually see and treat one another. But a careful study of the texts below will lead to a thorough academic knowledge of (primarily Christian) neighbor love as a field of study. I hope it also energizes and expands personal transformation and practice.

Entries are categorized into broad historical periods and then listed alphabetically. I roughly group sources according to their era of focus or original date of publication. It is noteworthy that, between 1992 and 2025, 2002 is the only year when I haven't found one or more significant text(s) in English focused explicitly or implicitly on neighbor love. It is encouraging that increasing attention and interdisciplinary study are being devoted to neighbor love.

I've compiled this nonexhaustive but extensive bibliography on neighbor love in the hopes that it will contribute to neighbor love becoming a more formalized, interdisciplinary field of study and practice—a "school of love" in bell hooks's words. Key questions here include: Who is our neighbor? How does love require us to see and treat our neighbors in the face of othering? Why? What are the practical implications? How does neighbor love connect to theology, spirituality, ethics, art, law, economics, health care, politics, technology, artificial intelligence, neurobiology, mental health, animal studies, environmental stewardship, gender, sexuality, identity, indigenous wisdom, globalization, space travel and the possibility of extraterrestrial forms of life, death, hope, human flourishing, and much beyond? I warmly welcome others to reach out (adecort@uchicago.edu) and help me develop this bibliography and ancient-yet-emerging field of study further.

The Hebrew Bible, Ancient Judaism, and Other Ancient Sources

Adam, Klaus-Peter, *Hate and Enmity in Biblical Law*. New York: T&T Clark, 2022.
    Chapter four looks at "brotherly love" in Leviticus 19.

Akiyama, Kengo. *The Love of Neighbour in Ancient Judaism: The Reception of Leviticus 19:18 in the Hebrew Bible, the Septuagint, the Book of Jubilees, the Dead Sea Scrolls, and the New Testament*. Leiden: Brill, 2018.

Anderson, Gary. *Charity: The Place of the Poor in the Biblical Tradition*. New Haven, CT: Yale University Press, 2013.

Brombacher, Shoshannah. "On One Foot." Chabad, accessed January 18, 2025. www.chabad.org/library/article_cdo/aid/689306/jewish/On-One-Foot.htm.

Clements, R. E. *Loving One's Neighbour: Old Testament Ethics in Context*. London: University of London Press, 1992.

Danby, Herbert, trans. *The Mishnah*. Peabody, MA: Hendrickson, 2011.

Green, Ronald. "Neighbor Love in the Jewish Tradition." In *Love and Christian Ethics: Tradition, Theory, and Society*, edited by Frederick Simmons and Brian Sorrels, 347-59. Washington, DC: Georgetown University Press, 2016.

Held, Shai. *Judaism Is About Love*. New York: Picado, 2025.

Kugel, James. *Traditions of the Bible: A Guide to the Bible as It Was at the Start of the Common Era*. Cambridge, MA: Harvard University Press, 1999.
    Pages 455-58 focus on ancient Jewish and Christian interpretations of neighbor love.

Kurlansky, Mark. *Non-violence: The History of a Dangerous Idea*. New York: Modern Library, 2008.
    Kurlansky traces appeals to love others and practice nonviolence from ancient times to the modern world.

Liebman, Sheldon. *The Evolution of Love: Theology and Morality in Ancient Judaism*. Eugene, Or: Wipf & Stock, 2021.

Middleton, J. Richard. *The Liberating Image: The Imago Dei in Genesis 1*. Grand Rapids, MI: Baker Academic, 2005.

Ramírez Kidd, José E. *Alterity and Identity in Israel: The "ger" in the Old Testament*. New York: de Gruyter, 1999.

Taittiriya Upanishad. Shlokam. 2024. https://shlokam.org/texts/taittiriya-1-11-2/.
    Hindu scripture on seeing the stranger as divine.

Jesus and the New Testament

Evans, Craig, and H. Daniel Zacharias, eds. *"What Does the Scripture Say?" Studies in the Function of Scripture in Early Judaism and Christianity*. New York: T&T Clark, 2012.
    Chapter two is titled "'Love Your Neighbor as Yourself' (Lev. 19.18b) in Early Jewish-Christian Exegetical Practice and Missional Formulation."

Ferguson, John. *The Politics of Love: The New Testament on Nonviolent Revolution.* Nyack, NY: Fellowship, 1979.

Furnish, Victor. *The Love Command in the New Testament.* Nashville: Abingdon, 1972.

Gianotto, Claudio. "The Lucan Parable of the Good Samaritan and Its Interpretations in Christian Antiquity." In *The Quest for a Common Humanity: Human Dignity and Otherness in the Religious Traditions of the Mediterranean,* edited by Katell Berthelot and Matthias Morgenstern, 125-38. Leiden: Brill, 2011.

Gray, Sherman. *The Least of My Brothers: Matthew 25:31-46: A History of Interpretation.* Atlanta: Scholars Press, 1989.

Klassen, William. "Coals of Fire: Symbol of Repentance or Revenge?" *New Testament Studies* 9 (1963): 337-50.

Nelson, Karen. *Hesed and the New Testament: An Intertextual Categorization Study.* University Park, PA: Eisenbrauns, 2023.

Perkins, Pheme. *Love Commands in the New Testament.* New York: Paulist Press, 1982.

Piper, John. *Love Your Enemies: Jesus's Love Command in the Synoptic Gospels and Early Christian Parenesis.* Cambridge: Cambridge University Press, 1979.

Ruzer, Serge. "From 'Love Your Neighbor' to 'Love Your Enemy.'" In *Mapping the New Testament: Early Christian Writings as a Witness for Jewish Biblical Exegesis,* 35-70. Leiden: Brill, 2007.

Ruzer, Serge. "The Double Love Precept: Between Pharisees, Jesus and Qumran Covenanters." In *Mapping the New Testament: Early Christian Writings as a Witness for Jewish Biblical Exegesis,* 71-99. Leiden: Brill, 2007.

Swartley, Willard M., ed. *The Love of Enemy and Nonretaliation in the New Testament.* Louisville, KY: Westminster John Knox, 1992.

Wall, Robert, and Eugene Lemcio. "The Commands to Love God and Neighbor: History, Redaction, and Canon." In *The New Testament as Canon: A Reader in Canonical Criticism,* 67-77. Sheffield: Sheffield Academic Press, 1992.

Wink, Walter. *Jesus and Nonviolence: A Third Way.* Minneapolis: Fortress, 2003.

Wink, Walter. *The Powers That Be: Theology for a New Millennium.* New York: Harmony, 1999.

Chapter five studies Jesus' teaching of enemy love and nonviolence.

Early Christianity

Chadwick, Henry, trans. *Origen: Contra Celsum.* Cambridge: Cambridge University Press, 1980.

"The Didache." In *The Apostolic Fathers I,* translated by Kirsopp Lake, 303-34 Cambridge, MA: Harvard University Press, 1985.

"The Epistle to Diognetus." In *The Apostolic Fathers,* translated by Kirsopp Lake, 2:347-79 New York: Macmillan, 1913.

Ferguson, Everett. "Love of Enemies and Nonretaliation in the Second Century." In *The Contentious Triangle: Church, State and University,* edited by Rodney Petersen and Calvin Pater, 81-96. Kirksville, MO: Truman State University Press, 1999.

Holmes, Augustine. *A Life Pleasing to God: The Spirituality of the Rules of St Basil.* Kalamazoo, MI: Cistercian Publications, 2000.

Chapter eight looks at Basil's views of neighbor love.

Justin Martyr. *First Apology.* In *The Ante-Nicene Fathers: Translations of the Writings of the Fathers down to A.D. 325*, edited by Alexander Roberts and James Donaldson, 1:159-87. New York: Scribner's Sons, 1905.

Lindberg, Carter. *Love: A Brief History Through Western Christianity.* Malden, MA: Blackwell, 2008.

Michael Long, ed. *Christian Peace and Nonviolence: A Documentary History.* Maryknoll, NY: Orbis Books, 2011.

Sider, Ronald. *The Early Church on Killing: A Comprehensive Sourcebook on War, Abortion, and Capital Punishment.* Grand Rapids, MI: Baker, 2012.

Siedentop, Larry. *Inventing the Individual: The Origins of Western Liberalism.* London: Penguin, 2015.

Tertullian. *Apology.* In *The Ante-Nicene Fathers: Translations of the Writings of the Fathers down to A.D. 325*, edited by Alexander Roberts and James Donaldson, 3:17-55. Buffalo, NY: Christian Literature, 1885.

Theissen, Gerd. *The Religion of the Earliest Churches: Creating a Symbolic World.* Minneapolis: Fortress, 1999.

Chapter four looks at neighbor love in early Christianity.

Rhee, Helen, ed. *Wealth and Poverty in Early Christianity.* Minneapolis: Fortress, 2017.

FIFTH- TO FIFTEENTH-CENTURY SOURCES

Aquinas, Thomas, *Summa Theologica.* New York: Benziger, 1948.

Augustine. *City of God.* Translated by Henry Bettenson. New York: Penguin Books, 1973. Especially books 14 and 19.

Augustine. *On Christian Teaching.* Translated by R. P. H. Green. New York: Oxford University Press, 1997.

Augustine. "Letter 155 to Macedonius (413/414)." In *Augustine: Political Writings*, edited by E. M. Atkins and R. J. Dodaro, 89-99. New York: Cambridge University Press, 2001.

Augustine. "Sermon 56." In *Sermons: III (51-94) on the New Testament*, translated by Edmund Hill, 95-108. New York: New City, 1992.

Augustine. "Sermon 90A." In *Sermons, III/11: Newly Discovered Sermons*, translated by Edmund Hill, 77-86. Hyde Park, NY: New City, 2000.

Augustine. *Ten Homilies on the First Epistle of St. John.* Translated by John Burnaby. Library of Christian Classics 8. Philadelphia: Westminster, 1955.

Julian of Norwich. *Revelations of Divine Love.* Translated by Barry Windeatt. New York: Oxford University Press, 2015.

Leirvik, Oddbjørn. "Aw qāla: 'Li-jārihi': Some Observations on Brotherhood and Neighborly Love in Islamic Tradition." *Islam and Christian-Muslim Relations* 21, no. 4 (2010): 357-72.

Melville, Gert, ed. *Aspects of Charity: Concern for One's Neighbour in Medieval Vita Religiosa.* Berlin: LIT, 2011.

Nirenberg, David, *Neighboring Faiths: Christianity, Islam, and Judaism in the Middle Ages and Today.* Chicago: University of Chicago Press, 2014.

Overweg, Cynthia. "Hildegard of Bingen: The Nun Who Loved the Earth." *Quest* 105, no. 3 (Summer 2017): 21-25.

Sachendina, Abdulaziz. *The Islamic Roots of Democratic Pluralism.* New York: Oxford University Press, 2001.

Especially part IIaIIae, questions 23-26.

Volf, Miroslav, Ghazi bin Muhammad, and Melissa Yarrington, eds. *A Common Word: Muslims and Christians on Loving God and Neighbor*. Grand Rapids, MI: Eerdmans, 2010.

Early Modern and Modern Sources

Anonymous ("By a Lady"). *A Poem on the Love of Our Neighbour: Published for the Benefit of a Person in Distress, Remarkable for Her Poetic Genius*. Cambridge: Cambridge University Press, 1783.
Barklay, Katie. *Caritas: Neighbourly Love and the Early Modern Self*. New York: Oxford University Press, 2021.
Barrow, Isaac. *Of the Love of God and Our Neighbour, in Several Sermons*. Vol. 3. London: Miles Flesher, 1680.
Brother Lawrence. *Practice of the Presence: A Revolutionary Translation*. Translated by Carmen Acevedo Butcher. Minneapolis: Broadleaf Books, 2022.
Bucer, Martin. *Instruction in Christian Love*. Translated by Paul Fuhrmann. Eugene, OR: Wipf & Stock, 2008.
Gowing, Laura, et al. *Love, Friendship, and Faith in Europe, 1300–1800*. New York: Palgrave Macmillan, 2005.
Hanley, Ryan. *Love's Enlightenment: Rethinking Charity in Modernity*. New York: Cambridge University Press, 2017.
Kierkegaard, Søren. *Works of Love*. Translated by Howard and Edna Hong. San Francisco: HarperCollins, 2009.
Legnani, Nicole Delia. *The Business of Conquest: Empire, Love, and Law in the Atlantic World*. Notre Dame, IN: University of Notre Dame Press, 2020.
Luther, Martin. "On the Jews and Their Lies." In *Martin Luther's Basic Theological Writings*, 2nd ed., edited by Timothy Lull, 25-32. Minneapolis: Fortress, 2005.
Luther, Martin. *What Luther Says: A Practical In-Home Anthology for the Active Christian*. Edited by Edwald Plass. St. Louis: Concordia, 1959.
Luther, Martin. "Whether One May Flee From a Deadly Plague." In *Martin Luther's Basic Theological Writings*, 2nd ed., edited by Timothy Lull, 479-91. Minneapolis: Fortress, 2005.
Mill, John Stuart. *On Liberty*. New York: Penguin, 1974.
Morgan, Joseph. *Love to Our Neighbour Recommended; and the Duties Thereof Importunately Urged: A Sermon Shewing What Is Required, and What Is Not Required in Loving Our Neighbours as Ourselves*. 1749.
Rinne, Pärttyli. *Kant on Love*. Boston: de Gruyter, 2018.
Schwartz, Regina. *Loving Justice, Living Shakespeare*. Oxford: Oxford University Press, 2016.

Twentieth-Century Sources

Andolsen, Barbara Hilkert. "Agape in Feminist Ethics." In *Feminist Theological Ethics*, edited by Lois Daly, 146-59. Louisville, KY: Westminster John Knox, 1994.
Arendt, Hannah. *Love and St. Augustine*. Chicago: University of Chicago Press, 1995.
Baldwin, James. *The Cross of Redemption: Uncollected Writings*. Edited by Randall Kenan. New York: Vintage Books, 2010.

Baldwin, James. *James Baldwin: Collected Essays*. Edited by Toni Morrison. New York: Library of America, 1998.

Bonhoeffer, Dietrich. "Letter to Hans-Walter Schleicher on June 2, 1944." In *Letters and Papers from Prison*, edited by John de Gruchy, translated by Christian Gremmels et al., 408-9. Minneapolis: Fortress, 2010.

Bonhoeffer, Dietrich. *Life Together*. Edited by Geffrey Kelly. Minneapolis: Fortress, 1996.

Bonhoeffer, Dietrich. "Outline for a Book." In *Letters and Papers from Prison*, edited by John de Gruchy, translated by Christian Gremmels et al., 499-504. Minneapolis: Fortress, 2010.

Bonhoeffer, Dietrich. "Sermon on 2 Corinthians 12:9 from London in 1934." In *London: 1933-1935*, edited by Keith Clements, 401-4. Minneapolis: Fortress, 2007.

Bonhoeffer, Dietrich. "Sermon on Genesis 32:25-32; 33:10 from March 13, 1932." In *Ecumenical, Academic & Pastoral Work: 1931-1932*, edited by Victoria Barnett et al, 428-33. Minneapolis: Fortress, 2012.

Bonhoeffer, Dietrich. "Sermon on John 8:32 from 1932." In *Ecumenical, Academic & Pastoral Work: 1931-1932*, edited by Victoria Barnett et al, 465-72. Minneapolis: Fortress, 2012.

Bonhoeffer, Dietrich. "Sermon on Luke 17:33 from October 21, 1928." In *Barcelona, Berlin, New York: 1928-1931*, edited by Clifford Green, 532-35. Minneapolis: Fortress, 2008.

Bonhoeffer, Dietrich. "Sermon on Matthew 28:20 from Barcelona on April 15, 1928." In *Barcelona, Berlin, New York: 1928-1931*, edited by Clifford Green, 490-94. Minneapolis: Fortress, 2008.

Brümmer, Vincent. *The Model of Love: A Study in Philosophical Theology*. New York: Cambridge University Press, 1993.

Burnham, Clint, and Paul Kingsbury. *Lacan and the Environment*. Cham: Palgrave Macmillan, 2021.

Chapter two explores loving the enemy in Jacques Lacan (1901–1981).

Cahill, Lisa. *Love Your Enemies: Pacifism, Discipleship, and Just War*. Minneapolis: Fortress, 1994.

Canon, Katie G. *Black Womanist Ethics*. Eugene, OR: Wipf & Stock, 1988.

Compton, John. *The End of Empathy: Why White Protestants Stopped Loving Their Neighbors*. New York: Oxford University Press, 2020.

Cone, James. *God of the Oppressed*. Rev. ed. Maryknoll, NY: Orbis, 1997.

Dilman, Ilham. *Love: Its Forms, Dimensions, and Paradoxes*. New York: St. Martin's, 1998.

Ellsburg, Robert, ed. *Dorothy Day: Selected Writings: By Little and by Little*. Maryknoll, NY: Orbis Books, 2005.

Forest, Jim. *Making Friends of Enemies: Reflections on the Teachings of Jesus*. New York: Crossroad, 1987.

Freud, Sigmund. *Civilization and Its Discontents*. Translated by Joan Riviere. New York: Doubleday, 1958.

Fromm, Erich. *The Art of Loving*. New York: Open Road Media, 2013.

Guenther, Titus. *Rahner and Metz: Transcendental Theology as Political Theology*. Lanham, MD: University Press of America, 1994.

Chapter three looks at neighbor love in the context of Karl Rahner and Johann Baptist Metz's political theology.

Hallett, Garth L. *Christian Neighbor-Love: An Assessment of Six Rival Versions*. Washington, DC: Georgetown University Press, 1989.

Hanh, Thich Nhat. *Love in Action: Writings on Nonviolent Social Change.* Berkeley, CA: Parallax, 1993.

Havel, Vaclav. *The Art of the Impossible: Politics as Morality in Practice.* New York: Knopf, 1997.

Hillesum, Etty. *Etty Hillesum: An Interrupted Life and Letters from Westerbork.* Translated by Arnold Pomerans. New York: Henry Holt, 1996.

hooks, bell. *All About Love: New Visions.* New York: William Morrow, 2018.

Isasi-Díaz, Ada María. "Solidarity: Love of Neighbor in the Twenty-First Century." In *Mujerista Theology: A Theology for the Twenty-First Century*, 86-104. Maryknoll, NY: Orbis Books, 1996.

Jackson, Peter. *Love Disconsoled: Meditations on Christian Charity.* New York: Cambridge University Press, 1999.

King, Martin Luther Jr. *A Testament to Hope: The Essential Writings and Speeches of Martin Luther King Jr.* Edited by James Washington. New York: HarperCollins, 1986.

King, Martin Luther Jr. *Strength to Love.* Minneapolis: Fortress, 2010.

Klassen, William. *Love of Enemies: The Way to Peace.* Philadelphia: Fortress, 1984.

Lewis, C. S. *The Weight of Glory and Other Addresses.* Grand Rapids, MI: Eerdmans, 1965.

Merton, Thomas. *Gandhi: On Nonviolence.* New York: New Directions, 2007.

Merton, Thomas. *A Life in Letters: The Essential Collection.* New York: HarperOne, 2008.

Merton, Thomas. *No Man Is an Island.* New York: Houghton Mifflin, 1983.

Merton, Thomas. *The Power and Meaning of Love.* London: SPCK, 2010.

Morrison, Toni. *Beloved.* New York: Vintage, 2004.

Morrison's novel explores self-love and healing from trauma.

Mother Teresa. *No Greater Love.* Edited by Becky Benenate and Joseph Durepos. Novato, CA: New World Library, 1989.

Mother Teresa. *Come Be My Light: The Private Writings of the "Saint of Calcutta."* Edited by Brian Kolodiejchuk. New York: Doubleday, 2007.

Nouwen, Henri. *The Inner Voice of Love: A Journey Through Anguish to Freedom.* New York: Image, 1999.

Nouwen, Henri. *Life of the Beloved: Spiritual Living in a Secular World.* New York: PublishDrive, 2002.

Nouwen, Henri. *The Wounded Healer.* New York: Image Books, 1979.

Nussbaum, Martha, et al. *For Love of Country: Debating the Limits of Patriotism.* Boston: Beacon, 1996.

Nygren, Anders. *Agape and Eros: A Study of the Christian Idea of Love.* New York: Harper & Row, 1956.

O'Donovan, Oliver. *The Problem of Self-Love in St. Augustine.* New Haven, CT: Yale University Press, 1980.

Outka, Gene. *Agape: An Ethical Analysis.* New Haven, CT: Yale University Press, 1972.

Pliskin, Zelig. *Love Your Neighbor: You and Your Fellow Man in Light of the Torah: A Practical Guide to Man's Relationship with His Fellow Man Culled from the Full Spectrum of Torah Readings.* Jerusalem: Aisha Ha Torah, 1977.

Rahner, Karl. *The Love of Jesus and the Love of Neighbor.* New York: Crossroad, 1983.

Ramsey, Paul. *Basic Christian Ethics.* Chicago: University of Chicago Press, 1977.

Romero, Óscar. "Christ Saves All People." Homily, January 15, 1978. Romero Trust. www.romerotrust.org.uk/homilies-and-writings/homilies/christ-saves-all-people-people.

Romero, Óscar. *The Church Cannot Remain Silent: Unpublished Letters and Other Writings*. Maryknoll, NY: Orbis Books, 2016.

Romero, Óscar. "Dedicated Love." Homily, March 17, 1977. Romero Trust. www.romerotrust.org.uk/sites/default/files/homilies/dedicated_love.pdf.

Romero, Óscar. "The Final Homily." Homily, March 24, 1980. Romero Trust. www.romerotrust.org.uk/homilies-and-writings/homilies/final-homily-archbishop-romero.

Romero, Óscar. "Motivation of Love." Homily, March 14, 1977. Romero Trust. www.romerotrust.org.uk/homilies-and-writings/homilies/motivation-love.

Romero, Óscar. "A Prophetic, Sacramental, Loving Church." Homily, September 10, 1978. Romero Trust. http://www.romerotrust.org.uk/homilies/116/116_pdf.pdf.

Romero, Óscar. *The Violence of Love*. Compiled and translated by James Brockman. Maryknoll, NY: Orbis, 2004.

Romero, Óscar. *Voice of the Voiceless: The Four Pastoral Letters and Other Statements*. Translated by Michael Walsh. Maryknoll, NY: Orbis Books, 1985.

Scanzoni, Letha Dawson, and Virginia Ramey Mollenkott. *Is the Homosexual My Neighbor? A Positive Christian Response*. New York: HarperCollins, 1994.

Smith, James K. A. "Healing the Imagination: Art Lessons from James Baldwin." *Image*, no. 107 (Winter 2020). https://imagejournal.org/article/healing-the-imagination-art-lessons-from-james-baldwin/.

Sweasey, Peter. *From Queer to Eternity: Spirituality in the Lives of Lesbian, Gay, and Bisexual People*. Washington, DC: Cassell, 1997.

Chapter seven looks at neighbor love in the context of sexual ethics.

Thekkinedath, Joseph. *Love of Neighbour in Mahatma Gandhi*. Alwaye, India: Pontifical Institute of Theology and Philosophy, 1973.

Thurman, Howard. *Jesus and the Disinherited*. Boston: Beacon, 1949.

Chapter five interprets Jesus' ethic of enemy love.

Trocme, Andre. *Jesus and the Nonviolent Revolution*. Walden, NY: Plough, 2014.

Vaderhaar, Gerard. *Enemies and How to Love Them*. Eugene, OR: Wipf & Stock, 2013.

Wattles, Jeffrey. *The Golden Rule*. New York: Oxford University Press, 1996.

Weil, Simone. "Forms of the Implicit Love of God: The Love of Our Neighbor." In *Waiting for God*, 83-142. New York: Putnam's Sons, 1951.

Weil, Simone. "Reflections on the Right Use of School Studies with a View to the Love of God." In *Waiting for God*, 57-66. New York: Putnam's Sons, 1951.

Williams, Dolores. *Sisters in the Wilderness: The Challenge of Womanist God*. Maryknoll, NY: Orbis Books, 1993.

Wolterstorff, Nicholas. *Lament for a Son*. Grand Rapids, MI: Eerdmans, 1987.

This meditation often reflects on the meaning of neighbor love in a context of grief.

Yao, Xinzhong. *Confucianism and Christianity: A Comparative Study of Jen and Agape*. Portland, OR: Sussex Academic Press, 1997.

Twenty-first-Century Sources

Abuelaish, Izzeldin. *I Shall Not Hate: A Gaza Doctor's Journey on the Road to Peace and Human Dignity*. New York: Bloomsbury, 2012.

Acevedo, Jorge. *Neighboring: Spiritual Practices for Building a Life of Faith*. Nashville: Abingdon Press, 2019.
   (Not nearly as focused on neighbor love as the title suggests.)
Appiah, Kwame Anthony. *Cosmopolitanism: Ethics in a World of Strangers*. New York: Allen Lane, 2006.
Augsburger, David. *Dissident Discipleship: A Spirituality of Self-Surrender, Love of God, and Love of Neighbor*. Grand Rapids, MI: Brazos, 2011.
Babie, Paul, and Vanja-Ivan Savić. *Law, Religion and Love: Seeking Ecumenical Justice for the Other*. New York: Routledge, 2018.
Badiou, Alain. *Saint Paul: The Foundation of Universalism*. Translated by Ray Brassier. Stanford, CA: Stanford University Press, 2003.
Bauman, Zygmunt. *Liquid Love: On the Frailty of Human Bonds*. Malden, MA: Polity, 2003.
Bell, Rob. *Love Wins: A Book About Heaven, Hell, and the Fate of Every Person Who Ever Lived*. New York: HarperOne, 2012.
Bernasol, Colton. "Theology After Symbolic Devastation: Method in the Liberation Theologies of Juan Luis Segundo, Jon Sobrino, and M. Shawn Copeland." MTS thesis, Garret-Evangelical Theological Seminary, 2022.
Berry, R. J. *The Care of Creation: Focusing Concern and Action*. Downers Grove, IL: InterVarsity Press, 2000.
   Chapter sixteen looks at neighbor love in the context of ecology and creation care.
Boursier, Helen. *Willful Ignorance: Overcoming the Limitations of (Christian) Love for Refugees Seeking Asylum*. Lanham, MD: Lexington Books, 2022.
Brooks, Arthur. *Love Your Enemies: How Decent People Can Save America from the Culture of Contempt*. New York: Broadside Books, 2019.
Burrell, Kathy. "Lost in the 'Churn'? Locating Neighbourliness in a Transient Neighbourhood." *Environment and Planning* 48, no. 8 (2016): 1599-1616.
Chapman, Tracy. "Save Us All." Track 3 on *Our Bright Future*. Elektra, 2008.
Chenoweth, Erica, and Maria Stephan. *Why Civil Resistance Works: The Strategic Logic of Nonviolent Conflict*. New York: Columbia University Press, 2012.
Clark, Kelly James, Aziz Abu Sarah, and Nancy Fuchs. *Strangers, Neighbors, Friends: Muslim-Christian-Jewish Reflections on Compassion and Peace*. Eugene, OR: Cascade Books, 2018.
Cochran, Robert, and Zachary Calo, eds. *Agape, Justice, and Law: How Might Christian Love Shape Law?* New York: Cambridge University Press, 2017.
Courtney, Jeremy. *Love Anyway: An Invitation Beyond a World That's Scary as Hell*. Grand Rapids, MI: Zondervan, 2019.
Curry, Michael. *Love Is the Way*. New York: Avery, 2020.
Dawkins, Richard. *The God Delusion*. Boston: Houghton Mifflin, 2008.
   Chapter 7 critiques neighbor love.
DeCort, Andrew. "Balinjeraye: Unity and Diversity Are Neighbors, and So Are We." *Ethiopia Insight*, April 26, 2020.
DeCort, Andrew. *Blessed Are the Others: Jesus' Way in a Violent World*. Washington, DC: BitterSweet Collective, 2024.
DeCort, Andrew. *Bonhoeffer's New Beginning: Ethics After Devastation*. Lanham, MD: Fortress Academic, 2018.

DeCort, Andrew. "Christian Nationalism Is Tearing Ethiopia Apart." *Foreign Policy*, June 17, 2022. https://foreignpolicy.com/2022/06/18/ethiopia-pentecostal-evangelical-abiy-ahmed-christian-nationalism/.

DeCort, Andrew. "Ethics During Crisis: From Missed Chances to Neighbor-Love." *The Ethiopian Herald* (Addis Ababa, Ethiopia), February 20, 2018.

DeCort, Andrew. *Flourishing on the Edge of Faith: Seven Practices for a New We*. Washington, DC: BitterSweet Collective, 2022.

DeCort, Andrew. "A Gospel of Violence." *Los Angeles Review of Books*, September 16, 2024. https://lareviewofbooks.org/article/a-gospel-of-violence/.

DeCort, Andrew. "On Human Flourishing: A Call for Public Responsibility in Contemporary Ethiopian Christianity." In *A Church for the World: The Church's Role in Fostering Democracy and Sustainable Development*, edited by Samuel Yonas Deressa and Josh de Keijzer, 37-63. Minneapolis: Fortress, 2020.

DeCort, Andrew. "Neighbor-Love Week for National Reconciliation." *Ethiopia Insight*, April 14, 2021. https://andrew-decort.com/essays/the-neighbor-love-week-for-national-reconciliation/.

DeCort, Andrew. "Othering: A Virus More Dangerous Than COVID-19." *Addis Fortune* (Addis Ababa, Ethiopia), February 23, 2020. https://andrew-decort.com/essays/othering/.

DeCort, Andrew. "Pain, Neighbor-Love, Intimacy." *Pace: The Art of Living Slowly* (Singapore), June 2022.

DeCort, Andrew. "Paul's Politics: Notes on a Letter from Prison." *The Other Journal* no. 30 (March 2021): 42-52.

DeCort, Andrew. "A Prayer for Enemies." May 16, 2021. https://andrew-decort.com/essays/a-prayer-for-enemies/.

DeCort, Andrew. "Protest: Love's Primal Vocation." *Offensis: An Online Magazine for Theology* (Germany), February 10, 2022. https://offensis.de/protest-loves-primal-vocation-%EF%BF%BC/.

DeCort, Andrew. "Public Theology in Ethiopia: State, Church, and Neighbor-Love." In *What Does Theology Do, Actually?*, edited by Matthew Ryan Robinson and Inja Inderst, 209-24. Leipzig: Evangelische Verlagsanstalt, 2020.

DeCort, Andrew. "Seeds of Contemplation and Revolution amid War: The Subversive Power of Attentive Presence." *Comment*, Winter 2023. https://comment.org/seeds-of-contemplation-and-revolution-amid-war/.

DeCort, Andrew, Lani Mireya Anaya Jiménez, Ikenna Paschal Okpaleke, and Matthew Ryan Robinson. *Enemy, Stranger, Neighbor, & Friend: A Rough Guide on Religion and Othering*. Geneva: World Council of Churches, 2023. www.oikoumene.org/resources/publications/enemy-stranger-neighbour-friend.

De Waal, Frans. *The Age of Empathy: Nature's Lessons for a Kinder Society*. New York: Crown, 2010.

Duffner, Jordan. *Islamophobia: What Christians Should Know (and Do) About Anti-Muslim Discrimination*. Maryknoll, NY: Orbis Books, 2021.
  Chapter ten discusses neighbor love.

Dunkelman, Marc. *The Vanishing Neighbor: The Transformation of American Community*. Princeton, NJ: Princeton University Press, 2014.

Ellethy, Yaser. *Islam, Context, Pluralism and Democracy: Classical and Modern Interpretations.* New York: Routledge, 2014.

Evans, Stephen. *Kierkegaard's Ethic of Love: Divine Commands and Moral Obligations.* New York: Oxford University Press, 2004.

Fisher, Helen. *Why We Love: The Nature and Chemistry of Romantic Love.* New York: Henry Holt, 2004.

Forest, Jim. *Loving Our Enemies: Reflections on the Hardest Commandment.* Maryknoll, NY: Orbis, 2014.

Gabbert, Echi Christina. "The Global Neighbourhood Concept: A Chance for Cooperative Development Or *Festina Lente.*" In *A Delicate Balance: Land Use, Minority Rights and Social Stability in the Horn of Africa,* edited by Mulugeta Gebrehiwot Berhe, 14-37. Addis Ababa, Ethiopia: Institute for Peace and Security Studies, Addis Ababa University, 2014.

Gabbert, Echi Christina, et al. *To Live with Others: Essays on Cultural Neighborhood in Southern Ethiopia.* Rüdiger Köppe, 2010.

Gensler, Harry. *Ethics and the Golden Rule.* New York: Routledge, 2013.

Glover, Jonathan. *Humanity: A Moral History of the Twentieth Century.* 2nd ed. New Haven, CT: Yale University Press, 2012.

Goff, Bob. *Everybody Always: Becoming Love in a World Full of Setbacks and Difficult People.* Nashville: Nelson, 2018.

Goodman, Lenn. *Love Thy Neighbor as Thyself.* New York: Oxford University Press, 2008.

Gordon, Wayne. *Who Is My Neighbor? Lessons Learned from a Man Left for Dead.* Ventura, CA: Regal, 2010.

Gordon, Wayne, and John Perkins. *Making Neighborhoods Whole: A Handbook for Christian Community Development.* Downers Grove, IL: InterVarsity Press, 2013.

Greaves, Mark. "Loving Thy Neighbor Is Priceless—But It's Also Worth £3 Billion." *The Times of London,* July 18, 2015.

Gregory, Eric. *Politics and the Order of Love: An Augustinian Ethic of Democratic Citizenship.* Chicago: University of Chicago Press, 2010.

Grob, Leonard, and John K. Roth, eds. *Encountering the Stranger: A Jewish-Christian-Muslim Trialogue.* Seattle: University of Washington Press, 2012.

Gushee, David. *The Sacredness of Human Life: Why an Ancient Biblical Vision Is Key to the World's Future.* Grand Rapids, MI: Eerdmans, 2013.

Gushee, David, and Colin Holtz. *Moral Leadership for a Divided Age: Fourteen People Who Dared to Change Our World.* Grand Rapids, MI: Brazos, 2018.

Hanh, Thich Nhat. *Essential Writings.* Maryknoll, NY: Orbis Books, 2001.

Hettiarachchi, Radhika. *Walking in Another's Shoes: Exchange, Empathy, and Dialogue.* Search for Common Ground, 2018. www.sfcg.org/wp-content/uploads/2018/02/Facilitation-guide-walking-in-anothers-shoes-final.pdf. Especially pages 7-12.

Hicks, Douglas, and Mark Valeri, eds. *Global Neighbors: Christian Faith and Moral Obligation in Today's Economy.* Grand Rapids, MI: Eerdmans, 2010.

Houston, Fleur. *You Shall Love the Stranger as Yourself: The Bible, Refugees and Asylum.* London: Routledge, 2015.

Huckins, Jon, and Jer Swigart. *Mending the Divides: Creative Love in a Conflicted World.* Downers Grove, IL: InterVarsity Press, 2017.

Hustinx, Lesley, et al. *Religion and Volunteering: Complex, Contested and Ambiguous Relationships*. Cham: Springer, 2014.

Iorio, Gennaro. *Sociology of Love*. Wilmington, DE: Vernon, 2014.

Isaac, Munther. *Christ in the Rubble: Faith, the Bible, and Genocide in Gaza*. Grand Rapids, MI: Eerdmans, 2025.

Jackson, Timothy. *Political Agape: Christian Love and Liberal Democracy*. Grand Rapids, MI: Eerdmans, 2015.

Jeanrond, Werner. *A Theology of Love*. New York: T&T Clark, 2010.

Jha, Sandhya Rani. *Transforming Communities: How People Like You Are Healing Their Neighborhoods*. Nashville: Chalice, 2017.

Kaur, Valarie. *See No Stranger: A Memoir and Manifesto of Revolutionary Love*. New York: One World, 2021.

Krishek, Sharon. *Kierkegaard on Faith and Love*. New York: Cambridge University Press, 2009.

Labberton, Mark. *The Dangerous Act of Loving Your Neighbor: Seeing Others Through the Eyes of Jesus*. Downers Grove, IL: InterVarsity Press, 2015.

Lepojärvi, Jason. "Love and the Winter: C. S. Lewis, Nigel Biggar, and Marc LiVecche on Enemy Love, Politics and Religion." *Politics and Religion* (2022): 1-17.

Lippitt, John. *Kierkegaard and the Problem of Self-Love*. New York: Cambridge University Press, 2013.

Mahn, Jason. *Neighbor Love Through Fearful Days: Finding Purpose and Meaning in a Time of Crisis*. Minneapolis: Fortress, 2021.

Marion, Jean-Luc. *The Erotic Phenomenon*. Translated by Stephen Lewis. Chicago: University of Chicago Press, 2007.

Mavis, Brian, and Rick Rusaw. *The Neighboring Church: Getting Better at What Jesus Says Matters Most*. Nashville: Thomas Nelson, 2016.

Mayer, Claude-Hélène, and Elisabeth Vanderheiden, eds. *International Handbook of Love: Transcultural and Transdisciplinary Perspectives*. Cham: Springer, 2021.

McCarthy, Eli, et al. *A Just Peace Ethic Primer: Building Sustainable Peace and Breaking Cycles of Violence*. Washington, DC: Georgetown University Press, 2020.

Mendes-Flohr, Paul. *Love, Accusative and Dative: Reflections on Leviticus 19:18*. Syracuse, NY: Syracuse University Press, 2007.

Mescher, Marcus. *The Ethics of Encounter: Christian Neighbor Love as a Practice of Solidarity*. Maryknoll, NY: Orbis Books, 2020.

Milburn, Josh. *Just Fodder: The Ethics of Feeding Animals*. Chicago: McGill-Queen's University Press, 2022.

Milbank, John, Slavoj Žižek, and Creston Davis. *Paul's New Moment: Continental Philosophy and the Future of Christian Theology*. Grand Rapids, MI: Brazos, 2010.

Mother Teresa. *Mother Teresa: Essential Writings*. Edited by Jean Maalouf. Maryknoll, NY: Orbis Books, 2001.

Mother Teresa. *Where There Is Love, There Is God*. Edited by Brian Kolodiejchuk. New York: Doubleday, 2010.

Mukwege, Dennis. *The Power of Women*. New York: Flatiron Books, 2021.

Munayer, Salim, and Lisa Loden. *Through the Eyes of My Enemy: Envisioning Reconciliation in Israel-Palestine*. London: Paternoster, 2013.

Munson, Derek. *Enemy Pie*. New York: Chronicle Books, 2000.

Nagler, Michael. *The Nonviolence Handbook: A Guide for Practical Action*. San Francisco: Berrett-Koehler, 2014.

Nega, Tekalign. *Balinjeraye [My Neighbor]*. Addis Ababa, Ethiopia: Faith and Flourishing Books, 2020.

Nelson, Tom. *The Economics of Neighborly Love: Investing in your Community's Compassion and Capacity*. Downers Grove, IL: InterVarsity Press, 2017.

Nussbaum, Martha. *The Cosmopolitan Tradition: A Noble but Flawed Ideal*. Cambridge, MA: Harvard University Press, 2019.

O'Connell, Maureen. *Compassion: Loving Our Neighbors in an Age of Globalization*. Maryknoll, NY: Orbis Books, 2009.

Owens, Lama Rod. *Love and Rage: The Path of Liberation Through Anger*. New York: North Atlantic Books, 2020.

Pathak, Jay, and Dave Runyon. *The Art of Neighboring: Building Genuine Relationships Right Outside Your Door*. Grand Rapids, MI: Baker Books, 2012.

powell, john, and Stephen Menendian. *Belonging Without Othering: How We Save Ourselves and the World*. Stanford, CA: Stanford University Press, 2024.

Reed, Esther. *Theology for International Law*. London: Bloomsbury, 2013.
   Chapter six is titled, "Nation-States, Borders and Love of Neighbour: Impartiality and the *Ordo Amoris*."

Rogers, Fred. *A Beautiful Day in the Neighborhood: Neighborly Words of Wisdom from Mister Rogers*. New York: Penguin Books, 2019.

Rohr, Richard. *The Universal Christ: How a Forgotten Reality Can Change Everything We See, Hope For, and Believe*. New York: Convergent Books, 2019.

Rosenblum, Nancy. *Good Neighbors: The Democracy of Everyday Life in America*. Princeton, NJ: Princeton University Press, 2016.

Rowling, J. K. *Harry Potter and the Deathly Hallows*. New York: Scholastic, 2009.

Ruthruff, Ron. "Loving and Forgiving Enemies." Street Psalms, February 2022. https://streetpsalms.org/loving-and-forgiving-enemies/.

Sacks, Jonathan. "Letting Go of Hate." *Covenant & Conversation*, August 28, 2012. https://rabbisacks.org/covenant-conversation/ki-teitse/letting-go-of-hate/.

Said, Yazid, and Lejla Demiri, eds. *The Future of Interfaith Dialogue: Muslim-Christian Encounters Through A Common Word*. New York: Cambridge University Press, 2018.

Santurri, Edmund, ed. *The Love Commandments: Essays in Christian Ethics and Moral Philosophy*. Eugene, OR: Wipf & Stock, 2009.

Schineller, Peter. "Without Love of Neighbor, There Is No Salvation." *America: The Jesuit Review*, December 4, 2018.

Sen, Amartya. *The Idea of Justice*. New York: Penguin, 2009.
   Pages 170-73 are on "Who Is Our Neighbour?"

Sider, Ronald. *If Jesus Is Lord: Loving Our Enemies in an Age of Violence*. Grand Rapids, MI: Baker Academic, 2019.

Simmons, Frederick, and Brian Sorrels, eds. *Love and Christian Ethics: Tradition, Theory, and Society*. Washington, DC: Georgetown University Press, 2016.

Soderstrom, Mary. *Frenemy Nations: Love and Hate Between Neighbo(u)ring States*. Regina, Saskatchewan: University of Regina Press, 2019.

Spencer, Nick. *The Political Samaritan: How Power Hijacked a Parable.* New York: Bloomsbury, 2017.

St. David, Gena. *The Brain and the Spirit: Unlocking the Transformative Potential of the Story of Christ.* Eugene, OR: Cascade Books, 2021.

Sun, Hyung Jin Kim. *Who Are Our Enemies and How Do We Love Them?* Harrisonburg, VA: Herald, 2020.

Telushkin, Joseph. *A Code of Jewish Ethics.* Vol. 2, *Love Your Neighbor as Yourself.* New York: Harmony, 2009.

Thompson, Kurt. *The Soul of Shame: Retelling the Stories We Believe About Ourselves.* Downers Grove, IL: InterVarsity Press, 2015.

Trotter, Elizabeth. "How Buddhism Taught Me to Love My Neighbors Better." A Life Overseas, October 28, 2016. www.alifeoverseas.com/how-buddhism-taught-me-to-love-my-neighbors-better/.

Tutu, Desmond. *No Future Without Forgiveness.* New York: Penguin, 2000.

Vanier, Jean. *Encountering "the Other."* Mahwah, NJ: Paulist Press, 2005.

Virji, Ayaz, and Alan Eisenstock. *Love Thy Neighbor: A Muslim Doctor's Struggle for Home in Rural America.* New York: Convergent Books, 2019.

Waldon, Jeremy. "Who Is My Neighbor? Humanity and Proximity." *The Monist* 86 (July 2003): 333-54.

Wallis, Jim. *The (Un)Common Good: How the Gospel Brings Hope to a World Divided.* Grand Rapids, MI: Brazos, 2014.

Walters, James. *Loving Your Neighbour in an Age of Religious Conflict: A New Agenda for Interfaith Relations.* London: Jessica Kingsley, 2019.

World Council of Churches. *The "Other" Is My Neighbour: Developing an Ecumenical Response to Migration.* Geneva: WCC Publications, 2015.

Žižek, Slavoj. *The Neighbor: Three Inquiries in Political Theology.* Chicago: University of Chicago Press, 2005.

OTHERING

A Brief Bibliography

I broadly define othering as seeing and treating others as unrelated or less than oneself and/or one's group. I see dehumanization as an extreme form of othering. The following texts focus on othering, caste, foreignness more broadly, hate, dehumanization, war, genocide, and related topics. They are listed in alphabetical order. Far from exhaustive, these few texts have been important for my understanding and articulation of othering.

Adam, Klaus-Peter. *Hate and Enmity in Biblical Law*. New York: T&T Clark, 2022.

Achenbach, Reinhard, et al., eds. *The Foreigner and the Law: Perspectives from the Hebrew Bible and the Ancient Near East*. Wiesbaden: Harrassowitz, 2011.

Arendt, Hannah. *The Origins of Totalitarianism*. New York: Schocken Books, 2004.

Baldwin, James. *The Cross of Redemption: Uncollected Writings*. Edited by Randall Kenan. New York: Vintage Books, 2010.

Baldwin, James. *James Baldwin: Collected Essays*. Edited by Toni Morrison. New York: Library of America, 1998.

Beck, Aaron. *Prisoners of Hate: The Cognitive Basis of Anger, Hostility, and Violence*. New York: Harper, 2000.

Bernasol, Colton. "Theology After Symbolic Devastation: Method in the Liberation Theologies of Juan Luis Segundo, Jon Sobrino, and M. Shawn Copeland." MTS thesis, Garret-Evangelical Theological Seminary, 2022.

Butler, Judith. *Frames of War: When Is Life Grievable?* New York: Verso, 2009.

Butler, Judith. *Precarious Life: The Powers of Mourning and Violence*. New York: Verso, 2004.

Carlson, Joanne Brown, and Crole R. Bohn, eds. *Christianity, Patriarchy, and Abuse: A Feminist Critique*. New York: Pilgrim, 1990.

DeCort, Andrew. "A Gospel of Violence." *Los Angeles Review of Books*, September 16, 2024. https://lareviewofbooks.org/article/a-gospel-of-violence/.

DeCort, Andrew. "Othering: A Virus More Dangerous Than COVID-19." *Addis Fortune* (Addis Ababa, Ethiopia), February 23, 2020.

Galtung, Johan. "Cultural Violence." *Journal of Peace Research* 27, no. 3 (August 1990): 291-305.

George, Cherian. *Hate Spin: The Manufacture of Religious Offense and Its Threat to Democracy*. Cambridge, MA: MIT Press, 2016.

Glover, Jonathan. *Humanity: A Moral History of the Twentieth Century*. 2nd ed. New Haven, CT: Yale University Press, 2012.

Goldenberg. David. *The Curse of Ham: Race and Slavery in Early Judaism, Christianity, and Islam*. New York: Oxford University Press, 2003.

Gross, Jan. *Neighbors: The Destruction of the Jewish Community in Jedwabne, Poland.* Princeton, NJ: Princeton University Press, 2022.

Hedges, Chris. *War Is a Force That Gives Us Meaning.* New York: PublicAffairs, 2014.

Isaac, Munther. *Christ in the Rubble: Faith, the Bible, and Genocide in Gaza.* Grand Rapids, MI: Eerdmans, 2025.

Keen, Sam. *Faces of the Enemy: Reflections of the Hostile Imagination.* New York: Harper & Row, 1986.

Legnani, Nicole Delia. *The Business of Conquest: Empire, Love, and Law in the Atlantic World.* Notre Dame, IN: University of Notre Dame Press, 2020.

Lindberg, Carter. *Love: A Brief History Through Western Christianity.* Malden, MA: Blackwell, 2008.

Lovin, Robin, and Frank Reynolds. *Cosmogony and Ethical Order: New Studies in Comparative Ethics.* Chicago: University of Chicago Press, 1985.

Luther, Martin. "On the Jews and Their Lies." In *Martin Luther's Basic Theological Writings*, 2nd ed., edited by Timothy Lull, 25-32. Minneapolis: Fortress, 2005.

Maas, Peter. *Love Thy Neighbor: A Story of War.* New York: Vintage, 1997.

Marin, Siobhan, and Andrew West. "What Is the Biblical Story of 'Amalek'? And Why Is It Being Used in South Africa's ICJ Case Against Israel?" ABC News, January 30, 2024. www.abc.net.au/news/2024-01-31/biblical-story-amalek-south-africa-icj-genocide-case-israel/103403552.

Morrison, Toni. *The Origin of Others.* Cambridge, MA: Harvard University Press, 2017.

Poo, M. C. *Enemies of Civilization: Attitudes Toward Foreigners in Ancient Mesopotamia, Egypt, and China.* Albany: State University of New York Press, 2005.

powell, john, and Stephen Menendian. *Belonging Without Othering: How We Save Ourselves and the World.* Stanford, CA: Stanford University Press, 2024.

Ramírez Kidd, José E. *Alterity and Identity in Israel: The "ger" in the Old Testament.* New York: de Gruyter, 1999.

Samuel, Kim. "How to Reverse the Psychology of Othering." *Psychology Today,* May 11, 2023. www.psychologytoday.com/us/blog/the-power-of-belonging/202305/how-to-reverse-the-psychology-of-othering.

Sen, Amartya. *Identity and Violence: The Illusion of Destiny.* New York: Norton, 2006.

Siedentop, Larry. *Inventing the Individual: The Origins of Western Liberalism.* London: Penguin, 2015.

Smith, David Livingstone. *On Inhumanity: Dehumanization and How to Resist It.* New York: Oxford University Press, 2020.

Smith, David Livingstone. *Less Than Human: Why We Demean, Enslave, and Exterminate Others.* New York: St. Martin's, 2011.

Smith, David Livingstone. *Making Monsters: The Uncanny Power of Dehumanization.* Cambridge, MA: Harvard University Press, 2021.

Smith, David Livingstone. *The Most Dangerous Animal: Human Nature and the Origins of War.* New York: St. Martin's, 2024.

Stern, P. D. *The Biblical Herem: A Window on the Religious Experience of Israel.* Atlanta: Scholars Press, 1991.

Wilkerson, Isabel. *Caste: The Origins of Our Discontents.* New York: Random House, 2023.

GENERAL BIBLIOGRAPHY

The following works referred to in this book are listed in alphabetical order.

Aristotle. *Politics*. Translated by Harris Rackham. Loeb Classical Library. Cambridge, MA: Harvard University Press, 1932.

Arendt, Hannah. *On Revolution*. New York: Viking, 1965.

Auden, W. H. "The Garrison." In *W. H. Auden: Collected Poems*, edited by Edward Mendelson, 844. New York: Random House, 1976.

———. "Musée des Beaux Arts." December 1938. www.poetryfoundation.org/poems/159364/musee-des-beaux-arts-63a1efde036cd.

Bacote, Vincent. *The Political Disciple: A Theology of Public Life*. Grand Rapids, MI: Zondervan, 2015.

Baldwin, James. *The Cross of Redemption: Uncollected Writings*. Edited by Randall Kenan. New York: Vintage Books, 2010.

———. *James Baldwin: Collected Essays*. Edited by Toni Morrison. New York: Library of America, 1998.

Bellah, Robert. *Religion in Human Evolution: From the Paleolithic to the Axial Age*. Cambridge, MA: Harvard University Press, 2011.

Bethge, Eberhard. *Dietrich Bonhoeffer: A Biography*. Rev. ed. Minneapolis: Fortress, 2000.

Bonhoeffer, Dietrich. *Sanctorum Communio: A Theological Study of the Sociology of the Church*. Edited by Clifford Green. Minneapolis: Fortress, 1998.

Brown, Peter. *Through the Eye of a Needle: Wealth, the Fall of Rome, and the Making of the Modern West, 350–550 AD*. Princeton, NJ: Princeton University Press, 2014.

Brueggemann, Walter. *The Prophetic Imagination*. 2nd ed. Minneapolis: Fortress, 2001.

Chenoweth, Erica. *Civil Resistance: What Everyone Needs to Know*. New York: Oxford University Press, 2021.

Chenoweth, Erica, and Maria Stephan. *Why Civil Resistance Works: The Strategic Logic of Nonviolent Conflict*. New York: Columbia University Press, 2012.

Cohen, Yoram. *Wisdom from the Late Bronze Age*. Atlanta: Society of Biblical Literature, 2013.

Common, Kate. *Undoing Conquest: Ancient Israel, the Bible, and the Future of Christianity*. Maryknoll, NY: Orbis Books, 2024.

Copan, Paul. *Is God a Moral Monster? Making Sense of the Old Testament God*. Grand Rapids, MI: Baker Books, 2011.

Cowles, C. S., et al. *Show Them No Mercy: Four Views on God and the Canaanite Genocide*. Grand Rapids, MI: Zondervan, 2003.

Crossan, John Dominic. *God and Empire: Jesus Against Rome, Then and Now*. New York: HarperOne, 2008.

Danby, Herbert, trans. *Tractate Baba Kamma*. In *The Mishnah*, 332-46. Peabody, MA: Hendrickson, 2011.

D'Emilio, Frances. "Pope: Vatican Will Shelter 2 Families Fleeing War, Hunger." Associated Press, September 6, 2015. https://apnews.com/general-news-9f9a61892ab74d e693b72641b42afeb1.

Ehrman, Bart. *The Triumph of Christianity: How a Forbidden Religion Swept the World.* New York: Simon & Schuster, 2019.

"Enuma Elish." In *The Babylonian Genesis: The Story of Creation*, 2nd ed. translated by Alexander Heidel, 1-60. Chicago: University of Chicago Press, 1963.

"Facts and Figures: Ending Violence Against Women." United Nations Agency for Women, November 24, 2024. www.unwomen.org/en/what-we-do/ending-violence-against-women/facts-and-figures.

Fishbane, Michael. *Biblical Myth and Rabbinic Mythmaking.* New York: Oxford University Press, 2003.

———. *The Garments of Torah: Essays in Biblical Hermeneutics.* Bloomington: Indiana University Press, 1989.

"Global Estimates of Modern Slavery: Forced Labour and Forced Marriage." International Labor Association, 2017. www.ilo.org/wcmsp5/groups/public/@dgreports/@dcomm/documents/publication/wcms_575540.pdf.

Gregory, Eric. "Agape and Global Economy." In *Global Neighbors: Christian Faith and Moral Obligation in Today's Economy*, edited by Douglas Hicks and Mark Valeri, 16-42. Grand Rapids, MI: Eerdmans, 2010.

Gutiérrez, Gustavo. *A Theology of Liberation.* Translated by Caridad Inda and John Eagleson. Maryknoll, NY: Orbis Books, 1973.

Hallo, William, and K. Lawson Younger, eds. *Contexts of Scripture.* Vol. 2, *Monumental Inscriptions from the Ancient World.* Leiden: Brill, 2000.

Harari, Yuval Noah. *Sapiens: A Brief History of Humankind.* London: Vintage, 2011.

Hendel, Ronald. *The Book of Genesis: A Biography.* Princeton, NJ: Princeton University Press, 2012.

Hersey, Tricia. *Rest Is Resistance: A Manifesto.* New York: Little Brown Spark, 2022.

Hesiod. *Theogony, Works and Days. Testimonia.* Cambridge, MA: Harvard University Press, 2007.

Hippolytus. *Refutation of All Heresies.* In Bruno Snell, *Heraklit: Fragmente,* 50-51. Munich: Heimeran, 1976.

Holland, Tom. *Dominion: How the Christian Revolution Remade the World.* New York: Basic Books, 2021.

Horsley, Richard. *Jesus and Empire: The Kingdom of God and the New World Disorder.* Minneapolis: Fortress, 2002.

Internal Displacement Monitoring Centre. "UNHCR Mid-Year Trends 2024." United Nations Refugee Agency, October 9, 2024. www.unhcr.org/en-us/figures-at-a-glance.html.

Josephus. *The Life, Against Apion.* Translated by H. St. John Thackeray. Loeb Classical Library. Cambridge, MA: Harvard University Press, 1929.

Kass, Leon. *The Beginning of Wisdom: Reading Genesis.* Chicago: University of Chicago Press, 2006.

King, Martin Luther Jr. *A Testament of Hope: The Essential Writings and Speeches of Martin Luther King Jr.*, ed. James Washington, 289-302. New York: HarperCollins, 1986.

Knoppers, Gary. *Jews and Samaritans: The Origins and History of Their Early Relations*. New York: Oxford University Press, 2013.

Kreider, Alan. *The Patient Ferment of the Early Church: The Improbable Rise of Christianity in the Roman Empire*. Grand Rapids, MI: Baker Academic, 2016.

Lederach, John Paul. "Spirituality and Religious Peacebuilding." In *The Oxford Handbook of Religion, Conflict, and Peacebuilding*, edited by Atalia Omer, R. Scott Appleby, and David Little, 541-68. New York: Oxford University Press, 2015.

Levenson, Jon. *Inheriting Abraham: The Legacy of the Patriarch in Judaism, Christianity, and Islam*. Princeton, NJ: Princeton University Press, 2014.

Lopez, Donald, Jr., ed. *Buddhist Scriptures*. New York: Penguin Classics, 2004.

Lorde, Audre. *The Master's Tools Will Never Dismantle the Master's House*. London: Penguin, 2018.

Lynch, Matthew. *Flood and Fury: Old Testament Violence and the Shalom of God*. Downers Grove, IL: IVP Academic, 2023.

Machiavelli, Niccolo. *The Prince*. 2nd ed. Translated by Robert Adams. New York: Norton, 1992.

"The Martyrdom of Polycarp." In *The Apostolic Fathers*, translated by Kirsopp Lake, 2:307-46. New York: Macmillan, 1923.

McEvoy, Claire, and Gergely Hideg. "Global Violent Deaths 2017: Time to Decide." Small Arms Survey, December 2017. www.smallarmssurvey.org/fileadmin/docs/U-Reports/SAS-Report-GVD2017.pdf.

McGinn, Bernard. *The Essential Writings of Christian Mysticism*. New York: Modern Library, 2006.

Middleton, J. Richard. "Reading Genesis 3 Attentive to Human Evolution." In *Evolution and the Fall*, edited by William Cavanaugh and James Smith, 67-97. Grand Rapids, MI: Eerdmans, 2017.

Milgrom, Jacob. *Leviticus 17–22*. Anchor Yale Bible Commentary. New Haven, CT: Yale University Press, 2000.

Munhall, Patricia, et al. *The Emergence of Man into the 21st Century*. Sudbury, MA: Jones & Bartlett, 2002.

"New Surgeon General Advisory Raises Alarm About the Devastating Impact of the Epidemic of Loneliness and Isolation in the United States." US Department of Health and Human Services, May 3, 2023. www.hhs.gov/about/news/2023/05/03/new-surgeon-general-advisory-raises-alarm-about-devastating-impact-epidemic-loneliness-isolation-united-states.html.

Nibley, Hugh. "From the Dead Sea Scrolls (1QS)." *Studies in the Bible and Antiquity* 2 (2010), article 5.

Nietzsche, Friedrich. *The Antichrist*. In *The Portable Nietzsche*, edited and translated by Walter Kaufmann, 565-56. New York: Penguin, 1982.

———. *Beyond Good and Evil*. Translated by Judith Norman. New York: Cambridge University Press, 2005.

———. *On the Genealogy of Morals*. Edited and translated by Walter Kaufmann. New York: Vintage, 1969.

———. *Thus Spoke Zarathustra*. In *The Portable Nietzsche*, edited and translated by Walter Kaufmann, 103-439. New York: Penguin, 1982.

Ogletree, Thomas. "Interpreting the Love Commands in Social Context." In *Love and Christian Ethics: Tradition, Theory, and Society*, edited by Frederick Simmons and Brian Sorrels, 19-35. Washington, DC: Georgetown University Press, 2016.

Plato. *The Republic*. 2nd ed. Translated by Allan Bloom. New York: Basic Books, 1991.

Rahner, Karl. "Epilogue: The Mystery of Unselfish Communion." In *The Love of Jesus and the Love of Neighbor*, 99-104. New York: Crossroad, 1983.

Rumi, Jalal al-Din. *The Essential Rumi*. Edited by Coleman Barks. San Francisco: HarperSanFrancisco, 2004.

Schneider, Johannes. "Homoia." In *Theological Dictionary of the New Testament*, edited by Gerhard Friedrich, 5:186-98. Grand Rapids, MI: Eerdmans, 1967.

Schweiker, William. "Loose Morals." *The Christian Century* 120, no. 10 (May 17, 2003). www.christiancentury.org/reviews/2003-05/loose-morals.

Seibert, Eric. *Redeeming Violent Verses: A Guide for Using Troublesome Texts in Church and Ministry*. Louisville, KY: Westminster John Knox, 2023.

Sen, Amartya. "More Than 100 Million Women Are Missing." *New York Times Review of Books*, December 1990.

Seneca. *On Anger*. Edited by Aubrey Stewart. London: George Bell and Sons, 1900. https://en.wikisource.org/wiki/Of_Anger.

———. *On Benefits*. Edited by Aubrey Stewart. Gutenberg ebook, 2010. www.gutenberg.org/files/3794/3794-h/3794-h.htm#link2H_4_0006.

———. *On the Firmness of the Wise Man*. Edited by Aubrey Stewart. https://en.wikisource.org/wiki/On_the_Firmness_of_the_Wise_Man#IV.

Smith, Mark. *The Priestly Vision of Genesis 1*. Minneapolis: Fortress, 2009.

Snell, Bruno. *Heraklit: Fragmente*. Munich: Heimeran, 1976.

Stark, Rodney. *The Rise of Christianity: How the Obscure, Marginal Jesus Movement Became the Dominant Religious Force in the Western World in a Few Centuries*. San Francisco: HarperSanFrancisco, 1997.

"Suicide: Key Facts." World Health Organization, August 24, 2024. www.who.int/news-room/fact-sheets/detail/suicide.

Taylor, Charles. *A Secular Age*. Cambridge, MA: Harvard University Press, 2018.

Tobin, Katie. "The Enigma of Simone Weil." *Verso Books*, February 28, 2024. www.versobooks.com/blogs/news/the-enigma-of-simone-weil.

Walton, John. *Genesis 1 as Ancient Cosmology*. University Park, PA: Eisenbrauns, 2009.

Walzer, Michael. *In God's Shadow: Politics in the Hebrew Bible*. New Haven, CT: Yale University Press, 2012.

Webb, William, and Gordon Oeste. *Bloody, Brutal, and Barbaric? Wrestling with Troubling War Texts*. Downers Grove, IL: IVP Academic, 2019.

Weil, Simone. *The Need for Roots: A Prelude Toward a Declaration of Duties to Mankind*. New York: Routledge, 2001.

———. *Oppression and Liberty*. New York: Routledge, 2001.

"What Is Genocide." United States Memorial Holocaust Museum, accessed January 19, 2025. www.ushmm.org/genocide-prevention/learn-about-genocide-and-other-mass-atrocities/what-is-genocide.

Whitehead, Alfred North. *Process and Reality*. New York: Free Press, 1979.

Wilkerson, Isabel. *The Warmth of Other Suns: The Epic Story of America's Great Migration*. New York: Vintage, 2011.

Wittgenstein, Ludwig. *Philosophical Investigations*. Translated by G. E. M. Anscombe. New York: Macmillan, 1958.
Wolin, Sheldon. *Politics and Vision: Continuity and Innovation in Western Political Thought*. Princeton, NJ: Princeton University Press, 2016.
Wright, N. T. *Jesus and the Victory of God*. Minneapolis: Fortress, 1996.
———. *The New Testament and the People of God*. Minneapolis: Fortress, 1996.
———. *Paul: A Biography*. San Francisco: HarperOne, 2020.
———. *The Resurrection of the Son of God*. Minneapolis: Fortress, 2003.
Younger, K. Lawson. *Contexts of Scripture*. Vol. 4, *Supplements*. Leiden: Brill, 2016.
Zak, Paul. *The Moral Molecule: How Trust Works*. New York: Penguin, 2013.

GENERAL INDEX

abolition (of othering), 4, 9, 11-13, 27, 55, 68-69, 71, 73, 76, 77-78, 80-82, 93, 97, 106, 108, 110, 112, 117-18, 130, 150, 151, 167, 192, 199-201, 208, 214, 218-19, 220-21
abortion, 25, 126, 154
abundance, 81, 88, 220
Abraham, 12, 36-38, 41, 51, 55-57, 60, 61, 78, 93, 96-97, 107, 119, 138, 152, 193, 214, 221
acceptance, 14, 62, 104-5, 115, 144, 167, 181, 190, 208-9, 220
action, 42, 44, 46, 55, 63-64, 69, 85-87, 89-90, 92, 98, 102, 108-9, 121, 134, 145, 149, 160, 165, 171, 176, 185-6, 189, 204, 207
addiction (of othering), 14, 104, 110, 197, 220
advocacy, 4, 95, 130, 162, 196, 215
agency, 18, 20, 25, 39, 64, 80, 98, 101, 108, 149, 216
altruism, 172-74, 183, 190, 206
Amalek(ites), 29-30, 41-43, 48, 52, 58, 63, 71, 199
anger, 17, 40, 52, 111, 113, 141, 196
antisemitism, 145-46, 152, 155, 156-57
apocalyptic, 61, 102-3, 199, 219
Aquinas, Thomas, 134-38, 139, 164, 173, 199, 212
Arendt, Hannah, 92, 191, 204
Aristotle, 10, 20-21, 25, 38, 40, 42, 45, 66, 73, 95, 135, 136, 138
attention (*see also* practice), 1-3, 11, 73, 85-86, 112, 116-17, 140, 166-69, 173, 190, 191, 200, 205-26, 209, 216
Auden, W.H., 5, 155
Augustine, 100, 131-35, 136, 208, 209
authoritarianism, 101, 105
awareness, 4-5, 47, 152, 199, 209
Baldwin, James, xii, 14, 97, 169, 171, 174, 175, 176, 220, 221
beauty, 15, 32, 60, 80, 93, 112, 118, 140, 141, 148, 161, 165, 186, 188, 191, 207, 210
beginning (new), 7, 14-17, 23, 31-37, 57, 67, 73, 92, 110, 113, 128, 140, 148, 157, 161, 168, 173, 182, 189, 191, 193, 198, 201, 209, 221-22
belief, 6, 88, 96, 120-21, 124, 137, 146, 147, 151, 219
belonging, 3, 13-15, 28, 30, 33-34, 36, 49, 56-58, 69, 72-75, 77, 80, 81, 86, 93, 98, 107, 111, 112, 116, 118, 122, 136, 152, 158, 163, 175, 182, 185, 200, 203, 212, 218, 220-21
belovedness, 26, 33, 35, 62, 67, 74, 78, 81, 112, 114, 139, 166, 176, 198, 208-9, 210-11, 213, 220, 221
Bible, biblical interpretation, 6, 8, 9, 29-31, 50, 53, 55, 57-58, 60-63, 70-71, 76-77, 78, 82-87, 95, 99-101, 131-32, 146, 154, 181
birth, 10, 55, 121, 199, 202, 210
blame, 35, 103, 131, 156
blessing, 12, 23, 32, 34, 36-38, 39-41, 45, 47, 49, 51, 53, 55-56, 57, 67, 71, 78, 80, 90, 92-93, 96, 98-99, 101, 118, 149, 152, 164, 193-94, 214, 221
Boaz, 12, 53-56, 58, 60, 66, 71, 199, 213

body, 35, 96, 106, 111, 113, 139, 141, 161, 194, 210-11
Bonhoeffer, Dietrich, 10-11, 155-62, 190, 191, 192, 202, 205, 210, 219, 221
Bucer, Martin, 142, 219
Buddhism, 14, 217-18
Caesar, 79, 100, 105
Canaanites, 38-41, 48, 57, 217
capital punishment. *See* death penalty
character, 42, 45, 54, 55, 67-69, 70, 72, 88, 128, 131, 148
caste (system), 3, 18-19, 184, 187-88, 191, 192
change, 8, 9, 29, 46, 64, 65, 72, 82, 99, 105, 120-21, 146, 154, 175, 177, 182, 186, 216, 218
charity, 21, 61, 121-22, 136, 137-38, 185
Chenoweth, Erica, 65, 216
children, 2-7, 12, 13, 17, 18-19, 20-21, 22, 25, 27, 29-30, 40-41, 48, 49, 50, 51, 58, 61, 67-70, 73, 75-76, 77, 93, 122, 123, 126-27, 128, 138, 141, 185, 187-88, 193, 215
choice, 3, 4, 11, 31, 37, 55, 62, 69, 86, 149, 198
Christ/God in the other/neighbor, 144-45, 157-59, 161-62, 179, 186-88, 192, 205, 213, 218, 221
Christian(ity), 1, 5, 6, 7, 9-10, 13-14, 27, 33, 39, 55, 59-60, 94-97, 100-102, 105, 114, 118, 120-25, 125-28, 128-30, 135, 137, 148, 161, 162, 198-99, 202, 205, 215, 216, 219
church, 1, 4, 5, 7, 121-22, 125-28, 142, 161, 162-63, 176, 181-82, 184, 199, 203
Cicero (philosopher), 22, 74, 98, 121
circle, 11-15, 16-17, 21, 23, 26-28, 33-34, 37, 43, 48, 51, 58, 59, 69, 73, 75, 78, 82, 86-87, 90, 93, 95, 178, 194, 104-5, 108, 112, 116-18, 124, 127, 130, 135, 138, 141, 146, 151-52, 162, 164, 169, 176, 178, 190, 192, 195, 202-3, 215, 221
citizen(ship), 13, 23, 75, 96, 105, 110, 112, 128-29, 181, 192, 201-2, 214, 218
civil rights movement, 170-72, 206
civilization, 21, 28, 33, 36, 134, 176, 183, 198
colonialism, 19, 152, 162
 neocolonialism, 24
commandment (greatest, of neighbor love), 8, 12, 31, 76-77, 79-80, 93, 100, 145, 221
community, 6, 11-12, 17, 40-41, 42-46, 49-50, 53-56, 58, 66-69, 95, 108, 113, 127, 159-60, 171-172, 179, 182, 211
compassion, 8, 13, 22-23, 30, 41, 45, 53, 68, 85-86, 93, 105, 112, 114, 117, 123, 140, 181, 185, 193-94, 208-9, 217, 220
competition (competitive mindset), 14, 22, 34, 36, 39, 49-50, 58, 71, 76, 133-34, 153, 208-9, 220
conflict, 7, 15, 17, 24, 30-31, 38, 39, 49, 63-65, 80, 82, 108, 173-76, 216, 218
  See also violence, war
connection (moral, spiritual, social), 3, 14, 27, 35, 58, 68, 70, 89, 149-50, 176, 187, 214
conscience, 4, 14, 101, 164, 171, 176, 177
cooperation, 14, 217, 220
cosmopolitanism, 22, 118, 128-30, 157, 164, 185, 202, 214

General Index

countercultural ethics of love, 12, 15, 31, 53-55, 61, 90, 95, 122, 129, 170, 174, 189, 202, 213
courage, 37, 52, 61, 64, 104, 148, 155, 156, 161, 174, 176, 179, 181, 194
creation (of the world, new), 15-17, 31-35, 57, 65, 90, 97, 103, 106, 109, 166-67, 200-201, 221
creation out of nothing as act of love, 62, 115, 139-40, 148, 166-68, 200-201, 213, 219
creative 32-33, 63-64, 72, 80, 98, 127, 166, 171, 176, 191, 215, 220
  See also resistance, nonviolence
critique of religion, Christianity, 22, 45, 71-73, 79-80, 124, 127, 134, 135, 137-38, 142, 145-46, 152-53, 156, 158, 159-60, 162-64, 169, 176, 181-82, 199, 202-3, 212-13
  See also prophets(s)
cross, 90-92, 106, 166-67, 201, 204
Crusades, 135, 137-38, 152, 164, 202
culture, 8, 12, 16, 21-23, 95-97, 119-25, 131, 213, 218
Day, Dorothy, 171, 189, 212, 213
death, 5, 10, 26, 36, 52, 59, 74, 83, 89-92, 106-7, 126, 127, 137, 159, 183, 185, 213-14
death penalty, 126, 134, 136-37
dehumanization, 2, 5, 7-8, 20, 24, 105, 136, 145-46, 156, 194, 196, 201
demonization. *See* dehumanization
desire, 8, 34-36, 38, 52, 67, 68, 69, 70-73, 101, 103, 108, 114, 130, 134, 189, 194, 220
devaluation (of others), 21, 75, 115, 117
Didache, 125-27, 151, 159, 175, 200
dignity, 18, 26-27, 31-34, 37, 42, 60, 64, 98, 122, 124, 162, 185, 187, 215
disability, 19, 21, 42, 126, 129
dogma (dead), 6, 7, 9, 15, 102, 128, 147, 170, 176
domination (lust for), 15-16, 20, 22, 39, 49, 51, 66, 104-5, 120, 129, 131-32, 156, 174-75, 198
earth (as our neighbor, sacred), 14, 32-34, 35, 57, 148, 167, 213, 221
economics, 24-25, 45, 74-75, 114-17, 120, 176, 182, 198, 215
embodiment, embodying love, 3, 27, 33, 45, 55, 65, 71, 78, 85-86, 89, 98, 130, 139, 145, 159, 165, 178, 183, 187, 193-94, 198, 205, 209-10, 216
empathy, 165, 173, 194
empire, emperor, 18, 35, 104, 110, 138, 197-99
enemy/enemies, 4, 8, 12, 51-53, 156, 212, 218
enemy love, 12, 51, 52-56, 60, 65-69, 72, 80-82, 82-86, 86-87, 89-90, 93, 97-99, 116, 119, 124, 125-26, 128-29, 134, 135-38, 139, 143, 149-50, 152, 173-75, 177, 179, 182-83, 192, 194, 200, 208, 213-14
enmity. *See* enemy/enemies
Enuma Elish, 15-16
envy. *See* jealousy
Epistle to Diognetus, 128-30, 164, 190, 202
equality (human), 3, 14, 21-22, 27, 33-34, 36, 45, 47, 49, 58, 65, 70-71, 73, 80, 95, 100-102, 107-8, 114, 115-17, 123, 134, 147, 149, 189, 208, 215, 220
essentializing (othering), 18, 66, 136, 173, 184
Esther, 51-52
eternal life, 68, 72-76, 79-80, 83-87, 88, 91-93, 136, 144, 151, 221
  See also salvation
ethics, 2, 5, 8, 11-15, 27, 33, 45, 52, 54, 62, 66, 68, 70-71, 78-79, 80-81, 87-88, 97-99, 100, 102, 105, 111, 115, 148, 156-57, 175, 207, 217-18

Ethiopia, 1, 4, 6-7, 8, 59-60, 72, 119-20, 154-55, 185, 193-97
ethnic cleansing, 59-60
eugenics, 18-19, 104, 126
evangelism, 5, 182
evil, 11, 52, 53, 67, 74, 81, 96, 98, 116, 134, 136, 168, 181-82, 191
evolution (of neighbor love), 9, 136, 154
exceptionalism. *See* nationalism (religious)
exclusion, 2, 11-13, 27, 19-21, 39, 49-50, 53-55, 61, 69, 79-80, 91, 107, 120, 133, 163, 220
exemplars of neighbor love, 155, 191-92
extermination. *See* genocide
Eyob, 1, 3-6, 14, 73, 144, 154, 197, 207, 222
Ezra, 49-50, 54, 84, 94
faith, 9, 37, 46, 58, 72-73, 107, 109, 115, 142, 148, 178, 217-18
fall, the, 35, 103, 141
family (humans as one), 11, 33-36, 67-69, 70, 96, 107, 110, 112, 129, 140, 155, 172, 197, 200, 221
fascism, 162
favor, favoritism, 1, 22, 38, 48, 50, 51, 53, 66, 80-81, 96, 115-17, 133, 137
fear/fearless, 6, 7, 10, 17, 39, 49-50, 58, 81, 92, 97, 141, 210, 220
feminist visions of neighbor love, 124
Ferdosa, 59-60, 119-20, 153, 154, 194, 197
Fishbane, Michael, 31
flourishing, 3, 8, 88, 129-30, 153, 193, 199, 215, 220
foreign/foreigner, 1, 13, 15, 19-21, 27, 34, 43-44, 47-50, 79, 93, 96, 110, 112, 128-29, 157, 202, 218
forgiveness, 81, 91-92, 112, 114, 134, 143, 173, 182-83, 194, 204, 209, 219
freedom, 17, 28, 31, 35, 64-65, 88, 91, 95, 108, 116-17, 124, 134, 177, 215
Freud, Sigmund, 151, 152
friends/friendship, 4, 13, 15, 23, 27, 44, 77, 90, 174-75, 178, 189, 210
fruit of the Spirit, 109-110
gay. *See* queer
Gaza, 29-30, 41
generosity, 8, 45, 47, 70-71, 74, 81, 88, 95, 98, 115, 122, 126-27, 190-91, 207
genocide, 2, 7-8, 10, 24, 29-30, 40-41, 50-52, 58, 146, 152, 156-57, 170, 199, 214, 217
gift, 5, 11, 15, 32, 34, 70, 74, 88, 110, 115-16, 126, 141, 148, 189, 210
globalization (of neighbor love), 37, 77-79, 92, 118, 151-153, 161, 202-3, 214-15, 220-22
God, 1, 5, 8, 9, 45, 52, 53, 67-69, 70, 72, 77, 91, 108, 130, 140, 148, 160, 166-67, 175, 187, 196, 200, 211, 212, 219
  Jesus' definition 80-83
God's will, 6, 8, 18, 22, 40, 62, 70-77, 84, 100, 102-3, 105, 126, 170-71, 181
golden circle (of love), 28, 192, 221
golden rule, 70-72, 74, 76, 80, 105
good/goodness (primal, human), 4, 20, 32, 34-35, 67, 80-81, 92, 98, 108-9, 114, 116, 130, 134, 136, 141, 172-73, 200, 210
  as arbiter of othering, 74-76
gospel, good news, 106-7, 133, 177, 181-82
Grande, Rutilio, 177, 178, 182, 206
Great Commission, 77-79, 93, 152, 182, 214, 221
grief, 2, 3, 8, 36, 178-79, 191, 196, 201, 208
  See also "ungrievability"

General Index

grudges, 42-43, 49, 53, 194, 214
Gushee, David, 33, 121, 127
Gutiérrez, Gustavo, 9, 179
happiness (humane), 23, 90, 129-30, 131-35, 151, 190, 199, 209, 212
Harari, Yuval, 26
hate, 12, 19, 35, 43, 51-52, 54, 66-70, 80, 84, 86, 99, 108, 125, 127, 129, 136, 146, 152, 157, 171, 174-75, 182, 194, 200-201, 218, 200
Havel, Vaclav, 35, 218
healing, xii, 7, 9, 10, 14, 15, 26-28, 37, 62, 69, 77-78, 92, 97, 103, 105, 111-12, 139-41, 155, 159, 184, 185, 191-92, 197, 201, 218, 219, 220
heaven (kingdom of, your Father in), 23, 61-62, 67, 70, 72, 74-75, 103, 110, 131, 139, 202, 212, 213
heteronaut/heteronautics, 37-38, 55, 61, 97, 193, 213
hierarchy, 3, 15, 18, 20-22, 33, 39-41, 45, 73-76, 89-90, 96, 105, 110, 114, 120, 137-38, 142, 148, 152, 180, 198
Hildegard of Bingen, 32, 221
Hinduism, 14, 218
Hitler, Adolf, 10, 146, 156-58, 160-61, 164, 169
Holocaust, 10, 13, 146, 152, 158, 160, 169
home, 15, 24-25, 33, 37, 38, 54, 75, 95, 118, 121, 129-31, 143, 163-64, 169, 185, 189, 199, 212, 221
hooks, bell, xii, 5, 8, 83, 209, 212
hope, 5, 10, 15, 56-57, 102-3, 109, 141, 151, 162, 169, 178, 191, 194, 219
hospitality, 8, 95, 98, 122, 128-29, 201, 207
human(s)/humanity, 5, 8, 11, 14, 16-17, 23, 27-28, 31-36, 37, 57, 67-68, 70, 78, 81, 95-97, 106-7, 100, 110-12, 114, 122, 128, 140, 183, 218, 221
human rights, 32-33, 120-21, 153, 198-99, 215
humility, 47, 80, 89, 108, 111, 113-14, 132, 141, 160, 220
hypocrisy. *See* critique of religion
identity, 2, 8, 11, 13, 37, 40, 46, 50, 55, 58, 68, 74, 80, 82, 84, 86, 89-90, 96, 106-7, 140, 159, 193, 198, 199-200, 214, 218
idols/idolatry, 32, 39, 52, 77, 108, 160
image of God (humans created in), 11, 30, 31-33, 34, 38, 40, 45, 56, 58, 93, 96, 133, 152, 173, 188, 190, 214, 221
imagination, 15, 17, 21, 22, 36, 56-57, 87, 124, 215
See also see/seeing
imperialism. *See* empire, emperor
inclusion, 4, 12, 14, 32-33, 48, 57, 61, 62-63, 77-78, 80, 87, 88, 90, 96, 100, 118, 125, 164, 167, 176, 202, 220
inequality. *See* hierarchy
inner life, 4, 71, 109-10, 111-12, 129, 148, 150, 173, 206-7
See also soul
innovation (ethical), 15, 31, 66, 68, 70, 96, 100, 120-21, 127, 136, 152, 182, 199, 215
insecurity (as source of othering), 34-36, 58, 81, 220
integrity, integration, 77-78, 82, 96, 111, 133, 155, 176, 195, 198, 216-17
interfaith (ethic, wisdom), 14, 217-18
Irenaeus, 124
irony (of othering), 13-14, 17, 23, 30, 34, 39-40, 50, 53, 58, 66, 73, 111, 137-38, 142, 146, 211-12, 219
Islam 14, 137, 138, 217
Israel
 biblical ethics, 63, 66-69, 71, 75, 94, 197
 nation of, 12, 29-31, 31-58
jealousy, 34-35, 58, 81, 103, 109, 113, 148, 194
Jesus, 3, 4, 8-9, 106-7, 112, 113, 118, 125, 127, 132, 135-36, 137, 139, 143-44, 148, 149, 152, 157, 166, 170, 173, 174, 181, 183, 185-87, 190, 196, 199, 200, 202, 208, 214, 215, 219, 221-22
 as mother, 140-41
 teachings and practices of neighbor love, 60-93
Judaism, 14, 31-58
 biblical ethics, 217
joy, 4-5, 10, 83, 90, 109, 140, 151, 190, 194, 212, 222
judgment, 12, 23, 74
 as arbiter of othering, 81-82, 116, 179, 188, 219
Julian of Norwich, 138-41, 148, 161, 184, 191, 193, 213, 221
justice, 8, 11, 18, 23, 28, 41-42, 46-48, 52, 98, 101, 117, 123, 165, 177, 179-81, 194, 198, 215-16
justification, 106-7
Kierkegaard, Søren, 146-51, 161, 200, 203-4
killing. *See* murder
kindness, 3, 45, 49, 52, 55, 65, 67, 70, 77, 80-82, 99, 109, 112-14, 140, 186, 189, 194, 200, 209, 219
King, Martin Luther, Jr., 28, 169-76, 183, 190, 191, 192, 198, 203, 206, 216
Lactantius, 123
law, 12, 20, 41-42, 45, 48, 55, 62, 63, 70, 76-77, 79, 83, 99-102, 108-10, 115-17, 161, 180-81, 199, 215
Lawrence, Brother, 67, 188, 207
Lewis, C. S., 27, 158
liberation, 20, 95-96, 115-17, 122, 177-78, 198, 215
limitations (in religious visions of others), 31, 57-58, 137-38, 199
listening. *See* practice, practitioner
loneliness, 26, 187-88
Lorde, Audre, 8-9, 105, 218
love, 4, 5, 44, 54, 88, 106-8, 131-32, 135, 141, 142, 144, 147, 149, 151, 152, 159, 163, 171-76, 180-81, 186, 189-90, 194, 198-99, 211
 negative limit of love (do no harm), 108-9, 110, 112-16, 121, 125, 127, 133, 135, 181
 See also neighbor love, enemy love
love in everything (see *mysticism*), 139-40, 148, 166-67, 201, 213-14
 See also mysticism
"love your enemy." *See* enemy love
"love your neighbor." *See* neighbor love
loving God (in relation to neighbor), 100, 108, 111, 123, 125, 132-34, 135, 148, 159, 168-69, 180, 188, 190
Luther, Martin, 14, 106, 142-46, 156, 199, 204
mandate (of neighbor love), 9, 14-15, 62, 102
marginalization. See *exclusion*
Marx, Karl, 151
meaning (of life), 4, 10-11, 15, 25, 28, 77, 85, 141, 157, 176, 180, 199
mercy, 11, 40, 48, 52, 56, 80-81, 85-86, 116, 146, 173
Merton, Thomas, 68, 163, 208
Messiah, 55, 90-91
Mill, John Stuart, 6, 7, 102, 147, 153, 197
mind (of Christ), 104, 109, 113, 176, 203, 207
Moabites, 49, 53-57, 69, 71
 See also Ruth
money, 11, 16, 22, 74, 85, 95, 108, 111, 114, 116-17, 121-23, 126-27, 130, 138, 151, 180, 188-89, 194
moral circle. *See* circle
morality, 6, 11-15, 12, 73, 125-28, 207, 218
Morrison, Toni, 2, 14, 206, 211
Moses, 12, 30, 39, 40-42, 45, 47, 49, 51, 54, 62-63, 66, 71, 199, 214
Mother Teresa, 28, 184-91, 219

General Index

movement (of neighbor love), 9, 10, 118, 120-25, 136, 139, 143, 152-53, 170, 191-92, 197, 211-20, 221-22
murder, 16-17, 19, 22, 24-25, 29, 32, 35-36, 52, 74, 89, 90-92, 99, 117, 126, 156, 180, 183, 216
Muslim (see *Islam*)
mystery, 5, 37, 95, 110, 140, 148
mysticism (of neighbor love), 32, 139-45, 148, 161, 165-67, 184, 188, 198, 213-14
mythology, 15-17, 22, 31-32, 36, 66
nationalism (religious), 12, 31, 38-39, 51-52, 56, 78, 83-84, 86, 90-91, 129, 154, 176, 197, 199, 203, 214
nature (human)/natural, 18, 136, 138, 173, 188, 199
Nehemiah, 50, 54, 84, 94
neighbor/neighbors, 7, 9, 11, 12, 14, 17, 19, 20, 22, 24, 26, 28, 40, 43, 46, 48, 55, 58, 75, 76, 77, 83-87, 93, 100, 104, 105, 108, 112-13, 116, 118, 121, 125, 127, 133, 143, 147-49, 152, 157, 172, 179, 187, 213, 218-19, 220
   definition, 3
   Jesus' definition, 61
   synthesis, 199-203
neighborhood (moral), 17, 78, 124, 167, 181, 193, 207, 215
neighbor love, 6, 7-9, 10, 11-14, 22-23, 26-28, 53-55, 57-58, 193-94, 197
   in Augustine, 131-34
   definition, 3-4
   in the Didache, 125-27
   in Dietrich Bonhoeffer, 156-62
   in the early Jesus movement, 120-25
   in the Epistle to Diognetus, 128-30
   feminist visions, 124
   in Jesus' teachings and practices of neighbor love, 60-93
   in Julian of Norwich, 138-41
   in Martin Luther, 142-46
   in Martin Luther King Jr., 169-76
   in Mother Teresa, 184-91
   in the New Testament outside the Gospels, 95-118
   origins in Leviticus 19, 41-46
   in Óscar Romero, 177-84
   perennial wisdom, 211-20
   in Simone Weil, 162-69
   in Søren Kierkegaard, 146-51
   synthesis, 198-211
   in Thomas Aquinas, 134-38
Neighbor-Love Covenant, 119, 193-94
Neighbor-Love Movement, 119, 153, 154-55, 193-97, 209-10, 217
Nietzsche, Friedrich, 124, 148, 151, 152
nonviolence, 51, 63-65, 69, 72, 77, 80-81, 92, 96, 98, 101, 103-6, 108, 126, 137, 162, 170-71, 172-76, 178, 197, 215-16
Nouwen, Henri, 188, 209
oppression, 20, 22-23, 45-47, 50, 56, 58, 64, 115-17, 157, 165, 179, 192, 199, 215
other(s), 1-3, 4-5, 7-8, 11, 22, 26, 27, 37, 38, 39, 47-50, 59, 61, 77, 79-80, 83-84, 87, 118, 122, 146, 150, 161, 167, 168, 170, 187, 195, 214, 218, 219-20
othering, 4-5, 7-8, 9, 10, 12-14, 32-33, 46, 47, 48, 50, 53-55, 59-60, 66-68, 74, 82-85, 90, 94-96, 102, 103, 109, 110, 113, 116, 120, 128, 133, 134, 135, 136, 138, 141, 142, 145-146, 147, 155, 160, 164, 168, 176, 183, 184, 190-191, 196-197, 211-12, 214, 218-20
   in America, 169-71
   ancient mythology, 15-17
   basic compulsion, 91
   Cain and Abel, 34-35
   classical philosophy, 17-21
   contemporary, 23-26
   core, 150
   curse of Ham, religious nationalism, 38-41
   definition, 1-3
   Greco-Roman culture, 21-23
   key to overcoming, 70-71
   self-othering, 208
pandemic, 143-44, 204
pain, 1, 4, 5, 26, 41, 84, 141, 163, 169, 170, 194, 201, 207, 209, 210
paradox of neighbor love, 13, 69, 72-73, 75, 77, 81-82, 87, 88, 93, 116, 129, 134, 136, 144, 152, 158, 163, 175, 187-88, 209, 212-13, 217
Parks, Rosa, 170
patriarchy, 25, 34, 96, 124, 138
patriotism, 164
peace(making), 23, 32, 35, 37, 51, 53, 62-65, 67, 69, 92, 96, 98, 104, 109-10, 126, 175, 190, 198, 201
philosophy, 17-21, 98, 110-11, 146
philoxenia (other-love, hospitality), 97-98, 201
plague. *See* pandemic
Plato, 18-19, 37, 40, 42, 66, 75, 95
politics, 3, 8, 12, 18, 20, 32-33, 45-46, 61, 79, 84-86, 101-2, 129, 135, 180-81, 191, 198, 215
Potter, Harry, 214
powell, john, 2, 3, 7-8, 49
power, 7, 14, 23, 27-28, 36, 42, 46, 51, 66, 68, 70-71, 88-90, 91, 162, 189, 194, 213
poverty, 13, 15, 21-22, 25, 42, 45, 47, 73-76, 96, 112, 115-17, 144, 151, 153, 155, 177, 184-88, 190, 192, 197, 215
practice, practitioner (of neighbor love), 3, 4, 7, 13, 44, 70, 81-82, 85, 89, 91, 179, 193-94, 200, 216
   attention, 167-69, 173, 190, 216
   listening, 119, 159-60, 173, 186-91, 194, 216
   helping (see *service*), 160-61
   suffering, 160-61, 172, 190, 219-20
   "small things" (kind words, smiles, touch), 186, 188-89, 194, 206-7, 216
prayer, 42, 69, 77, 127, 166, 184, 188, 194, 200, 201
prejudice, 101, 128-29, 203
   See also othering
presence, 14, 28, 32-33, 57, 64, 69, 91, 101, 138, 140, 165-67, 179, 211, 219
prison (also *prisoners*), 10, 123, 157, 179, 181
privilege, 28, 33, 70-71, 101, 129, 138, 213
prophet(s), 23, 30, 36, 46, 48, 56-57, 62, 70, 76, 78-80, 104, 117, 126-27, 154, 159, 169, 171, 176, 179, 180-84, 212-13, 216
protest, 65, 162, 165, 169, 171, 176, 178, 191
public life, 21, 131, 145, 191
public policy 145
purity, 19, 49-50, 55, 84, 89, 95, 140
queer, 15, 156
question(s), 10-11, 135, 159, 174
race, 8, 49, 128-30, 156, 172, 176, 190
racism, 19, 39, 49-50, 156
   See also othering
rage, 35, 38, 87, 94-95, 196
rationality, 20-21, 23, 138
reconciliation, 37, 51, 56-57, 96, 177, 182
refugees, 24, 61, 123

relationship (see also *belonging*), 8, 34-36, 38, 53-56, 60, 64-65, 67, 74-75, 77, 91, 98, 101, 106, 113, 115, 127, 157, 173, 195, 198, 216
  See also belonging
religion, 5, 8, 71, 78, 79, 115-17, 130, 176, 217
  See also critique of religion
repentance, 99, 181-82
resentment, 41, 47, 54, 59, 218
resistance, 10, 63, 65, 104, 156, 161, 175-76, 191, 194-95
responsibility, 11, 14-15, 26, 31, 32-33, 68, 71, 77, 86, 101, 159, 162, 189, 191, 203
resurrection, 76, 79, 91-92, 94, 110, 139, 141, 144, 219
retribution, retributive justice, 32, 37, 63-64, 216
revenge, 17, 42-43, 52, 63, 92, 98, 194, 214
  See also grudges, retribution, retributive justice
reviving (neighbor love), 7, 10, 107, 153, 197, 221
revolution(ary), xii, 8-9, 12-13, 15, 23, 79, 97, 120, 124, 127, 162, 183, 186-87, 201, 215, 218-19, 221
risks (of neighbor love), 143-44, 172-73, 183-84, 194, 206
Romero, Óscar, 177-84, 190, 191, 192, 198, 208, 215
Rowling, J. K., 214
Rumi, 26
Ruth, 12, 53-56, 58, 60, 66, 69, 78, 199
sadness, 23, 40, 197
  See also grief
salvation, 105-6, 114, 127, 136, 143-44, 174, 176, 204
  See also eternal life, universal salvation
Samaritan, parable of, 3, 82-87, 149, 160, 167, 172, 219
"Save yourself," 91-93, 161, 207
Scripture. *See* Bible, biblical interpretation
secular ethics, 14, 218
security, 37, 45, 60, 151, 204, 217
see/seeing, 1-5, 7, 9, 10, 12, 15, 31, 36, 68, 81, 83, 85, 155, 159, 169, 186-88, 194, 201, 222
segregation, 49-50, 169-71, 214
self. *See* inner life
self-care. *See* self-love
self-love, 26, 132-33, 150, 159, 186, 204, 207-11, 216
selfishness, 103, 113, 147, 150, 180-81, 203-7
separation, 1, 9, 18, 35, 43, 50, 54, 73, 96, 106, 111, 140-41, 150, 163, 211, 219
Sermon on the Mount, 23, 62-73, 75, 99, 115, 139, 212
service, 11, 32, 45, 87, 89-90, 108, 116, 120, 123, 131, 143-45, 159-61, 183, 185-86, 188-90, 194, 209
  See also practice, practitioner
sex, 10, 107, 124, 142, 151
shame, 4, 34-36, 52, 103, 107, 141, 210
siblings (humanity as sacred), 34, 68-70, 73, 180, 201
sickness, the sick, 19, 22, 45, 126, 139, 143-45, 157-58, 185, 187, 190
Sider, Ronald, 21, 126, 216
Siedentop, Larry, 21-22, 120, 151
sin, 181-82
  See also evil
sinner, 13, 80, 136-38, 219
slavery, 12, 16-17, 19-20, 25, 27, 33, 36, 38-39, 45, 48-49, 53, 56, 59, 95-96, 107, 114, 122-23, 148, 152, 170, 199
Smith, David Livingstone, 2
solidarity, 14, 43, 124, 153, 163, 165, 213, 217, 220
soul, 76-77, 127, 129, 135, 139, 141, 166, 172-74, 206
Spirit, spiritual(ity), 10, 70, 78, 81, 109, 148, 159, 100, 200
  See also presence

status, 3, 32, 35, 74-75, 108, 114, 130, 160, 194
story/stories, 4, 9, 15-17, 29-30, 31-32, 35-36, 38-39, 51-52, 53-56, 82-86, 92, 128, 203, 213, 214, 220
stranger(s), 4, 7, 12, 15, 21, 27, 48, 85, 110, 122, 128, 135, 138, 148, 179, 218
suffering, 2, 4, 5, 9, 144, 160-61, 166, 179, 187, 190, 192, 194, 219-20
  See also practice, practitioner
suicide, 25-26
superiority, 1, 13, 19-21, 35, 38-39, 58, 69, 74, 81, 89, 96, 98, 111, 113, 129-30, 141, 146, 150, 153, 203, 208, 211, 220
supremacy, 14, 36, 41, 111, 129-30, 169-70, 184, 217
surrender, 37, 58, 64, 69, 71, 81, 128, 161, 165, 214
technology, 36, 194
Tertullian, 104, 117, 122-23, 199
theology, 9, 33, 63, 65, 74, 77, 103, 106, 107, 110, 115, 116, 124, 128, 134, 136, 138, 170, 178-79, 215
  See also God
together(ness), 10-11, 15, 161-62, 199, 221
  See also solidarity
trauma, 41, 47
trust, 81, 88, 113, 116, 140, 148
truth, 6, 7, 11, 111, 113, 114, 169, 194
Tutu, Desmond, 20-21, 30, 158, 183
"ungrievability," 2, 8, 201
union, unity, 14, 88-89, 166-67, 213, 220
universal salvation, 140-41, 163-65
  hopeful universalism, 219
universality of neighbor love, morality, 12, 133, 149-50, 152, 167, 172, 187, 190, 192, 199-201, 214, 217, 221
universe, 28, 88, 110, 118, 139-40, 164, 166, 167, 213-14
us versus them, 13-14, 15, 25, 27, 74, 164, 196
value, 3-5, 9, 13, 21-22, 27, 32-32, 68, 140-41, 151, 182-83, 192, 193, 208, 215, 220
vibrations of love, 166-67, 200-201, 213
violence, 2, 8, 15-17, 19, 24-26, 29-31, 36-37, 40-41, 51-52, 63-65, 90-92, 104-5, 126, 129, 131, 137-38, 146, 162, 164, 173, 178-83, 198, 216-17
vision. *See* see/seeing
vocation, 11, 37, 53, 163, 183, 184-85, 194, 218
vulnerability, 35, 37, 42, 45-46, 49, 50, 91, 97, 115, 127, 147, 158, 177, 188, 205
war, 8, 13, 15-17, 19, 24, 25, 29, 36, 41, 104, 126, 135, 165, 191, 216
  See also violence, nonviolence
we, 13, 15, 73, 164, 166, 183, 202, 214, 216, 218
  See also belonging
weakness, the weak, 15, 16, 19-20, 22, 27, 45, 104-5, 111-12, 113, 114, 126, 129-30, 141, 156, 162, 179, 185
Weil, Simone, 162-69, 190, 191, 192, 198, 200, 202, 205, 213, 219
Wilkerson, Isabel, 17, 60, 170
wisdom, 14, 27, 31, 66, 70, 82, 110, 140, 166
  perennial wisdom of neighbor love, 211-20
women, 2, 12, 13, 19-22, 24-25, 27, 32, 34, 40-41, 48, 51-52, 53-56, 96, 122, 124, 138-41, 153, 162-69, 183, 184-91, 193, 215, 217
world. *See* earth
work, 111-12, 114, 116-17, 149, 165-66, 194
workers, 17-18, 20, 45, 54, 123, 155, 177, 195
worth. *See* value
xenophobia, 19, 49-50

SCRIPTURE INDEX

OLD TESTAMENT

Genesis
1, *31, 32, 33, 45, 49, 54, 57, 67, 136, 214*
1–2, *56, 107, 200*
1–12, *39*
1:26-27, *31*
1:28, *37*
1:28-31, *67*
1:31, *32*
2, *33, 34, 52*
2–3, *33*
2:17, *52*
2:18, *34*
2:25, *34*
3, *34, 35*
3–4, *103*
3:1-7, *81*
3:5, *34*
3:7, *35*
3:9, *52*
3:21, *52*
4, *35, 36, 52, 117*
4:4-5, *81*
4:6-7, *52*
4:9, *36*
4:10, *35*
4:10-12, *52*
4:15-16, *52*
4:21-22, *36*
6:11, *37*
9, *37, 38, 39, 181*
9:6, *32, 63*
9:25-26, *38*
11, *36*
11–12, *36*
12, *37, 38*
12:1-3, *139*
12:2-3, *37*
12:3, *12, 37, 63*
12:7, *37, 38*
15:5-21, *38*
15:6, *37*
17:4-8, *38*
18:18, *38*
18:18-19, *38*
19:36-38, *54*
22:17-18, *38*
22:18, *38*
26:2-4, *38*
26:4, *38*
28, *38*
28:13-15, *38*
28:14, *38*
32:25-32, *158, 205*
33:10, *158, 205*
35:11-12, *38*
46:4, *38*

Exodus
1:15-22, *41*
3:6-8, *38*
6:2-8, *38*
12:48, *48*
15:15, *54*
17:14-16, *41, 48*
20:10, *48*
21:24, *63*
21:35, *46*
22:21, *47*
23:4, *52*
23:12, *48*
23:22, *39, 51, 66*
32, *46*
34:6, *54*

Leviticus
16:29, *48*
17–22, *44*
19, *41, 44*
19:9-10, *42*
19:10, *47*
19:13, *42*
19:14, *42*
19:15, *42*
19:18, *12, 42, 43, 46, 76, 199, 214*
19:33-34, *42*
19:34, *47, 48*
22:10, *48*
23:22, *47*
24:17-21, *63*
24:19, *46*
24:22, *48*
25:6, *47*
25:35, *47*
25:44-46, *49*
26:7-8, *51*
26:8, *66*

Numbers
9:14, *48*
15:14, *48*
15:15, *48*
21:35, *40*
24, *54*
24:20, *41, 48*
25:1, *54*
31, *40*
31:15-17, *41*

Deuteronomy
2:34, *40*
3:3-6, *40*
3:6, *73*
4:6-8, *42*
5:14, *48*
6:4, *72*
6:5, *76*
6:10-11, *40*
7, *38, 40, 146*
7:1-6, *48*
7:2, *40*
7:14, *39, 71*
7:14-26, *48*
7:16, *40*
7:24, *40*
9:3, *41*
10:14-15, *40*
10:18-19, *43, 44, 47*
10:23, *41*
11:1, *44*
12:31, *73*
14:29, *47*
15:3, *49*
15:10, *45*
15:12, *49*
19:21, *63*
20:3-4, *41*
20:16-17, *41*
23:3-6, *49, 54*
23:7, *47*
23:15-16, *45*
23:20, *49*
24:14, *48*
24:14-22, *47*
25, *41*
25:17-19, *48*
26:12, *47*
27:19, *47*
28, *38*
28:9-10, *39*
28:13, *39*
28:43-44, *50*
32:42, *51*
33:29, *41*

Joshua
6:21, *40*
8:22-25, *40*
24:12-13, *40*

Judges
3:12-14, *54*
3:28-30, *54*

Ruth
1:4, *54*
1:8, *55*
1:22, *54*
2:2, *54*
2:6, *54*
2:13, *54*
2:20, *54*
2:21, *54*
3:10, *54*
3:11, *55*
4:5, *54*
4:10, *54*
4:13, *54*
4:15, *54*
4:22, *55*

1 Samuel
11:18-26, *54*
14:47, *54*
15, *41, 48*
15:2, *40*
15:3, *73*
18:1, *42*
20:17, *42*
24, *52*
24:19, *52*
27:9, *40*

2 Samuel
1, *41*
1:1-16, *48*
8:2, *40, 49, 54, 69*
20:24, *49*
22:35-49, *51*

1 Kings
5:1, *44*
8:41-43, *48*
16:21-24, *84*

2 Kings
3, *54*
6:21-23, *52*
17:24, *84*
17:25-41, *84*

1 Chronicles
1:8, *39*
1:13, *39*
22:2, *49*

2 Chronicles
6:32, *48*
6:34, *51*
19:2, *44*
20, *54*
24:26-27, *54*
28:15, *52*
30:25, *48*

Ezra
2:64-65, *49*
4:3, *84*
9:2, *49*
10, *50, 54*

Nehemiah
7:64, *49*
9:7-8, *38*
13, *54*
13:1-3, *54*
13:23, *54*
13:25, *50*
13:30-31, *50*

Esther
3:10, *52*
8–9, *41, 48*
9:5, *52*
9:16, *52*

Job
31:32, *48*

Psalms
68:21-23, *51*
72, *38*
72:17, *38*
139:19, *66*
139:22, *66*

Proverbs
16:7, *53*
24:17, *53*
25, *53*
25:21-22, *53*

Song of Solomon
8:6, *92*

Isaiah
1:13-18, *79*
11:9, *57*
14:1-2, *56*
15:1, *54*
19:23-25, *57*
25:10, *54*
49:6, *57*
60:10-12, *56*
61:5-6, *56*
66:22-23, *57*

Jeremiah
7:3, *46*
7:5-7, *46, 79*
7:6, *48*
22:3, *48*
25:21, *54*
48, *54*

Ezekiel
9:5-7, *51*
22:7, *48*
22:29, *48*
25:8-11, *54*
37, *56*
39:21-22, *56*
47:22, *48*

Hosea
6:6, *79*

Amos
2:1-2, *54*
5:21-24, *79*

Micah
6:5, *54*
6:6-8, *79*

Zephaniah
1:8, *50*
2:8-9, *54*

Zechariah
2:8, *57*
2:11, *57*

7:10, *48*
14:21, *57*

NEW TESTAMENT

Malachi
3:5, *48*
3:12, *38*

Matthew
1:1-2, *60*
1:5, *55, 60*
3:13-17, *62, 226*
3:17, *78, 139, 208*
4:23-25, *63*
5, *79, 87, 89, 110, 114, 125, 126*
5–7, *62*
5:1-12, *115*
5:1-16, *23*
5:10-12, *23*
5:38, *63*
5:38-42, *63*
5:39-42, *63*
5:43, *62, 66, 97*
5:43-45, *214*
5:43-48, *66, 139*
5:44, *12, 69, 200*
5:44-48, *67*
5:45, *13, 77*
5:48, *68, 74*
7, *79, 90, 127*
7:1, *219*
7:7-12, *62*
7:11, *70*
7:12, *70, 76, 144, 227*
7:21-23, *72*
7:21-24, *71*
7:23, *77*
7:24, *72*
7:28-29, *73*
13:52, *61*
15:21-28, *217*
17:5, *208*
19, *73, 79, 83*
19:14, *73*
19:16, *74*
19:17, *74*
19:17-19, *227*
19:19, *62, 74, 97*
19:21, *74, 77*
19:30, *75*
20:20-28, *89*
22, *76*
22:36, *76*
22:36-40, *227*
22:37-40, *76*
22:39, *145*
22:40, *77*
23:39, *62, 97*
25, *144, 179, 187, 205, 218*
25:31-46, *179, 187, 213*
25:40, *145, 157*
28, *77, 89, 227*
28:18-20, *78, 92, 221*
28:19-20, *152*
28:20, *158*

Mark
1:11, *208*
2:13-17, *80*
5:23, *83*
9:7, *208*
10:42-45, *89*
12, *79, 83*
12:28, *79*
12:28-34, *227*
12:29-31, *79*
12:31, *62, 97*
12:33, *62, 79, 97*
12:34, *79*

Luke
3:22, *81, 208*
3:38, *60*
6, *80, 87, 89, 90, 110, 114, 126, 141*
6:27, *108, 200*
6:27-28, *80, 89*
6:27-36, *62*
6:31, *80*
6:35, *13, 200, 219*
6:35-36, *80, 115*
6:37, *116, 219*
6:37-38, *81*
6:40, *81*
6:46, *82*
6:46-49, *82*
6:47-48, *82*
6:49, *82*
9:35, *208*
9:51-56, *84*
10, *4, 82, 86, 227*
10:25, *83*
10:26, *83*
10:27, *62, 97*
10:28, *8, 83, 92, 93, 133, 212, 220, 227, 231*
10:29, *62, 83, 97*
10:31, *85*
10:32, *85*
10:33, *85, 86*
10:34, *85*
10:35, *85*
10:36, *62, 85, 97*
10:37, *85, 86*
17:33, *159*
23, *90*
23:2, *91*
23:34, *91, 204, 219*
23:35, *91*
23:36, *91*
23:39, *91*

John
1:1-5, *88*
1:14, *88*
3, *88*
3:16, *190*
3:16-17, *88*
4:9, *84*
8:32, *162*
8:48, *87*
10, *88*
10:1, *88*
10:3, *88*
10:10, *88*
10:11, *88*
10:16, *88*
10:17-18, *88*
10:18, *89*
12:24, *92*
13, *113*
13:1, *89*
13:3, *89*
13:4-5, *89*
13:14-15, *89*
13:34, *90*
13:34-35, *62, 89, 90*
14:6, *88*
15:9, *90*
15:9-17, *62*
15:11-13, *90*
15:17, *90*
20:21, *92*
20:23, *92*
21:15-19, *92*

Acts
2:24, *92*
3:24-26, *92*
3:25, *37*
4:34, *95*
7:27, *62*
9:1-6, *139*
9:2, *94*
9:4, *95*
10:28, *95*
11:26, *94*
17:26, *34*
19:9, *94*
19:23, *94*
22:3, *118*
22:3-5, *95*
22:4, *94*
24:14, *94*
24:22, *94*

Romans
2:11, *96*
4:3, *37*
4:16, *96, 97*
5:9, *99*
8:38-39, *140, 219*
8:39, *106*
9:3, *164, 165*
10:9, *72, 105*
10:12, *96*
10:12-13, *100*
12, *97, 99*
12:9, *97, 201*
12:9-21, *97, 201*
12:13, *97*
12:14-21, *98*
12:15, *201*
12:21, *101*
13, *99, 101, 102, 103, 108, 109, 111, 133, 180, 228*
13:1, *101*
13:3, *101*
13:3-4, *101*
13:4, *101*
13:5, *101*
13:8, *101*
13:8-10, *99, 101, 227*
13:9, *100*
13:9-10, *62, 97*
13:10, *101, 108, 125, 216*
13:11-12, *103*
13:13, *103*
13:14, *103*
15, *103, 113, 228*
15:1-3, *104*
15:2, *62, 97*
15:5, *104*
15:7, *104, 105*
15:9, *104*
16:7, *96*

1 Corinthians
8, *113*
8:1, *113*
8:9, *113*
12:13, *96*
12:22-23, *113*
12:31, *113*
13, *97*
13:4-8, *113*
13:7-8, *219*
16:14, *97, 114*

2 Corinthians
5:14-15, *114*
8:7, *114*
8:13-14, *114*
8:14, *95*
12:9, *162*
13:9, *114*

Galatians
2–3, *106*
2:16, *106*
2:20, *106, 107*
3:7-9, *92*
3:8, *37*
3:26-28, *107*
3:28, *96, 107, 108, 228*
5, *109, 111*
5–6, *107*
5:6, *107, 109*
5:13, *108*
5:13-15, *108, 228*
5:14, *62, 97, 108*
5:15, *108*
5:19-21, *108*
5:22, *109*
5:22-23, *109*
5:26, *109*
6:1-5, *97*
6:2, *109*
6:3, *110*
6:9-10, *109*
6:10, *108*
6:15, *109*

Ephesians
2–5, *110*
2:4, *110*
2:8, *110*
2:11-20, *228*
2:14-15, *201, 228*
2:14-16, *97, 218*
2:15, *95, 110*
2:16, *201*
2:19, *110, 112, 201*
3:14-16, *201*
3:17, *110*
3:17-19, *201*
3:18, *110, 118*
3:18-19, *139*
3:19, *110*
3:19-20, *110*
3:20-21, *201*
4:1-2, *111*
4:15, *111*
4:20-21, *111*
4:22-23, *111*
4:25, *62, 97, 111*
4:25-31, *111*
4:28, *111*
4:29, *112*
4:32, *112*
5:1-2, *112*

Philippians
2, *113*
2:2, *113*
2:3, *113*
2:3-7, *113*
3:20, *202*

Colossians
3:9-14, *96*
3:11, *96, 228*
3:12-14, *114*

1 Thessalonians
4:9-12, *97*

1 Timothy
1:5, *114*
2:3-4, *114, 219*
6:2, *114*

Titus
3:14, *114*

Philemon
1:16, *95*

James
1:17, *115*
1:27, *115*
2:1, *115*
2:5-6, *115*
2:8, *62, 97*
2:8-9, *115*
2:12, *116, 215, 228*
2:12-13, *116*
4:12, *62, 97, 116*
5:1, *117*
5:3-6, *117*

1 Peter
1:22-23, *97, 118*
3:8-9, *97, 118*
4:7-10, *97, 118*
5:14, *97, 118*

2 Peter
1:5-9, *97, 118*
1:17, *208*

1 John
2:9-11, *97*
3:11, *97, 118*
4:7-21, *97*
4:8, *118, 212*
4:16, *118, 212*
7, *134*

2 John
5–6, *97, 118*